EMPIRE NEWS

SUNY series in the History of Books, Publishing, and the Book Trades
——————
Ann R. Hawkins, Sean C. Grass, and E. Leigh Bonds, editors

EMPIRE NEWS
THE ANGLO-INDIAN PRESS WRITES INDIA

PRITI JOSHI

Cover Image: *Kohinoor* by Mita Mahato.

Published by State University of New York Press, Albany

© 2021 State University of New York

All rights reserved

Printed in the United States of America

No part of this book may be used or reproduced in any manner whatsoever without written permission. No part of this book may be stored in a retrieval system or transmitted in any form or by any means including electronic, electrostatic, magnetic tape, mechanical, photocopying, recording, or otherwise without the prior permission in writing of the publisher.

For information, contact State University of New York Press, Albany, NY
www.sunypress.edu

Library of Congress Cataloging-in-Publication Data

Names: Joshi, Priti, 1967– author.
Title: Empire news : the Anglo-Indian press writes India / Priti Joshi.
Description: Albany : State University of New York, [2021] | Series: SUNY series in the history of books, publishing, and the book trades | Includes bibliographical references and index.
Identifiers: LCCN 2021000806 (print) | LCCN 2021000807 (ebook) | ISBN 9781438484136 (hardcover : alk. paper) | ISBN 9781438484129 (pbk. : alk. paper) | ISBN 9781438484143 (ebook)
Subjects: LCSH: Press—India—History—19th century. | Government and the press—India—History—19th century. | English newspapers—India—History—19th century. | Press and politics—India—History—19th century. | Great Britain—Colonies—Asia—Administration—History—19th century.
Classification: LCC PN5373 .J67 2021 (print) | LCC PN5373 (ebook) | DDC 079/.5409034—dc23
LC record available at https://lccn.loc.gov/2021000806
LC ebook record available at https://lccn.loc.gov/2021000807

10 9 8 7 6 5 4 3 2 1

Contents

LIST OF ILLUSTRATIONS	vii
NOTE ON USAGE AND TRANSLITERATION	ix
ACKNOWLEDGMENTS	xi

INTRODUCTION
Circulating Crisis: Colonial Newspapers and Print Culture … 1

CHAPTER 1
Bibliographical, Periodical, and Imperial Codes … 29
   An Archive—With Many Gaps … 29
   Materiality: Communicating through Form, Format, and
      Organization … 38
   In Good Company: Colonial Critique and Imperial Certitude
      in the *Mofussilite* … 71

CHAPTER 2
Through a Glass Darkly: The Great Exhibition and the
Great Indian Contractor … 87
   Rocks in Paxton's Glass Palace … 90
   "Full of Novelty and Interest": The Great Exhibition Overtaken … 98
   The Trial in Many Mirrors … 117

CHAPTER 3
The Uprising in the Anglo-Indian Press … 127
   Editorial Turbulence … 129
   Extracting News: Improvisation and Chaos … 138
   The *Hindoo Patriot* in the Balance … 162

Chapter 4
Wanderings and Textual Travels 173
  House Rules 178
  Indigenizing Brand Dickens 192
  Independent *Wanderings* 201

Conclusion
Mofussil News 219

Appendix
Press Regulations and Significant Events in Indian Press History, 1780–1857 229

Bibliography 233

Index 249

Illustrations

Figure 1.1	*Mofussilite* 1845 masthead.	41
Figure 1.2	*Mofussilite* 1847 masthead.	41
Figure 1.3	*Friend of India* 1854 masthead.	41
Figure 1.4	*Bombay Times* 1857 masthead.	42
Figure 1.5	*Bengal Hurkaru and Chronicle* 1829 masthead.	42
Figure 1.6	*Hindoo Patriot* 1859 endcap.	44
Figure 1.7	Editors of the *Mofussilite*, 1845–60.	73
Figure 4.1	The Geographic and Linguistic Journey of the Magistrate's Tale of Pillage.	177
Figure 4.2	"Wanderings in India" in *Household Words*, November 1857.	205
Figure 4.3	*Wanderings in India and Other Sketches of Life in Hindostan*, 1859.	206
Figure 4.4	*Wanderings in India* title page and frontispiece.	213
Figure 4.5	*Wanderings in India* frontispiece.	213
Figure 4.6	"Nana Sahib" from *Illustrated London News*, September 1857.	215

Note on Usage and Transliteration

Throughout this book, I use "Anglo-Indian" as it was in the nineteenth century: for Britons resident in India (not in its twentieth-century designation for mixed-race or Christian Indians). While some have rejected the use of "Anglo-Indian" for Britons living in India as it implies greater integration than pertained, I use the term because it marked an identity distinct from both Britons and Indians. As this book details, the hyphen signals not hybridity, but a transactional relation.

The transliteration and Anglicization of Indian names and words is notoriously messy, and a scholar is continually toggling between clarity and fealty to non-Anglicized sounds. In chapter 2, I discuss the many variants on the name of the Indian businessman whose legal case lies at the center of the chapter. In this volume, except when quoting, I have opted for transliterations that are current among scholars writing in English. Thus, Awadh, not Oude; Ambala, not Umballah. The exception is that when referred to in the nineteenth century, Bombay and Calcutta are not altered to Mumbai and Kolkata as the latter are name changes effected in the last two decades, not orthographical corrections of Anglicizations.

I have not altered proper names either: thus, the Serampore Press is not corrected to Srirampur for the simple reason that the proper name of the press *is* Serampore Press notwithstanding that the spelling is an Anglicization of the town's name. Similarly, I spell Harish Chandra Mukherjee's *Hindoo Patriot* as he elected to in the masthead of his newspaper, as well as refer to the Calcutta daily as the *Bengal Hurkaru* (not "Harkaru," as one prominent scholar does, notwithstanding the masthead).

Acknowledgments

This book has been a long time in the making, and for long I was eager to get to this page; now here, it feels like the hardest writing of all, my words inadequate to the task.

I am grateful for the funding I received over the years from my institution, the University of Puget Sound, including summer funds to travel to London and, most preciously, a Lantz sabbatical year that allowed me the headspace and time to develop the argument and write a draft. I stumbled upon this project when I discovered that our library had a microfilm of the full run of *Household Words*. The acquisition was no doubt thanks to my predecessor at Puget Sound, Rosemary VanArsdel, who all those years ago gifted me, a "novel person," a copy of the volume she co-edited, *Periodicals of Queen Victoria's Empire*. Rosemary followed my work and always encouraged me; I am only sorry that I cannot present her with the fruits of my work in periodicals of the empire that she seeded.

The Research Society for Victorian Periodicals (RSVP) supported this project, both financially and in that more intangible but essential of ways: with fellowship and a community of like-minded scholars. A Curran Fellowship allowed me to spend several weeks in the British Library during which time much of the archival work that appears here was collected and this volume started to take shape. RSVP was also one of the first places I presented work on the *Mofussilite* and I am thankful for the support of scholars like Laurel Brake, Margaret Beetham, Patrick Leary, Brian Maidment, Jim Mussell, Catherine Waters, and many others. A special shout-out to Patrick Leary who, one day in 1992 or thereabouts, out of thin air it seemed, conjured VICTORIA, that community of scholars who share, collaborate, discuss, and exchange, always generously, always insightfully.

No institution has been more fundamental to my intellectual development since I left grad school than the Dickens Universe, that remarkable portal into all things nineteenth century that John Jordan keeps conjuring up year after year and balletically managing. In that universe, my profound gratitude goes to Helena Michie, who took seriously my remark at the lunch line at NAVSA one year about *A Tale of Two Cities* and the Indian "Mutiny" and invited me to give a keynote at the Universe. Helena was instrumental in helping me revise that talk into a publication; as I was putting the final touches on that paper, I did a quick check in *Household Words*, where I discovered a series called "Wanderings in India," penned by an Australian who edited a newspaper in India. The rest is . . . this book. Helena's incisive questions continued over the years and the "Form and Reform" group she led was formative as my ideas were gelling.

Over seventeen summers at the Dickens Universe, I have had brilliantly enriching conversations with many folks who have taught me how to think deeply and offered equally deep friendship. My suitemates and co-teachers, Sara Hackenberg and Susan Zieger, not only stocked the fridge and arranged mood lighting in our institutional suite, but kept me continually thinking about institutional politics and gender and race in and out of Victorian studies. Co-editing a special issue of a journal with Susan was both energizing and painless. I have learned gallons from another co-teacher, Daniel Pollack-Pelzner: about restaurant-review limericks, expiring frogs, musicals, *Middlemarch*, and finding the courage to write in new media. If I were a better student, this acknowledgment would be in the form of a clever rhyme, set to a reggaeton beat no less. It was another co-teacher, John Jordan, from whom I first learned to pay attention to seriality when he brought in part-publications of *David Copperfield* to our class. The three J's—Jim Adams, John Bowen, and Jim Buzard—welcomed me into that strange universe that coalesces and disbands every summer and made me feel like I belonged. The meals, meandering conversations, exploration of Santa Cruz's restaurants (*we* discovered Lailli's, right?) and wines, late-night discussions of the year's novel, teaching, university politics, US and UK politics—these are some of my most treasured Dickens moments. My deep thanks to John—who will, I hope, appreciate my proper usage and restraint here!—for his advice about presses when I felt stressed one summer, and to Jim B. who patiently listened over many hours as I played sleuth through the archival mysteries of the *Mofussilite*. At Dickens there are so many from whom I learned styles of argumentation and ways of thinking about literature, theory, teaching, the profession, and everything in between: the incomparable Ian Duncan, whose brilliance is accompanied by the greatest kindness and unmatched oenological expertise; suitemates Summer Star, Sharon Aronofsky Weltman, Sukanya Banerjee, Cornelia Pearsall, and Ruth Livesey; Pete Capuano, Jill Galvan, Jonathan Grossman, Teresa Mangum, Jason Rudy, Tricia Lootens, Robyn Warhol, Carolyn Williams—these names just scratch the surface.

Over the years, I have presented parts of this project at many venues and received helpful feedback that sharpened my ideas and argument. Many thanks to Vanessa Warne, who invited me to write a short piece for the *Victorian Review*'s topics-in-exploration section; my essay on mastheads for the journal seeded several ideas that are developed further here. Ross Forman's invitation to the University of Warwick to speak at the "Print Culture and Gender in the British Empire" conference was the boost I needed as the project was kicking into high gear. At Warwick, I was lucky to be bookended with Tanya Agathocleous, my end-of-century accomplice in Indian newspapers. Mary Ellis Gibson's invitation to present at the "Second Cities of Empire" conference in Glasgow was a rich experience that put me in conversation with scholars in the UK and India thinking about marginality. Thanks as well to Jennifer Dubrow who organized an MLA panel on Indian print culture. As I was bringing the project to a close, Matt Poland invited me to speak at the University of Washington's 18th/19th Century Graduate Research Cluster; the faculty and graduate students there asked me tough questions that helped me hone arguments I was taking for granted. I have presented portions of this work at many NAVSAs as well and always come away grateful for the community and camaraderie there: whether in Venice or Victoria, Banff or Columbus, London (Ontario) or Florence (Italy), we somehow always managed to ask big questions and solve the world's problems over four intense days.

Any archival project is only as good as the librarians who collect, archive, process, and provide the materials. At the British Library, I am grateful to Patrick Casey, curator of Asian and African newspapers, who first helped me unravel some of the mysteries of Indian newspapers. Hedley Sutton was generous in sharing his list of English-language newspapers, a resource that helped me broaden the project. My heartfelt thanks go to John Chignoli, librarian and friend par excellence; every year John patiently showed me updates and upgrades, suggested resources I might look at, and one year tracked down a few pages I had foolishly forgotten to copy while there. John also showed me the rooftop garden—lunch hour at the BL was never the same!—and brought into the many studious weeks on the fourth floor a lot of smiles. Gratitude as well to the many friends one makes at the library, particularly Noel Gunther of the British Indian Genealogical Society, who suggested dozens of resources I might consult to track down leads.

At SUNY Press, many thanks to the series' editors Sean Grass, Ann R. Hawkins, and E. Leigh Bonds, who promptly adopted the project and were stalwart supporters throughout. The anonymous readers were enormously generous, helped me see the larger stakes of the project, and pushed me to articulate them. I am tremendously grateful to Catherine Blackwell of the press's editorial team who generously shared her personal copy of the masthead of the *Bengal Hurkaru and Chronicle* from 1829; it was a joy and assurance to have someone who has spent as much time in the archive supervise this aspect of the final copy. They say the art of copyediting is dying; they haven't met Brian Kuhl, sharpest and most tactful of editors whose eagle eyes saved me from many an error.

In Mussoorie: thanks to Hugh and Coleen Gantzer, who arranged for me to visit Camel's Back Cemetery; to Prem Singh, longtime caretaker, who took several hours of his day to lead me to Lang's tombstone and gave me a tour of the cemetery and its fascinating history; and to Surbhi Aggarwal, who maintains the splendid Mussoorie Heritage Centre and invited me to give a talk on Lang and Mussoorie. The special place that Landour has in the heart of this *pahari* girl has much to do with the many leisurely afternoons and vibrant conversations I had with Pawan Gupta and Anuradha Joshi in their lovely home.

I have lived longer in Tacoma—occupying the lands of the Twulshootseed-speaking Puyallup people—than any other one place in my peripatetic life. I have here so many friends who have broken bread and raised a glass with me, discussed, argued, and plotted, who have nurtured me and helped me find an unexpected home in this corner of the Pacific Northwest. Foremost amongst these is the talented and witty Mita Mahato, without whom Wyatt 3 feels that much lonelier. Mita's cut-paper collages have long had pride-of-place on my mantelpiece; I am thrilled that her newspaper collage now graces the cover of this book and deeply touched that she created this lovely image for me. Other friends who sustain me include: Barry Goldstein, who, good geologist that he is, knew where to dig and the questions to ask; Jeff Matthews, who kept at me to write and modeled discipline with his own books; Kate Stirling, who just makes me happy with her big laugh; Diane Kelley, Laura Krughoff, and Elise Richman, who shared walks, wine, and wonderful company. The final stages of this book's preparation coincided with Covid, when all our lives shrank. I was lucky to have two pods—Erin Colbert-White, Monica DeHart, and Robin Jacobson; Yige Dong and Yan Liu—who, whether in a backyard or walking, in the glorious Northwest summer or its soggy rain, kept me anchored with vibrant conversations about the news, the state of higher education, race politics, food and food politics, virtual teaching, book covers, and so much more.

My parents gave me the most precious gift of all: books and a love of reading. I thank them for it every day: with books in my corner, I can never be bored. Many moons ago, as I was completing my dissertation under deadline, I sent my mother—via snail mail—each chapter which she meticulously proofread and returned; the only error in that document was on the acknowledgements page, which she did not read. As I completed the final version of this book, I sat in a room not far from my now-fading mother. I think she would like this book—its style is less Chadwickian!—and I hope she knows that I could never be where I am were it were not for the love and confidence she unstintingly gave me.

To my sister Chaya and to Sameer, whose house has been home for so many years: "thank you" hardly scratches the surface. LaP is the gathering place where we all come together and can be ourselves; your house stands for chaotic mealtimes, a lush vegetable garden, board games, 29, and . . . love and acceptance. My other sister Priya led the way multiple times over and I am deeply grateful for the model, the encouragement, the advice, but most of all the laughter; you showed me that this "writing-shiting thing" could be fun and insisted: celebrate every step of the way. And to Orfeo, who quietly makes sure that we all somehow have drinks in our hands no matter what, and Nestor, who manages to hold his own in this *tamasha*.

To the boys go my thanks for everything and everything else. Akshay and Amal came to London one summer, and while they could not understand how on earth I could turn my back on the city to pour over old newspapers all day, they made the most of a strike at the BL and showed me London in new ways. Akshay gave this work the highest praise when he printed out a chapter, read it on the BART home, and said, "This is actually interesting and makes sense." I hope you infect every reader of this book with that sentiment! Amal: all those long, long, long conversations where I watched you grow and grew myself, along with our kitchen escapades that produced *gobi manchurian* and grandpa's *baigan* biryani. You've always kept my mind and palate buzzing! Anuj: your courage, wit, persistence, and intuitive feel for when someone needs a hug blow me away. And yes, Wigs, you're my AE! And to Parul, the newest member of the family: you're a saint!

For over thirty years I have been in deep and enriching conversation with Farid Abdel-Nour; from him I learned to think about politics and Palestine, political theory and the public sphere, nationalism and dissent in ways that have left their stamp on every page of this book. I hope that makes up for the culinary *haram* I continue to commit daily.

My deepest gratitude goes to Monica DeHart. It was Monica who first suggested that my "John Lang article" might be a book; Monica who read early drafts and drew out what was buried under the messiness; Monica who talked me through every idea, who read too many pages, and who encouraged and insisted I have something to say; Monica who advised me at every stage; Monica who gently pointed out at the eleventh hour that though *Mofussil News* might be the perfect title, it needed to be set aside. I could ask for no more brilliant—and stalwart—intellectual interlocutor. And yet I got more: a friend for triangle trips and wine nights; for plotting, grousing, and whining; for seminars and curricula we dreamed up; for weekly dinners and all those gatherings we arranged; for endless conversations that clarified my thinking on so many matters. This book would not exist were it not for her, and I am thankful to have her in my corner.

Introduction

Circulating Crisis:
Colonial Newspapers and Print Culture

At the start of Eleanor Catton's *The Luminaries* (2013), Walter Moody, an upper-crust Briton newly arrived in New Zealand in 1866 to try his hand prospecting in the gold fields, makes his way to the town of Hokitika. Worn after a harrowing journey through a storm, he checks into the shabby Crown Hotel and calls for refreshments. After his first pot of tea, Moody takes stock:

> The maid had left yesterday's newspaper beneath the teapot—how thin it was, for a sixpenny broadsheet! Moody smiled as he took it up. He had a fondness for cheap news, and was amused to see that the town's *Most Alluring Dancer* also advertised her services as the town's *Most Discreet Accoucheuse*. A whole column of the paper was devoted to missing prospectors (*If this should reach the eyes of* EMERY STAINES, *or any who know of his whereabouts . . .*) and an entire page to Barmaids Wanted. Moody read the document twice over, including the shipping notices, the advertisements for lodging and small fare, and several very dull campaign speeches, printed in full. He found that he was disappointed: the *West Coast Times* read like a parish gazette. But what had he expected? (22–23)

A parish gazette: Moody's condescension telescopes the metropole's dismissal of both the settlement on the edge of empire and its threadbare print culture. But what to Moody looks "thin," "amusing," and pedestrian is the stuff of powerfully entwined histories he is incapable of perceiving; it takes a Catton to unfurl these stories. Over eight hundred pages, each of the items Moody patronizingly ridicules—the dancer, prospector, barmaids; shipping notices, advertisements, and campaign speeches—blossoms under Catton's expert hands to produce a rich narrative of the personal, financial, emotional, and ethical negotiations of life on the edge of empire. That Catton's tale—which the *New York Times* calls "a lively parody of a 19th-century novel" (Roorbach)—begins with a newspaper whose every section the novelist will tease apart and use to imaginatively reconstruct a colonial world speaks to the importance of newspapers as her source material, as well as to a twenty-first-century sensibility towards this particular form of print culture that is finally receiving its scholarly due.[1]

Like Catton's, this book plumbs the depths of newspapers, though it is neither fiction nor eight hundred pages long. *Empire News* is an account of Anglo-Indian newspapers in the years preceding and immediately following the Uprising of 1857.[2] Unlike existing accounts of Indian newspapers, which concentrate on the press of the presidency capitals of Calcutta, Bombay, and Madras, this book's focal point is an English-language newspaper from an "upcountry" province—a "parish gazette" twice over—with a cluster of Calcutta newspapers serving to situate and augment the analysis. The questions that animate my study of these newspapers between 1845 and 1860 are shaped by Book History, as well as by the intellectual dispensation I will shorthand as postcolonial.[3] As I examine some half dozen Anglo-Indian newspapers in the period before the high noon of the

---

1. During a visit to Hokitika, after the book had won the Man Booker Prize, Catton "said she did most of her research while she lived overseas, aided by online newspaper archives from the National Library of New Zealand" (Mussen).

2. Deeptanil Ray and Abhijit Gupta eschew "Anglo-Indian" because it "implies a sense of integration never realised in the field of newspapers and periodicals in nineteenth-century colonial India" (245, n. 1). Their use of "British" is unsatisfactory, however, for it fails to distinguish between colonial and metropolitan domains, a central thrust of this book; I also refrain from "native," their preferred term for Indian newspapers. The events of 1857 have been referred to as the Sepoy Mutiny or First War of Independence; for the limitations of these terms, see Priti Joshi, "1857." Indian contemporaries referred to the events as *ghadar*, an Urdu word meaning outburst or disturbance (Farooqui 394).

3. See Loomba et al. for a number of excellent essays on whether postcolonial studies is or should be behind us, whether it has been superseded by "globalization," or whether it should be replaced by "transnational studies."

Raj and anti-colonial challenges to it, my emphasis is on circulation and rupture, connection and crisis. Newspapers are material objects dependent on movement. Their circulation can coalesce communities, as well as produce collisions. This book traces the material circulation of a set of Anglo-Indian newspapers—their circuits and routes, editors and printers, exchanges and borrowings—even as it is alert to the gap that lies between physical movement and claims about circulatory effects. (While editors and publishers often declaim the range and influence of their prints, the transmission of ideas is difficult to trace and requires care on the part of a scholar.) If circulation is the lifeblood of newspapers, impediments to their transmission can be a death knell. This book trains its attention on moments of rupture as well, when newspapers were literally blocked, unable to access sources or readers. For newspapers, ruptures often occur at moments of historical upheaval. In British India, the narratives of empire that emerged at such moments of crisis are as central to grasping the workings of the British Empire in India as moments when the flow of print was relatively stable. Of the crises I address in this book, one, the Uprising of 1857, received widespread attention and was understood as globally significant in the annals of the British Empire; the second, a sensational 1851 trial that pitted the East India Company[4] against an Indian, registered more locally, though the "parish gazettes" read it through the prism of and as a test of empire. Attending to both global and local-global crises and their coverage in the Anglo-Indian press, this book examines the making and breaking of empire.

Though newspapers were central to the dissemination of print culture and the development of modernity—birthing the growth of the bourgeoisie, class consciousness, nationalism, and, in India, vernacular languages and literature, as well as anti-colonial nationalism—they are only now beginning to receive the attention that has been bestowed on books. Some of this belatedness is an archival matter, an issue we shall return to in a moment; some is the outcome of an Anglo-American academy that has been book-focused. Yet, as scholars of print and reading culture repeatedly remind us, newspapers, journals, and reviews circulated more widely than

---

4. Also referred to as simply "the Company" or EIC.

books. In nineteenth-century Britain, for instance, more people consumed newspapers or periodicals more often and more consistently than they did books (Hughes 1; McKitterick 50). While books and serials existed in overlapping, not separate, spheres, most of the innovations of the period—the serialization of fiction, illustrations, developments in the steam press—had their trial run in the periodical press (Brake, *Print* 11–16; Law and Patten 144). Graham Law and Robert Patten write, "The emergence in Britain of print-capitalism ... is apparent rather earlier in the part and periodical sectors than in that for books themselves, where the first edition tended to remain something of a limited circulation luxury item until relatively late in the century" (147). Unsurprisingly, the periodical press was also more lucrative than the book industry. As Patrick Leary and Andrew Nash note, "Even the most successful novelists, including Dickens, turned to the expanding periodical press as an outlet, not simply for their fiction, but for stories and non-fiction of various kinds, as well as for the steady income promised by staff and editorial positions" (178).

The number of newspapers and periodicals published in Britain in the nineteenth century was colossal. The *Waterloo Directory of English Newspapers and Periodicals* lists approximately 73,000 distinct titles of newspapers and periodicals published between 1800 and 1900. By comparison, the number of novels that appeared during Victoria's reign was approximately 50,000 (Leary and Nash 174). And while newspapers and periodicals are frequently catalogued together—to wit, the *Waterloo Directory*—the differences between them are considerable. Most prominent is that newspapers have a built-in obsolescence and fleeting life span. Newspapers are, in Benedict Anderson's memorable phrase, "one-day bestsellers" (35), with the date stamp at the head of each issue announcing its shelf life. Laurel Brake notes that this transience is central to the business model of newspapers as "editors had an interest in purveying the impression of the alleged 'ephemerality'" of their product in order "to ensure that the last issue was abandoned when its more topical and news-rich successor was 'ready' for purchase" ("Longevity" 7). For a researcher, as Linda Hughes soberly puts it, nineteenth-century newspapers and periodicals represent "a materiality so massive that it exceeds scholarly ability to document it" (5).

Painstakingly documenting and analyzing this staggering archive over the last twenty-five years, scholars have noted its many gaps. In an essay that moved the study of periodicals from specialist journals to the mainstream of literary studies, Sean Latham and Robert Scholes direct us to study periodicals not "merely as containers of discreet bits of information," but as "autonomous objects of study" (517–18). As we do, they caution that the surviving archive contains many "holes," the largest one being advertisements that were stripped when periodicals were preserved. Brake, a pioneer in the study of Victorian periodicals, and James Mussell, the visionaries behind the digitization of nineteenth-century periodicals and newspapers, add discarded wrappers and supplements or multiple runs of a day's paper to the list of holes. The archive we access today, they equally soberly note, is merely "the remains" (Brake and Mussell). In pointing to the material gaps in the archive, these scholars underscore Derrida's insight that the "nostalgic desire for the archive" as a place of origin or "absolute commencement" or completion is a fever ("*mal d'archive*") and is misguided (57).

Compounding the gaps in the archive of down-market print is its fragility, which David McKitterick captures in this passage:

> There remains a largely uncharted mass of cheap literature, printed on low-grade brownish wood-pulp paper from worn stereos and often reusing materials that had begun their existence somewhat further up the economic scale. Much of this kind of mass-produced literature, for which no-one expected a long life, has disappeared completely. Much of it has no doubt been pulped. Much of it has simply disintegrated. Even when it was new, little found its way into the contemporary surveys of press output. It is difficult now to recover much of its manufacture, circulation and use. (16)

In other words: the archive is staggeringly vast on the one hand and also gap-filled and disintegrating on the other. In Margaret Beetham's succinct phrasing, "we have both a bewildering excess of material and some crucial absences" (97).

Yet against McKitterick's gloomy appraisal of so much lost print is this passage from an article entitled "Starting a Paper in India" that appeared in *Household Words* in 1853:

> Then the type. I could not think of allowing my manuscript to be "set up" in anything but Figgins. A particular friend of mine, called Iniquity Smith, had once remarked to me that a little production of mine looked "uncommon tidy" in Figgins, and the conversation to which that remark led informed me

of the fact that Figgins was the prince of type-founders. Now there happened to be plenty of every other sort of Figgins's type in Calcutta, except Figgins's long primer, not a letter of which was to be had for love or money; and the long primer was absolutely necessary for the leading article. There were founts of types cast by other founders in the market, but they would not "make up" with Figgins, and therefore were of no use to me. At last I heard of a second-hand fount, or set of types, and bought it for fifty pounds. The heading of the paper, the column rules, the leads, and the chases or iron frames within which the type is jammed were soon got ready by native artisans, and nothing now remained but to engage the establishment. (94)

The juxtaposition of these remarks with McKitterick's is fruitful: if McKitterick is haunted by ephemerality, the second passage is imbued with the material and tangible. While McKitterick takes up metaphorically weighty matters of survival, access, and preservation, *Household Words'* playful piece is preoccupied with the literal weight of typefaces and reminds us that the even commodities that were not expected to survive were designed with considerable care. And while McKitterick's passage lacks agents ("simply disintegrated"), the second bustles with characters, from the speaker himself to the font-setter Figgins to the shadow "native artisans" who produced the newspaper. While differences abound, both passages grapple with movement—the first through time, the second across space. Between them, these passages capture several conceptual issues *Empire News* takes up and that hinge on the two senses of "transitory": fleeting and in transition.[5] Throughout the course of this book we will encounter caesuras in the archive. These gaps are the result of factors intrinsic and extrinsic to newspapers: their material fragility, their inconsistent preservation and marginality in the universe of print, and their susceptibility to state regulation. Working with the gaps requires flexibility and reading methods that call for ingenuity.

Scholarly attention to nineteenth-century Indian newspapers is tied to the burgeoning scholarship on British newspapers and periodicals in

---

5. The *Oxford English Dictionary* lists "of the nature of a passage or transition" as a rare usage of the word, last used in 1592 ("Transitory." *OED Online*, Oxford University Press, 1989. Accessed 13 July 2017).

the Anglo-American academy. With the launch of the Research Society for Victorian Periodicals in 1968, the scholarship on British newspapers and periodicals grew rapidly. Richard Altick's *Punch: The Lively Youth of a British Institution, 1841–1851* (1997) and Andrew King's *The London Journal 1845–83: Periodicals, Production, and Gender* (2004) focus on single journals, while others have attended to networks of editors and publishers (Humpherys and James; Leary); the radical or popular press (Allen and Ashton; Conboy; Gilmartin; Jones); national identity (Connors and MacDonald; de Nie; Legg; Potter); and gender (Brake; Onslow). With digitization, the field has grown further, particularly in newspaper studies.[6] The pioneering work in the Anglo-American academy on periodicals and the British Empire was J. Don Vann and Rosemary VanArsdel's 1996 *Periodicals of Queen Victoria's Empire*; the volume's subtitle "An Exploration" is a salutary reminder that but two decades ago colonial periodicals were largely uncharted territory. The scholarship on India that followed in the wake of their edited volume concentrated primarily on India and Indians in British periodicals. Chandrika Kaul's *Reporting the Raj: The British Press and India, c. 1880–1922* (2003) offers an in-depth analysis of the relations between Fleet Street and the Foreign Office in London, while David Finkelstein and Douglas Peers's *Negotiating India in the Nineteenth-Century Media* (2000) includes essays on the coverage of India in the *Indian Magazine*, *Englishwoman's Domestic Magazine*, *Illustrated London News*, and *Household Words*. Javed Majeed's essay in the latter volume on two Urdu periodicals from India is the exception. Not until 2004 did the study of periodicals published in India receive a boost in the Anglo-American academy with a *Victorian Periodicals Review* special issue, *The Nineteenth-Century Press in India* (edited by Julie Codell), that included essays by Máire Ní Fhlathúin, Edwin Hirschmann, and Debapriya Paul on Calcutta's newspapers.[7]

---

6. More data and greater access do not equal better scholarship; Jerome McGann writes that today we face vast amounts of data and the ability to "quickly annotate just about anything we've never heard of" (*New Republic* 14). Paul Fyfe warns that "digital collections inevitably condition much of the research we undertake" and urges conversations about methodologies to sort, access, and analyze this plethora (716).

7. Hirschmann's biography of Robert Knight, editor of both the (Calcutta) *Statesman* and Bombay-based *Times of India*, has subsequently appeared in print, while Deborah Logan's *The Indian Ladies Magazine, 1901–1938* attends to an Indian periodical of the twentieth century.

The first printing press was brought to the Indian subcontinent by Portuguese Jesuits in 1556; by the end of the eighteenth century, India had over forty printing presses, a type foundry, and a paper mill (Dharwadker 108). Print took off and flourished in the nineteenth century, never, however, replacing preprint cultural traditions.[8] Vinay Dharwadker puts the number of newspapers and periodicals published in India in the nineteenth century at 14,000 (126). These include papers edited by Indians and non-Indians, and represent print in some forty languages. Ephemerality and vulnerability haunt this archive as well: most of those 14,000 journals, Dharwadker reports, failed, but "hundreds" survived and some "even reached large regional and national audiences" (126). Mrinal Kanti Chanda, the indefatigable chronicler of the Bengal press, however, laments that "the files of old newspapers . . . are completely going out of use for scholars for want of scientific preservation in the libraries" (*History* [2008] xiii). Those that survive are often missing numbers and of poor quality. In *An Empire of Books: The Naval Kishore Press and the Diffusion of the Printed Word in Colonial India*, Ulrike Stark adds that the challenges of Book History on the Indian subcontinent include "the scarcity of basic empirical data on just about every aspect of production, transmission, and consumption. Factual knowledge of material, infrastructural, and operational aspects of the regional-language book trade, of author-publisher and publisher-bookseller relations, of readership and consumption practices is still limited. Seldom extant, Indian publishers' and booksellers' archives are not readily accessible and lie mostly untapped" (7). Notwithstanding such onerous archival challenges, a handful of Indian and Pakistani scholars have studied the nineteenth-century Indian press, though much of the work on newspapers is almost a half century old or older.[9]

Newspapers were a form of information gathering and dissemination introduced into the subcontinent by the British. Christopher Bayly's *Empire*

---

8. Ghosh argues that "residues of preprint era were to continue to impinge on the world of Bengali print well into the early twentieth century" and that "early book producers—authors and printers—therefore conformed to preprint tastes" (35, 37). She makes a strong case for the "continuing importance of oral and preprint traditions that prevented the printed text from being fixed in certain ways" (44).

9. Today, scholarship on Indian print culture and the book trade is flourishing at Presidency and Jadavpur Universities under the guidance of Swapan Chakravorty and Abhijit Gupta. Others who have produced rich accounts of print culture in India include Priya Joshi and Francesca Orsini.

and Information: Intelligence Gathering and Social Communication in India, 1780–1870 is a formidable account of information networks and social communication in the nineteenth century and offers a rich history of the epistemological shifts wrought in the encounter between Britons and the peoples of the subcontinent. Newspapers initially rivaled and ultimately displaced scribal and court-sponsored newsletters, or *akhbarats*. When print newspapers first started to appear in late eighteenth-century India, they overlapped with the *akhbarat*, which had a distinct system of knowledge production and dissemination. Careful not to idealize these newsletters, Bayly describes them as "documents of almost tedious detail, describing court ritual and gossip" (72); yet they also contained "a good deal of social information" that rulers used "to create a climate of opinion or justify a political move" (72). Bayly characterizes the knowledge newsletters contained as "the deep knowledge acquired by magnates with roots in the villages and political sympathy which comes from ties of belief, of marriage and from a sense of inhabiting the same moral realm" (144). The differences between *akhbarats* and newspapers were material—scribal versus print— and linguistic, as well as socio-epistemological, with disparate conceptions of what counted as news, newsworthiness, and an audience. Newspapers, Bayly writes, represented "institutional knowledge" (144) in contrast to the "embodied" or "affective and patrimonial knowledges" of *akhbarats* (55).

The first print newspaper on the subcontinent appeared in 1780. Unlike the court-sponsored *akhbarats*, *Hicky's Bengal Gazette* was brought out by a man with a long-standing grudge against the Government of India (effectively, the EIC), the governor general (Warren Hastings), and the chief justice of the Supreme Court (Elijah Impey). By all accounts, James Augustus Hicky's attitude towards the authorities was irreverent, vitriolic, and, from the perspective of the governors, libelous. The adjective often used to describe him was "scurrilous" (Chakraborti 5; Otis xi), and even one of the newspaper's friendliest biographers describes the newspaper as a place for "ventilating grievances" (Nair, *History* 42). By contrast, Partha Chatterjee, whose project in *The Black Hole of Empire* is to chart the appearance of mechanisms that permitted the expression of colonial citizenship, sums up the contribution of *Hicky's Bengal Gazette* as "offer[ing] the first forum in Bengal where the government's policies could be publicly debated" (112).[10]

---

10. Two book-length studies of *Hicky's Bengal Gazette* have appeared recently: P. T. Nair's 2001 volume and Andrew Otis's 2018 book.

Rivals to *Hicky's* sprung up quickly, and the newspapers and periodicals of the next two decades were chiefly published and edited by Anglo-Indians. The explosion of newspapers, however, only occurred downstream of two events: the establishment of the Baptist Mission's type foundry and press in Srirampur (Serampore, in British accounts) in 1800 and the lifting of government interventions in and censorship of print, first in 1818 and then more substantially in 1835. In the first forty years of its establishment, the Baptist Mission Press cast types in over forty languages and brought out materials in thirty Indian languages and dialects, as well as in Arabic, Armenian, Burmese, Malay, and Thai (Chakravorty 319; Dharwadker 111). By the 1820s, vernacular-language newspapers in Bengali, Hindi, Gujarati, and Urdu started to appear. The effects of the press and its technology gradually transformed the intellectual and social landscape of the subcontinent: "One of the most far-reaching effects of print between about 1800 and 1835 was the more or less simultaneous invention of modern prose in various languages, including Bengali, Hindi, Marathi, Tamil, Telugu, and Urdu" (Dharwadker 112). Newspapers were at the forefront of this invention. In the second half of the nineteenth century, Indian-owned and -edited newspapers, both in English and vernacular languages, flourished and, with the rise of the nationalist movement in the 1870s, assumed an increasingly anti-colonial and largely nationalist stance.

Accounts of the press on the Indian subcontinent fall into roughly three categories. Studies of the late eighteenth century focus primarily on the emergence of the press and on the government's tense relations with and wavering support for a free press.[11] A second set of studies attends to the rise of periodicals published and edited by Indians and in an Indian language. Due to the subcontinent's linguistic diversity, much of the scholarship on the Indian press focuses on the emergence and growth of a single vernacular tradition.[12] Lastly, numerous studies have appeared on the role of the press in the anti-colonial, nationalist struggle.[13] Monitored and suppressed by the ratcheting-up of anti-nationalist censorship laws such as the Vernacular Press Act of 1878, Indian-owned and -edited newspapers have survived archivally as a result of being policed. The trials of the *Amrita Bazar Patrika* and the *Bangabosi* in the

---

11. See Boyce; Nair, *History*; Mukhopadhyay.
12. See Chakraborti, N. A. Khan, Ramakrishnan, Stark.
13. See Agathocleous, Hofmeyr, Narain.

final decades of the nineteenth century capture anti-colonial resistance and have received considerable attention from scholars. As this schematic suggests, the literature on the nineteenth-century press in India consists of gaps, most notably in the forty years between 1835—when Charles Metcalfe repealed censorship laws—and 1878 when a jittery Government of India passed the Vernacular Press Act that imposed restrictions on the non-English-language press. From the colorful fates of James Hicky (the pioneer), James Silk Buckingham (who allied himself with Indian editors in the 1820s and was deported for critiques of the government), and J. Stocqueler (who purchased the Tory *John Bull* with Dwarkanath Tagore in 1833 and transformed it into the Whig *Englishman*), the historiography of India newspapers skips some half a century to anti-colonial outlets such as the *Amrita Bazar Patrika*.

Empire News steps into this gap to analyze English-language newspapers between 1845 and 1860. Situated between the pioneering years of the news media and the ferment of the anti-colonial struggle, these middle years have been neglected. Bhrahma Chaudhuri, an early scholar of Indian newspapers, considers 1830 to 1850 the "formative years of Indian periodicals" (178), while Bayly refers to the 1830s and 1840s as the "age of hiatus, when social change was crippled by economic depression and government penury . . . [and] the deepest changes of this era can be seen in the information order: the rapid diffusion of print media into north Indian society" (212). Yet no scholarly account of the newspapers of this period exists. In attending to English-language and Anglo-Indian newspapers, this book offers a history of the role of the press at a moment when British territorial expansion was slowing and its colonial bureaucracy expanding. The standard account of Anglo-Indian newspapers is that they were belligerent bullhorns for empire and functioned in isolation from their vernacular-language contemporaries. While there is some accuracy to the description, several Anglo-Indian newsmen worked in conjunction with Indians and fostered the growth of Indian newspapers.

The most prominent example of such transactional exchange is embodied in Rammohan Roy, the Bengali reformer who, in addition to owning and editing the Bengali-language *Sambad Kamudi* (est. 1821), worked with Anglo-Indians in press ventures such as the *Unitarian Repository* (est. 1823) and the *Bengal Herald* (est. 1829).[14] The latter was a joint

---

14. Chanda (*History* [1987]:84–85, 115–17).

venture of Roy, Dwarkanath Tagore (the landowner, industrialist, banker, and grandfather of the litterateur, Rabindranath), Prasanna Kumar Tagore, Nilratan Haldar, Rajkishan Singh, and Robert Montgomery Martin.[15] Most of these men played an active role in multiple newspapers, but none more so than Dwarkanath Tagore, who was proprietor or financial supporter of two of Calcutta's most important and rival newspapers, the *Englishman* (from 1833) and the *Bengal Hurkaru* (from 1834). While Tagore's involvement in newspapers was largely financial—he left the editing to Anglo-Indians such as Stocqueler and James Sutherland—Roy's involvement was both more intellectual and personal. Chatterjee writes that Roy's transformation of "freedom of belief into the legal-constitutional form of the individual subject's right to liberty . . . could not have happened without [his] association with the emergent public sphere in Bengal of free traders and freethinkers," including Anglo-Indian interlocutors (*Black Hole* 140).

Besides elites such as Roy and Tagore, numerous Indians working in Anglo-Indian presses—as printers and compositors, occasionally as correspondents—learned the trade in these workshops before moving on to establish their own newspapers or periodicals. Many of those who labored in the presses are lost to history, but some writers, such as Harish Chandra Mukherjee, who went on to own and edit the *Hindoo Patriot*, are known and we will turn to the cross-fertilization he represents in chapter 3. Anindita Ghosh summarizes the association between Indians and Anglo-Indians in the arena of print thus: "The pioneering Indian proprietors of vernacular presses were men who had been associated with European ventures for some time as teachers, authors, and printers of vernacular works. Having gained some knowledge of the trade, they moved on to establish their own businesses" (27).[16] Though this symbiosis ruptured, Swaminath Natarajan, an early historian of the Indian press, indicates that the two press cultures severed at a later date than scholars have allowed: "The Mutiny was responsible for driving a wedge between

---

15. See Chanda (*History* [1987], 115–16); Chatterjee (119); Ahmed (70).

16. Ghosh's earliest example of such interactions is from 1807, and her most "dynamic" example is Gangakishore Bhattacharya, who worked as a compositor at the Serampore Press (27). Robert Fraser describes "early publishing in Bengal" as "collaborative" (18). Antoinette Burton, writing about imperial archives generally, argues that their contents are "likely to have been the collaborative product, as the India Office collections themselves are, of 'native' agency and state-sponsored information collection. They are hybrids rather than hegemons" (95).

English-owned and Indian newspapers and creating a distinction between the English language and Indian languages [sic] journals" (50). Prior to 1857, as we shall see, the traffic between Anglo-Indian and vernacular-language presses, though often difficult to tease out, was not negligible.

※

This book examines several Anglo-Indian newspapers, leaning heavily on one paper, the *Mofussilite*, with four additional newspapers—the *Bengal Hurkaru*, the *Friend of India*, the *Englishman*, and the *Hindoo Patriot*—forming the core of the sample and augmenting the analysis. On occasion, I draw on newspapers such as the *Agra Messenger*, crucial to the story I develop in chapter 2, or two London-based steamship newspapers, *Allen's Indian Mail* and *Atlas for India*, that were busy in the circulation of news in 1857. The five papers comprising the core represent a range of types of newspapers and coverage: three papers were Calcutta-based (the *Englishman*, *Hindoo Patriot*, and *Bengal Hurkaru*), one from the Serampore Press in Srirampur, outside Calcutta (the *Friend of India*), one from the "mofussil" or provinces (*Mofussilite*). Two, in mid-century, were dailies (the *Englishman* and the *Hurkaru*); one, the *Mofussilite*, was twice weekly (for a time, it was triweekly); and two appeared once a week (the *Friend* and the *Hindoo Patriot*). With the exception of the *Hindoo Patriot*, all were edited by Anglo-Indians of various political stripes. From 1834 until his death in 1846, Dwarkanath Tagore owned the *Bengal Hurkaru* while also providing considerable "financial assistance" to its rival, the *Englishman* (Chanda *History* [1987] 35; Natarajan 47). The *Hindoo Patriot*, on the other hand, was kept barely alive by its editor and proprietor, Harish Chandra Mukherjee, who subsidized it with his meager salary working at the military auditor's office.

Print runs and circulation numbers are always difficult to ascertain, particularly so in the landscape of Indian newspapers where office books have not survived.[17] Chanda offers some numbers in his *History of the English Press in Bengal, 1780–1857*. Culled painstakingly from newspapers themselves and seldom comparative, these numbers provide nothing like

---

17. See Stark (7). The biographer of John Lang, the founder of the *Mofussilite*, bemoans the lack of office books or business papers: "There are no diaries and practically no letters. He is seldom mentioned in the writings of his many friends and acquaintances" (Crittenden, *John Lang* xii).

a systematic portrait, merely glimpses and hints. In 1839, the Serampore-based *Friend of India* had over 500 subscribers, a number that climbed to almost 3,500 in 1860 (Chanda, *History* [1987] 49; *History* [2008] 5). It boasted a subscriber base all over the subcontinent, in Britain, even the Strait Settlements, and was the Anglo-Indian newspaper best regarded by Bengal's young elite; Chanda writes that it was "uniformly in demand by the natives," with over 100 Indian subscribers in the mid-1850s (*History* [1987] 50). By contrast, the *Hurkaru* and the *Englishman*, Chanda writes, "[never] could . . . become popular with the natives," with approximately 20 Indian subscribers each in 1843 (*History* [1987] 34). What they lacked in Indian readers, they made up in Anglo-Indian readers: in 1833, the daily *Hurkaru* had 726 subscribers, while the *Englishman* in 1837 had a postal circulation of 376 copies, a number Chanda characterizes as "respectable" (*History* [1987] 403, 169). The *Hindoo Patriot*, by contrast, at its height in 1857 had only 36 subscribers, almost all Indian (Chanda, *History* [1987] 334–37). The *Mofussilite*, publishing from outside the region and one of only a handful of English-language papers in the North-Western Provinces, had, by its own account, 133 subscribers at the end of its first year in 1846 and "upwards of eleven hundred" in 1850; its published tally of subscribers in 1852 lists 738 names.[18]

Why the *Mofussilite* as anchor? The name of the newspaper is derived by adding the Latinate suffix "-ite" to the word "mofussil," itself an Anglicization of an Urdu word whose Persian and Arabic root, *mufaṣṣal*, meant "to divide or classify."[19] By the late eighteenth century, "mofussil" had been absorbed into the Anglo-Indian vernacular and was used to refer to parts of India outside the presidency capitals of Calcutta, Bombay, and Madras, or more generally, provincial India. The *OED*'s first reference to "mofussil" appears in 1781 in that first print newspaper, *Hicky's Bengal Gazette*, which included the following sentence: "A gentleman in the Mofussil, Mr.

---

18. *Mofussilite*, 10 January 1851, and *Mofussilite*, 2 March 1852. Subscribers and postal circulation tell only a partial story: James Long, who studied the Indian press in 1859, estimated ten "readers or hearers" for each copy of a book or issue of a newspaper (xv, xxxiv).

19. The nineteenth-century Hindustani suffix would have been "mofussil-walla" [masc.] or, in the "vulgarized" Hindi that was emerging in the central plains of the subcontinent, "mofussil-ka." For the growing usage of "ka/ki" in the 1840s, see Bayly (286).

P., fell out of his chaise and broke his leg."[20] The unfortunate Mr. P. who cannot manage to maintain himself in his vehicle captures the disparaging connotation attached to the term in common parlance, something akin to country bumpkin. The mofussil—or a posting in the mofussil—could strike despair in many an Anglo-Indian official's heart. Yet, in 1845, the term got a makeover with the appearance of the *Mofussilite*. Proudly donning a mantle of marginality, the newspaper claimed the secondary status and perceived invisibility of the provinces; its founding assumption was that a "parish gazette," distant from the center of power permitted it autonomy and the ability to express itself without constraints. A mofussilite, in this reworking, was a person who challenged the Government of India *and* a mentality. It is this oppositional stance that interests me: What did it look like to inhabit the margins of empire? How was this identity fashioned and how did it conceive of itself? Did a space for critical distance to colonialism exist in colonial communities in mid-nineteenth-century India? What might such distance look like? Is marginality as a member of a powerful empire a chimera?

The *Mofussilite* was launched in 1845 by John Lang, who served as its fiery and caustic editor for several years. Lang was born and raised in Australia, the son of a Glaswegian trader and his Australian-born wife, who was the daughter of a transported convict.[21] The senior Lang died eight months before his son was born (Crittenden 13–14); despite his attenuated connection to Britain, Lang junior developed a love–hate relationship with the "mother country," variably desiring recognition from it and holding himself aloof from it. An ambitious young man, Lang entered Trinity College, Cambridge, for law, but was expelled within months for blasphemy, drunkenness, and "Botany Bay" exploits (Crittenden 38). He

---

20. *Hobson-Jobson*, the compendium of the Anglo-Indian vernacular, offers a comparative definition: "If, in Calcutta, one talks of the Mofussil, he means anywhere in Bengal out of Calcutta" (Yule and Burnell 570).

21. Lang's mother, Elizabeth Harris Lang Underwood, was the daughter of John Harris, a transported convict, who never married Elizabeth's mother in Australia as he already had a wife in England (Crittenden, *John Lang* 12). Harris was Jewish and it is unclear if Elizabeth's mother was Jewish as well. When Elizabeth was young, Harris left her to be brought up in the home of a distant relation, James Larra, a man of "French Jewish extraction" (14, 51; this and all further citations for Crittenden refer to the book *John Lang* unless otherwise noted).

read law at Middle Temple in London instead, was called to the bar, and returned to Australia with an English wife. Unable to establish a practice in Sydney—related to a combination of his hotheadedness and injudicious participation in debates on the governance of the colony[22]—Lang decamped for India in 1842. The reason he chose India is unclear, though it seems overdetermined: his biological father's family did business in India, as did his stepfather, and his English wife had a brother living in India.[23] Lang's marriage did not last, nor did he practice much law, but he settled in India where he became a prolific writer, publishing some dozen novels and volumes of poetry, as well as editing the *Mofussilite*. Though it is said that Lang was a resident of India all his adult life, in fact, he spent a good portion of the next twenty-two years shuttling between the mofussil of India and London, an expert on India in London and a gadfly to imperial powers in the mofussil. He died in India and is buried in Mussoorie, the hill station he often retired to for his health.

Lang is experiencing something of a renaissance in India these days: in 2014, India's prime minister, Narendra Modi, presented his Australian counterpart, Tony Abbott, a "commemorative photo collage" consisting of Lang's writings and archival documents from his life in India, a gesture seen as something of a détente between the two countries.[24] And in 2015, an elegant volume entitled *In the Court of the Ranee of Jhansi and Other Travels in India* by John Lang appeared in India. Brought out by a young publishing house with solid credentials, Speaking Tiger, the volume was reviewed positively by academics in respectable newspapers and magazines.[25] In the accounts of Lang that have appeared recently, both

---

22. Though earlier biographers (Roderick and Earnshaw) emphasized the prejudice in Sydney against emancipists (convicts and their descendants) and Jews, Lang's more recent biographers deny that either anti-Semitism or anti-emancipist sentiment played a role in his disgrace (Crittenden 53–57; Keesing 43–55). Keesing writes, "[Lang] was undoubtedly amusing and brilliant; he was also flashy, conceited and when drunk at best silly, at worst objectionable" (32).

23. For Walter Lang's family trade with India and Australia, see Crittenden (13); for Joseph Underwood, Lang's mother's second husband, see Hainsworth. For Lang's brother-in-law, Andrew Turton Peterson, see Crittenden (63) and Keesing (39).

24. See Medcalf and "PM Gifts."

25. Speaking Tiger Books is co-directed by Ravi Singh, formerly of the Aleph Book Company, which he left following the politicized withdrawal of Wendy Doiger's *On Hinduism*, and Manas Saikia, who headed Cambridge University Press India. The

in India and in Australia, he is portrayed, in the words of Amit Ranjan, a Delhi-based researcher, as "a hero with the Indians."[26] This reputation rests on Lang's arguing—and winning—the blockbuster case of an Indian against the Government of India in 1851 (an episode I delve into in chapter 2), his defense of the Rani of Jhansi in 1854 (taken up in chapter 4), and his newspaper. Referring to the *Mofussilite*, Ranjan declares that Lang was "an anti-colonialist, with his constant lampoons, sometimes even harpoons directed against the East India Company."[27]

Though *Empire News* is far more than an account of Lang and the *Mofussilite*, Lang's revival and current stature in certain circles can serve as a barometer of the legacy of the British in India today, as well as provide a portal into shifts in the critical analyses of the colonial period. Whether Lang *was* the champion of Indians as he is celebrated in some circles is a matter I shall address in the course of this book. Here it bears noting that his life and work mirrors that of another famous India-based journalist and writer: Rudyard Kipling. In some respects, we might think of Lang as "Kipling in a minor key," the former's life a precursor to his more famous successor's. As if serially picking up where Lang left off, Kipling was born in Bombay in 1865, sixteen months after Lang died in Mussoorie. Like Lang, Kipling began his career in journalism, and both men used their day jobs as a springboard for their literary productions. Though the landscape of Anglo-Indian newspapers had altered considerably between 1845 when Lang started the *Mofussilite* and 1882 when Kipling stared writing for the *Civil and Military Gazette* in Lahore, the two outlets were very literally linked: a dozen years after Lang's death, his newspaper was absorbed into the *Civil and Military Gazette*. Much of Lang's fiction was serialized in the *Mofussilite*, just as dozens of Kipling's early stories appeared in the *Civil and Military Gazette*, where he served as assistant editor from 1882 to 1886. Their careers, of course, diverged considerably—Lang was no Nobel Prize winner and never wrote as widely or achieved the renown Kipling did—but their journalistic writings have more than a hint of similarity.

---

editorial team includes some of Indian publishing's top names drawn from Penguin India, Roli, and Rupa Books. For reviews of the Lang volume published by Speaking Tiger, see Kanjilal, A. Kaul, and Venkatachalapathy.

26. Lang's Australian biographer, Victor Crittenden, writes of his "sympathetic depictions" of the lives of "the native Indian people" (xii).

27. In "The Aussie Who Took On the British for Rani Laxmibai," Archana Masih cites Ranjan as saying: "His novels had characters displaying resistance against the British."

Moreover, Kipling's fissured stature—denounced as a strong imperialist by many critics, viewed by others as a clear-eyed commentator on the excesses of empire, and popular among readers—points to the ambiguous legacy of such figures who served as internal critics-*cum*-beneficiaries of empire.

Controversy about a Kipling—or a Lang or Anglo-Indian newspapers—rehearses debates inaugurated by postcolonial studies, debates that have subjected the analytic framework itself to scrutiny. Questions about postcolonial studies, its putative demise—premature to some, belated for others—and its continued utility have played out since at least the early 2000s. One critic has dated postcolonial studies to the years between Edward Said's 1978 *Orientalism* and Michael Hardt and Antonio Negri's 2000 *Empire*, while another cites the same dates, though the reference points are Said and Dipesh Chakrabarty's *Provincializing Europe* (Loomba et al. 2; Helgesson 165). For many, postcolonial criticism's focus on the discursive, cultural, and epistemological has surpassed its utility, outpaced by a globalization that, they argue, requires new critical tools and approaches. Arif Dirlik, an early critic, writes that postcolonial studies' "preoccupation with colonialism and its legacies makes for an exaggerated view of the hold of the past over contemporary realities, and an obliviousness to the reconfiguration of past legacies by contemporary restructurings of power" (429). In his 1991 essay "Is the Post- in Postmodernism the Post- in Postcolonial?" Kwame Anthony Appiah addressed the preoccupation with the legacy of colonialism and argues that while postcolonial scholars—in the West and in universities in formerly colonized places—adopt "the binarism of Self and Other . . . [as a] shibboleth," the lives and art of ordinary folk tell a different story: that "the broad shape of th[e] circulation of cultures . . . is surely that we are all already contaminated by each other" (354).

David Scott is more sympathetic than Dirlik or Appiah and values a postcolonial approach for its "strategy for investigating the trace of colonial effects in our postcolonial time" (386) and for "incisively and relentlessly demonstrat[ing] the essentialisms at work in older paradigms" (393). Nevertheless, he asks

> whether the questions that have animated postcolonialism's genealogical critique of colonial knowledge continue to be questions worth having answers to. I wonder whether the historical context of problems that produced the postcolonial effect as a critical effect has not now altered such that the yield of these questions is no longer what it was. I wonder, in

other words, whether postcolonialism has not lost its point and become normalized as a strategy for the mere accumulation of meaning. (392)

He concludes that it *has* lost its "point" and transformed from criticism to method (394). Jim Masselos, in his critique of Subaltern Studies—a field distinct, in its early days, from postcolonial studies but later more aligned with it—makes a similar argument: "once the basic point is made and accepted, that language reflects power and the systems of knowledge, and that knowledge is determined by the needs of power and is formulated through those needs, then perhaps there is little more to be said. The explanation may become mechanical and deterministic—and even circular . . . Because it has happened therefore it is a product of power and that is essentially all that can be said. The explanation ceases to explain and tends towards reflex cliché and dogma" (115–16).

None—not Dirlik, Appiah, Scott, or Masselos—is an "Occidentalist" and none minimizes the significance or value of postcolonial studies; they merely believe its moment or intellectual ferment has passed.[28] The historian Fredrick Cooper too has argued that postcolonial studies "needs a shot in the arm," but he believes that its lassitude can be rectified by giving "more weight to the specificity of colonial situations and the importance of struggles in colonies, in metropoles, and between the two" (401). Cooper, with Ann Stoler, has been advocating such a reorientation since their edited collection *Tensions of Empire*. In that volume, Stoler and Cooper caution against essentializing "the colonial" or "coloniality" as globally and historically singular. Even particular colonial regimes, they argue, "were neither monolithic nor omnipotent" (6), but "shot through with conflicts" (21). Attending to such conflicts exposes the precarity of colonial regimes (even while acknowledging their immense power). Like Stoler and Cooper, Cheryl Beredo, a historian of US–Philippines relations, describes "the colonial project as simultaneously powerful and fragile, as at once repressive and unsure, as both ideally ordered and manifestly unruly"

---

28. Critics of Subaltern Studies have charged *it* with losing its ferment when it abandoned the focus on reconstructing the lives and experiences of subalterns and took a turn towards colonial discourse analysis. Ludden characterizes this shift as "[c]olonial representations had begun to overwhelm subaltern activity" (19). Sumit Sarkar, himself a former member of the Subaltern Studies Group, articulated these criticisms most sharply in his 1997 essay "The Decline of the Subaltern in *Subaltern Studies*."

(13). Thus, in contrast to the view that colonial power was all-pervasive, such critiques suggest that we approach colonial power as constructed, debated, up for grabs.

The conflicts Stoler and Cooper urge us to be alert to only become visible when we examine the "colonial domain [as] distinct from the metropolitan one" (3). In the colonies, as Nathan Hensley elegantly puts it, the

> particular shape and strategies [of imperial policies] on the ground derived . . . from an ensemble of *ad hoc* responses to local conditions. Key decisions were made not just by grand strategists, but politicians responding to domestic necessities, bureaucrats buried in paperwork, and governors in the field seeking to advance their own careers. The Empire was not, as Sir John Seeley put it in 1883, acquired in a 'fit of absence of mind,' but it was nevertheless generated from an array of competing motivations, and at no point was its achievement guaranteed. (522)

The work of postcolonial studies today is to attend to these ad hoc responses and competing motivations, to what Stoler and Cooper call the "protracted debate . . . [that] went into defining dichotomies and distinctions that did not have the predicted effect" (8).[29]

Such interventions, particularly Cooper's, are precipitated by the field's tendency to repudiate the Enlightenment and with the "occlusion that results from turning the centuries of European colonization overseas into a critique of the Enlightenment, democracy, or modernity" (403). Rather, the goal and challenge is to

> *really* provincialize Europe. To do that is not to invert the narrative of progress to expose its underbelly, but to examine the limits as well as the power of European domination, the unevenness and conflict within Europe itself; it is to study systems of power and representation in interaction with each other, neither presuming the centrality of modern Europe as a reference point nor shying away from analysis of power as it actually was exercised. (Cooper 416)

---

29. In many postcolonial accounts, Stoler and Cooper write, "European agency too often remains undifferentiated, assumed, and unexplored" (16).

The value of such second-wave postcolonial analysis is that it neither shrouds the violence and power of colonialisms, nor jettisons reason, modernity, truth, or democratic values as "Western" impositions. Concerns that postcolonial studies' critiques of Enlightenment rationalism provide ready ammunition to retrogressive forces in the formerly colonized world and Euro-America have been voiced throughout the 1990s. In the Indian landscape, Sumit Sarkar wrote about the dangers of Hindutva as early as 1997; and in 2012, Partha Chatterjee, writing of the mass agitation in India at the time, noted "it would be a mistake to try to understand these activities of contemporary mass politics within the theoretical paradigm of peasant insurgency . . . I think a theoretical framework such as, let us say, populism . . . might be more appropriate for our purposes" ("After Subaltern Studies" 47). At a moment when, across the globe, sweepingly retrogressive nationalisms, populisms, and tribalisms—religious, white nationalist, majoritarian, purist—are riding to power on platforms that sweep aside reason, truth, and modernity (in some cases positing these values as "Western," in others as "elite"), we must secure the baby as we toss out the putative bathwater. As Cooper writes in regards to a value that is especially imperiled today, "Postcolonial studies has a strong stake in not carrying the contextualization of truth claims into a dismissal of truth as just another Western conceit" (414).

This book is animated by such questions and attends to the protracted debates about empire that are visible in newspapers, which Sean Latham and Robert Scholes refer to as "the first rough draft of history" (520). *Empire News* is situated in the colonial domain and alert to moments when the colonial regime's self-assurance wavered. Anglo-Indian newspapers' haphazard, sometimes near-hysterical, attempts to traverse and manage moments of crisis suggest that colonial power was neither omnipotent nor univocal. To say this is not to deny the power of the colonial state, particularly of its armed and fiduciary wings. But it is to explore the ad hoc nature of the Indian empire. These newspapers are some of the most intriguing sites to capture and scrutinize the instability, the tug-and-pull, the inconsistencies, reversals, and protracted debates among imperialists about the fate and future of the British Indian empire. Unlike the celebratory accounts of Lang sprouting in India, this book does not attempt to discover or rehabilitate hitherto neglected "good" colonialists. The Anglo-Indians we will encounter in this account are men—and they were, to a person, men—of their time and place, mirroring the ideologies of their class and position and, at moments, like Forster's Cyril Fielding, squirming against it. There are no hidden press heroes here; my aim is to explore a portion of the Anglo-Indian press at a moment when it was in flux, between the conclusion of empire's territorial expansion and the cementing of its imperial identity and policy.

Neither does this book seek to locate and showcase resisting Indians. Critics have warned us not to "celebrate 'resistance'" or "heroic anticolonialism" (Cooper 403, 412) nor ignore that many Indian elites "share[d] common purpose" with colonial authorities (O'Hanlon and Washbrook 125). As numberless accounts have demonstrated, in encounters between Britons and Indians, the latter were neither merely passive nor resistors. Many of the Indians who worked with or for Anglo-Indians approached their encounters as, to use Priya Joshi's rich metaphor, a transaction from which they intended to absorb and learn.[30] What they absorbed, they altered as they translated or grafted ideas into a different soil. Chatterjee discusses Rammohan Roy's and Dwarkanath Tagore's engagements with the "colonial early modern" before it came to a close in 1830 (*Black Hole* 134–58). Given the nature of their engagements, these men, particularly the latter, have tended to be shunted aside in nationalist accounts; as Chatterjee, one of the founding members of the Subaltern Studies Collective, laconically puts it, "Early modernity in India does not sit easily with the nationalist modern" (*Black Hole* 158). The historian Tapti Roy similarly seeks to avoid a Manichean model of colonial relations in her discussion of restrictions on Bengali literature; in an essay whose subtitle is "Colonial and Nationalist Surveillance of Bengali Literature," she notes that the Rev. James Long's dismissal of "exotic" vernacular books was echoed, even extended, by Bengali elites. Many of the Indians in my study who entered into relations with Anglo-Indians were neither subverting colonial power nor colluding with it, neither victims of false consciousness nor subalterns; rather they had, in Stoler and Cooper's terms, "a vantage point on modernity" (8).[31]

---

30. Priya Joshi writes, "my image of the British Empire in India is of two sides facing each other with their arms outstretched, each side taking, snatching, pilfering, plundering what and when it could, but also giving, exchanging, and unevenly borrowing, fitfully and sporadically, but persistently, from the other" (*In Another Country* 7).

31. In her subtle essay on the circulation of books at the Madras/Chennai public library between 1996 and 2003, Priya Joshi argues that "the bilingual reading practices of this new generation . . . reveal an embrace of global realities *simultaneous with* an embrace of local conditions. Each *enables* the other, unlike the post-colonial framework, according to whose formulation one obliterated the other" ("Globalizing" 37).

While postcolonial studies writ large serves as the intellectual sign under which this project appears, "circulation" is one of its structuring principles. Recently critics such as Sukanya Banerjee, Kapil Raj, Ryan Cordell, and James Mulholland have criticized the overuse of the trope of circulation. Mulholland points out that the term is often deployed as a "generic placeholder" for mobility, effacing the structures that produce—or prevent—movement ("Indian It-Narrative" 374). Kapil Raj, a historian of science, encourages a more robust use of circulation such that it serves as "a strong counterpoint to the unidirectionality of 'diffusion' or even of 'dissemination' or 'transmission,' . . . which all imply a producer and an end user. 'Circulation' suggests a more open flow—and especially the possibility of the mutations and reconfigurations coming back to the point of origin" (344). Rather than a synonym for "influence," Raj suggests, circulation might more fruitfully be considered the start of transformation, while Mulholland considers circulation as "the process of creating cultural meaning" (377).

Ryan Cordell has produced some of the richest work examining both the structures that enable circulation—in his case study, newspaper reprints—and the transformations that circulation engenders. Deploying the analogy of "virality," Cordell asks of a text, "How far and in what forms did it spread? In which communities did it circulate? How was this text modified, remixed, responded to, or commented upon?" ("Viral Textuality" 32). In a similar vein, but different archive, Priya Joshi works with circulation records of Indian libraries to tease out "how ideas and ideologies are dispersed, mutate, and are reauthorized far from their source"; this approach leads her to access "a deep archive of . . . the extensive half-life of things Victorian" ("Globalizing" 22). While Cordell's and Joshi's works are devoted to reception and consumption, Banerjee and Mulholland have drawn attention to the uneven trajectory of circulation itself: they trace moments when the vectors of mobility, rather than proceeding in a linear or unbroken fashion, are interrupted or blocked. As Mulholland asks, what happens when "movement is interrupted, accidental, disorganized, or angular"? When relations are "entangled" and flows stop, when "currents" are "arrested or redirected"? ("Indian It-Narrative" 377–78).

Empire News is informed by such questions. It takes up literal and material circulation—newspapers traverse space—as well as obstruction. The circulation of newspapers depended on the labor of many and was the outcome of particular technological, legal, and political forces—type foundries and presses, licenses, censorship, oversight and deposit requirements—that allowed English-language newspapers to survive in archives while so many Indian-language newspapers from the same period either never survived or are in extremely deteriorated condition. But even the surviving archive of these circulating objects is filled with gaps, which makes movement through it uneven and piecemeal. Even as I tackle the technologies and routes of flow, I will also interrogate stasis, blockage, and obstruction. In short, this book examines the mechanisms and structures of circulation, as well as the *failures* of circulation. In each chapter, I will examine who or what is mobile, as well as the historical moments when circulation was impeded, blocked, or obstructed by material and ideological forces and when mobility was constricted. As I attend to the physical movement of newspapers and newsmen, I remain cautious in making claims about non-material circulation, the flow of ideas or influence.

Circulatory obstruction occurred during what I have been referring to as moments of "crisis." A few words about the term, particularly as it relates to the media, are in order. In his comprehensive, keyword-style analysis of "crisis," Reinhart Koselleck refers to it as "a structural signature of modernity" (372), a concept that, beginning in the nineteenth century, functioned as "a truly autonomous concept of history" (377). Charting the term's usage in the works of Schiller, Rousseau, Burke, Paine, and Diderot, Koselleck illustrates that crisis came to be conceptualized as "both structurally recurring and utterly unique" (374), an "iterative concept" *and* "a singular, epochal challenge," evolution *and* revolution (378), referring to "long-term changes as well as occasional outbursts" (381). In the twentieth century, he notes, the term's usage has expanded so considerably that "crisis" has become a "catchword" (397), used widely in the human and social sciences. But "[a]bove all, it is the media which have inflated the use of the term" such that "crisis" has "transformed to fit the uncertainties of whatever might be favored at a given moment" (399).

Though the media Koselleck castigates lies in the future of the newspapers we analyze here, the media's affinity for "crisis" is virtually woven into its DNA. Not all that appears in newsprint is or is presented as crisis, of course, but newspapers' business model, their need to generate the next number before the ink on the first is dry, means that they rely heavily on the novel, the calamitous, the catastrophic. Crisis is central to circulation. For this reason, Janet Roitman's insight in *Anti-Crisis* is pertinent: "there is not 'crisis' versus 'noncrisis,' both of which can be observed empirically; rather, crisis is a logical observation that generates meaning in a self-referential system, a non-locus from which to signify contingency and paradox" (10). In the chapters that follow, I will trace both the making and managing of crisis in my sample newspapers as I ask: What do newspapers mark as crises that require decisive action or explanation? How do they write about crises that lie outside their making? How does naming an event a crisis assert local independence over global affairs?

———

As no history of Anglo-Indian newspapers in the period leading up to the Uprising of 1857 exists, broad generalizations abound: that the Anglo-Indian press was insular, isolationist, and, in 1857 particularly, racially inflammatory. As the chapters that follow illustrate, some of these characterizations were accurate—some of the time. But as I also detail, the sample of the Bengal and mofussil press I examine was less monolithic and unanimous as such generalizations would indicate. It was, in fact, marked by instability, uncertainty, and infighting. As a body, the Anglo-Indian press rarely transmitted imperial certitude. Most newspapers were vocal in their critiques of the Company and vociferously debated almost every aspect of the British administration of India—though not British rule or presence on the subcontinent. Newspapers' editorial commentary was frequently aggressive in tone, but antagonism was disbursed equitably across the board to print rivals, the government, fellow Anglo-Indian civilians and officials, Indian rulers, and Indians. Rather than correcting (mis)impressions of the Anglo-Indian press of this period, the purpose of *Empire News* is to offer a granular account of the connections and disruptions that the press forged and that shaped it between 1845 and 1860. Chapters will trace circuits of relations between news outlets within India, between Anglo-Indians and Indians, and between Britons and Anglo-Indians, attentive throughout to moments of crisis when these circuits malfunctioned or when colonial consensus disintegrated.

The arguments of this book emerge inductively, through the accretion of stories it tells about Anglo-Indian newspapers, about the men who wrote and produced them, and about the events they responded and reacted to. To this history, a Peter Stone D'Rozario matters for the glimpse he provides into the world of heritage-Portuguese printers, while a G. H. Wilby serves as a portal into the network of Anglo-Indian editors and subeditors. Working in a ruptured archive, some of these stories are themselves truncated and can only be explored so far. Throughout, I foreground the gaps, absences, and silences in the archive, as well as moments when the argument relies on speculation and conjecture.

Chapter 1 lays the groundwork by offering a bird's-eye view of the ecosystem of Anglo-Indian newspapers of the period. The archival fissures of the *Mofussilite* will serve as an entry into the reading strategies required for navigating a colonial archive dotted with caesuras. The chapter's focus is a McKenzie-esque attention to bibliography, particularly those bibliographic codes that shape newspapers and periodicals: format, fonts, masthead and layout; news, commentary, and letters; local and extra-local coverage; reprints and their deployment by editors; and the relation between printers and editors, correspondents and readers. My attention to such bibliographic features serves to draw out the sociocultural environment of Anglo-Indian newspapers, one shaped and fed by an animus towards the colonial governing authority, the East India Company. The chapter concludes with a discussion of the convoluted politics of one newspaper that simultaneously critiqued the empire and advocated an imperial mission.

In May 1851, Victoria inaugurated the Great Exhibition in London's Hyde Park. A showcase of "the Works of Industry of All Nations," the exhibition displayed thousands of items from around the world. The most popular item on display was the Kohinoor diamond, the glittering spoil of the annexation of Punjab. The newspapers in our sample eagerly covered preparations for the exhibition—then suddenly drop the topic. In place of promised reports on displays and goods, the columns of Anglo-Indian newspapers are dominated with lengthy accounts of the trial of Jyoti Prasad, a businessman who had provisioned the British India army during the Anglo-Sikh wars. The case of *East India Company v. Jootee Persuad* consumed the Anglo-Indian press not least because his legal counsel was a newspaper owner and editor, John Lang of the *Mofussilite*. In chapter 2, I read the displacement of the exhibition and its substitution by the trial as a gloss on the exhibition's celebration of "industry"; in a colonial context, as Lang's defense of Prasad suggested, industry is indistinguishable from plunder. Anglo-Indian newspaper coverage of the trial is a story of the physical circulation of news—battles over court transcripts, reprints, and editorial commentary—and the recirculation and reprisal of the Burke-Hastings trials of the late eighteenth century that attempted to put the imperial mission on trial. Newspaper accounts of the Jyoti Prasad case enable us to hear the colony—mediated through an Australian-born, British-trained, mofussil-inhabiting barrister—speaking back to the metropole as the latter celebrated its global ascendency.

By the early summer of 1857, discontent among Indian soldiers, or sepoys, of the British army was growing, and on May 10 troops at

Meerut mutinied. Disaffection quickly spread to other units and among the civilian population, and for the next twelve months large portions of the North-Western Provinces were in turmoil. Chapter 3 examines Anglo-Indian newspapers' coverage of the events of 1857–58, coverage riven with gaps as well as dizzying shifts. The gaps we encounter in the archival record are the outcome of physical obstructions—chaotic and blocked roads brought the circulation of people, goods, mail, and news to a virtual standstill—as well as government censorship. As access to copy withered, editors improvised and their temporary solutions led to an unprecedented *expansion* of sources. This chapter details some of the ways blocked circuits counterintuitively led to an explosion of types of sources and voices. As editorial control slipped—due both to a high level of turnover at the helm of newspapers and to the additional voices included—so did newspapers' consistency: throughout 1857, Anglo-Indian newspapers expressed a bewildering array of political explanations for the Uprising, some anticipating twentieth-century historians' understandings. This chapter highlights the ways crisis and the *failure* of circulation produced new circuits of information and accounts of empire.

When sepoys at the Meerut cantonment mutinied, Lang had the great misfortune of being in London. For a journalist to be absent when the biggest story of his lifetime breaks is sheer bad luck. Though far away, Lang continued to write about India: when Dickens asked him for copy on the day's hot news, Lang obliged . . . by recycling travel essays from his earliest days in India over a decade earlier. The essays Lang repurposed had been penned in a politically different India, and in a genre, the picturesque, that was at odds with the political role they were pressed into. Chapter 4 traces the circulation of Lang's essays from mid-1840s India to the twelve-part "Wanderings in India" in Dickens's *Household Words* to volume publication in London to its most recent guise in an abridged reprint from Delhi. Focusing on the journey of this text from an Anglo-Indian newspaper to a metropolitan weekly to a volume in a railway reading series to a postcolonial revisionist series, I offer an account of the ways the site of publication alters the meaning and reading of a text. Highlighting as well the faint traces of indigenous voices in Lang's account, the chapter examines what Ranjit Guha calls the "braided temporalities" of colonial relations (335).

As a whole, this book traces the movement of print, peoples, and occasionally ideas across numerous boundaries. Chapters 1 and 4 focus on circulation in local and transnational registers, respectively, while chapters 2 and 3 highlight narratives of failed or blocked circulation during moments of crisis. Neither the trajectory nor the business of the Anglo-India news media in this period was straightforward or well preserved; consequently, *Empire News* is throughout attentive to archival gaps which it uses to illuminate nineteenth-century colonial relations, as well as shape our scholarly strategies for working in such ruptured archives.

Chapter 1

Bibliographical, Periodical, and Imperial Codes

In March 1853, Dickens's *Household Words* carried a lighthearted essay entitled "Starting a Paper in India." The piece jauntily narrates the mishaps—workmen demanding exorbitant pay, half-drunk pressmen, a compositor devoured by a crocodile, the short supply of bullock carts and even shorter supply of the capital letter "H" in a set of fonts—an enterprising young editor faced as he set out to start a paper in the interior of India, "upwards of eight hundred miles from a sea-port town."[1] Published anonymously, as was customary, the essay, we now know from *Household Words*' office books, is by John Lang, and although it claims to narrate the experiences of "a friend of mine," it is in fact an embellished account of Lang's own experience. Buoyant and self-aggrandizing, "Starting a Paper" presents life in India as the stuff of adventure and romance. Putting out a newspaper in India was, in reality, a less romantic affair; it was a business with many moving parts and a high mortality rate. This chapter, with that newspaper Lang started as its focal point, will illuminate some of those moving parts of the Anglo-Indian newspaper industry of nineteenth-century India.

An Archive—With Many Gaps

Unlike most of its Anglo-Indian rivals, Lang's newspaper adopted a non-English name for its title; the name *Mofussilite* is a linguistic hybrid formed by adding a Latin suffix to the Anglicized Urdu word "mofussil"

---

1. "Starting a Paper in India," *Household Words*, 26 March 1853, 94.

that meant "the provinces." In selecting this name, Lang was signaling the newspaper's intention of speaking from a remove, of distancing itself from the centers of power. A promotional advertisement that appeared two weeks before its inaugural appearance in August 1845 proclaimed the *Mofussilite* a newspaper "for the people in the Mofussil" and pledged to devote attention to "Oriental Literature and other materials intimately connected with 'the land we live in'" (Chanda, *History* [1987] 261). Though it neglects to specify *which* "people in the Mofussil"—Britons and Europeans or Indians? Company officials or private citizens?—the quotes around "the land we live in" alert us to some disquiet about the newspaper's sense of belonging. Yet, despite its name and promise to represent "the people in the Mofussil," the *Mofussilite* did not appear from what was generally conceived of at the time as the provinces. Rather, as the masthead of its first number on 2 August 1845 announced, the newspaper was published in Calcutta, the capital and administrative center of the British Empire in India. For four months, the paper appeared every Saturday from Calcutta, until it suddenly announced that it was relocating, and "after the 1st of March next, the *Mofussilite* will issue, twice in every week, from *Umballah*."[2] Only in making this move, some 1,000 miles west to the frontier of British India, did the newspaper's geographical location come to reflect its name.[3]

What are we to make of the newspaper's four-month cameo in Calcutta? Did this period serve as a dry run? Was Lang testing the waters? Establishing a reputation? Gathering subscriptions? Training a crew? Was the move to the mofussil precipitated by some failure in Calcutta? Was the name of the paper initially metaphoric and only later fused with its geographic location? Lang left no private papers and none of the business materials of the newspaper have surfaced, so we do not have immediate answers to these questions. Though such gaps may seem like a handicap in a study that draws on the newspaper, they serve as an apt emblem of the colonial archive: an artifact pockmarked by absences. This section draws on the *Mofussilite* to illuminate the discontinuities a researcher encounters in the colonial archive and the strategies required to surmount such gaps. The next section will turn to a range of Anglo-Indian newspapers—including the Calcutta-based dailies the *Bengal Hurkaru* and the

---

2. *Mofussilite*, 22 November 1845, 231.

3. The *Englishman* noted the inconsistency between the paper's name and place of publication: "the *Mofussilite*, a weekly paper, lately published here, is determined to realize its name, and move up to Umballah" (20 November 1845; qtd. in *Allen's Indian Mail*, 21 January 1846, 36).

Englishman and the Serampore-based weekly the *Friend of India*—and examine their material features and circulation. The chapter will close by delving into the politics of the *Mofussilite* to ascertain what a critique of empire looked like in the mid-century Anglo-Indian press. Overall, the chapter seeks to establish a baseline for the materiality and substance of my sample of newspapers. In contrast to the next two chapters that take up crises, this one emphasizes circulation in the everyday.

If the *Mofussilite*'s four months in Calcutta were not a trial run, they were, from a market perspective, a risky undertaking: in 1844, the year before the *Mofussilite*'s appearance in Calcutta, the city boasted three English dailies and seven weeklies or semiweeklies.[4] Standing out in such a populated sphere required substantial skill, not to mention cash. In the mofussil, by contrast, there was far less competition: the *Bengal and Agra Directory* of 1847 lists one English paper from Meerut (the *Mofussilite*), one from Agra, and one from Benares. In the mofussil, potential readers were spread out over a vast region that extended from Allahabad to Bijnor, Kanpur to Kumaon. In faraway garrison towns, Anglo-Indians were eager for news from the "wider" world. In *The Good Old Days of the Honorable John Company* (1882), W. H. Carey wrote that due to the scarcity of papers in the 1840s, readers in the North-Western Provinces "clutched at" any news source they could (160).[5] Thus, in addition to promoting a "mofussil mentality"—that is, distance from the centers of power—the *Mofussilite*'s move up-country in mid-century reflected a sound business decision.

If the Calcutta months were a trial run preparatory to moving to the mofussil, one detail from these early months raises a conundrum: when the *Mofussilite* appeared on 2 August 1845, its printer and publisher was listed as P. S. D'Rozario of 8, Tank Square in Calcutta. After a mere four issues, the 30 August paper listed a new printer and publisher, Thomas Andrews of 5, Esplanade Row, who continued in that role until the final Calcutta number of 22 November.[6] What are we to make of this turnover? The requirement that the name of the printer and publisher be listed on

---

4. See *The Bengal and Agra Directory and Annual Register for the Year 1844* (342–33). The population of Calcutta in 1840 was approximately 360,000, the British population some three to four thousand (Nair, "Growth" 23).

5. Meerut got its first newspaper, the *Meerut Observer*, in 1831; it expired in 1837 or thereabouts (Carey 156–57). See also "The Newspaper Press of the North-west Provinces," *Allen's Indian Mail*, 22 October 1859, 870.

6. In the *Bengal and Agra Directory and Annual Register* of 1846 the "Publisher" column for the *Mofussilite* is left blank (343).

all printed materials dates to 1799 when Lord Wellesley, the governor general, imposed the first press regulations in India.[7] These regulations—and the many revisions and reversals to them—reflect the Government of India's uncertainty in the early nineteenth century about the value of a free press. Mrinal Kanti Chanda notes that in the early years of the Indian press—when newspapers and journals were run almost exclusively by Anglo-Indians—the government preferred to deal with editors (*History* [1987] 362–63). They were held responsible for the content of the paper and, in a number of notorious cases such as that of William Duane in 1794, Charles Maclean in 1798, and James Silk Buckingham in 1823, deported for violating restrictions imposed by the government. (For a summary of press regulations in India from 1780 to 1860, see the appendix.) In time, as increasing numbers of Indians entered the business and extradition to England proved impossible, the government shifted its surveillance efforts from editors to printers and publishers.[8]

The Press Act of 1835 lifted the draconian Press Regulations of 1823, which had imposed direct censorship. The 1835 act stipulated only that the printer and publisher declare themselves to a magistrate and that their name and address be listed on publications (Cassels 376–78).[9] Though declaration before a magistrate was not an onerous burden, it was a chore that a new paper, trying to raise subscriptions and revenue, work out distribution networks, and compose a paper on deadline, might wish to avoid. Yet, after only four numbers, the *Mofussilite* changed its printer and publisher from P. S. D'Rozario to Thomas Andrews. Why?

---

7. Wellesley's 1799 regulations—which also required that all papers be "inspected" by the government—prompted the proprietor of the *Bengal Hurkaru* to write the government to point out that the printer's name had always appeared at the bottom of newspapers and to inquire how and where inspection was to occur given subscribers expected the paper in the morning (Cassels 366). The requirement in Britain that every newspaper publish the name of the printer and publisher dates to a 1798 act (H. Barker 69).

8. For printers, see Chanda (*History* [1987] 415–18) and Ahmed (56). Jacob Heatley, editor of the *Calcutta Morning Post*, had an English father and Indian mother, as did Francis Sandys, whom Buckingham handed the *Calcutta Journal* over to when he was deported in 1823 (Ahmed 56, 62; Chanda, *History* [1987] 429; Sanial, "History" [III] 92–96).

9. Boyce writes, "The Act was based on a single principle: that the existence of liberty in the shadow of immediately employable force was both safe and permissible. No one doubted that the government could control, influence, or shut down any press at any time" (39).

We do not know for certain and must speculate by drawing on resources outside the newspaper's pages.

The name "D'Rozario" indicates Portuguese ancestry. Portuguese Jesuits had introduced the printing press to India in 1556, and into the eighteenth and nineteenth centuries most compositors and many printers were of Portuguese descent (Dharwadker 2; Chanda, *History* [1987] 388–89). P. S. D'Rozario & Co. in Calcutta was a well-established printing, publishing, bookbinding, and bookselling firm, located in Tank Square, one of the most prestigious business districts of the city.[10] The firm's origins date back to at least April 1823, as S. C. Sanial relates in his 1908 "History of Journalism in India, III": "a license was granted to Mr. John Sandys, the editor, Messers. John Palmer and George Ballard, the managing proprietors, and Mr. Peter Stone De Rozario, to publish the *Calcutta Journal*" (92).[11] Every Bengal directory from 1838 onwards lists P. S. D'Rozario as a Calcutta printer and publisher,[12] and the Rev. James Long, in his famous 1859 *Report on the Native Press in Bengal*, cites the D'Rozario firm as an agent for the Vernacular Literature Society's publications (83). So prominent and successful was the firm of P. S. D'Rozario that even the most cursory glance at the advertising pages of any English-language periodical of India at mid-century brings up numerous references to its publications and library.[13]

Thomas Andrews, on the other hand, proves harder to trace. His name does not appear in any Bengal and Agra directory in a twenty-year span. *Granth*, Jadavpur University's mammoth open-access site on book history in South Asia, lists a Thomas Andrews as deputy superintendent of the

---

10. See https://granthsouthasia.wordpress.com/sabti/sabt-index-d/. Accessed 10 September 2014.

11. This license Sanial refers to was brought out to comply with the 1823 Press Regulations, which was used to deport Buckingham; Sandys, being mixed race, could not be deported despite the journal's continuing to run afoul of regulations (Sanial, "History" [III] 92–96; Chanda, *History* [1987] 429).

12. The 1825 Bengal Directory lists a "P.S. DeRozario" as a printer in Mirzapore, halfway between Delhi and Calcutta on the banks of the Ganges. Whether this is the same Peter Stone D'Rozario as the Calcutta printer is unclear, although *Granth* lists them as the same.

13. Two examples: *Mofussilite*, 17 March 1848, 176, for "P.S. D'Rozario & Co.'s Library" and *Mofussilite*, 8 September 1848, 572, about a volume in "English, Bengalee, and Hindee" published by the firm.

Government Press in Allahabad in 1862 and a T. Andrews as printer at the Secundra Orphan Press in Agra in 1857.[14] The dates allow that either of these men—who could be the same person—could have been in Calcutta in 1845 and the *Mofussilite*'s printer between September and November of that year. Yet another possibility presents itself: the *Mofussilite*'s 2 March 1852 record of subscribers lists a T. Andrews as "Principal Sudeer Ameen, Jaloun." A "sudder amen" is, in the words of *Hobson-Jobson*, "a second class of native Judge" (Yule and Burnell 862). If this T. Andrews was the *Mofussilite*'s second Calcutta printer, then the paper's printer was mixed race or Christian-Indian (or both) and moved into the legal profession not long after. The absence of leads on Andrews, however, only deepens the mystery: why would the *Mofussilite* switch from one of Calcutta's most renowned and established English-language publishers to an unknown entity? We can only speculate: perhaps Lang quarreled with D'Rozario or perhaps D'Rozario caught wind of Lang's intention to move the operation to the mofussil and chose not to invest further in an operation with little future for him. Another possibility is that Lang switched to a printer who was more willing to move to the mofussil: P. S. D'Rozario, an established firm in one of Calcutta's most desirable commercial districts, was not mobile. The shift in printer adds one more mystery to the perplexing tale of a newspaper whose origins are consistently misrepresented.[15]

If we are to credit Lang's 1853 *Household Words* account of starting a paper in India, in December 1845 he traveled some 900 miles across the Gangetic Plain with a crew of pressmen and box of typefaces to establish a press up-country. Of the printer he engaged in Calcutta at the start of the journey, Lang wrote, "I at length selected a young man who had been a foreman in one of the Calcutta printing-offices. I was aware that his character could not bear investigation; but I had no alternative" (95). We do not know who this young man of questionable character was—Thomas Andrews or someone else?—but from its 1 January 1847 number onwards, the *Mofussilite* was printed and published by John A. Gibbons. That Gibbons was a highly

---

14. See http://granthsouthasia.wordpress.com/sabti/sabt-index-a/. Accessed 10 September 2014.

15. Many claim that the *Mofussilite* started in Meerut in 1845 (see Yule and Burnell 570; *Granth* at https://granthsouthasia.wordpress.com/print-bibliography/bib-index-l/; Chanda, *History* [2008] 252; even Lang in his thinly disguised *Household Words* essay). Aside from the paper itself, the only source that accurately identifies the *Mofussilite*'s start in Calcutta is W. H. Carey's *The Good Old Day of the Honorable John Company* (160).

reliable and steady hand is indicated by the longevity of his tenure at the *Mofussilite* and the increasing responsibility that devolved upon him. To wit: an 1851 announcement signed "John Lang, Sole Proprietor" announces that Gibbons was authorized to "receive money for and on account of the *Mofussilite Press*, and to grant receipts for the same."[16] And by 1862, two years before Lang's death, Gibbons' roles had expanded to publisher and manager of the Mofussilite Press.[17] If Gibbons was the printer Lang enticed to the mofussil in 1845, he developed a remarkable steadiness of character over time. A more likely scenario is that Lang jettisoned that young man of questionable character and hired the responsible Gibbons—or that the tale Lang related in *Household Words* was simply a good yarn.

The puzzle about printers and relocation are the tip of a deeper mystery, an archival caesura. In announcing the move to Ambala, the *Mofussilite* warned readers: "It is *possible* we may be able to commence operations before [the 1st of March 1846]; but, taking into consideration the delay necessarily attendant on the transfer of printing material, we do not think it *probable*."[18] Whether the paper made its deadline seems unclear as no copies from 1846 exist in the archives. No explanation exists for the missing year, and Crittenden speculates that the *Mofussilite* went dark in 1846 (90).[19] However, evidence from the body of the *Mofussilite* suggests that the newspaper *did*, in fact, appear in 1846. The first number of 1847, dated Friday, 1 January, includes "Col. Outram's Book" with "(*Continued*

---

16. *Mofussilite*, 21 January 1851, 44. See also the announcement in 1850 that due to ill-health the editor was moving to Shimla to edit the paper, while "the mechanical part of the duties [of the paper] will be carried on by Mr. Gibbons" (*Mofussilite*, 16 April 1850, 244).

17. http://granthsouthasia.wordpress.com/sabti/sabt-index-g/. It is unclear when Gibbons arrived on the subcontinent; no John A. Gibbons appears on any ship arrivals list I have consulted and his first appearance in a Bengal directory is in 1847. Over a quarter century later, *Allen's Indian Mail* announced the 1874 marriage of John A. Gibbons "formerly of Agra and Meerut, N.W.P. of India" at St. George's in Hanover Square, London (9 March 1874).

18. *Mofussilite*, 22 November 1845, 321.

19. Crittenden bases his argument on bibliography: the 1847 newspapers are numbered "Vol. 2"; had the *Mofussilite* continued publishing in 1846, the 1847 editions would have been numbered Volume 3. Closer scrutiny, however, indicates that the numbering is inconsistent: the first number of 1847 is listed as "Vol. 2, No. 88," while the last number in 1845 was No. 18, suggesting that 69 issues of the *Mofussilite* appeared in 1846.

from last Tues)" below the title (8).[20] And in an 1851 item recounting its growth, the editor writes, "The *Mofussilite* on the 4th of March 1846, commenced with 133 actual Subscribers, and in the month of August of the same year it bore upon its list upwards of 800."[21] In addition to such internal evidence, other newspapers serve as a resource as well. In March 1846, the *Friend of India* carried a notice on its front page of the "first number of the *Mofussilite*" and "offer[ed] the Editor our cordial congratulations on his resurrection."[22] The *Friend* even reprints the *Mofussilite*'s "manifesto," which is dated 4 March.[23] In short, it appears that the *Mofussilite*'s editor met his promise to commence operations on or about 1 March 1846.

Having solved one mystery—the *Mofussilite* did indeed publish in 1846—we are left with another: the absence of any numbers from 1846 in the archive. In a brief notice, Crittenden speculates that the paper was censored for publishing "sexually explicit" Persian tales (Crittenden, "Missing" 10). As the tales Crittenden refers to are not particularly explicit and as the government had pulled back from active censorship following Metcalfe's Press Act XI of 1835, this suggestion seems like a stretch. A more plausible explanation for the archival gap is the *Mofussilite*'s new location: the Ambala Cantonment was established in 1843 following the first Anglo-Sikh War, and the Ambala District came into existence as an administrative unit in 1847. Thus, in 1846 Ambala would certainly have been the mofussil—perhaps excessively so. As a military garrison, it lay within the Company's sphere of influence, but was a distant satellite. This

---

20. Two weeks later, the Irish Relief Agency advertised a subscription for victims of the potato famine that noted, "For an account of the reasons which have led to the formation of the Agency see the *Mofussilite* of the 29th December." *Mofussilite*, 15 January 1847, 34.

21. *Mofussilite*, 10 January 1851, 21.

22. *Friend of India*, 19 March 1846, 177. Throughout the year, the *Friend of India* regularly cites from the pages of the *Mofussilite*. See *Friend of India*, 4 June 1846, 353; 9 July 1846, 435; 30 July 1846, 481; 24 December 1846, 819. *Allen's Indian Mail*, a London-based steamship newspaper, also regularly cited news stories from the *Mofussilite*. See 6 May 1846, 299; 5 June 1846, 365; 13 August 1846, 495; 24 September 1846, 587–88; 27 October 1846, 655; 5 November 1846, 684; 30 November 1846, 717; 4 December 1846, 765; 30 December 1846, 778.

23. The manifesto closes with "We confess, we are hardly prepared to renew our labours: for, as yet, our arrangements are far from complete: but we prefer making our reappearance on the day fixed, rather than delay publication." See *Friend of India*, 19 March 1846, 178.

remoteness might explain the missing copies of the *Mofussilite*. Although the 1818 press regulations required all newspapers to register with a magistrate and deposit copies with the secretary of the government, it is possible that as a distant outpost Ambala was not yet firmly within administrative surveillance. Though this speculation for the missing 1846 numbers is precisely that, it sheds some light on the magnitude of Lang's ambition to produce a paper from the mofussil and the market he was hoping to capture.[24] It also explains why the operation moved again. For move once again it did: in January 1847, the *Mofussilite* began to appear as a biweekly from Meerut, where it settled for some half a dozen years.

What can we learn from this checkered history of gaps, absences, and uncertainties? First, quite simply, that the newspaper business was not a steady or stable one. Chanda highlights the "high rate of mortality of journals in their infancy"; most newspapers and periodicals born between 1780 and 1857, he writes, "languished for want of sufficient nourishment" (*History* [1987] xix). The primary nourishment they lacked was an audience: Chanda points to the small size of the Anglo-Indian community, its lack of interest in local affairs, and its tendency to prefer British periodicals, notwithstanding the delay in their arrival (xx–xxi). Harish Chandra Mukherjee, owner and editor of the *Hindoo Patriot*, wrote in 1855 that the English press in India was limited because most were "merely organs of the different services which maintain them . . . Hence they are totally devoid of any influence over any section of the community" (qtd. in Chanda, *History* [1987] xxi). Not only did the *Mofussilite* not "languish," it flourished: between March and August 1846, its subscription list grew from 133 to 800, signaling a population eager for nourishment.[25] The *Mofussilite*

---

24. A dozen years later, *Allen's Indian Mail* wrote, "[The *Mofussilite*] commenced its existence at a very critical time—Affghanistan [sic], Persia, Scinde, and the Punjab, were all in a ferment. The avidity for Mofussil news was at its highest pitch . . . and this eagerness for intelligence from the seat of strife, in combination with the ability and vivacity of its proprietor and editor, enabled the *Moff* at once to gain a footing" (22 October 1859, 870). One final possibility (which does not shed light on the missing numbers from 1846): perhaps the *Mofussilite* never relocated to Ambala at all, but moved instead directly from Calcutta to Meerut. This would explain the oft-repeated claim that the *Mofussilite* commenced in Meerut.

25. To place these numbers in context, an 1833 estimate of the subscribers of all the Calcutta news outlets placed them at 2,200; by the 1840s, the number of subscribers to Calcutta papers was believed to be lower, largely due to the growth of up-country newspapers such as the *Mofussilite* and *Delhi Gazette* (see Chanda, *History* [1987] 403–05).

found a niche and provided readers with a product they desired; as H. G. Keene wrote in his 1897 memoir, *A Servant of "John Company,"* Lang was "a general favourite [of] the Anglo-Indian public" (123), which relished his sharp tongue and humor. That the *Mofussilite* survived, flourished, and developed a robust following should not obscure the challenges of running a newspaper, challenges whose traces are registered in its uneven and fragmented archive.

The lacunae thrown up by the case of the *Mofussilite* offer a lesson in archival methods. Faced with an archive of missing or unavailable data, we must adopt flexible reading methods, akin to sleuthing, and develop informed speculations. Every historian does this, of course, seeks to tell a history despite what the historian Michel-Rolph Trouillot calls the many "silences" in the archive. Every historical record, Trouillot maintains, "is a particular bundle of silences, the result of a unique process, and the operation required to deconstruct these silences will vary accordingly" (27). In a similar vein and working in a different archive, Antoinette Burton writes that "[i]f feminist work . . . has taught us anything it is to be creative about what counts as an archive and to learn to recognize that history resides in any number of locations" (104). I have applied such insights to the study of colonial Book History and drawn on a range of tools and resources to develop a profile of print and place: anywhere from ships' arrivals and departures lists to local directories to passing references in other journals to advertisements to maps of a colonial city. Piecing together the history of a colonial newspaper requires a researcher to look in myriad and unexpected places, as well as embrace a degree of uncertainty and ambiguity. While this section modeled some of these reading strategies with the *Mofussilite*, the next broadens the discussion to examine additional Anglo-Indian newspapers, focusing on the bibliographic and formal features of my sample of Anglo-Indian newspapers. The final section returns to the *Mofussilite* to examine the politics of one mid-century newspaper that positioned itself as critical of the Government of India.

Materiality: Communicating through Form, Format, and Organization

In his seminal essay "What Is the History of Books?" (1982), Robert Darnton notes the variety of "ephemera" that fall under the study of Book History and the many subfields a book historian has to consider: "the history of libraries, of publishing, of paper, type, and reading" which "would have him [the book historian] collating editions, compiling statistics, decoding copyright law, wading through reams of manuscript, heaving at the bar of a reconstructed common press, and psychoanalyzing the mental processes of readers" (66–67). Instead of such "interdisciplinarity run riot," Darnton offers a streamlined "communications circuit" to disaggregate and locate key points in the journey of a print text (67). By inviting us to think of the relations between author, publisher, printer, shipper, bookseller, and reader, Darnton locates a piece of print in economic, social, political, and cultural contexts. In many cases, the records necessary to trace the circuit Darnton sketches are available, in others they have simply disappeared (if they existed at all). In the case of colonial newspapers, where the detailed records of the book trade that form one basis of Book History are scarce, D. F. McKenzie's work in *Bibliography and the Sociology of Texts* (1986), with its capacious definition of bibliography, offers direction. McKenzie rejects the notion that bibliography examines merely the "arbitrary marks" on a page and eschews meaning; he insists that bibliography includes the study of, among other things, "the composition, formal design, and transmission of texts by writers, printers, and publishers" (12). For McKenzie, the composition and design work of printers and publishers are "social," signs of the human context in which books are produced, and worthy of attention for that reason.

Jerome McGann's *The Textual Condition* (1991) develops McKenzie's framework and offers further direction. Drawing our attention away from both the textual and paratextual (prefaces, dedications, advertisements, footnotes) features of a text, McGann highlights "bibliographic codes": "typefaces, bindings, book prices, page format" (13). These physical features, McGann argues, are as central to a text's "symbolic and signifying dimensions" (56) as its "linguistic codes" where meaning has traditionally been sought. For McGann, "Meaning is transmitted through bibliographic as well as linguistic codes" (57), simply because for authors "[t]he physical presence of these printed texts has been made to serve aesthetic ends" (78). McGann, like McKenzie whose insights he builds on, seeks to reorient and expand scholars' attention solely from the textual, linguistic, or aesthetic to the bibliographic as well. McGann's object of analysis is literary texts, and he himself hesitates to extend his argument about bibliographic codes to historical documents (69–76), though others inspired by McKenzie's "sociology of texts" have expanded the analysis of bibliographic codes beyond the Romantic and Modernist poems and novels McGann limits himself to.

Peter Brooker and Andrew Thacker adapt the notion of bibliographic codes for the study of periodicals. Their "periodical codes" include features such as "page layout, typefaces, price, size of volume . . . , periodicity of publication . . . , use of illustrations . . . , use and placement of advertisements, quality of paper and binding, networks of distribution and sale, modes of financial support, payment practices towards contributors, editorial arrangements, or the type of material published" (6). As with McGann, Brooker and Thacker argue that such features are not ancillary to the meaning of the text, but central to it, and they encourage attention to the relation between "internal" (typeface, layout) and "external" (distribution networks, commercial relations) codes to understand the ways periodicals positioned themselves and were positioned in their environment.[26] The survey of bibliographic and periodical codes that follows applies bibliographic tools—developed in what Kate Ozmet calls "a haven of racial and gendered sameness" (160)—to the landscape of mid-century Anglo-Indian newspapers. Attending to the bibliographic features of these texts, I aim to unpack both their function, particularly their role in establishing an identity for the newspaper, and the social context in which they functioned.

Facing Out: Typography and Appearance

In appearance, the 1845 Calcutta-based *Mofussilite* is strikingly dissimilar from its post-1847 version. Its two "looks" capture the predominant styles of English-language newspapers of the day. The title in the 1845 masthead (figure 1.1) is in a bold, serif typeface (likely Scotch Modern or a precursor) spanning the width of the page with "The Mofussilite" followed by a dark period.[27] The 1847 masthead (figure 1.2), by contrast, uses a highly ornate Gothic-medieval typeface, most likely Old English, the (London) *Times*' typeface since 18 March 1788. Unlike the *Times*,

---

26. In his analysis of the steamship press, Rooney fleshes out this work and writes of social codes, compositional and material codes, economic codes, and temporal codes.

27. The word "masthead," according to the *OED*, originated in the US and its earliest appearance dates to 1838. The term refers *both* to the banner of a newspaper—"[t]he title, motto, or similar device, of a newspaper or journal, printed . . . usually at the top of the first page"—and "the section in a newspaper or journal . . . giving information relating to the publication, such as the owner's name, a list of the editors, etc." In nineteenth-century newspapers, publication data is generally at the tail end of the paper. For clarity, I will use "masthead" (or "nameplate," an anachronism that only appeared in 1954) for the title and "endcap" for publisher information.

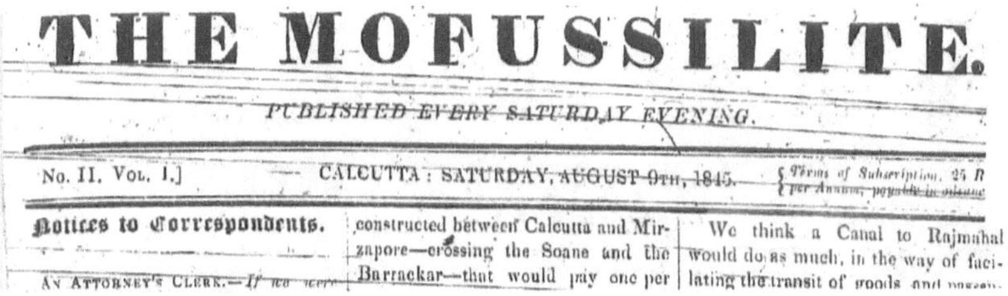

THE MOFUSSILITE.

PUBLISHED EVERY SATURDAY EVENING.

No. II. Vol. I.] CALCUTTA: SATURDAY, AUGUST 9th, 1845.

Notices to Correspondents.

AN ATTORNEY'S CLERK.—

constructed between Calcutta and Mirzapore—crossing the Soane and the Barrackar—that would pay one per

We think a Canal to Rajmahal would do as much, in the way of facilitating the transit of goods and

Figure 1.1. *Mofussilite* 1845 masthead (courtesy of the British Library SM 56).

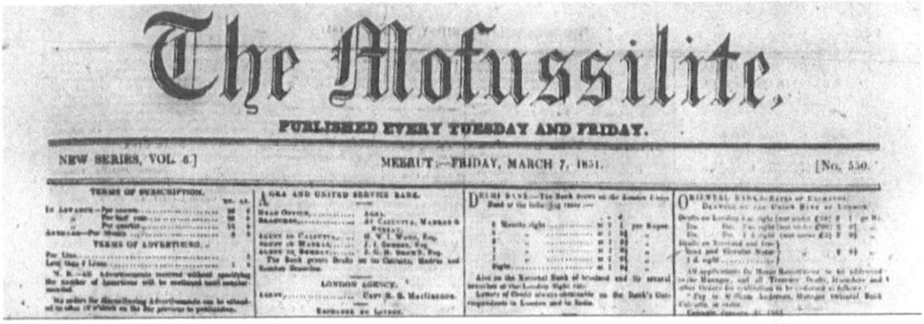

The Mofussilite,

PUBLISHED EVERY TUESDAY AND FRIDAY.

NEW SERIES, VOL. 6.] MEERUT,—FRIDAY, MARCH 7, 1851. [No. 550.

Figure 1.2. *Mofussilite* 1847 masthead (courtesy of the British Library SM 56).

which followed its name with a period, the *Mofussilite* inserted a comma at the end of its name.

These two fonts—blocky, serif versus white-lined, Old English typeface—fairly evenly capture the styles that Indian newspaper mastheads adopted. The *Friend of India*, a weekly from the Serampore Press with one of the highest circulations of English-language newspapers in the first half of the century, opted for the blocky, serif style, down to the final period (figure 1.3), as did the *India Gazette* (est. 1780), one of the subcontinent's

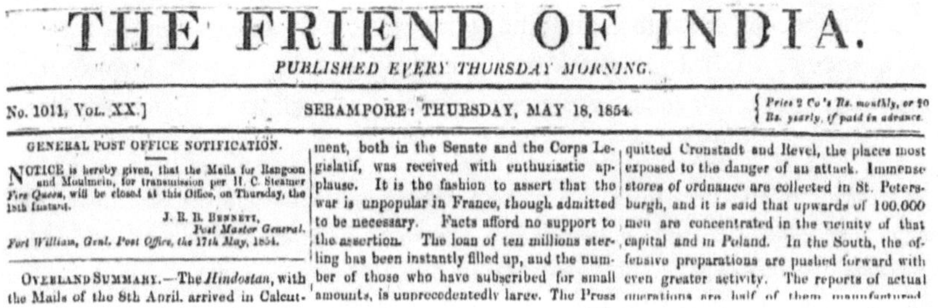

THE FRIEND OF INDIA.

PUBLISHED EVERY THURSDAY MORNING.

No. 1011, Vol. XX.] SERAMPORE: THURSDAY, MAY 18, 1854. *Price 2 Co's Rs. monthly, or 20 Rs. yearly, if paid in advance.*

GENERAL POST OFFICE NOTIFICATION.

NOTICE is hereby given, that the Mails for Rangoon and Moulmein, for transmission per H. C. Steamer *Fire Queen*, will be closed at this Office, on Thursday, the 18th instant.

J. R. B. Bennett,
Post Master General.

Fort William, Genl. Post Office, the 17th May, 1854.

Overland Summary.—The *Hindostan*, with the Mails of the 8th April, arrived in Calcut-

ment, both in the Senate and the Corps Legislatif, was received with enthusiastic applause. It is the fashion to assert that the war is unpopular in France, though admitted to be necessary. Facts afford no support to the assertion. The loan of ten millions sterling has been instantly filled up, and the number of those who have subscribed for small amounts, is unprecedentedly large. The Press

quitted Cronstadt and Revel, the places most exposed to the danger of an attack. Immense stores of ordnance are collected in St. Petersburgh, and it is said that upwards of 100,000 men are concentrated in the vicinity of that capital and in Poland. In the South, the offensive preparations are pushed forward with even greater activity. The reports of actual

Figure 1.3. *Friend of India* 1854 masthead (courtesy of the British Library SM 141).

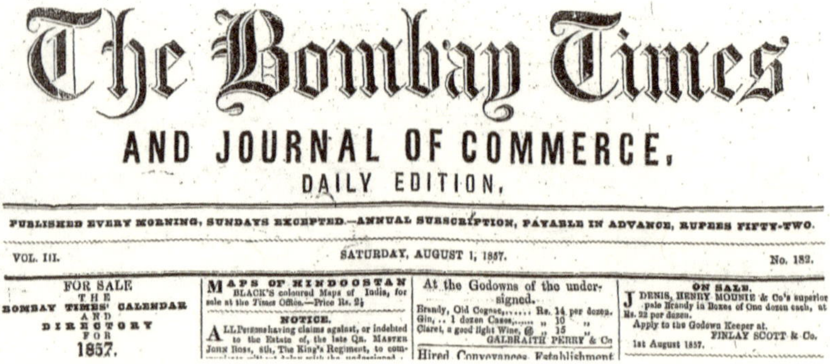
The Bombay Times
AND JOURNAL OF COMMERCE,
DAILY EDITION,

PUBLISHED EVERY MORNING, SUNDAYS EXCEPTED.—ANNUAL SUBSCRIPTION, PAYABLE IN ADVANCE, RUPEES FIFTY-TWO.

VOL. III. SATURDAY, AUGUST 1, 1857. No. 182.

FOR SALE THE BOMBAY TIMES' CALENDAR AND DIRECTORY FOR 1857.

MAPS OF HINDOOSTAN BLACK'S coloured Maps of India, for sale at the Times Office.—Price Rs. 2½

NOTICE.
ALL Persons having claims against, or indebted to the Estate of, the late Qr. Master John Ross, 8th, The King's Regiment, to com-

At the Godowns of the undersigned.
Brandy, Old Cognac,...... Rs. 14 per dozen.
Gin, .. 1 dozen Cases,...... " 10 "
Claret, a good light Wine, @ " 15 "
GALBRAITH PERRY & Co

Hired Conveyances Establishment

ON SALE.
J DENIS, HENRY MOUNIE & Co's superior pale Brandy in Boxes of One dozen each, at Rs. 22 per dozen.
Apply to the Godown Keeper at.
FINLAY SCOTT & Co.
1st August 1857.

Figure 1.4. *Bombay Times* 1857 masthead (courtesy of the British Library SM 73).

The Bengal HURKARU and Chronicle.

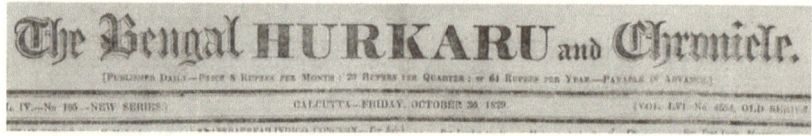

Figure 1.5. *Bengal Hurkaru and Chronicle* 1829 masthead (from the personal collection of Catherine Blackwell, shared with the author).

first newspapers; the *John Bull* (est. 1821); the *Reformer* (est. 1831); and the *Hindoo Patriot* (est. 1853).[28] The *Bombay Times* opted for the *Times*' look (figure 1.4), though it added a typeface for the second part of its long name. For a brief period between 1827 and 1834, the *Bengal Hurkaru and Chronicle* also amalgamated two fonts, though its innovation—to include two radically different typefaces on the same line—made for a dramatic look (figure 1.5). (By the 1840s, the *Hurkaru* abandoned both the blocky and Old English typefaces, opting for a light, serif font; by 1857, it reverted to two typefaces, though not on the same line).

The masthead is the face of a newspaper; along with the type size, the number of columns, and the general "look" of the sheet, it serves as a species of branding. Notwithstanding the impetus to brand in a crowded marketplace, newspapers in India (as well as in Britain[29]) drew

28. Images of the first three newspapers appear in Benoy Ghose's *Selections from English Periodicals of 19th Century Bengal, Volume I (1815–33)*; an image of the *Hindoo Patriot*'s masthead appears in volume IV of the same series.

29. Following the *Times*' adoption of the Old English typeface for its nameplate, the *Leeds Mercury* followed in 1807, then the *Manchester Guardian* in 1821 (Hutt 38–39).

on a narrow range of options in crafting their appearance. By the early years of the nineteenth century, the *Times'* Old English typeface seemed to telescope heft and serious intent, and though the occasional Indian newspaper experimented or played with alternatives, the desire to, as Andrew King puts it, "clai[m] an ancestry" (51) prevailed and most Anglo-Indian newspapers did as the *Mofussilite* did: they opted for some version of that more "serious" nameplate. By 1857, almost all English-language newspapers from the Bengal Presidency and the North-Western Provinces mirrored, in part or in whole, the white-lined, blackletter typeface of the *Times* in their nameplate.

If a masthead is the first thing readers see, the publisher's name and address—the endcap—printed at the bottom right of the last page, is the final word in each newspaper. In the previous section, I discussed the legal requirements for this information and the Government of India's increased surveillance of printers and publishers in the aftermath of the 1835 Press Act. As illustrated in the discussion of the *Mofussilite*'s swap of printers from the well-established P. S. D'Rozario to the untraceable Thomas Andrews, much information can be harvested about the newspaper business by paying careful attention to the endcap of newspapers. I will not pursue a similarly detailed analysis of the printers of every other newspaper in my sample, but will briefly mention a few salient details, pointers towards further study of printers and presses. Unlike the *Mofussilite*, which in the space of twenty-five years had ten different printers,[30] the *Bengal Hurkaru* was more stable, both in terms of location and personnel: during much of the period under review, it was published by John Gray, until its new proprietors, Samuel Smith and Co., brought in a new printer, James E. Gomes, in October 1856. The press office, however, never moved and the paper continued to publish from No. 1 Hare Street in Calcutta. The *Hurkaru*'s rival, the *Englishman*, published next door from No. 2 Hare Street, with J. F. Bellamy as its printer. While D'Rozario's press—the *Mofussilite*'s printer for its first four issues—was

---

30. After the early hiccup of printers, from 1847 onwards, whether from Meerut or Agra, Tuesday and Friday or Monday and Thursday, the newspaper was consistently printed and published by John A. Gibbons, who remained in his post until 1862. He was replaced by a revolving door of printers whose rapid turnover—seven in eight years—underscores the stability Gibbons provided: F. W. Moore, K. Keightley, Sookhun Lall, then, following Lang's passing in August 1864, C. H. Voss, R. Williams, Wilton Robert Hodges, and Sookhun Lall once again. During this time, the press also moved several times, including to Delhi in 1868 and to Ambala in 1870.

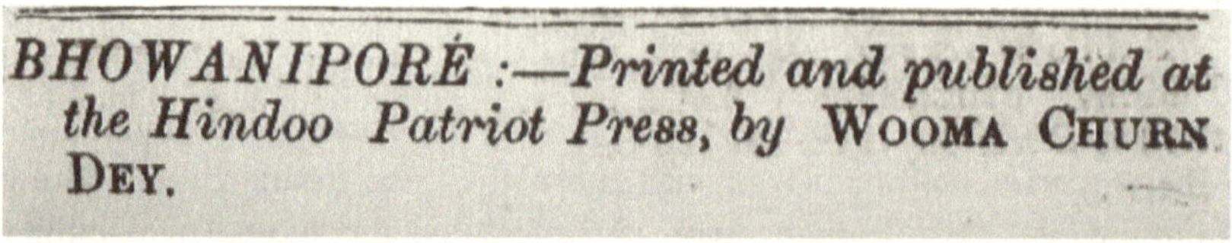

> *BHOWANIPORE :—Printed and published at the Hindoo Patriot Press, by* WOOMA CHURN DEY.

Figure 1.6. *Hindoo Patriot* 1859 endcap (courtesy of the British Library MFM. MC1108).

located in Tank Square, almost directly across from Government House, Hare Street was in the shadow of Hindu College, the bookish center of English-language learning. At a remove, twenty miles north in the former Danish enclave of Srirampur, the weekly *Friend of India* was printed and published at the Serampore Press under the supervision of John Cashman.

The *Hindoo Patriot*'s endcap was something of a declaration of independence: its place of publication is listed as "Bhowanipore" and its printer and publisher, like its owner and editor, an Indian, Wooma Churn Dey (figure 1.6). Bhowinpore (today Bhabanipur) was a neighborhood of Calcutta south of Fort William, an area popular among men of the "Bengal Renaissance" and middle-class Bengalis with legal training.[31] Listing its place of publication as "Bhowanipore"—rather than Calcutta—the *Hindoo Patriot* was signaling its independence from the Anglo-Indian newspapers of Calcutta, as well as aligning itself with the Bengali intelligentsia of the city.[32]

Between its 1845 and 1847 iterations, the *Mofussilite* morphed from a weekly paper (Saturdays) of twenty pages with three columns to

---

31. The *Hindoo Patriot* moved to Bhowanipore in 1855 and Nakazato credits the move as a "turning point" for the newspaper which had been struggling in its first years; the move gave the paper local readers who had a local pride in the paper (255–56). The area north of Fort William was known as "Indian Town" or "Black Town" and was home to those identified with the "Bengal Renaissance" such as Rammohan Roy and the Tagores; it also housed Battala (or Bartala), where vernacular presses congregated (N. Sarkar 133; Ghosh, 27–28). By mid-century, "Indian Town" extended south of Fort William as well, into Bhowanipore (P. T. Nair, "Growth" 16; S. Sarkar, "Calcutta" 100).

32. The masthead makes a concession by explaining that Bhowanipore is "in the suburbs of Calcutta." The endcap of the Bengali-language daily, *Sambād Prabhākar*, is even more deliberate in its assertion of independence and singularity: "This Prabhakar newspaper is published every day excepting Sundays from house No. 44/3, situated in the lane on the southern end of the open road appearing on the south side of Calcutta's Simuliya Hendua pond" (qtd. in R. Chaudhuri, 65).

a semiweekly (Tuesdays and Fridays) with eight crowded pages of four columns.[33] In its earlier iteration, the *Mofussilite* looked much like India's most prominent weekly, the *Friend of India*, which consisted of sixteen three-columned pages. With less of the burden to report "news" in a timely fashion, weeklies included lengthier commentary and tended to opt for the less cramped three-columned page with more white space. Dailies, by contrast, included a greater variety of material and had more of a miscellaneous character; consequently, they sought to utilize space more efficiently and accomplished this by shrinking margins.[34] The *Bengal Hurkaru*, a daily (except Saturday and Sunday), was four pages long, each with six, tightly packed columns, while its rival daily (except Sunday), the *Englishman*, also consisted of four pages, each sliced into seven columns.

The price of the newspapers roughly correlated to frequency: the weekly *Friend of India* cost Rs. 20 yearly, while the biweekly *Mofussilite*'s subscription rate was Rs. 36 per annum—a discount attributable to its mofussil origins. Calcutta's dominant dailies, the *Hurkaru* and the *Englishman*, both charged Rs. 64 for a yearly subscription. The *Hindoo Patriot* stands out: although a weekly, it charged half of what the other weekly in our sample, the *Friend of India* charged: Rs. 10 per year. Subscriptions and sales, however, were not the largest source of revenue: most of these newspapers relied far more on advertisements. By my calculation, roughly forty percent of the *Mofussilite*'s revenue came from subscriptions and sixty percent from advertisements. Though subscription, sales, and ad revenue for the other newspapers are difficult to ascertain, I conjecture that their balance was roughly similar. Because advertisements were such a large portion of revenues—far larger than income from subscriptions or sales—they consumed a large proportion of the real estate of each newspaper. Lucy Brown's analysis of English newspapers of 1882 shows that major London dailies devoted anywhere from forty-six to sixty-three percent of their space to advertisements (16). (By contrast, newspapers in 1960 devoted only forty-one percent of space to advertisements.) With the exception of the *Friend of India*, the newspapers in my sample fall within this spectrum, with something in the range of fifty percent of their

---

33. Though for a brief six months in 1849 the *Mofussilite* appeared three times a week, it reverted to semiweekly for the remainder of the period under review.

34. In the 1820s, London's cheap, radical periodical press first experimented with using multiple columns and small margins to maximize space and reduce costs (Topham 83–84, 89, 97).

real estate devoted to advertisements.[35] Though both readers and scholars can profit from advertisements, they were also an annoyance, as this wry comment from one reader illustrates: "The first page of the Mof (advertisements) has little effect on those not immediately concerned, beyond regret that three double barrelled guns do not meet with a purchaser . . ."[36] So onerous could advertisements and a newspaper's reliance on them be that the *Friend of India*, as soon as its coffers allowed, determined to limit the number of advertisements it would accept.[37]

INSIDE: LEADERS AND DIVISIONS

What distinguished each newspaper—and generated those subscription lists—was its "leaders." Generally beginning on page 2, 3, or 4—after the advertisements, government and market notices, and letters from readers—the section containing the newspaper's leading articles is marked by the paper's name set off between heavy rules and the current date. This section could run anywhere from three-quarters to a page long. In "Who Invented the 'Leading Article'? Reconstructing the History and Prehistory of a Victorian Newspaper Genre," Dallas Liddle distinguishes between two types of leading articles: the pre-Victorian "digest of news and commentary paragraphs" and the "long, authoritative" opinion essay (7). The latter, he writes, "occupied more than a full column (between 20 and 25 column inches, or perhaps 1500 words) of a six-column broadsheet, and newspapers generally ran three or four of them every day" (6). This opinion-oriented type of leader replaced the digest style that dominated in the eighteenth and early nineteenth centuries: paragraphs that consisted of "principal or late-breaking items of news, news commentaries, and translated items from foreign papers" (Liddle 6).[38] Liddle credits the *Edinburgh Review*

---

35. Though newspapers varied in their practice, many used the front page for smaller and more "personal" ads, while the back page was reserved for ads from larger firms such as Holloway's or library and booksellers' ads.

36. *Mofussilite*, 21 September 1858, 599. See Priti Joshi ("Audience") for the ways advertisements can help us discern the readership of a journal.

37. The newspaper had a wide readership, in India and Britain, and cut back on ads in 1846 (Chanda, *History* [1987] 50).

38. Henry Crabb Robinson, one of the *Times*' two leader writers in 1809, described his work of writing "the Leading Article as consist[ing] in the compiling of the little articles of information" (qtd. in Liddle 7).

from its earliest days in 1802 with creating the conditions for the opinion form of the leading article, but also underscores that "the shift to longer, opinion-oriented leaders in these years was not clearly either abrupt or gradual, but rather uneven and discontinuous" (10).

Such uneven development is manifest in my sample of mid-century Anglo-Indian newspapers. With the exception of the two weeklies—the *Friend of India* and *Hindoo Patriot*—all the newspapers' leader sections consist primarily of the earlier digest-style leading paragraphs that summarized reports and briefly commented on the day's or week's events. On occasion, particularly at moments of rupture, the commentaries, with their mix of synthesized report and opinion, could be several columns long. But as a general rule the leader section consisted of multiple short, digest-style pieces, each separated by a thin line or rule.[39] The transition from disjointed opinion paragraphs into the familiar close-packed Victorian leaders, each a "column and a bit" (Liddle 14), is evident in Indian newspapers over our period, though Liddle contends that the process was complete in Britain by the 1830s. Why the lag? As Liddle examines the cultural work the Victorian-style leader performed, he argues that, even as it offered "ready-to-speak opinions on the topics of the day," it had to appear to "express or crystalize the already-existing opinion of the nation as a whole" (11). The shift, in other words, marks a transition from the "press as public instructor" to the press as the "Voice of Public Opinion" (12). As we trace moments of crisis in the colonial public sphere in the next two chapters, we shall determine whether such moments served to expand the "leading paragraph" into something like the more expansive Victorian leader that expressed a collective opinion.

In my sample, the section of each newspaper that contains "leaders"—whether of the short form or more expansive editorial opinion—is set off against the rest of the letterpress with the newspaper's title centered on the column in a typeface that sometimes echoes the masthead, though not always. The *Mofussilite*'s leader section is singular in this sample as the paper's name and date are followed by an epigraph from Junius: "Let it be impressed upon your minds, let it be instilled into your children, that the liberty of the press is the palladium of all the civil, political, and

---

39. Liddle cites a 1796 source that suggests that the term "leader" came about because of the thin, lead strips compositors lay between such paragraphs (6). The same source also wrote that giving "greater space than usual between lines" was known as giving a prominent article a "lead" (15n13).

religious rights of an Englishman."[40] The declaration indicates some of the ways Lang, the paper's inaugural editor, viewed his role in taking up the mantle of press independence. Each "leading paragraph" or item in this section is separated by a thin line and a small amount of whitespace.

All our papers eschew headlines. The *Mofussilite* and the *Hindoo Patriot* used small caps for the first line of a new piece. Though these opening words have been used by indexers as "headlines," they hardly serve that function, either visually or as a synthesis of what follows. For illustrative purpose, the following is a randomly selected leader:

> ABSURD AND UNJUST AS EVERY ONE FEELS THE imputations cast by the *Times* on the character of the Indian Army, to be, we must expect that they will be believed by a very large portion of society at home.[41]

The *Hurkaru* and the *Englishman* both held out against even the small caps for the first line. The *Friend of India* was the only newspaper that used something like headlines, though they were not accorded an extra line and simply folded into the body of the leader itself, as in the following:

> THE NEW MARRIAGE ACT FOR INDIA.—We have at length the opinion of most of our contemporaries on the New Marriage Act . . .[42]

The emergence of headlines—which can attract readers—contended with the scarcity of a precious commodity, space, and the impulse to maximize it. As a result, our daily and biweekly newspapers sported very little white space on a page.

While the "leader section" contained a newspaper's explicit editorial content and perspective, not as much real estate was devoted to it as one might expect. A number of additional sections were standard issue in our daily and biweekly newspaper (less so in the weeklies), giving these newspapers their vaunted miscellaneous character. (Of the miscellany, Benedict Anderson writes, "Reading a newspaper is like reading a novel

---

40. The *Bombay Gazette* also included an epigraph (from Milton: "Give me the liberty to know, to utter, and to argue freely according to conscience, above all liberties") and like the *Times* included a clock face, in this case set at 12:34.
41. *Mofussilite*, 1 April 1851, 205.
42. *Friend of India*, 25 September 1851, 609.

whose author has abandoned any thought of a coherent plot" [33n54].[43]) Our sample newspapers include some version of the following sections: Domestic Occurrences (birth, marriage, and death announcements); Government Notifications (orders of the governor general); Military Gazette (appointments and troop movements); Commercial or Market Gazette; Shipping Intelligence (arrivals and departures); and Correspondence (comprising letters from readers).[44] These sections generally preceded the day's leaders; following the leader section was the editor's compilation of news items from other newspapers. Both the *Mofussilite* and the *Friend of India* had two sections devoted to excerpts from other newspapers (an "Epitome of News" and "Spirit of the Press" in the former and a "Weekly Epitome of News" and "Contemporary Selections" in the latter). Other newspapers had only one section: the *Bengal Hurkaru*'s was sorted by region (Mofussil Press, European Press), while the *Hindoo Patriot* often began with a section called "Weekly Register of Intelligence."

SCISSORS-AND-PASTE JOURNALISM

Reprinting items from other news outlets was a common, if belittled, feature of the nineteenth-century newspaper trade, earning the disparaging moniker of "scissors-and-paste journalism." Culling and reprinting articles or excerpts from other journals was, in essence, a sourcing technique that predated syndication. The method was pervasive in the industry—in Britain, India, the US.[45] By some accounts, the job of an editor consisted of little more than rapidly scanning dozens of other newspapers, marking

---

43. Anderson's description of early newspapers in the Americas is famous: "Early gazettes contained—aside from news from the metropole—commercial news (when ships would arrive and depart, what prices were current for what commodities in what ports), as well as colonial political appointments, marriages of the wealthy, so forth. In other words, what brought together on the same page, *this* marriage with *that* ship, *this* price with *that* bishop, was the very structure of the colonial administration and market-system itself. In this way, the newspaper of Caracas quite naturally, and even apolitically, created an imagined community among a specific assemblage of fellow-readers, to whom *these* ships, brides, bishops and prices belonged" (62).

44. For a time both the *Hurkaru* and *Mofussilite* included a dedicated section called "Native States," but it shrank and eventually disappeared as the number of such states diminished.

45. McGill and Cordell have produced nuanced work on the culture of reprints as they pertain to copyright and authorship in the US newspaper business; Slauter has done the same for UK newspapers.

sections, and handing them to the typesetter for resetting in the frames of one's own columns (Brown 85; Brake, "'Time's Turbulence'" 119). Though an exaggeration, this characterization is not entirely inaccurate: a quick glance at nineteenth-century newspapers indicates that the object that circulated under the title *The Mofussilite* or *The Bengal Hurkaru* was a compendium of recirculated and repackaged copy from a variety of other newspapers. The material object that circulated, in short, was the next step in an ongoing textual circulation. The term "scissors-and-paste" was used as a synonym for "hack"; it signaled a lack of originality and a derivative approach to newsgathering. Notwithstanding commentators' withering contempt for editors who relied on this technique to compile their newspapers (see Topham 77, 86), the use of "scissors-and-paste journalism" was both wider and more complicated than the pejorative term suggests.

In Britain, the historical origins of scissors-and-paste journalism lay in efforts to undermine the stamp taxes. The radical, unstamped press, in the 1820s and 1830s, reprinted reports from the stamped dailies, thus evading taxes (J. Wiener 163–65).[46] When charged with violating copyright, "unstamped publishers retorted . . . that the daily newspapers frequently appropriated news from each other without permission and that legal Sunday weeklies . . . indulged in this practice at the expense of the dailies" (J. Wiener 164). The *Mirror*, a two-penny weekly miscellany, pointed to the ubiquity of the practice in 1824:

> The public will learn with surprise that we have been threatened with a suit in Chancery, by Messrs. Baldwin, Cradock, and Joy, for quoting, from a periodical work they publish, an account of the last moments of Lord Byron, although we acknowledged the source whence we derived it. It is the more remarkable, as the article had previously been copied into all the London, and most of the country papers. Why the MIRROR has been thus invidiously selected for a Chancery suit will perhaps hereafter appear, and the real motive be made known. (qtd. in Topham 94)

---

46. Ironically, one of the earliest instances of reprinting material published elsewhere occurred in 1816, when William Cobbett issued an abridged edition of his own *Political Register* in order to evade the stamp tax (Topham 78).

As the *Mirror* notes, every newspaper in the business participated in textual borrowing, yet contemporaries and many historians have identified scissors-and-paste journalism with provincial or "country papers." Hannah Barker writes, "Historians have largely accepted that provincial newspapers were small-scale, amateurish, 'scissors-and-paste' operations" (112), offering no more "than a delayed and passive replica of attitudes in the capital" (114).[47] Though the provincial press was berated for excerpting and recycling from publications higher up in the food chain, the practice was in fact commonplace across the spectrum.

Scissors-and-paste journalism was pervasive in the Anglo-Indian media sphere. The pages of the *Mofussilite, Bengal Hurkaru, Friend of India, Englishman,* and *Hindoo Patriot* all bulge with copy taken—with citation—from other newspapers and periodicals. Excerpts range anywhere from a short passage to a lengthy, multiple-column quote. In a sample year, the *Hurkaru*, drew on over fifty different news outlets, and in the course of fifteen years, the *Mofussilite* referenced over 125 different journals in its pages. Some sources are cited from only once or twice, other cited and commented on regularly. The British media that tended to appear regularly in my sample include the *Times, Daily News, Household Words, Punch, Weekly News, Fraser's Magazine, Blackwood's, Illustrated London News,* and *Atlas for India* (a steamship journal that compiled news specifically for Anglo-Indian readers[48]). Each newspaper in my sample consistently drew on some journals more than others, but none ignored the *Times*.

Though British newspapers were cited, Anglo-Indian newspapers cited far more frequently and regularly from other Anglo-Indian newspapers, a fact that repudiates the charge that the "provincial" press relied on and merely recycled news from metropolitan papers. In this sample, certain newspapers dominated the reprint columns: the *Bengal Hurkaru, Friend of India, Englishman, Delhi Gazette* and *Bombay Times* were most frequently referenced. The *Mofussilite,* (Lahore) *Chronicle, Bombay Gazette, Agra Messenger,* and *Madras Athenaeum* belonged to the second tier, while the *Bangalore Herald, Lucknow Herald, Dacca News, Ceylon Times, Hindoo Patriot,* and *Poona Observer* came in for occasional reference.

---

47. The entry for "News" in the *Dictionary of Nineteenth-Century Journalism* states that provincial papers "raided" metropolitan newspapers for copy (Brake and Demoor 450).

48. For steamship journals, in particular their modes of synthesizing and circulating news, see Rooney.

Topic-focused journals such as the *Indian Sporting Review*, the *East India Army Magazine*, or the *Indian Annals of Medical Science* are cited, though mostly to announce their emergence.

Two other types of newspapers make an occasional appearance in my sample: vernacular-language newspapers and prints from across the British Empire. The *Hurkaru* quoted from a broader range of vernacular-language papers than any other newspaper in my sample. In the early 1850s, it drew primarily on Bengali-language newspapers such as the *Poornoochundrodoy*, the *Chundrika*, and the *Bhaskar*; by the mid-1850s, it quoted from Urdu-language newspapers from farther afield as well: the *Koh-i-noor* from Lahore, *Urdu Akbar* from Delhi, *Multa-ool-Akbar* from Agra. The cited material was always in English with a headnote: "translated for the Bengal Hurkaru," indicating that the press had in-house translators. Newspapers from beyond the subcontinent and Britain were cited as the occasion called for it: the *Journal de Constantinople* (during the Crimean War), the *Singapore Free Press*, or the *Sydney Herald*. If our newspapers received copies of all the newspapers and journals they cited from, the editor's office must have been a cluttered space indeed! (Most newspapers had an exchange agreement with contemporaries of their class).

My sample newspapers drew on their sources in multiple ways, few of which look like the caricature of scissors-and-paste journalism as filler or barely concealed theft. Reprinting was an active editorial function that served the industry, readers, and community.[49] The most ordinary reference to other newspapers—which did not necessarily include cutting and pasting or quoting from them at length—comes in the form of announcements about the birth and demise of journals. Thus, on 4 March 1851, the *Mofussilite* notes that the *Bengalee Penny Magazine* is to appear in Calcutta "under the editorship of Baboo Rajendralal Mittra, the able Librarian of the Asiatic Society. It is to be illustrated by electrotypes executed in England of woodcuts which have already appeared in the *Penny Magazine*, the *Saturday Magazine*, and the *Illustrated News*" (140).[50] As for closures, the *Mofussilite* announced that the *Calcutta Sporting Review* had ceased

---

49. For an analysis of scissors-and-paste as a form of archiving that predated digitization, see Priti Joshi ("Scissors-and-Paste").

50. The *Hurkaru* waited until it had something more definitive and announced in July that it had received a copy of *Satyarmob*, "or as we may descriptively term it, the Bengali 'Penny Magazine'" (5 July 1851, 18).

and in its place was born a journal called *Field*, while the *Hurkaru* noted the demise of the *Morning Chronicle* in dramatically anthropomorphic language.[51] At various points we learn from other papers that the *Hurkaru* has a new editor, that the *Calcutta Review* will now be led by the former editor of the *Friend of India*, that the *Phoenix* will shortly become a daily.[52]

Reporting on the birth and death of journals was a matter of professional interest and courtesy. For scholars, in a landscape where many journals had a short lifespan, most have not survived, and no office books are extant, such announcements serve as critical data to recreate the media landscape. Thus, it is only from notices in the *Hurkaru* that we know that between August and October 1851, John Lang issued a paper called the *Optimist* from Calcutta.[53] Chanda's chronicle of Bengal's English-language newspapers relies on the immensely painstaking work of collecting, cross-checking, and assessing such announcements. Similarly, Nadir Ali Khan is only able to trace the dozens of Urdu newspapers of the 1840s, of which not a single copy is extant, because of notices of their birth and death in surviving Urdu journals and newspapers (175–80). Were it not for such notices, we would have a far more impoverished sense of the size and vitality of the nineteenth-century periodical marketplace in India.

Beyond announcements, the most straightforward manner in which newspapers in our sample drew on material from other sources was to report regional news from a regional source. Thus, the *Mofussilite*'s report on the problems with Calcutta's ice supplies came from the *Friend of India* (just outside Calcutta).[54] More substantially, every newspaper's coverage of the *East India Company v. Jootee Persuad*, a case tried in an Agra court, came from the *Agra Messenger*. Similarly, the *Mofussilite* drew its reports of the fall of Multan from the *Delhi Gazette*,[55] news of the fall of Kars from

---

51. For the *Sporting Review*, see *Mofussilite*, 5 March 1856, 143; for the *Morning Chronicle*, see *Bengal Hurkaru* 20 August 1856, 175: "After a lingering illness borne with exemplary patience, the *Morning Chronicle* is at length dead!"

52. *Mofussilite*, 8 January 1856; 11 January 1856; and 8 January 1856, respectively.

53. In the *Hurkaru*, see the advertisement on 3 July 1851, 9; the brief notice on 4 August 1851, 138; the reprint of the *Bombay Telegraph*'s review of the first number on 26 August 1851, 226; and the small leader announcing the paper's discontinuation on 16 October 1851, 430.

54. *Mofussilite*, 4 March 1851, 140.

55. *Mofussilite*, 28 January 1849.

the *Journal de Constantinople*,⁵⁶ and the report of the arrival in Britain of a fugitive slave from Virginia from the *Liverpool Mercury*.⁵⁷ The *Hurkaru*, meanwhile, with its robust translation department, reported on the household of the former king of Awadh [Oude, in Anglicized form], following the annexation of that territory, from the *Aftab-i-Hind (*Benares) and the Delhi-based *Urdoo Akbar*, both geographically closer to the scene and with greater access to the dispersed court.⁵⁸ Anglo-Indian newspapers drew on an astonishingly wide range of sources to expand their coverage—which included news from "provincial" towns as often as it did metropolitan-based coverage. Reprinting served as an in-house news service not unlike Reuters and the Press Association (which were born in 1851 and 1868, respectively, and beyond the budget of most smaller newspapers).

Excerpts, particularly longer ones, included in a "Spirit of the Press" or "Contemporary Selections" section, more than broadened readers' vistas. Every editor used reprints and excerpts as a launching pad for debate, discussion, and scrutiny. The following is a typical example: on 5 February 1858, the *Mofussilite* cited a report from the 21 January 1858 number of the *Friend of India* on the relocation of the capital of the North-Western Provinces from Agra to Allahabad. The excerpt from the *Friend* appears in the *Mofussilite*'s "Spirit of the Press" section and is approximately half a column in length. In the excerpted report, the *Friend* announces the move, reports on opposition to the relocation from Agra-wallahs, and concludes with its reasons for supporting the move: "If the mutinies have revealed anything, it is the unfitness of Agra for a seat of Government."⁵⁹ The *Mofussilite*'s leader—which *precedes* the reprinted story—challenges the *Friend*'s position, is more than double the length of the excerpt and, as is customary, appears in larger type than the reprinted item. The *Mofussilite* rebuts the *Friend*'s assertions point by point and challenges its claims about Agra's suitability and Allahabad's virtues. To the *Friend*'s assertion that Agra is too far from the sea, the *Mofussilite* retorts, "On this principle Kedgeree rather than Calcutta ought to be the metropolis of India, and Lahore should be abandoned in favor of Kurrachee, or of

---

56. *Mofussilite*, 1 February 1856, 78.

57. *Mofussilite*, 3 January 1851, 6.

58. *Bengal Hurkaru*, 5 March 1856, 224.

59. *Mofussilite*, 5 February 1858, 81.

Mooltan" (81).⁶⁰ Far from a passive exercise, reprinting was the catalyst for engagement and debate.⁶¹

Such reprinting and commentary were a feature of every newspaper in my sample, a type of circulation embedded in the form and business model of nineteenth-century newspapers.⁶² While not every editor took as aggressive or confrontational a stance as the *Mofussilite*'s editor tended to, every paper included excerpts from other sources that it commented on in its own leaders. Sometimes the commentary would appear days after the reprinted story first appeared, sometimes in the same number; sometimes an editorial commentary was prompted by a reader's letter responding to an excerpt, at other times a third newspaper's commentary might prompt the paper to take a stance. As a result, items developed a "tail" or shelf life that exceeded their immediate "newsworthiness."⁶³ While not every report from another newspaper was commented on, about half to two-thirds were cited in order to be probed, challenged, supported, or engaged in one form or the other.⁶⁴ The result was a robust, if raucous, style of engagement that lends these newspapers their particular polyvocality. Such engagement gives the lie to the charge that scissors-and-paste was a passive act; indeed, rather than "reprinting," we might consider the practice as one of repurposing.

The inclusion of so many excerpts from an array of sources makes explicit that the function of a newspaper editor at the time aligned with this *OED* definition of the term: "One who prepares the literary work of

---

60. The *Mofussilite* is referring here to "the village and police station on the low lands near the mouth of the Hoogly, on the west bank, and 68 miles below Calcutta" (Yule and Burnell 477), not to the dish of rice and lentils.

61. McGill writes that editors of nineteenth-century US periodicals "repeatedly invoke[d] editing as a principle of refinement that sifts out essays of lesser worth and those that are too local in their field of reference" (26).

62. Slauter discusses shifts in the business of news between the eighteenth and mid-nineteenth centuries such that copying was no longer viewed as "welcome publicity . . . [but] unwelcome appropriation" (122).

63. For more on the endurance of and circulation of news stories, see Priti Joshi ("Scissors-and-Paste"). Writing of US newspapers in the 1840s, McGill identifies "the sense of up-to-dateness that is achieved by reperiodizing" previous pieces" (26).

64. Generally, there was far less commentary on reports from British papers—with the exception of items on India, particularly the EIC charter renewal.

another person, or number of persons for publication, *by selecting, revising, and arranging the material*" (emphasis added).⁶⁵ In selecting and weighing excerpts, the editor played an active role in shaping each day's newspaper. J. H. Stocqueler, the editor of the *Englishman*, described an Anglo-Indian newspaper editor's typical day in 1833 thus:

> Rise at half past five;—open the daily journals directly they arrive. Read, learn and inwardly digest;—note for extract;—write dissent, assent, or reflections suggested by contemporary's correspondents. Ablution and *la-toilette* . . . Breakfast, brief and spare—toast, tea and a *periodical*—off to business at 9 A.M. . . . At office summon the printer supply him with extracts from English and Asiatic papers, made with care the previous night . . . At ten, the "busy hum" begins—and as you prepare to write an article, two or three notes successively enter bearing reference to some of your sins of omission or commission in that day's paper. You answer them—and continue your article . . . (qtd. in Chanda, *History* [1987] 371; emphases in original).

And so on until his noon task, which was "a Parliamentary précis, wading through not less than 100 columns of the *Times* . . . " (371–72). The multitasking required of an editor was endless, leading one to complain that "[e]veryone gets a holiday except an editor" (Chanda, *History* [1987] 374). Scholars who dismiss such editors as mere compliers have neglected the critical role they played both in forging a unique identity for their journal and in deploying strategies of compilation to make specific arguments. Hannah Barker insists that although "provincial papers made extensive use of material from London," they did so "on a selective basis" that "display[ed] a uniquely local set of political preoccupations and opinions" (112); selections met local needs and politics, not London's. In short, the choice of material was never neutral or unmediated; excerpts were deliberately selected to make an argument—and the editorial commentary offered a gloss on the selection.

In *The Anthology and the Rise of the Novel*, Leah Price examines the burgeoning market for anthologies—texts that compiled excerpts or

---

65. "Editor." *OED Online*, Oxford University Press, September 2014. Accessed 17 October 2014.

digests of a lengthy work or an author's oeuvre—in the nineteenth century. Though her focus is on anthologies of literary texts, Price's insights on excerpting and the service editors provided is relevant to the news trade. Editors of literary anthologies were seen as lacking in originality (Price 74–75). Yet, as Price notes, a legal ruling—the end of perpetual copyright in 1774—fueled the market for anthologies, which stepped in to "respond to a surfeit of accessible texts" (77). "Information overload," she writes, "creates a demand for editors, even for censors—not simply to limit the data available, but to order it" (77). In a flooded market, the editor who compiled an anthology served an important function: to cull and select material so as to give shape to what appears as chaos.[66] The surfeit Price refers to was particularly staggering in the periodical marketplace; no reader could afford the budget required to subscribe to even a quarter of the news sources cited in my sample of papers, much less read and absorb their contents. Newspaper editors culled in order to create a coherent narrative or political position.

To illustrate, let me return to the *Mofussilite*'s reprinting of the *Friend*'s report on the relocation of the capital from Agra to Allahabad. Readers in Agra—where the *Mofussilite* was located in 1858—already knew the news. What Agraites wanted—or the *Mofussilite* believed they needed—was *arguments* against the move. Excerpting from the *Friend* provided the *Mofussilite* the pretext to make its own case and to offer its readers a set of debate points. Forming and informing opinion in this manner, the commentary is a prime example of what Liddle argues was the function of the nineteenth-century leading article: "commodified and ready-to-speak opinions on the topics of the day" (11). While sourcing news was one reason editors turned to scissors-and-paste, they utilized reprints in a far more active and robust fashion: as fodder for debate and with an eye to forming opinion.

It takes reading only a few numbers in this sample to recognize that editors took their opinion-forming function as of equal if not greater importance to their news-reporting one. That some readers valued such editorials and opinion over news is evident in a short letter that appeared in the *Mofussilite*. The writer complains that the editors of Calcutta dailies change so frequently that it is not possible to "rely" on any paper,

---

66. Cordell makes a similar argument about US newspapers: "In large part, antebellum newspaper reprinting privileged texts for their edification or usefulness to readers, not their originality" ("Reprinting" 427).

particularly as the "Editorials of the Calcutta Daily Papers of the day, are generally scanty, the columns being often filled with contributions of correspondents.—Shameful affairs!—The Editors are either too busy or too idle to write much in their paper."[67] Though the view of one reader, the letter suggests that the editorial—that is, opinion-forming—function of newspapers was highly valued, while the news-gathering and reporting function was viewed as secondary.[68]

Readers and Writers; or Correspondence and Correspondents

Readers are often one of the more challenging nodes to access in Darnton's communication circuit. Letters, handled carefully, can provide insight into a newspaper's readership. The *Mofussilite*'s letters, for instance, appear to be primarily from Anglo-Indians (though writers generally assumed—or were assigned—pen names such as EMPE) who, like the newspaper, were disgruntled with the Government of India. The *Bengal Hurkaru*'s letter writers, on the other hand, were evidently prosperous citizens of Calcutta or established bureaucrats. The *Hurkaru* also had more Indian letter writers—they either signed their names or identified themselves as Indian[69]—than any other paper in my sample. The Correspondence sections brim with letters that touch upon the mundane, the momentous, and much in between. At the quotidian end is a letter complaining that the name of a lady who participated in a school's activities was left out of the paper's report; this letter, in turn, prompted another reader to supply further information that had been left out in the initial coverage.[70] A writer asks the editor for advice on handling his sixteen-year-old daughter's elopement with a soldier;[71] another shared a cure for sunstroke,[72] while

---

67. *Mofussilite*, 29 February 1856, 139.

68. The *Mofussilite*'s editor, in an uncharacteristically brief response to this letter, wrote, "We are not in favor of Daily Papers at all. The fault complained of by our correspondent is caused by the frequency of publication" (29 February 1856, 139).

69. See, for instance, the letter from "A Native" correcting the newspaper's ignorance in regards to Indians wearing shoes (*Bengal Hurkaru*, 17 March 1856, 262).

70. *Mofussilite*, 1 January 1856 and 8 January 1856, respectively.

71. *Mofussilite*, 15 April 1859.

72. *Mofussilite*, 18 June 1858.

a series of dueling letters debated the benefits of Peake's over Holloway's pills (prompting the editor to complain of the "deluge" of letters he had received on the topic[73]). Such letters are deeply local and also deeply felt; though seemingly trivial, they indicate that subscribers were not passive consumers of a finished product, but engaged participants, part of an emergent public sphere. Letters can offer a glimpse into the fabric of lives that are not often registered for being too ordinary or transitory. For instance, a letter on the Peake's versus Holloway's fray includes these rich details:

> The other night I eat for dinner, mock turtle soup, salmon, beef, turkey, and ham, trouffled partridges, pate de fori gras [sic], jellies, custards, tarts, cherry and apple—to say nothing of fruits and dessert—and as for wines I indiscriminately mixed every one on the table and they were not a few. You may judge that I did not pay for such a dinner, but in one sense you may think I *must* have paid for it: viz. with a racking headache the next day: from this I was saved by six Peake's pills at bed time—got up in the morning as right as a trivet! (412)

The prose, errors, excess, and glee remind us that this was a historical moment when men with few options in Britain could make the East a lucrative career that allowed such indulgences.

Other letters are so of their time and place that no amount of diligent sleuthing decodes them. In May 1852, a series of letters about a "Clara Ellis" appear in the *Mofussilite*. The letters offer little context and I am unable to trace Ellis or why a spate of letters on her appear suddenly and then subside after four or five numbers. Other letters are easier to situate, if also of their time and place: a letter from the unfortunately named Fitzherbert Kight about his failed balloon attempts are clearly a response to the *Bengal Hurkaru*'s mockery of his efforts.[74] The letter from "J. Long," thanking those who supported a vernacular lending library, is not hard to identify as coming from the pen of James Long, the missionary and educator who supported Indian education in vernacular languages.[75] An

---

73. *Mofussilite*, 4 July 1853, 413.

74. For the mockery, see *Bengal Hurkaru*, 28 January 1851, 78; for Kight's response, see *Hurkaru*, 29 January 1851, 114.

75. *Bengal Hurkaru*, 11 January 1851, 45.

acrimonious exchange between L. E. Rees and Martin Gubbins about the siege of Lucknow is also readily identifiable, in part because Gubbins was a high-ranking civil official and his book *An Account of the Mutinies in Oude* (1858) one of the earliest personal accounts of the Uprising.[76] This exchange, as well as letters like the one complaining of the new commander in chief, William Gomm, illustrate that, contrary to perception, the EIC and the governing elites of India were continually scrutinized by ordinary rank-and-file Anglo-Indians even after the more colorful Hickys and Buckinghams were removed.[77] Any notion of a homogeneous or monologic response to India is put into question when we read such letters. They reveal both that a significant segment of the Anglo-Indian population was critical of the EIC and that the critical stance, particularly of a paper such as the *Mofussilite*, was shared *and* formed by its readers.[78]

Letter writers could also be overzealous and a source of trouble for editors. In 1852, the *Mofussilite* was obliged to inform readers that it would only publish letters about soldiers' rations that were "temperately and concisely expressed . . . others have been too long, and too diffuse, for publication and others,—though only in one or two instances,—we have considered to be objectionable from the terms in which they were expressed."[79] The *Hurkaru* in 1856 was similarly moved to publicly reprimand writers on two separate occasions: first informing "Caleb Quotem and others that we do not publish unauthenticated letters containing attacks upon public men,"[80] and a few weeks later notifying "Head-Ache and others" that "[w]e do not publish all letters sent to us, nor do we consider ourselves bound to give a reason for not doing so. When therefore a correspondent's letter does not appear, he is to know that it has been destroyed."[81] The necessity for such warnings indicates that readers were engaged and, paradoxical though it might sound given the last two refer-

---

76. *Mofussilite*, 17 September 1858.

77. *Mofussilite*, 17 January 1851.

78. An uncharacteristic defense of the EIC appears in the same number that includes the Gubbins's exchange: in a letter titled "A Plea for John Company," the writer laments the demise of the EIC, noting that "[i]t was I regret to say too common a custom to abuse the old gentleman" (*Mofussilite*, 17 September 1858, 591).

79. *Mofussilite*, 30 July 1852, 485.

80. *Bengal Hurkaru*, 21 January 1856, 70.

81. *Bengal Hurkaru*, 4 February 1856, 118.

ences, that newspapers had been successful in forging a community. That such community found an outlet in the pages of newspapers illustrates the growing importance of the medium in the formation of a public sphere.

If letter writers could be reckless or intemperate, editors could opt for the expedient of publishing, under a pseudonym, letters they themselves wrote. The practice was not uncommon in Britain, going back at least to Edward Moore's *World* of the mid-eighteenth century in which he published letters from "Rebecca Blameless" and "Toby Frettabit" that he had written himself.[82] An editor publishing a letter under a pseudonym was one way to ensure that the paper took a consistent stance on issues, even while giving the appearance of obliging readers and encouraging a community forum. Or it was a way to express the editor's views without endangering the newspaper.[83] I do not know if the newspapers in my sample practiced this deceit, but the evidence is suggestive. Throughout 1858, in the aftermath of the Uprising, the *Mofussilite* printed a series of letters signed "EMPE."[84] Their regularity, length, and breadth indicates that they were written by someone the editor trusted. Also in 1858, the newspaper included numerous letters from "Junius Indicus," including a six-part series on the Rebellion and its causes.[85] That the writer was connected to the editor, if not the editor or proprietor himself, is suggested by the fact that the "Mofussilite" section of the newspaper begins with an epigraph from Junius about the freedom of the press.

Though the Uprising and ensuing censorship brought the matter of letter writers to a head (discussed in greater detail in chapter 3), concerns

---

82. See "Letters/Correspondence" in Brake and Demoor (358–59). Liddle writes that in the late eighteenth century, it was customary for political analysis to appear as "letters *to* the paper from pseudonymous correspondents signing themselves Decius or Britannius (or, famously, Junius), who were either really or fictionally readers rather than editors or employees" (5).

83. In the 1820s, James Silk Buckingham, the soon-to-be-deported editor of the *Calcutta Journal*, published criticisms of the Company in the form of the anonymous letters (Ahmed 59).

84. *Mofussilite*, 7 May 1858, 285 (two letters on same page); 1 June 1858, 343–44; 8 June 1858, 359; 11 June 1858, 370; 15 June 1858, 375; 22 June 1858, 391; 6 July 1858, 423; 9 July 1858, 431; 17 August 1858, 521; 17 September 1858, 591; 21 September 1858, 599; 29 October 1858, 687.

85. *Mofussilite*, 9 February 1858, 87; 23 February 1858, 119; 6 July 1858, 423; 23 July 1858, 463; 3 August 1858, 487; 13 August 1858, 511–12; 27 August 1858, 546.

about the dependability and veracity of writers had been growing for some years. During the period under review, in response to these concerns, a new professional figure, the "correspondent," emerged. The term is unstable at this moment in newspaper history, just as often indicating a person who submitted a letter to the editor—published in the "Correspondence" section—as someone like a "reporter."[86] In the pages of the *Mofussilite* in these years, we can trace this shift from letters to leaders from its very first year, as items move from the "Correspondence" to the "Mofussilite" section of the paper. In one report, the paper informs us that a letter from a reader claiming that the education of "native children" outside Calcutta is "barbarous" prompted the paper to investigate, resulting in a leader on "Native Education in the Mofussil."[87] A few weeks later, a story on the near sati of the Rani of Vizianagram comes from a "valued correspondent at Benares, who promises to give us weekly favors."[88] The writer followed through and two weeks later, an item in the "Mofussilite" section begins, "The following is from our Benares Correspondent."[89] Whether these "correspondents" were paid is unclear, but given the language—"weekly favors"—it seems unlikely.

With time, the *Mofussilite* started to grow a cadre of interlocutors or "correspondents" on whom it increasingly relied to send reports from various locations. There appears to be a regular Calcutta correspondent, and in 1856, prior to and following the annexation of Awadh, the *Mofussilite* published reports from "our Distinguished Correspondent" *in the letters*

---

86. The term "reporter" itself is unstable: Brown writes that while "journalist" dates to the seventeenth century, "reporter" in the sense of "an uninvolved person sent to some public occasion to make a record for publication" did not appear until the early years of the nineteenth century (85). H. Barker writes that in Britain, "Often termed 'newsgatherers' rather than reporters, such individuals were unlikely to have been regularly employed by newspapers in the first half of the eighteenth century, but were paid on a casual, freelance basis" (101); only by the second half of the eighteenth century and only in London, might a newsgatherer have graduated to drawing a salary from one newspaper (101). Black cites the singular example of an editor from 1719 who announced that he had settled English correspondents on the Continent at his expense (90); the journal, Black notes, did not survive long.

87. *Mofussilite*, 16 August 1845, 42.

88. *Mofussilite*, 6 September 1845, 101.

89. *Mofussilite*, 20 September 1845, 142.

section of the paper.⁹⁰ Despite the editor's note that this correspondent was a "chartered libertine" who refused "to modify his very improper personality," it continued to publish his letters throughout May and June. At various times, the *Mofussilite* has a London correspondent—almost certainly Lang while he was in England. Over the course of fifteen years, the newspaper increasingly came to include items in its leader or letter-press section by "correspondents" from all over the subcontinent, including the following: [I have spelt the names here as the newspaper does] Scinde and Lahor, Umballa and Jullunder; Camp Kusmere, Futtergure, Kotah, and Camp Nuwabgunge; Patna, Rajpootana, Joudhpoor, Dinaporr, Loohooghaut and Sealkote; Saharunpore, Gwalior, Etwah, Meerut, Allyghur, Etawah, Nowedah, and Kumoan. The list confirms that the newspaper took seriously its responsibility to speak for and to the mofussil—and that it worked hard to cultivate "correspondents" in a broad swath of the North-Western Provinces. Whether any these "correspondents" were paid is again unclear—but given the brief nature of their reports, it seems unlikely.⁹¹ Moreover, the occasional nature of their reports suggests that such "correspondents" were more like "newsgatherers"—acquaintances who wrote from where they were domiciled—rather than "reporters" *sent* to cover an event.

While the *Bengal Hurkaru* and the *Englishman*, larger and more established newspapers, regularly included items marked "from our Correspondent in [place name]," it is not clear whether their correspondents were trusted, locally situated newsgatherers or persons sent by the newspaper to a location. The latter sense of the professional, paid "correspondent" only appears in Anglo-Indian prints with the arrival of William Howard Russell to cover the Uprisings. The *Englishman* reported that "Mr. Russell, the special correspondent of the *Times*" has arrived in Calcutta, "rather too late in the day to harrow the readers of that journal with thrilling

---

90. *Mofussilite*, 27 May 1856, 341.

91. Chanda notes that between 1780 and 1857 "reporters had no very respectable standing in the Press establishment" (*History* [1987] 394). Those who were remunerated appear to be freelance agents paid per line. A report from Buckingham's *Calcutta Journal* of 1822 lists the monthly "Allowance for Reporter & Corrector" at Rs. 300; by contrast, the editor's allowance is Rs. 1,200, the head printer's is Rs. 135, and the "Printer's bill, for wages etc." amounts to Rs. 1,300 (400). That the task of reporter was often combined with another job appears to be the case in several establishments: in 1833, *John Bull* listed the salary of head printer and reporter at Rs. 300 per month (401).

narratives of the mutiny, but not too late to make the state of India better known to the people of England. Mr. Russell has been elected an honorary member of the Bengal Club, and invited to take up his residence there, a proof that its members are keenly alive to the effect which this gentleman's letters may have in England."[92] The reference to Russell's "letters" reminds us that the origins of the "correspondent" lay in the epistolary form; before too long the term of art for this person would be "reporter," a title that professionalized an activity that had its origins in a community forum.

A final word on correspondents: on a very few occasions, both the *Hurkaru* and the *Mofussilite* indicate that a report came from a non-European. In 1848, a *Mofussilite* leader begins, "Our native newswriter at Lahore writes . . ."[93] And the *Hurkaru* included a report "from our esteemed correspondent in Hyderabad" and indicated that it was "Translated for the Bengal Hurkaru."[94] Recall that the *Bengal Hurkaru* was the only Anglo-Indian newspaper in this sample that regularly included reprints from the vernacular press that were evidently translated in-house. That the *Hurkaru* also had an occasional, vernacular-speaking correspondent is unexpected. The occasions on which correspondents named as Indian appear in these newspapers are so few as to suggest that "native correspondents" were the exception that proved the rule that correspondents were always Britons.

Literature: Vernacular, Local, and Pirated

If translated material from Indian prints appeared scarcely in Anglo-Indian newspapers, material in an Indian language is scarcer still. The few times text in a non-romanized script appears, it is noteworthy and serves as a barometer of shifting relations across racial lines. The *Mofussilite*, on half a dozen occasions—seven in fifteen years, to be precise—included material in *nasta'liq* (or Perso-Arabic) script. In mid-century India, the script was used for both Persian—the language of the Mughal court—and "Hindustani," the amalgamated language that preceded the parting of ways between Hindi and Urdu.[95] In 1848 and again in 1849, the *Mofussilite* included

---

92. See *Mofussilite*, 9 February 1858, 87.

93. *Mofussilite*, 1 August 1848, 483.

94. *Bengal Hurkaru*, 18 July 1856, 64.

95. Das offers this deft précis of the division: "[T]he linguistic base of Hindi and Urdu is almost identical. It is generally believed that the distinction between Hindi and Urdu never existed except on the stylistic level and it was the language policy of the

a full-page insert of a manuscript in *nasta'liq* script; no explanation or translation of the lithographed page is offered in the letterpress. Not until 1853 do we again encounter *nasta'liq* in the pages of the *Mofussilite*; this time it appears in the letterpress and is a typeset poem in Hindustani, with only its title ("Barney Brallaghan! Or Murder in Irish!!!") and an attribution ("Le Juif Errant") in Latin script.[96]

These documents suggest that it was not until 1853 that the Mofussilite Press had access to *nasta'liq* types, a rather late date.[97] In 1847, the year the *Mofussilite* started operating in Meerut, the town got its first vernacular-language newspaper, the Urdu-language *Jam-e-Jamshed* (N. A. Khan 227–28). Though never mentioned in the pages of the *Mofussilite*, the *Jam-e-Jamshed* was likely known to Lang who had an interest in Indian languages and was reputed to be a "friend of Indians." Given the circulation and exchange of pressmen between printing houses, it certainly lies within the realm of possibility that the two presses shared compositors or typesetters, the nimble-fingered men who set text "backwards" in a language that was often foreign to them.[98] The appearance of material in *nasta'liq* type in the *Mofussilite* suggests that Lang had contacts at presses that owned the expensive types[99]; it moreover suggests either that some sector of his newspaper's cliental could read Hindustani or that the newspaper took it upon itself to tutor its readers on "native languages." An early leading article had bemoaned that "Native Languages are not

---

College of Fort William that led to the division of a popular language [Hindustani] into modern Hindi and modern Urdu" (141).

96. *Mofussilite*, 4 August 1853, 487. Crittenden speculates that "Le Juif Errant" is a pseudonym for Lang himself (51, 128–29).

97. Mulholland discusses Calcutta and Madras newspapers that, already by 1785, include Roman, *nasta'liq*, and Bengali type side by side ("Translocal" 279–85). But the Presidency capitals were not the mofussil: Orsini writes that moveable-type printing presses with *nasta'liq* fonts were introduced into the mofussil in the 1820s, but most presses publishing in Urdu or Persian preferred lithography as it was "cheap and easy to operate, and it reproduced the elegant hand of calligraphers . . . without having to buy a full set of type fonts" ("Pandits" 106).

98. In his essay in *Household Words*, Lang wrote that many compositors "do not know a single word of English; many cannot tell you the names of the letters; but they will fill a case as speedily and accurately as any European" ("Starting" 95).

99. That Lang had contacts in Indian presses at an even earlier date than 1853 is indicated by the note "Printed at the College Press" that appeared below the *Mofussilite's* 25 October 1849 lithographed insert in Hindustani.

studied sufficiently by those whose duty it is to conduct judicial and other proceedings in them."[100] If such inserts were attempts to exhort readers, they were half-hearted efforts and not often repeated.[101]

By contrast, the *Mofussilite*'s promotional promise to attend to "Oriental Literature and other materials intimately connected with 'the land we live in'" got some attention in its early days (qtd. in Chanda, *History* [1987] 261). The first number included a ballad from the "Gulistan," a Persian collection of stories and poems from the thirteenth century.[102] And over a few weeks in November 1845, the newspaper ran a series called "Translation of the 1st Book of Anwari Soheily." The *Anvar-i Suhayli* is a late fifteenth-century illustrated Persian text by Husayn Vaiz-i Kashifi. An instantiation of the global transmission of texts and ideas, Kashifi's text drew on tales and fables of talking monkeys and other anthropomorphic animals that had originated on the Indian subcontinent and traveled to Persia in the tenth century. These fables were repatriated to the subcontinent in the nineteenth century when, as the scholar Christine van Ruymbeke writes, "the text [of *Anvar-i Suhayli*] was considered an excellent tool for practicing the Persian language, and it is a well-known fact that it was on the program for the Persian examination in the Indian Civil Service" (574).[103] That the *Mofussilite* included a translated excerpt from the *Anvar-i Suhayli* suggests that the translator was studying for the Indian Civil Service or perhaps tutoring those who were. (The translation in the *Mofussilite* was undertaken by a person knowledgeable in Persian,

---

100. 5 October 1845, 102–03. The writer urges greater knowledge of vernacular languages because lack of such knowledge "renders officers [in]capable of detecting the very many frauds which native officers are known to practice" (103).

101. In addition to material in *nasta'liq*, on three occasions the newspaper printed a poem or letter in Hindustani transcribed into Roman script (30 August 1845, 91; 13 May 1851, 302; 29 October 1851, 683). The paper also regularly included untranslated Hindustani words, a reminder of the ways Hindustani became incorporated into English.

102. "Sadoean Ballads. By the Editor. Gulistan Chap. 1—Tale 3" in *Mofussilite*, 2 August 1845, 14. The *Encyclopædia Iranica* indicates that "[i]n 1771, Sir William Jones advised students of Persian to pick as their first exercise in the language an easy chapter of the *Golestān* to translate. Thus, the *Golestān* became the primary text of Persian instruction for officials of British India at Fort William College (est. 1801) and at Haileybury College in England (est. 1806), with selections of the text being repeatedly published in primer form" (Lewis). See Mulholland for translations of Persian texts appearing in Anglo-Indian newspapers ("Translocal" 276).

103. Van Ruymbeke writes that the first full translation to appear in India was in 1854 (572).

but not an accomplished translator; the text is heavily annotated with explanations of words and phrases and the narrative clunky and lacking fluidity or poetry.)

The inclusion of the *Golestān* and *Anvar-i Suhaylī* in the pages of the early *Mofussilite* indicates that the newspaper's editor or translator of excerpts was participating in a project that was begun by Orientalists at Fort William College in Calcutta. Since the late eighteenth century, Calcutta had been the center of Orientalist learning. The philological work of William Jones and the Asiatic Society focused on Sanskrit and its relation to ancient Greek and Latin, while in nearby Srirampur, William Carey and his fellow missionaries translated and produced grammars of numerous Indian languages. These efforts culminated with the inauguration, in 1800, of both Fort William College, a facility to train British officials in Indian languages, and the Serampore Mission Press, dedicated to translating scripture into Bengali and other Indian languages. The emphasis on Sanskrit and vernacular languages had the effect of displacing Persian, the language of the Mughal court. Aamir Mufti writes that in the "process of indigenizing" the language landscape of India, William Jones and the Orientalists of the Asiatic Society produced the "Sanskritization of tradition, on the one hand, and the invention of the modern vernaculars, on the other" (478). The outcome of this indigenization was the "disappearance of Indo-Persian civilization, whose forms of cosmopolitanism . . . could now only appear under the sign of the non-indigenous, the elite, and thus alien" (Mufti 478). In short, Persian—and its cognate Urdu—were framed as alien, while Sanskrit and vernaculars such as Bengali were promoted as "indigenous."

By the 1840s, the Orientalist star was waning as another rose: the Anglicist. The goal of studying subcontinental languages, literatures, cultures, and customs was gradually eroded by the infusion of evangelical officers and civilians who headed east to change the world. If the 1780s to 1820s were the period of Orientalist learning, the 1830s onwards saw the growth of an Anglicist movement that emphasized the English language, Christianity, and European cultural mores.[104] If "White Mughals"—British men who settled in India, partnered with local women, and started families with them—are the symbol of that earlier period, Macaulay's infamous 1835 Minute on Education, in which he urged the Government of India to support education in English over vernacular languages, is the icon of this shift. As the Company and government annexed larger portions of

---

104. For a synthesis of this shift, see Viswanathan (101–04).

the subcontinent, it and its functionaries became increasingly distant from locals, more absorbed in administering subjects and lands.

The early *Mofussilite* and Lang were cut of Orientalist cloth. Lang was fluent in both Persian and Hindustani, and his impulse to know the "land we live in"—primarily for purposes of better administering it—had animated his newspaper in its early days. But that impulse did not survive, either because Lang altered or because his audience did. In the provinces, where Britons were primarily Company servants in garrisons and cantonments, the newspaper's readers leaned towards military and civil servants in secondary rungs of service, generally younger recruits who were more likely to have been in India a shorter time and almost certainly carried the arrogance of conquerors. Few would be conversant in vernacular languages (beyond the smattering required for the civil service exam). This explains both the increasingly infrequent use of Indian languages in the paper and the cessation of the early experiment in publishing "Oriental literature."

Non-"Oriental" literature, however, the newspaper offered plenty of. The first number begins with a poem—"Go boldly forth, 'Mofussilite,'/ My glory, and my great delight!"[105]—and a short story called "Recollections of the Late Jack Weatherly, by his brother Jeffrey." The first was signed "J.L."; the second was unsigned, but Crittenden makes a persuasive case that the writing is Lang's (89). In the course of its run, the *Mofussilite* published a good bit of Lang's literary output, including his best-regarded novel, *Too Clever by Half*. As in that first number, some of his work appeared signed, some unsigned. And, as was customary at the time, many of Lang's writings that appeared serially in the newspaper were reprinted in volume form, sometimes in Britain, sometimes in India.[106] That "Australia's first novelist," as Lang is often referred to, wrote and published much of his work serially in an Indian mofussil newspaper is one of the ironies of the global circulation of people and the transmission of ideas that this project sheds light on.

Aside from works by Lang, the Literature section of the *Mofussilite* featured fiction and nonfiction prose by numerous British writers. Some are unsigned—"A Week in Vienna Last Winter. By an English Gentle-

---

105. *Mofussilite*, 2 August 1845, 14.

106. *Passages in the Life of an Undergraduate* appeared in the *Mofussilite* in 1846–47 and was reprinted in volume form by the Mofussilite Press in late 1847 (Crittenden 109); *Too Clever by Half* appeared serially in the newspaper in 1848 and then in London in 1853 (114). For a complete list of Lang's works and their publication history, see Crittenden (223–26).

man"[107]—some signed but unattributed: "How I Got Married by Proxy!!!" by E____B____.[108] Others are drawn from British journals: the paper ran a story from *Chambers Edinburgh Journal* called "Mrs. Alfred Augustus Potts—A Tale of the Influenza," by Mrs. Frank Elliot, and in 1855 the topical "The Story of the Campaign; Written in a Tent in the Crimea," reprinted from *Blackwood's Magazine*.[109] Reprints from *Household Words* appeared from time to time: "The Road in India," signed "S.L.B.," appeared in 1856,[110] while Dickens's and Wilkie Collins's Christmas number "The Perils of Certain English Prisoners, and their Treasure in Women, Children, Silver, and Jewels" appeared on 2 March 1858. On 18 June 1858, "An Indian Court Martial," also attributed to *Household Words*, appears, although I have been unable to trace this essay to Dickens's journal.

The *Mofussilite*, with its literary pretensions, was not alone in reprinting literature from British periodicals; the Calcutta dailies did as well. On 2 January 1851, the *Bengal Hurkaru*'s Literature section included "Horace's Military Life" from the *Edinburgh Review* and a poem about the British Museum from *Punch*. The copyright status of these reprints is unclear: British law applied to Britons in India, but the ubiquity of reprints suggests that colonial newspapers were either exempt from or given a free pass by enforcers of the Copyright Act of 1842 and the Colonial Copyright Act of 1847. Notwithstanding the legal standing of reprints, certain forms of reprinting seemed to violate norms. In 1851, the *Mofussilite* rapped the *Lahore Chronicle* on its knuckles for its "literary piracy" of Edward Bulwer Lytton's *My Novel*:

> We may while about it say a word for poor Mr. Dickens, whose "Household Words" our contemporary is in the habit of republishing almost from beginning to end. The offence, thought thoughtless, is a very grievous one. We have no doubt whatever that the *Chronicle's* very considerable circulation deprives Mr. Dickens of many subscribers in this country, and this is "wrong." Our contemporary must have read about a superior class of highwaymen who made it a point of honor never to

---

107. *Mofussilite*, 26 February 1856.

108. *Mofussilite*, 11 May 1855.

109. *Mofussilite*, 1 August 1848 and 6 February 1855, respectively.

110. *Mofussilite*, 11 April 1856. The essay by Sidney Laman Blanchard appeared in *Household Words* on 29 December 1855.

> rob the same man twice.... [W]e would at least suggest to our contemporary a little variety in his victims. This is what we always aim at. We have the same contempt which every enterprising Editor must have for the laws of literary property; but we always attempt to steal decorously, and with an eye to the equitable distribution of our knaveries.[111]

Notably, not only does this editor not oppose "literary piracy," he even goes so far as to declare that, along with "every enterprising Editor," he has "contempt . . . for the laws of literary property." Perhaps because news was never covered by copyright, editors such as Lang and his ilk were flippant about the tussles over copyright that preoccupied authors of literary works.[112]

Five years after advising the *Lahore Chronicle* to "steal decorously," however, the *Mofussilite* found itself issuing a warning, this time about the pillage of literature from its own pages:

> The pressure of European news induces us to postpone the publication of the third number of Mr. Lang's tale, "Plot and Passion," until our next issue. This will be inconvenient, we fear to the conductors of the *Indian Times*, who are stealing the tale in question, and publishing it in their own columns. But perhaps it will be better for them in the end, as they will receive notice during the interval that we have given instructions to our Attorney in Calcutta to commence an action at law against the journal for literary piracy. Unless therefore our contemporary means to hoist the black flag *en permanence*, we would advise an immediate discontinuance of this dishonest and disreputable proceeding.[113]

---

111. *Mofussilite*, 20 January 1851, 60.

112. See Slauter on newspapers and copyright and Catherine Seville on copyright law in the nineteenth century more broadly.

113. *Mofussilite*, 11 January 1856, 36. The paper was not always so stern: four years earlier, it accused the *Delhi Gazette* of plagiarizing a review that had appeared in the *Mofussilite* in January 1847, placing its contemporary's review beside its own 1847 review. Despite this evidence, the *Mofussilite* urged readers to have "mercy" on the *Delhi Gazette* (11 February 1851, 93).

For the vantage point of the editor turned novelist, literary property rights look different. Perhaps, too, Lang had been won over to the cause of copyright during his years in London when his own essays appeared in Dickens's *Household Words* (six in 1853). By the end of the decade, Lang's policy on borrowing had taken a sharp turn from the "decorous stealing" he advised in 1851: in the autumn of 1859, upon resuming editorship of the *Mofussilite* after a furlough in London, Lang halted the serialization of *A Tale of Two Cities* that had been initiated by his predecessor because the *Mofussilite* "did not own the copyright" (Crittenden 194). In less than a decade, then, Anglo-Indian newspapers shifted their practice to align with the increasing pressure to protect authors' intellectual property rights, notwithstanding the ease with which authors' words could circulate and appear in their pages.

This section has foregrounded bibliographic codes of my data set in order to examine the circulating objects that were Anglo-Indian newspapers and to illuminate the environment and ecosystem these newspapers functioned within. Focusing on physical and material features—mastheads, endcaps, columns, etc. that Brooker and Thacker call internal periodical codes—the section has sought to recreate the contexts and histories embedded in what might otherwise remain inert marks on the page. In the discussion of each code, I have sought to explicate it by embedding it in contexts large and small, from press regulations in India to newspapers' relations with readers, from connections between newspapers to tensions within them. My attention to letters and leaders, reprints and rates, as *features*—rather than as content or substance—serves as a portal into a world of print in flux: tolerated by the authorities but unsure of the "people" or public they spoke for, expanding and expansive in their reach but stretching their resources and technologies. This focus on bibliographic features establishes a baseline of practices; in the coming chapters, we will return to some of these features as they fracture and tilt in the face of crises. In order to make sense of those crises, the final section of this chapter turns from bibliography to content analysis of one newspaper.

In Good Company:
Colonial Critique and Imperial Certitude in the *Mofussilite*

Anglo-Indian newspapers of the middle years of the nineteenth century have received little attention from scholars. From the emergence of print newspapers in the late eighteenth century and collaborations in the 1820s between Indians such as Rammohan Roy or Dwarkanath Tagore and editors of liberal presses, the story of Indian newspapers skips almost fifty years to the last quarter of the century. In the absence of any detailed studies, Anglo-Indian newspapers of the middle years of the century have almost uniformly been characterized as vociferous handmaidens of the imperial project. In this section, I will drill into one newspaper's views on the governing authorities of British India. Of the papers in my sample, the *Mofussilite* was by far the most "radical." Proudly embracing its marginality from the centers of power, the newspaper viewed itself as a voice of opposition to the Government of India. Its relation and reaction to the authorities offers a glimpse into what a critique of empire looked like at the heart of empire. The discussion will set the stage for the exploration of crises the next two chapters take up.

Any attempt to characterize the politics of Anglo-Indian newspapers is complicated by the fact that editors had a large hand in determining a newspaper's politics, and, like other Anglo-Indian newspapers, the *Mofussilite*'s editorial chair saw steady turnover. During the period under review, the *Mofussilite* had multiple editors: Lang founded the *Mofussilite* and edited it from its inception in 1845 to 1851. In early 1851 he went on a "furlough" and left the newspaper in the hands of G. R. Wilby, who had previously worked at the *Hurkaru*.[114] Lang stepped back into the role briefly in 1854 before handing the reins over to Sidney Laman Blanchard in mid-1854. There is some confusion about how long Blanchard served as editor;[115] my own investigation—drawing, in part, on other newspapers' reports—indicates that Blanchard took over the reins at the *Mofussilite* in May 1854 and remained at the helm until January 1857. The occupant of the editor's chair between January 1857 and April 1858—the period of the Uprising—remains a mystery (which we shall drill into in chapter 3), but we know that Blanchard returned in 1858 and remained in the office for approximately a year.[116] He was followed by Lang, who resumed editorial duties in August 1859. To sum up: between 1845 and 1860, the *Mofussilite*'s editor changed at least six times.

---

114. Crittenden erroneously refers to this editor as "Wylie" (117).

115. Crittenden writes that Blanchard was editor of the *Mofussilite* from 1854 to 1859 (159–60, 169, 192); S. C. Sanial, by contrast, reports that Blanchard was editor of the *Bengal Hurkaru* from 1854 to June 1857 ("History" [IV] 202).

116. Chanda (*History* [2008] 247, 253; *History* [1987] 35–36).

Editorial Turnover at the Mofussilite, 1845–60

From	To	Editor	Length in Chair
Aug 1845	Jan 1851	John Lang	5½ years
Jan 1851	early 1852	G. R. Wilby	1 year
1852	1854	Unknown	(2 years)
Feb 1854	May 1854	John Lang	~ 4 months
May 1854	Jan 1857	Sidney Laman Blanchard	2½ years
Jan 1857	April 1858	Unknown	(16 months)
April 1858	Aug 1859	Sidney Laman Blanchard	16 months
Aug 1859	1862	John Lang	3 years

Figure 1.7. Editors of the *Mofussilite*, 1845–60.

Despite these shifts, the *Mofussilite* was very much "Lang's newspaper," in part because even when not occupying the editorial seat, Lang remained a frequent contributor, and was from March 1850 the newspaper's owner and proprietor.[117] While the tenor of the paper altered slightly each time Lang stepped down as editor, its politics did not change dramatically over the course of fifteen years. That Lang's shadow was long is evident in this lengthy leader from 1851:

> Mr. Lang has from this day ceased to be the editor of the *Mofussilite*. We (individually Mr. G. R. Wilby) are very glad of it, because we succeed to so honorable a position. But it is just possible that many readers of this paper may be very sorry for it, since during the past five years (with occasional interruptions) the public has been instructed, reasoned with, and entertained by a writer who never took any one for his model and is not likely to find a successful imitator. . . .
>
> The rapid rise of the *Mofussilite* and its continued prosperity excited no wonder in those who knew Mr. Lang, his talents, his erudition, his illimitable resources, and above all his peculiar vein of wit and humour . . .

---

117. The notice appeared in the paper: "[T]he entire property of *Mofussilite* Newspaper and Press has passed into the hands of the Editor—who fully intends (D.V.) to drive his own coach, and be his own guard, for the next five years to come" (*Mofussilite*, 5 March 1850, 148).

> But while we award to Mr. Lang as an instructive and amusing journalist the highest order of praise, we are not blind to the many faults of his Editorial career. On looking over the files of the *Mofussilite* we frequently find him sacrificing noble principles . . . to a love of jocularity and to an apparently affected superciliousness . . . In short, whatever may be Mr. Lang's logical powers, they have always been subservient to his love of ridicule, of which there can be no doubt he was and is a perfect master.
>
> To take charge of a newspaper, edited as this paper has been, is by no means an easy matter, but . . . let us hope for the best. We do not mean to be an imitator of Mr. Lang, but we shall do our best to emulate him. His success as a newspaper Editor being without precedent in the history of the Indian Press, we shall never forget the sterling principles which have guided his career, nor lose sight of the policy which has led him on to fortune. Taking over the *Mofussilite* as a *carte blanche*, we shall henceforth do our best to fill it up to the satisfaction of its readers.[118]

I have quoted this appreciation at length because it provides a sense of the personality it took to put out an oppositional newspaper and the energy Lang brought to his task. Editors were expected to teach and amuse, to lead and simultaneously camouflage their instruction. An ideal editor was equal parts pedagogue, parent, and performer. Lang, by all accounts instructed and he certainly entertained his readers; it is less clear that he reasoned. For those who were disinclined to share his views, Lang had nothing but contempt and ridicule. He had a loyal following, but also enemies: government officials towards whom he directed the firehose of his criticisms and fellow editors whom he mocked for their fawning of authorities.

As Wilby hints, the *Mofussilite* was a vocal critic of the East India Company, the de facto Government of India, which the newspaper called a "shop-keeping government."[119] Many of its criticisms were leveled at the

---

118. *Mofussilite*, 10 January 1851, 21.

119. *Mofussilite*, 21 February 1851, 117. The Company was a trading enterprise that in 1765 acquired, from the Mughal emperor, the *diwani*, or right to collect taxes in Bengal. Shortly thereafter, in 1773, the British Parliament started to regulate it more

government's nepotism and promotion of ill-qualified candidates for plum positions. In only its fourth number, the paper opined, "We are sorry to find that the claims of Mr. Prinsep, the oldest, and most respected practitioner at the Calcutta bar,—who has for many years served the E. I. Company as Standing Counsel,—and on two occasions acted as their Advocate General,—have been passed over in order to make room for a Mr. Colville,—a youth, quite as 'unknown to fame,' in England, as he is in India. These appointments are excessively disgusting."[120] A few years later, the *Mofussilite* lashed out again, this time castigating the Company's board in London and not just for nepotism:

> Men who have been educated for the Indian service, who have spent their lives in acquiring a knowledge of the languages, habits and interests of the people—who have gained their confidence and ruled them with success—may in a few rare instances be appointed to a subordinate Government; but for the last half century not a single servant of the Company has held permanently the Supreme Government of this country . . . If a Governor General is required, the War Office, the Admiralty, the Board of Trade, or the Royal household are ransacked for a peer whose ambition can be tickled, or cupidity tempted by the Viceroyship of Hindostan! A knowledge of the country, its people, its vast and varied political relations with princes and potentates, of unknown regions . . . are never thought of. It suits the leaders to get rid of a troublesome member of the Cabinet, or it is a good card to play with the public to nominate a new very powerful or staunch opponent who has acquired a temporary popularity on a not very solid foundation . . . Did time and space permit, we think it would not be difficult to trace most of the public difficulties and dangers, in which this country has been involved during [the last thirty years] to the peculiar unfitness of the Governor General to meet each successive crisis in which difficulties have occurred or dangers

---

closely and required the Company's charter to be periodically renewed. With each renewal, Parliament imposed further oversight and regulations on the Company's administration of India; sovereignty over India was eventually transferred from the Company to the Crown in August 1858.

120. *Mofussilite*, 23 August 1845, 62.

have arisen. Would the Affghan [sic] war have ever been a blot on the page of the British Indian histories or would the Sutlej campaign, or the most recent Punjab campaign have ever been the causes of woe to India, had a Metcalfe ruled her at the one period, or a Clarke at the other?[121]

The charge that colonial appointments served political ends leads the writer all the way to the top to denounce "the peculiar unfitness of the Governor General," a claim that would have been actionable not too long before.

Not every paper in my sample was so strong or stinging in its criticisms, but neither was the *Mofussilite* unique in its takedown of the EIC, nor was its anti-establishment stance novel in the history of Indian journalism. As I noted in the introductory chapter, the rise of the news media in India is filled with accounts of skirmishes between newspapers and the Company. The first print newspaper to appear in India, *Hicky's Bengal Gazette* (est. 1780), was written and edited by James Augustus Hicky, who viewed the Company as despotic; he used his newspaper to expose the corruption he believed existed at every level up to the governor general, Warren Hastings.[122] Hicky's tone and attacks on officials tended to be personal, and after less than two years he was imprisoned on charges of libel and his typefaces confiscated. James Silk Buckingham, the venerated editor of the *Calcutta Journal* (est. 1818), on the other hand, was both a scrupulous journalist and fierce critic of the Company and its administration of India. But he, too, learned that exposing Company policies did not pay, and he was extradited to England in 1823. (In 1834, the House of Commons recommended recompense and the Company granted him a pension of £200 per year.[123]) The historian Nadir Ali Khan writes that "[j]ournalism in India owed its origin to the fact that certain dismissed employees of the East India Company had a grouse against the administration and wished to express it through effective public propaganda" (1). Partha Chatterjee, as we saw in the introduction, reads this early history not in terms of personalities, but in terms of the space early newspapers opened up for public debate about government policies (*Black Hole* 112).

But what of such debate in the 1840s and 1850s? Anglo-Indian society in this period was more conservative—separatist and Anglicist—

---

121. *Mofussilite*, 10 July 1849, 445.
122. See Nair (*Hicky*); Chakraborti; N. A. Khan; Mukhopadhyay; Otis.
123. See G. F. R. Barker.

than the world Hicky and Buckingham inhabited (which was marginally more integrationist and Orientalist). Though more conservative, the mid-century Anglo-Indian press did not shy away from criticisms of the Company and its governance of India. And these criticisms were tolerated at this juncture. Why? Partly because of the change in press regulations: in 1835, Charles Metcalfe, acting governor general, had lifted the increasingly draconian press regulations that had been imposed on the press since 1799. Consequently, between 1835 and 1857, newspapers and journals had only to register with the government, but their content was not censored. Criticisms of the sort that landed Hicky, Buckingham, and others in trouble, were now ignored; sentiments that prior to Act XI of 1835 would have led to a reprimand, the revocation of the publication's license, or deportation of the editor, the government was now indifferent to. The new policy about censorship was the result, in part, of the increasing scrutiny and regulation of the Company itself. Beginning in 1773, the Company's charter regularly came up for parliamentary renewal (renewal years were 1784, 1793, 1813, and 1853). Prior to each renewal, the British press—and increasingly the Anglo-Indian press—fiercely debated the administration of India. For instance, although the charter was not up for renewal again until 1853, as early as 1845 the *Mofussilite* ran a piece entitled "Will the East India Company's Lease of India be Renewed in 1853, or Will it Not?" The leader contemplated the "entire dissolution [of the Company] as a governing body" and wondered what would happen if "the government of India were assumed by the crown."[124] That precisely such a transfer occurred thirteen years on speaks less to the perspicacity of the *Mofussilite* as to the culture of debating the Company's suitability to govern India that flourished in Anglo-Indian prints. (Notably, the *Mofussilite* does not question the British presence in India, only the Company's administration of it.)

Such criticisms were also countenanced partly because stopping them would be like trying to stop a tidal wave. Well before its burial in 1858, the Company was cut and stabbed so often in public prints that one might wonder it survived as long as it did. In 1851, the *Mofussilite* wrote of the "changes that must take place in the Government . . . [which] presents so great a mass of anomalies—and is in so many of its details so unsuited to the spirit of the age, and the altered condition of the country—that many and great changes must take place . . . both in the mode of governing and

---

124. *Mofussilite*, 27 September 1845, 164.

in the form of Government."[125] What were some of the changes needed to make the governance of India more "suited to the spirit of the age"? One answer, not surprising for a man trained to the bar as Lang was, was reform of the judiciary. An 1851 leader charged,

> Under the present construction of the Mofussil Courts it is unreasonable to expect an honest or independent bar. It will be many years before the Government is disinterested enough to confer the higher judicial appointments on natives, and perhaps longer still before the natives are qualified for them; but were the bar made the stepping stone to subordinate judicial offices, we should soon see an improvement in the character of pleaders and the efficiency of Sudder Ameens [the highest position an Indian judge could aspire to] . . . It cannot however be supposed that the office of vakeel [attorney] will ever become respectable until Civil servants are taught to treat those who plead before them with respect.[126]

This editorial is remarkable as much for what it does not say as for what it does. The writer—most likely Lang—does not disparage Indians, nor rely on a racial explanation for their lack, nor blame Indian officials for lies told in court (common accusations found in other prints). Instead, he views the lack of Indians' skills as the direct result of the government's actions. The notion that Indians' lack of judicial skills is due to infrastructure—the "present construction of the Mofussil Courts," as well as the government's and Civil servants' treatment of Indians—is unexpected and singular in our sample. Coupled with the newspaper's unrelenting criticisms of the government for incompetence and nepotism, this defense of Indian attorneys and judges and call for their promotion provides one clue as to why Lang was considered a friend by many Indians of the day.

At other times, the *Mofussilite*'s views towards Indians was of its moment. The same year the newspaper defended Indian court officials, it also ran a leader that, even as it seemed to disparage Britons who came to India, took a pointedly imperial turn. "The Saxon race," the editorial

---

125. *Mofussilite*, 4 March 1851, 141.
126. *Mofussilite*, 11 March 1851, 156–57.

ran, "cannot look on India as a home and hence feels only a traveller's interest in the institutions and prospects of the country through which he is sojourning. To popularize the Government of this land is a dream from which the wildest enthusiast would soon awaken were he to have but a few months experience of the country and the people."[127] Even as it accepts that "popularizing" British rule is a pipe dream, the editorial continues, "[i]t is the mission of England to train up the people of India to become partakers of the civilization of the 19th century—and to pave the way for the overthrow of that debasing faith, which disgraces the character and debases the mental faculties of the people."[128] The civilizational certitude, along with the missionary arrogance, are not singular; in the years of this study, countless leaders in newspapers upbraid the Government of India for neglecting its "duty" to improve the country.[129] This is the civilizing mission, unapologetic and writ large.

Civilizing India meant "rescuing" Indians, whether from their religion or education or rulers. Indeed, nowhere was the *Mofussilite* sharper in its

---

127. *Mofussilite*, 4 March 1851, 141.

128. *Mofussilite*, 4 March 1851, 141.

129. To wit: "The people of India are still many hundred years behind almost any portion of the European family: yet they form an admirable soil for the philanthropy of modern legislation to work its works on. . . . [I]t is both the duty and the interest of those in whose hands the Government of this great country is entrusted, to lay the foundation of a system which may afterwards be expanded to its full dimensions . . . [F]or till the moral and intellectual faculties of the population are advanced . . . till the body of the nation can be brought to consider every improvement, as a boon impending on themselves—and that can only be done by a general and judiciously conducted system of education carried into every village and hamlet throughout the land—all the efforts which can be made to extend to India, the benefits of modern improvements, will fall far short of the sanguine expectations of those who now anticipate so many advantages from the extension of steam in all its branches to this country" (*Mofussilite*, 19 November 1847, 740). And: "The question is *not* whether India is better off under British Rule than it would be under a Native dynasty . . . The question is this. Has the British Government, during the term of its occupancy, made those gigantic strides which might have been naturally expected of it? Have we availed ourselves of the opportunities which have constantly been offered? Have we introduced to the full extent of our power and ability, the 'arts of peace' which are common to all civilized countries in Europe? He would be a bold man who would rise up and answer all, or any, of these questions in the affirmative" (*Mofussilite*, 20 March 1849, 181).

indictment of the Government of India than in its management of "native" states. Throughout the nineteenth and into the twentieth century, the subcontinent was dotted with Indian principalities under the jurisdiction of an Indian rajah or nawab. Most were nominally "independent," but paid for that independence with fealty—and taxes—to the British. Most were also gradually absorbed into the empire on any number of pretexts. The Punjab was the EIC's last major territorial conquest; following that costly war, the Company's administrative arm devised alternatives such as the "doctrine of lapse" to annex other principalities. Awadh was an independent state in the central plains on good terms with the British until the government annexed it in 1856, claiming that its elites were profligate. This 1849 leader that appeared seven years prior to the annexation of Awadh (Oudh) bears quoting at length:

> The British Government might solemnly bind itself never to go into the Oudh territory provided a certain annual sum was paid regularly. But would any moralist in the world blame the British for breaking its treaty, for the purpose of suppressing cruelty, and affording protection to thousands of ground-down subjects? . . . But since . . . we know that the people would be more contented, and their property more secure, under the British power, since we are certain that on a handsome pension the Boy King[130] would lead a far more pleasurable life; and since we can see that nothing short of absolute possession will repay the British Government the money justly due and owning—why, we have not the slightest compunction in recommending that the land of the five rivers be "absorbed." There are cases, between men, even, where agreements are more honored in the breach than in the observance. For instance, we may voluntarily agree to pay a man so much per month for life. But if we find that he applies the stipend to improper purposes, surely we have a right to withhold it, if we think it proper. And so with states. If the first party—(that is the *strongest*) finds it inexpedient and improper to keep to its treaty with the second party, we cannot see the smallest particle of harm in departing at once. . . . Treaties are so much waste of

---

130. Dalip Singh, the young maharaja of defeated Punjab.

paper.... Let us hope that the British Government in India will never again be beguiled into making Treaties. There will, then, be no occasion for *breaking* them.[131]

"Treaties are so much waste of paper": an apt imperialist formula. In the newspaper's logic, the government's duty to protect "thousands of ground-down subjects" leads it quite inexorably to argue that reneging on its word is the "moral" thing to do. The *Mofussilite*'s distance from the corridors of power amounted to hostility to the colonial government—but not to the imperial project itself.[132] The imperial formula it articulates is all too familiar to any student of nineteenth-century empire; what is noteworthy in this instance is that such views appeared in a newspaper edited and owned by a man considered a supporter of Indians in their struggles against the government.

If the *Mofussilite* considered the Government of India one obstacle to realizing the muscular imperial vision it endorsed, public opinion in Britain was another: "It has been in our power to silence every potentate and to subjugate his dominions. The great mistake we have committed has been doing this by piece meal . . . fearing public opinion *in England*—by wondering what the people in Exeter Hall would say."[133] Exeter Hall: the metonym for the evangelically inspired political movements whose greatest success was the abolition of slavery. Thomas Carlyle used the shorthand contemptuously and to potent purpose in his December 1849 "Occasional Discourse on the Nigger Question," a virulent essay that prompted John Stuart Mill's response, "The Negro Question," a few months later.[134] The reference to Exeter Hall raises that long-standing conundrum: how a historical moment that in Britain witnessed the greatest expansion of liberties and liberal principles—a commitment to the rule of law, individual rights, an accountable and representative government—was paralleled with the abrogation of those same rights and principles in its colonies? The contradiction is unabashedly articulated in Mill's opposing declarations

---

131. *Mofussilite*, 16 January 1849, 36.
132. See Loomba for a discussion of the distinction between colonialism and imperialism (4–6). A useful heuristic is that imperialism is the ideology and colonialism the implementation of that ideology in specific places.
133. *Mofussilite*, 20 March 1849, 181.
134. For an analysis of the debate, see Goldberg.

in *On Liberty*: "whatever crushes individuality is despotism, by whatever name it may be called, and whether it professes to be enforcing the will of God or the injunctions of men" (193) and "[d]espotism is a legitimate mode of government in dealing with barbarians, provided the end be their improvement, and the means justified by actually effecting that end" (136).[135]

Partha Chatterjee argues that Mill accepted this contradiction because he made a distinction between political despotism and paternal despotism. The former is the despotism of absolute rulers that, in Europe, was replaced with "[d]eliberative politics[,] . . . exchange of opinions and persuasive process[,] . . . the practice of self-government" (*Black Hole* 181). Paternal despotism, on the other hand, was the "protection and guidance of a European power over non-European peoples" (181). The result, writes Chatterjee, of this "liberal justification of paternal despotism in the colonies," was twofold: to bring "colonial governance under some sort of parliamentary control" and to "create a sphere ruled by experts who would both demand and enjoy a degree of autonomy from supervision by an ignorant and uncomprehending metropolitan public along with its elected representatives" (182). The *Mofussilite*'s editorials cited above, dating to the late 1840s and 1850s, express both Mill's paternal justification and the repudiation of metropolitan opinion: only "[m]en who have been educated for the Indian service, who have spent their lives in acquiring a knowledge of the languages, habits and interests of the people" ought to speak on Indian question and govern India.[136]

Addressing liberalism's contradictions more broadly, the political theorists Uday Singh Mehta and Jennifer Pitts analyze the relations and tensions between liberalism and empire in the late eighteenth and nineteenth centuries. Both Mehta, in *Liberalism and Empire: A Study in Nineteenth-Century British Liberal Thought* (1999), and Pitts, in *A Turn to Empire: The Rise of Liberal Imperialism in Britain and France* (2005), scrutinize the writings of Edmund Burke and the Mills (father and son), among others, but they arrive at different conclusions. For Mehta, "strategies of exclusion" lie at the core of liberalism and are not antithetical to

---

135. Any student of the East India Company routinely encounters the father of liberalism in the archive, where almost every document received in the Company's office in London is signed "(True Copies) J. S. Mill, Examiner of Indian Correspondence."
136. *Mofussilite*, 10 July 1849, 445.

it; exclusions were used to justify differential treatment and suspension of rights when dealing with those considered different.[137] Pitts, by contrast, identifies eighteenth-century critics of European imperial expansion—Adam Smith, Edmund Burke, Jeremy Bentham—and concludes that "liberalism does not lead ineluctably either to imperialism or anti-imperialism" (4). The liberal "turn" to empire occurred, she writes, in the 1820s and 1830s when thinkers like the Mills (and Tocqueville in France) began to express greater "civilizational self-confidence" (240).

In the early years of the nineteenth century, Pitts argues, the ideas of eighteenth-century theorists were extricated from their opposition to imperial expansion and used to make a case for empire. Thus, Scottish historians' complex gradations of human societies or Smith's stage theory of historical progress which "refus[ed] to rank societies" (25) and "resist[ed] any implication that non-Europeans ought to be excluded from ordinary standards of political respect, inclusion, or reciprocity" (21) were reduced to a dichotomy of "civilization–barbarism" (130). While the Scottish historians who had influenced Smith and Burke viewed institutions in other societies as rational responses to circumstance and experiences, James Mill "repeatedly argued that the practices of rude peoples in general, and Indians and Chinese in particular . . . , illustrated the debility of their minds, their inability to recognize their interests, and the enslavement of their reason to whim or passion" (Pitts 131). For Pitts, the nineteenth-century turn is significant; it is what led John Stuart Mill to conclude that Indians' social and political differences were indicative of their intellectual deficiencies and character (133–37) and liberals more broadly to conclude that "moral and political standards that governed relations within Europe [could be] suspended in dealings with other peoples" (240–41). Pitts demonstrates that liberal political thought that "appeared . . . to hold the promise of a critical approach to European expansion" transformed in the nineteenth century into "an imperial liberalism that by the 1830s provided some of the most insistent and well-developed arguments in favor of the conquest of non-European peoples and territories" (2).

---

137. More recently, Lowe offers a similar reading of liberalism: "The genealogy of modern liberalism is thus also a genealogy of modern race; racial differences and distinctions designate the boundaries of the human and endure as remainders attesting to the violence of liberal universality" (7).

Whether one concludes that violence lies at the heart of liberalism itself or that liberalism's exclusions are a repudiation of its principles, the contradiction between extending liberty to some and denying it to others lay at the heart of the nineteenth-century British state and empire.[138] The *Mofussilite* did not break rank and its views about the governance of India were staunchly liberal imperialist: better governance so as to provide for and improve the lot of those "unable" to do so for themselves. It got there by drawing on a smorgasbord of views: paternalist notions about the happiness of the people are drawn from a Utilitarian toolbox (Macaulay is often cited positively in the newspaper), while the language of rescuing victims from the tyranny of their rulers draws on evangelical rhetoric (which is simultaneously castigated as the stumbling block to the realization of these principles). As an articulation of an imperial stance, the *Mofussilite*'s belief that "native" states could and should be annexed is unexceptional. What is puzzling is that this position did not bar John Lang from taking a leave of absence as editor from his own newspaper in order to provide counsel to Rani Laxmibai when her principality, Jhansi, was annexed in 1854 and she sought his counsel (discussed in chapter 4).

Such messiness interests me. Chatterjee has written that "empire was not just about power politics, the logic of capital, or the civilizing mission but instead was something that had to be practiced, as a normal everyday business as well as at moments of extraordinary crisis, by real people in real time" (*Black Hole* xi–xii). His notion that "the irreducible contingency of historical events . . . can never be fully encompassed by conceptual abstractions" leads him to attend to "actual practices of empire as engaged in in real time" (xii). And "real time" was messy and filled with contradictions. This is a point Douglas Peers makes in a subtle essay on J. W. Kaye, the first chronicler of the 1857 Uprising: "Kaye's articles, reviews, and books collectively reveal the often hybrid quality of imperial discourse. It could never be hegemonic when it had to contend with so

---

138. Said captures the contradiction in reference to Conrad: "Conrad's tragic limitation is that even though he could see clearly that on one level imperialism was essentially pure dominance and land-grabbing, he could not then conclude that imperialism had to end so that 'natives' could lead lives free from European domination. As a creature of his time, Conrad could not grant the natives their freedom, despite his severe critique of the imperialism that enslaved them" (30).

many voices, ideologies and positions" (294). Stoler and Cooper, too, warn us against totalizing stances; writing of the "tensions of empire," they argue that "the colonial" is a notion that "homogenizes a power relationship whose limitations and contingencies need to be examined" (33). In many accounts, they insist, "European agency too often remains undifferentiated, assumed, and unexplored" (16). They are concerned that their discipline "[remains] surprisingly silent about the plurality of competing visions by which Europeans in the colonies fashioned their distinctions, conjured up their 'whiteness,' and reinvented themselves" (16). Newspapers, as "the first rough draft of history" (Latham and Scholes 520), are one of the richest sites to capture the instability, the tug-and-pull of numerous voices, the inconsistencies and reversals, the braiding of a discourse of "duty" along with the urge to give voice to Indians.

Indeed, what *of* Indians in the *Mofussilite*'s pages? I close this section on the politics of the *Mofussilite* with a letter that appeared in the body of the paper in early 1851 when Lang was still editor. Under the header "(From our own Correspondent with the Camp of the Governor General)" appeared this singular text:

> My dear Sir, — I am very sorry whitch you are not heair To see the darbar of Mahrag Glob Sing [the Maharajah of Kashmir] and the Governor General and all the gentleman and all the armeys and the first Mahrag Glob Sing came to see the Governor Ginarl and G. G. gave him great kheluth and G. G. bin to see the Mahrag Glob Sing and Glob Sing gave him great kheluth and G. G. was rid on eleyphant and silver houda and my master and all the gentleman was ful dreas and their was great fun and wear quite well and I hope your onor will be quite well and I am very sorry for your things which you hav lost by majester [Magistrate Denison?] and Mr. Gubeen behave very il with you and if I was G. G. then I shall sint him jeal for 14 years or turnhinm out from his sirvis and whitch you wish To giv me your wark of nues paper I shall do it, and if I cant do it then I shall kipe a baboo under me and I shall giv him 100 rupees a munth and if your ornor will gav me to do it I shall Do it proper by my dear Sir Mr. Lang and my great complement to you and God will mak you Governor genlr of India then will bee very well and in Wuzibad was very rain

that for I cant sint you this letter befour and Afread is very well agen and sint your ornor great compliment and shela giv you great Shalam

Mahomed Usghur[139]

This letter is utterly anomalous in the pages of the *Mofussilite*—or any newspaper in my sample. Both the *Mofussilite* and *Bengal Hurkaru* had a small number of "native" correspondents whose reports are marked with a "Our native newswriter at Lahore writes . . ." or "A native correspondent from Oude writes as follows . . ."[140] These correspondents' reports appear in standard English and read so much like the remainder of the newspaper that, notwithstanding the quotation marks, one suspects the copy was revised by a heavy editorial hand. Nothing like this letter with its nonstandard spelling, imperfect grammar, and the correspondent's name appears in any Anglo-Indian newspaper of the period I have consulted. Nothing of such a private nature—referring to "your things which you hav lost," to "my dear Sir Mr. Lang," or the offer to "To giv me your wark of nues paper I shall do it"—nothing so *like a letter* appears in these newspapers. Who is Mahomed Usghur, what made him "our own Correspondent," and why does Lang publish a signed and unedited letter from Usghur? By this point the reader will not be surprised to learn that the answers to those questions require considerable sleuthing and some speculation. I will return to Usghur in the next chapter and again in the final one. For now, I close with this letter that hints at a closeness between Lang and Usghur, a man who, though not wealthy (he serves a master who attends the durbar between the governor general and Maharaja Gulab Singh of Kashmir), can afford to pay a "baboo" a hundred rupees a month, a considerable sum of money.[141] The *Mofussilite*'s unapologetic imperialism was, to at least some of its Indian readers, not in contradiction to its editor's support for and giving voice to Indians.

---

139. *Mofussilite*, 7 January 1851, 12.

140. *Mofussilite*, 1 August 1848, 483; *Bengal Hurkaru*, 8 September 1856, 239.

141. An Indian office clerk generally earned from Rs. 20 to Rs. 60 a month, while a British clerk earned something in the vicinity of Rs. 100 a month. For more on salaries, see Priti Joshi ("Audience" 262–63).

Chapter 2

Through a Glass Darkly

The Great Exhibition and the Great Indian Contractor

On 7 January 1851, a small notice appeared in the *Mofussilite*: "It is quite true that 'we'—the Proprietor—intend ere long to become 'our own London Correspondent'—and possibly we may address our constituents from Windsor Castle or Buckingham palace. We hope to arrive in time to chronicle 'the great Exhibition of Arts.'" The proprietor of the newspaper was John Lang, as confirmed by this small announcement two weeks later: "Notice.—The undersigned hereby authorizes Mr. J. A. Gibbons, until further notice, to receive money for and on account of the *Mofussilite Press*, and to grant receipts for the same. John Lang, Sole Proprietor" (21 January).[1] Confirming Lang's departure, a lengthy editorial appeared on 10 January (discussed in the previous chapter) announcing, "Mr. Lang has from this day ceased to be the editor of the *Mofussilite*. We (individually Mr. G. R. Wilby) are very glad of it, because we succeed to so honorable a position." Thus it was that an era came to a close as John Lang, the founder and editor of the *Mofussilite* since 1845, announced his intention to step down as editor—but not proprietor—and travel to London from where he would file stories, including on the Great Exhibition.

That Lang proposed visiting London to report on the Great Exhibition, scheduled to open on 1 May in London, is unremarkable. Indian newspapers anticipated the opening of the royally sponsored experiment

---

1. Unless otherwise noted, all citations from newspapers in this chapter will refer to 1851. To limit parenthetical interruptions and promote flow, dates will appear in the narrative.

with as much interest as their British counterparts. Moreover, Lang was an ambitious journalist and writer with literary aspirations that included the desire to see his stories in print at "home." But something happened on the way to Hyde Park. Lang's biographer Victor Crittenden writes that "Lang arrived in London early in 1851. He had hardly unpacked his bags and settled in to a leisurely life in the city when he received an urgent letter from India. It was from a wealthy Indian banker and entrepreneur who asked Lang if he would come back to India to defend him in an important court case . . . [Lang] left England in May 1851 travelling via the Cape of Good Hope in one of Green's celebrated liners, the *Nile*" (118–19).

Crittenden's account contains slivers of accuracy—a steamer named *Nile* did indeed arrive in Calcutta from London—but is incorrect in almost every detail: were Lang to have left England in May 1851 to return to India, he would have missed the trial Crittenden refers to which commenced on the 27th of March 1851 in Agra, some eight hundred miles inland from Calcutta, and concluded on April 9. Moreover, no ship's arrival or departure lists between Calcutta and London in 1850 or 1851 lists a passenger named "John Lang."[2] All evidence suggests that Lang never, in fact, left India, much less arrived in London or returned to Calcutta in 1851. Crittenden is correct, however, in terms of the defense: Lang *did* represent the "wealthy Indian banker and entrepreneur" at his trial in March 1851 in Agra. This is a matter of public record: dozens of Anglo-Indian and British newspapers, including the *Times* (which repeatedly spelled his name "Laing") reported on Lang's pugnacious defense of his client and sensational closing arguments. Lang, fairly peripatetic in his life, did not, in this case, circulate but remained local. As this chapter elaborates, his relinquishing the global story for the local is a mirror of Anglo-Indian newspapers' reporting in 1851 when they too largely abandoned the global story of the Great Exhibition in favor of a local one.

Rather than the much-anticipated Great Exhibition, the trial of "Lalla Joteepershad" became *the* sensation of the day where Anglo-Indian newspapers were concerned.[3] Coverage of this trial, which the *Times*

---

2. Lang's name appears in ships' lists for travel between India and Britain for other years. The resource of ships' departure and arrival lists is invaluable. Many newspapers carried such lists, as did annual directories. Families in British India Society (FIBIS) volunteers have transcribed records from these and additional sources and made them available on their searchable site.

3. The irregularities in the spelling of the man's first and last names are legion, with multiple versions in a single print source, often within the same item. "Lalla" is a title

and the *Bengal Hurkaru* called "the monster trial," dominated the pages of Anglo-Indian newspapers for much of 1851, easily edging out the column inches devoted to the Crystal Palace.[4] The case distilled the ills of the British judiciary in India, raised concerns about the governance of the colonized subcontinent, and revived memories of past cases and injustices, reaching back to the early days of the East India Company's rule and Edmund Burke's challenge to that rule. The trial of Jyoti Prasad was a version of the Burke-Hastings impeachment hearings—though briefer, fought on colonial terrain, and more conclusive. As is the way with repetitions, version 2.0 was a pale simulacrum, a crisis averted, one might say. For the Anglo-Indian press, the trial coalesced its role as an independent watchdog. In this analysis of the press coverage of the trial, I will have occasion to trace the workings of technologies and practices I discussed in the previous chapter: reprinting, editorial opinion-making, the circulation of goods and ideas about the empire, and tussles between colonizers in the metropole and the colony. The trial of Jyoti Prasad captures the relation between the global and the local as mediated by a local press network.

Particular to the case itself, two questions animate this chapter: Why did stories of the Jyoti Prasad trial and its many spin-offs come to displace stories of the Great Exhibition? What can this substitution tell us? Today, this trial is mostly forgotten, mentioned briefly in the odd scholarly account. Only a focus on newspapers—the "first rough draft of history"—brings the case to life. This chapter will examine the trial of Jyoti Prasad as it was covered in Anglo-Indian newspapers. In the British world of news and print, the Great Exhibition was *the* story of 1851; not so in India where Paxton's palace was largely dislodged by a trial that was no more than a footnote in the metropolitan center. My attention to this case brings to the foreground a marginal story, one that preoccupied Indians and Anglo-Indians far more than the contemporaneous Crystal Palace did. Their attention to the trial throws an unexpected light on the

---

for a respectable merchant; the merchant's name itself appears as Jotee Persaud, Jotee Persad, Jotee Pérshad, Jotee Pershaud, Jotee Persand, Jutee Persad, Joti Prasad, as well as Ajoodia Pershad. One twentieth-century historian spells his name "Ajodhya Prasad" (Misra 136); "Jyoti" is a likely short form of "Ajodhya." In this chapter, unless quoting from a source, I transcribe the Lalla's name as Jyoti Prasad.

4. *Times*, 16 April 1851; *Hurkaru*, 18 April 1851. The phrase "monster trial" appears to have originated in the *Delhi Gazette* and it quickly became the hashtag-like handle for the case.

Great Exhibition, a landmark event that has been examined from every conceivable angle. My focus on this moment in Anglo-India print media and its substitution of the exhibition for the trial dramatizes the wealth lying within colonial newspapers. Attention to such neglected sources allows us to trace an alternative history and to illuminate a body of colonials and their relation to empire.

To mark the kindred nature of the exhibition and trial, events at some remove from one another, I have taken as the title of this chapter "Through a Glass Darkly," Paul's evocative phrase of knowing God and his Kingdom only dimly and in parts, never whole.[5] In Britain in 1850–51, "glass" more often than not conjured up the Crystal Palace, Paxton's monument of glass in Hyde Park. The notion of partial sight or cognition—captured in the metaphors of both glass and mirror—is relevant for the argument I pursue here about how Britain saw itself, or wanted to, and the role its colonies played in that self-imaging. The colonial mirror often reflected back something "dark," whether because the glass was smudged and the image in it partial, or because it reflected something "dark" or undesirable in the collective national psyche. In this chapter, I examine the coverage of the 1851 Great Exhibition in my sample of Anglo-Indian newspapers and place that coverage in conversation with their reporting on the Jyoti Prasad trial.[6] If the exhibition was intended as a celebration of the "industry of all nations," the trial 6,000 miles away exposed another meaning of "industry" apropos to a colonial context: the very literal indigenous labor required to keep the empire functioning and the price of that labor.

Rocks in Paxton's Glass Palace

Anglo-Indian newspapers energetically debated and anticipated the upcoming Great Exhibition. As early as 3 January 1850, the *Friend of India* wrote enthusiastically about the exhibition's "immense importance to the interests

---

5. 1 Corinthians 13:12, King James Version. In the New International Version, the phrase is translated as "For now we see only a reflection as in a mirror."

6. In addition to the *Bengal Hurkaru*, *Englishman*, *Friend of India*, and *Mofussilite* (the *Hindoo Patriot* did not commence until 1853), a number of additional newspapers are discussed as well, including *Allen's Indian Mail*, a steamship newspaper, and the *Agra Messenger*.

of the different members of the European family," and declared that that "[t]o this Collection it is desirable that Asia, and, more especially, the British empire in the East, should send its contributions." So keen was the newspaper about the exhibition that it attempted to prod readers within the subcontinent into rivalry by reporting that already "the Presidency of Bombay is preparing to transmit its quota of interesting productions to London." "It will not do," the *Friend* declared, "for us, in this Presidency, which claims the pre-eminence in India, to allow ourselves to be outdone at the sister Presidency." Newspapers reported on the exhibition throughout 1850 and into 1851. On 14 January 1851, the *Mofussilite* ran a two-page supplement that included reprints from journals as various as the *Home News*, the Berlin *Times*, the Canada *Pearl*, and the *Dispatch*. The topics covered were both local and global in scope, with an article on "Discontented Workers" at the building site and another on the "Effects of a Continental War on the Great Exhibition of 1851." The *Bengal Hurkaru* and the *Friend of India* also printed a steady stream of articles on the event, including a satiric piece from *Punch* about the exhibition bringing on "another Great Plague of London."[7]

Anglo-Indian outlets published their own commentaries on the upcoming exhibition as well. Much of the coverage prior to the 1 May opening was concerned with the constitution and work of committees charged with selecting items to represent India in London. Thus, an 18 July 1850 report in the *Friend of India* describes in detail items collected by the Bengal Committee, including carved ivory chairs, embroidered cashmere shawls, a cushion with the names of Victoria and Albert embroidered in diamonds and pearls, and sundry jewels. Of these items, the *Friend* declares simply, "none of these articles are exactly calculated to display either the resources or peculiarities of India. Indeed we would rather that these magnificent presents had not been sent, as they will tend to revive the old assertion—not yet extinct—that India is a land, where gold and diamonds are the most common specimens of the mineral world." The *Mofussilite*, the gadfly newspaper, was more explicit in its criticisms, declaring that "those who imagine that Dr. McLelland's collection of property represents the industry of the country will be woefully mistaken."[8] Who represented

---

7. *Bengal Hurkaru*, 2 January.

8. *Mofussilite*, 28 March 1851. For additional critiques of items sent forward, see *Friend of India*, 20 March, and *Bengal Hurkaru*, 22 March.

India and how was a matter of some debate in the Anglo-Indian press—which rejected exoticized India and promoted India-as-resource.[9]

Despite such censure, the final India exhibit included many exotic, "Orientalized" goods.[10] Contemporaries spoke of the splendor of the India Court, as in this 15 May review in the *Times*: "Those jewels, that rich display of mineral and vegetable produce, those shawls and carpets in which the harmony of colours is so admirably represented; filigree work in silver and gold, brocaded stuffs, curiously executed carvings, rude models of machinery, musical instruments, arms, elephant trappings, naval architecture—how suggestive they all are, and what stories they tell." Notwithstanding this *Arabian Nights*-style evocation, the *Times* never lost sight that one item in this list—the "mineral and vegetable" products—were, as far as British industry was concerned, India's most significant contribution. The jewels and elaborate works, the paper declared, were "trophies of ancient civilization and arts . . . evidences of barbaric pomp . . . that belong to the natives, to the traditions of the past." By contrast, it declared, "Our [Indian] part of the collection is the raw produce—the mineral, vegetable, and animal treasures undiscovered and unused till our commerce and the wants of our manufactures sought them out." Our . . . our . . . our . . . While the minerals and vegetables were overshadowed by the showier items on display, the raw materials in fact exceeded the luxury products in number; and yet commentators had to continually remind viewers of the greater strategic value of the pulses, oils, and woods on display.[11] Paul Young cites the *Crystal Palace*, an English weekly journal, that warned its readers, "The various objects of natural produce, vegetable, animal, and mineral, [must not] be overlooked; for though less striking,

---

9. This debate gives the lie to the narrative that the India exhibit was put together by one man in London, John Forbes Royle (see Priti Joshi, "Miles").

10. Breckenridge highlights the "palanquins, elephant trappings, thrones, crowns, scepters and vestments . . . [the] metal vessels, weapons, woven and printed textiles, and shawls . . . the ivory throne of the Raja of Travancore . . . the crown of the Raja of Oudh and the regal dress of the Raja of Bundi" (203–04).

11. Kriegel writes, "Ultimately, the Company assembled an exhaustive display of raw materials that attested to the financial benefits of empire, a splendid array of artisanal manufactures that catered to contemporary fantasies of Oriental splendor, and exhibits of jewels and models that represented a domesticated India" (150). The latter categories—artisanal goods and luxury items—were the attention grabbers, though they were not in fact the foremost items collected and displayed.

upon picturesque grounds . . . they are perhaps of even higher interest to the future destinies of our vast Indian empire" (350). Jeffrey Auerbach notes that the exhibition's official *Catalogue* as well as many guidebooks "downplayed the inclusion of colonial handicrafts. What mattered, for Britain and for other countries with colonial or imperial ambitions, was to find new sources of raw materials and, later on, new markets for their manufactured goods" (101).[12]

Notwithstanding the official emphasis on utility, on the floor, India's "sumptuous objects made a splash" (Breckenridge 203). And no item was more dazzling than the Kohinoor diamond, though it appeared neither in the India galleries nor in the India section of the *Official Descriptive and Illustrated Catalogue of the Great Exhibition* (hereafter *Catalogue*). Displayed in the transept across the hall from the India Court along with other big-ticket, attention-grabbing items, the Kohinoor diamond, reputed to be the world's largest "rock," was displayed behind a heavily guarded fence-and-glass enclosure in a "neutral," non-national space as if to indicate that it belonged to all humankind. (Scores of visitors were drawn to the case—but almost all expressed disappointment [Young 345–46].) The gem had an uncertain status. Classified under "Articles Exhibited by Her Majesty the Queen" and given pride of place as the third item listed in the *Catalogue*, it is described as "The Great Diamond of Runjeet Singh, called 'Koh-i-noor,' or Mountain of Light. (Class 23)." Two prepositions—"by" and "of"—capture the instability that lay at the heart of this object and that provoked debate and dispute that summer. Exhibited *by* the Queen, but the diamond *of* Ranjit Singh: the language of the *Catalogue* conjures a cordial, even harmonious, camaraderie between royals.

The truth was more complicated: Ranjit Singh had died more than a decade earlier in 1839 and bequeathed the diamond to a temple. Instead, within ten years his empire had become the property of the Company's holdings and the diamond was now housed in a very different sort of temple. The Kohinoor's appearance in London in 1851 was the outcome of two Anglo-Sikh wars. The first (1845–46) left the Sikhs nominally independent but effectively under the management of the Company and its resident at Lahore. The second war (1848–49) concluded with the

---

12. Auerbach's characterization is broadly correct: the pages and detail devoted to raw materials in the *Official Catalogue* far outweigh those on machines, arms, fabrics, utensils, furniture, jewels, vehicles, and the fine arts. Nevertheless, the pages devoted to the latter include illustrations, thus presenting the artifacts as more visually compelling.

annexation of the Punjab, the largest remaining independent territory on the Indian subcontinent. These wars were the last of the Company's major armed conquests.[13] Ranjit Singh, the founder of the Sikh empire, had acquired the diamond from an emir of Afghanistan in the early nineteenth century; when the Company annexed his kingdom in 1849, they announced that Ranjit's ten-year-old successor, Dalip Singh, had "surrendered" the Kohinoor to Queen Victoria. The young Dalip, escorted by Company-appointed handlers, traveled to England with the stone and presented it to the Queen only a few months before the opening of the Great Exhibition.

The *Catalogue*'s obfuscating language deceived nobody. The question of the day, as the *Mofussilite* bluntly put it, was "Who Owns the Koh-i-noor?"[14] The *Times* devoted a lengthy commentary to the question of ownership on 27 May that begins by declaring that "[i]t is rather amusing that the proprietorship of the great Koh-i-noor should be discussed at the moment that a hundred thousand eyes are staring at the precious jewel with such unsated interest." The newspaper continues, "Fifty times at least every morning are questions asked as to the capture, sale, purchase, or conveyance of this priceless treasure. Nobody appears to know exactly how it passed from the jewel-room of Lahore to its present resting place—whether it became British property by seizure or forfeit, or whether it fell to the QUEEN by tribute or right." The *Times*'s editorial was prompted by a debate that occurred in the House of Lords the previous day and that the paper covered at length in the "Parliamentary Intelligence" section of the 27 May edition. Although the Kohinoor itself is never mentioned in the debate, the member who introduced the topic, Lord Ellenborough, argued that the property that came into British hands as the result of the fall of Lahore on 17 September 1848 was stolen—from the British soldiers who fought the Anglo-Sikh war. Ellenborough had been president of the Board of Control (the London-based body appointed by Parliament to oversee the East India Company) three times between 1828 and 1841, and had briefly served as governor general of India between 1842 and 1844, prior to the First Anglo-Sikh War. He was a fierce supporter of British troops in India and was notorious for raising thorny issues on the floor

---

13. The Company continued to acquire territory, but principally through legal maneuvers such as the "doctrine of lapse." The conquests of Sindh and Punjab brought to a close almost a hundred years of armed acquisition of territory.

14. *Mofussilite*, 15 July.

of the Lords. On this occasion, Ellenborough argued that because the "property taken in the field" in Lahore was acquired in war, it ought to be treated as "prize-property" and distributed to the officers and soldiers who fought in the war.

"Prize property" (or prize money) is a British militarism that requires explanation: the archivist Anthony Farrington notes that "[p]rize consisted of property taken as loot in an action, which was subsequently sold, the money received being divided among the troops taking part according to their rank" (53). Farrington's use of "loot" and description are not presentist judgment; the *Times*'s headline on the debate in the Lords about such property is titled "The Punjab Booty"; and Ellenborough, as well as those who disputed his claims, including the Duke of Wellington, all used the term "booty" to describe the spoils of war. Proponents viewed "prize property" as a synonym—not euphemism—for booty or spoils of war. Every war on the Indian subcontinent was followed by a public auction of jewels and other portable property taken from the defeated; proceeds from the auctions were then distributed to those who fought in the war. The advertisement sections of Anglo-Indian newspapers regularly listed upcoming prize-property auctions.[15] The India Office Military Department kept meticulous records of the distribution of prize money for every war on the subcontinent in neatly written, precisely columned pages, listing the name of each officer, his rank, the amount of prize money paid down to shillings and pennies, the date of payment, and the name of the person who collected the money. The department's document for the battle of Multan, crucial to British success in the Second Anglo-Sikh War, for instance, begins with "H. Gough," the commander in chief of the Bengal army, and works its way down the ranks.[16] Prize money was not only an expectation; it was judged to be the *right* of every officer and soldier for having endangered his life. The military dutifully fulfilled the expectation throughout the century.

On the floor of the House of Lords, Ellenborough argued that, by rights, the property seized at Lahore—including, though he never

---

15. Advertisements for the "Grand Sale of the Scinde Prize Property" appeared in 1849, for Punjab prize money in 1851, and for Lucknow prize jewels in 1858. See Priti Joshi ("Audience").

16. The Siege of Multan occurred in April 1848; the India Office account of the distribution of prize money for this battle dates to 1854. See *Prize and Batta Rolls, 1793-c1886*.

mentions it by name, the Kohinoor—ought to be auctioned and the proceeds distributed to the British officers and soldiers who fought the war. Ellenborough's argument rested on the claim that the property that fell into British hands belonged not to the East India Company—which had gifted it to the Queen—but to the Crown, and therefore should be distributed as prize money to troops. Lord Broughton, the president of the Board of Control, responded that the EIC "were trustees for the Crown." Broughton was not alone in expressing bafflement at the legal distinction and leap Ellenborough made from Crown possession to prize money: the *Bengal Hurkaru*'s London correspondent, though he believed that Ellenborough "h[eld] forth manfully on the claims of the army to the Koh-i-noor," nevertheless concluded "that there are not many officers in the army, who would grudge the Queen and the people of England the possession of a jewel which now glitters as one of the chief attractions of the 'World's Fair.'"[17] The debate on the floor finally concluded when the Lord Chancellor intervened to declare that "in 1848 no war arose between the Maharajah of Lahore [ten-year-old Dalip Singh] and the British Government in India." Instead, the government had "interfered to protect [the Maharajah] . . . as an ally and friend, not as an enemy." Consequently, the Lord Chancellor declared, "the property seized on the 17th of September, 1848, was seized for the purpose of protection," not in war.[18]

The twists and sleight of hand in the debate in the Lords might bring to mind Burke's speeches in the impeachment of Warren Hastings, the first governor general of India, who was charged with crimes of fraud, plunder, bribery, peculation, oppression, and tyranny. At the 1788 opening, Burke extended his indictment beyond the man to the nation he was representative of when he stormed, "An opinion has been insidiously circulated through this kingdom, and through foreign nations too, that in order to cover our participation in guilt, and our common interest in the plunder of the East, we have invented a set of scholastic distinctions, abhorrent to the common sense and unpropitious to the common necessities of mankind, by which we are to deny ourselves the knowledge of what the rest of the world knows" (274–75). There is no better instanti-

---

17. *Hurkaru*, 14 July. The *Mofussilite* wrote angrily of the "booty which the Court of Directors are so evidently determined to hold fast" and declared that "no political sophistry, however, can convince the Army that it has not been unjustly defrauded of money, which by all usages of war it has fairly earned" (11 July).

18. *Times*, 27 May.

ation of the "scholastic distinctions" or legalisms Burke excoriated than the Lord Chancellor's intervention that 1848 was "interference" not war, the property seized "protection" not theft. Burke had charged that "we have [hitherto] moved within the narrow circle of municipal justice" and he exhorted colleagues "to enlarge the circle of national justice to the necessities of the empire we have obtained" (275). Burke's appeals—as with his impeachment efforts—fell on deaf ears; half a century later, questions of justice and legality arose again, this time on behalf of British troops. Indians or questions of colonial plunder are absent in the debate on the floor of the Lords in 1851. Municipal justice held sway.[19]

The debate on the Kohinoor in Parliament introduces themes central to this chapter: issues of representation (expressed by the *Friend of India* in its commentary about items sent to represent the subcontinent) and ownership (the *Times*'s confidence that "our commerce" draws out the "undiscovered and unused" in the land or Ellenborough's insistence that property seized in Lahore belongs to British soldiers). Both were central to the trial of Jyoti Prasad that the next section of this chapter explores. In the logic of municipal justice that Burke despaired of, "Who or what represents India?" is imbricated with "Who owns India?" The *Times* grasped this relation and put its imperial spin on the question when it declared that the luxuries "belong to natives" and the past, but the minerals and vegetables that had been "discovered" by Britain made it the owners of these. The paper's reasoning in regard to the natural resources was apposite Ellenborough's, which took the soldiers' presence on the battlefield to signify their ownership of the region's property. Though the *Times* pitched its rhetorical battle between "natives" and Britain, and Ellenborough between the imperial state and its military men, both wrote off the indigenous peoples of the land. Such questions of representation and ownership reappear in the trial of Jyoti Prasad; with an Indian at its center, the dismissal of indigenous peoples would seem difficulty to maintain. Let us see.

---

19. See Mithi Mukherjee's analysis of Burke's effort in the impeachment to develop a "supranational deterritorialized theory of justice" and his reliance on natural law over a narrower, national/territorial common law. Relatedly, Pitts writes that Burke called on the nation to "exercise moral imagination and to extend sympathy beyond their traditional circle of moral concern" (71). For Burke, "the British had an obligation to extend universally the fundamental standards of respect, lawfulness, and humanity that applied at home" (Pitts 78).

"Full of Novelty and Interest": The Great Exhibition Overtaken

Despite their early enthusiasm for the Great Exhibition, once the doors of Paxton's palace opened, Anglo-Indian newspapers' coverage of the event was notably sparser than one might have expected of an event described as "the grandest and most extraordinary [spectacle] that the world has ever gazed upon."[20] Rather than a cascade of reports on the Great Exhibition, coverage was tepid: excerpts of the opening from the *Times* or *Home News*, a small report on shilling days, a disappointed account of prizes awarded. Not only did the coverage shrink, but it was replaced with a bevy of complaints that the Great Exhibition was crowding out more important news. As early as 14 June, the *Bengal Hurkaru* groaned that "the subject [of the Great Exhibition] meets us in every variety of form, and is somehow or other introduced into every discussion." By 11 July, the *Mofussilite* griped that "[t]he Great Exhibition continues to keep the British public too busy to manufacture news," a sentiment echoed by the *Hurkaru*, whose London correspondent grumbled that the exhibition has "crushed and pressed down by its weight, anything that is very well worth discoursing about . . . Politics have become a dead letter" (14 July). Politics had not in fact become a dead letter in London. The *Hurkaru*'s correspondent concedes that a few items on India had come up in Parliament: Ellenborough's charge that the Company defrauded the troops of Punjab prize money and "this business of Jotee Persaud's [that has] come inopportunely to damage the Indian Government, and again to raise an outcry against it on the score of tyranny and oppression."

Though but an afterthought in Parliament and the English prints, it was, in fact, "this business of Jotee Persaud's" that dominated the pages of Anglo-Indian newspapers and edged out coverage of the Great Exhibition, which had received considerable attention prior to March 1851. For instance, the *Bengal Hurkaru*, a daily, carried a notice or commentary on the Jyoti Prasad case in virtually every number in April; by contrast, though it had carried nine stories in the run-up to the Great Exhibition, the *Hurkaru* carried only four stories following the 1 May opening (one of which complained that the exhibition had swallowed up all other stories). Even the *Friend of India*, which ran a dozen stories on the exhibition in

---

20. *Bengal Hurkaru*, 14 June.

1850, included only two substantial reports after the opening and through the year. Once the "business of Jotee Persaud's" became public, it consumed most of the Anglo-Indian press's attention in 1851, far outstripping the attention Bengal's newspapers bestowed on the exhibition. In short, the local trial of an Indian bumped *the* global story of the day off the "front page" of Anglo-Indian newspapers. The exhibition, which is often described as the dawn of British ascendency and preening on the world stage, at this moment in the Anglo-Indian press took a back seat to a case about payment and fraud, theft and avarice.[21]

In the introduction, I referred to the simultaneous fragility and excess of the newsprint archive. And in the previous chapter, I developed some of the ways that fragility played out in the archive of Anglo-Indian newspapers, which is dotted with gaps and absences, of missing newspapers and issues, of office books and other supporting materials book historians rely on. While such materials remain elusive, the newspaper record in regard to the Jyoti Prasad case of 1851 is marked by excess. The buildup, trial itself, and aftermath were covered so widely and exhaustively that the volume of materials threatens to overwhelm. Many Anglo-Indian newspapers published the transcript of the trial (in a crushingly miniscule type size); reported on the day's or week's events; ran multiple opinion-style leaders on the case in almost every number; excerpted other newspapers' editorial leaders; and engaged these commentaries in their own leaders. These materials provide an opportunity: in each paper in my core sample, both the ambition and scope of leaders and number of reprints from rival papers rose dramatically. This episode allows us to study a moment when newspapers adapted their practices for the exigency of the moment and adopted an aggressive editorial style, something akin to the public opinion-style leader Dallas Liddle identifies as a Victorian invention.

In the account that follows, I will synthesize the case, trace the media's coverage of the trial, and probe this coverage. That I draw largely on print media itself for my account of the case might seem like a methodological weakness, as I examine that very coverage to analyze Anglo-Indian perspectives. I rely on newspaper accounts because, despite the significance

---

21. The trial of Jyoti Prasad was covered by British news outlets as well, though it never displaced the exhibition. Excerpts from either the *Times* or a steamship journal or the Overland Supplement of the *Hurkaru* were reprinted in a wide range of British newspapers, from the *Morning Chronicle* to the *Glasgow Herald*, the *Northern Star* to the *Nottinghamshire Guardian*.

of this case that raised the specter of Burke's impeachment of Hastings and misgivings about the imperial project, no scholarship on or historical accounts of the Jyoti Prasad case exist. In navigating the danger of using the media as both source and object of study, I am guided by Michel-Rolph Trouillot, who, in his account of the making and narrating of history, writes that human actors are engaged "simultaneously in the sociohistorical process and in narrative constructions about that process" (24). In practice this means sifting through source materials carefully, seeking corroboration from multiple sources, and charting and analyzing differences between newspapers and their collective effect.

Jyoti Prasad was a businessman and contractor who had provisioned the Company's army with food, fuel, and vehicles during the Afghan campaigns and the Anglo-Sikh wars. His bills from these campaigns were, as of 1851, yet outstanding. In a classic colonial twist, as the Kohinoor, the symbolic spoil of the second Sikh war, was prepared to make its English debut under Paxton's glass dome, the Indian supplier who had made that war possible and successful for the British prepared to face trial in an East India Company court. For in July 1850, the government charged Prasad with accounting fraud and brought criminal charges against him. John Lang, the *Mofussilite*'s combative editor and a trained barrister-at-law, undertook Prasad's defense in a case that the *Bombay Times* called "that most stupendous of blunders."[22] The trial filled columns of Anglo-Indian newsprint and provoked sharp criticisms of the Company both for bringing the case and for its handling of it. The extensive commentary on the case in Anglo-Indian prints points to a vigorous media culture marked by dissent from the government and debate among news outlets. All the newspapers in my sample subscribed to an imperial vision; within that mindset, they demonstrated considerable independence.

The earliest mention of the Jyoti Prasad case in the Bengal newspapers I have been able to track appears in the *Friend of India* on 1 August 1850. In a brief report, the *Friend* refers to a notice that appeared in the *Lahore Chronicle* that "the Editor of the *Mofussilite* has been retained to defend the cause of Jotee Purshad, a Commissariat official, accused of malversation before the Sudder Court at Agra." The *Lahore Chronicle* had reported that Lang has been retained at a very high price, but the *Friend* counters, "Mr. Lang is, we are informed, to receive only 30,000 rupees—but

---

22. See *Bengal Hurkaru*, 8 May 1851.

even *that* is not so bad a retaining fee."[23] This brief notice (only ten lines) encapsulates many of the features of the trial's coverage that recur in the coming months: an attraction to legalese, a preoccupation with monetary sums, and the site of the trial at the "Sudder Court at Agra." The last is a detail whose import Anglo-Indian readers would have grasped instantly, though it is unlikely that British readers without India experience would have. (I shall turn to it momentarily.)

The date of the brief notice, August 1850, is worth noting: recall that in January 1851, five months after these reports that Lang had agreed to serve as Prasad's attorney, Lang announced in the pages of his newspaper that he was traveling to London to cover the Great Exhibition. His biographer took him at his word and went so far as to report that Lang arrived in London only to be recalled to defend Prasad. As we saw at the start of this chapter, Lang never left India in 1851, much less returned. That Crittenden was credulous is understandable;[24] what is harder to explain is why Lang would fib. The case was newsworthy and covered in all the Anglo-Indian newspapers—the *Delhi Gazette*, the *Lahore Chronicle*, the *Bengal Hurkaru*, the *Friend of India*, the *Englishman*—as far back as August 1850. The case had too much publicity and Lang could not possibly have thought he was throwing anyone off the scent. His fake announcement in January 1851 that I opened this chapter with remains a mystery.

Towards the end of 1850, the London *Times* had picked up the story of Jyoti Prasad, with a small notice that "the alleged frauds in the Bengal Commissariat have lately occupied a large space in the Indian papers."[25] Throughout 1851, the story and its rhizome-like extensions occupied much newspaper real estate. What made the case so newsworthy? Two interconnected factors: the details of the case evoked ghosts of Britain's misdeeds in India and the prestige of the Government of India appeared at stake. A host of lesser factors played a role in the case's ongoing notoriety: Lang's reputation as an outspoken, even intemperate, foe of all he quibbled with;

---

23. Crittenden cites the sum as 30,000 pound sterling (125), suggesting that he did not make the rate conversion.

24. Crittenden appears to have relied on Lang's announcement in the *Mofussilite* and on Forbes-Mitchell's 1910 *Reminiscences of the Great Mutiny* in which he wrote, "John Lang left England in May, 1851, and came out round the Cape in one of Green's celebrated liners, the *Nile*, and he reached Meerut about December, when the trial commenced" (155). In fact, the trial commenced on 27 March 1851 and concluded on 9 April.

25. 2 November 1850.

the racial spectacle of an English-trained barrister defending a "native" against the Company; the conflict between the Crown's and Company's courts; the implementation of a law altering the rules of legal representation; the role of an independent news media; and the relation between Britons—the Company, civilians, the news media—and the Indians they relied on to oil the machinery of state.

The trial of Jyoti Prasad commenced in late March 1851, but it was preceded by an episode that initially caused much amusement in the press but soon birthed suits of its own. The episode is worth pursuing for a moment as it illustrates the argument about legalese I trace. At his arraignment in the summer of 1850, Prasad posted bail and was released on his own recognizance with Lang undertaking surety or security. In September or October 1850, Prasad was summoned to appear in court in Agra on 19 November; he and his attorney were in Calcutta and neither made the court date.[26] By some accounts the time allowed was not sufficient to make the journey, by others Prasad and Lang chose to "linger" in Calcutta, thus not arriving until the deadline had passed and thereby forfeiting the recognizance they had posted.[27] The magistrate in Agra, Martin Gubbins, moved to seize both Prasad's and Lang's property. Officials went to Prasad's residence and, according to the *Friend of India*, an outlet otherwise entirely unsympathetic to Prasad's case, "entered the zenana, and insulted the women," snatching from Prasad's wife "the ring on [her] nose."[28] Lang's property too was "estreated," though accounts of what was confiscated vary: the *Friend*, clearly enjoying itself, wrote that "Mr. Lang's breeches and toothbrush" were taken and dubbed the affair the "*sans-culotte* situation."[29] It also reported that Gubbins had ordered the *Mofussilite*'s presses to be shut down, but did not enforce an order that, in the newspaper's view, "wears so vindictive an appearance." Six months later, Ellenborough of the Punjab prize property debates, berated the East India Company in the House of Lords, claiming that Gubbins "laid

---

26. *Times*, 2 November 1850.

27. For insufficient time, see *Times*, 17 January 1851; for dallying, see *Friend of India*, 19 December 1850. Accounts of the bond vary: at one point the *Times* reported the bond at 400*0l*. (2 November 1850), though later it referred to it as 200*0l*. (17 January 1851). The *Mofussilite* names the figure as 10,000 rupees or £1,000 (6 May 1851).

28. *Friend of India*, 19 December 1850; Ellenborough repeated this account of the violation of the zenana in the Lords on 24 June (*Times*, 25 June 1851).

29. *Friend of India*, 19 December 1850.

an embargo on [Lang's] printing press and prevented the publication of his newspaper."[30] Whether the press was confiscated or only shut down remains uncertain; what is clear is that in the archives, all but one of the December 1850 numbers of the *Mofussilite* are marked as "missing."

The only reference to the Gubbins episode in the extant pages of the *Mofussilite* appears in the 7 January 1851 letter by Mahomed Usghur that I cited at the close of the previous chapter. The letter appeared in the "Mofussilite" section of the newspaper and is introduced with a headnote "From our own Correspondent with the Camp of the Governor General." In the midst of the report of the durbar appear these words about Gubbins and the continuation of Lang's newspaper:

> I am very sorry for your things which you hav lost by majester and Mr. Gubeen behave very il with you and if I was G. G. [governor general] then I shall sint him jeal for 14 years or turnhinm out from his sirvis and whitch you wish To giv me your wark of nues paper I shall do it, and if I cant do it then I shall kipe a baboo under me and I shall giv him 100 rupees a munth and if your ornor will gav me to do it I shall Do it proper by my dear Sir Mr. Lang.[31]

Lang's explicit use of an indigenous correspondent and publication of his letter in nonstandard English were unprecedented. That this letter/report appears in the final number Lang edited before he stepped down to undertake Prasad's defense suggests an act of defiance as well as a declaration of alliance: Lang was announcing that he had support and friends among Indians.

I have quoted again from Mahomed Usghur's letter because it speaks to questions of language and usage in a multilingual space, topics that were to arise in the Jyoti Prasad trial in an unexpected manner. On 17 January 1851, still referring to the recognizance phase of events, the *Times* reported

---

30. *Times*, 25 June 1851. Three days later, Ellenborough clarified that by "embargo" he "did not mean to say that the press was carried away, but only that Mr. Laing [sic] was not permitted to make use of it" (*Times*, 28 June). The *Bengal Hurkaru* cited the *Delhi Gazette*—a paper that Lang and the *Mofussilite* conducted open warfare with—as denying that "it was ever intended to seize the *Mofussilite Press* in satisfaction of Mr. Lang's estreated recognizances" (10 January 1851).

31. *Mofussilite*, 7 January 1851.

that when Lang appeared before a judge "and was about to address the Court on the part of his client, he was stopped by an order to say all he had to say in Hindoostanee, which was the only language recognized by the Court. 'Thus' (says the *Delhi Gazette*) 'ended the first essay of the first English barrister who has sought to exercise his vocation in the Courts of the Mofussil.'" Ellenborough repeated this story on the floor of Lords on 24 June, adding that Lang "understood not a word" of Hindustani, an assertion that, based on all the evidence we have, is inaccurate.[32] In "Wanderings in India," the twelve-part series he published in Dickens's *Household Words*, Lang wrote that when he arrived in India "[m]y first step was to acquire a knowledge of Hindoostanee and of Persian. By dint of hard study, at the end of six months I found myself capable, not only of holding a conversation, but of arguing a point in either of these languages."[33]

Moreover, as we saw in the previous chapter, Lang published—under the pseudonym "Le Juif Errant"—in the *Mofussilite* texts he translated, if clumsily, from Hindustani into English, and on occasion he included material in Hindustani in the pages of the newspaper. Lang had been living in central India since at least 1846; in 1837, the Government of India replaced Persian with Urdu as the language of law and revenue in the North-Western Provinces (Das 141). Given that Urdu—colloquially referred to as Hindustani—was the official language of the region, there is every reason to believe that Lang, although not in the civil service, would have maintained his skills in this language, not allowed them to atrophy. It is possible that Lang's Hindustani, despite his claims in *Household Words*,

---

32. *Times*, 25 June. In the nineteenth century, "Hindustani" was written in *nasta'liq*, included a preponderance of loanwords from Persian and Arabic, and was spoken broadly across the Gangetic Plain (Das 140–41). *Hobson-Jobson* defines it as "the language of the Mahommedans of Upper India . . . It is also called Oordoo" (Yule and Burnell 417). The first part of the definition reflects the communalization of India, but in the second they were correct: "Hindustani" and Urdu were used interchangeably. Post-1947 and Partition, Hindi and Urdu were claimed the national languages of India and Pakistan, respectively, and declared distinct. But even today's sanitized versions are closer in kind than nationalists in either country allow: they utilize distinct scripts (Urdu uses *nasta'liq*, a variant of Perso-Arabic, while Hindi uses Devnagari) and each incorporates loanwords from different sources (Urdu from Persian and Arabic, Hindi from Sanskrit). But linguists consider them "mutually intelligible" rather than distinct languages.

33. *Household Words*, 14 November 1857, 399. Persian was the language of the Mughal court.

was not strong enough for him argue a case[34]; or perhaps he simply wished to make a point about speaking in a tongue not one's own. This minor fracas throws a new light on the letter by Mohamed Usghur: appearing as it does after Lang was reprimanded in the EIC's court for not speaking in Hindustani, it is tempting to read the letter as Lang's way of inviting readers to experience what it might sound like to speak in a language that is not one's native tongue. As it were, the matter of the language Lang used in court was dropped and he proceeded to argue his case, both at this hearing and at the trial itself, in English.[35]

The trial of Jyoti Prasad began in Agra on 27 March 1851; twelve days of testimony and arguments followed and a verdict—Prasad was acquitted—rendered on 9 April. The Anglo-Indian print media covered the trial extensively. The *Bengal Hurkaru*, for instance, carried nineteen days of continual coverage when the trial started, and over the course of the year had, conservatively counting, almost ninety separate reports of varying lengths on the case and its spin-offs. (By contrast, the same paper carried a total of sixteen reports on the Great Exhibition during the entirety of 1851, most excerpts from English newspapers.) The coverage in Anglo-Indian newspapers consisted of several types of materials: all or substantial amounts of the transcript of the trial; short reports that synthesized events; and longer leaders or commentary either on the case or other newspapers' editorials on it. The transcripts of the trial all came from one source: the *Agra Messenger*.[36] In chapter 1, I noted that, given

---

34. On 12 April, the *Delhi Gazette* wrote that at the start of the trial, "Mr. Lang stated that he needed the services of a native in parts of the examination" and that he was granted one (qtd. in *Allen's Indian Mail*, 3 June, 315).

35. At the trial, Indian witnesses were examined by a "Serishtadar," an officer of the court "whose duty it is to receive plaints and see that they are in proper form and duly stamped" (Yule and Burnell 826).

36. On 12 April, the *Delhi Gazette* announced that, seeing that the trial is "full of novelty and interest" and that only a full report could do it justice, it would publish the proceedings shortly in a "pamphlet" (qtd. in *Hurkaru*, 18 April). The full testimony of the trial appeared in a volume titled *The Trial of Lalla Jotee Pershad and Others. Reported for the Delhi Gazette*. The contents are identical to the transcripts that appeared in the *Agra Messenger*, which was a branch of the *Delhi Gazette* (the former's endcap reads "Printed at the Agra Messenger Press, for the Proprietors/ Delhi Gazette Press, by R. Miller"). When citing from the trial, I will reference both the newspaper that serves as my source and the day the testimony occurred for those who wish to consult the volume.

limited resources and the yet-to-be-developed profession of correspondents, Anglo-Indian newspapers adopted the practice of excerpting local news from local outlets. In this case, the custom became a necessity as the *Agra Messenger* was the only newspaper allowed by the judge to take notes at the trial and publish them. The culture of scissors-and-paste was ready-made for the legal restriction on who could publish the proceedings, and the constraint complemented newspapers' limited human resources.[37]

The *Agra Messenger*'s transcripts of the hearings started to appear on 29 March, two days after the case commenced. A few days into the trial, when the judge imposed a ban on publication of witnesses' testimony until the conclusion of the trial, the transcripts continued only after the trial concluded. Given the prohibition and lag, as well as the editorial practice of reprinting and commenting on rival newspapers' views, the Jyoti Prasad trial echoed in newspapers long after the verdict had been announced. This is one reason that this local story with a strong local interest developed a very long tail and dominated news columns for months. Additionally, relying on the *Messenger*'s trial transcripts allowed other newspapers to reserve their resources for editorial commentaries on the trial. In his discussion of the leading article, Dallas Liddle traces its development from short digests of news to opinion essays as paralleling a shift from "press as public instructor" to press as the "Voice of Public Opinion" (12). During the Jyoti Prasad trial, the Anglo-Indian press published more and increasingly lengthy opinion-style essays. These appeared in a style that Liddle, speaking of English newspapers, described as "crystaliz[ing] the already-existing opinion of the nation as a whole" (11). The trial, a moment of rupture for Anglo-Indians as it raised questions about the character of British rule in India, served as a defining moment; editors stepped into the opening and offered ready-made views for their readers to adopt. The shift from digest to opinion is evident in the forcefulness and consistency of editorial reactions and in the virtual absence of dissenting letters from readers.

Prasad was charged by the Government of India and tried in criminal court in Agra for fraud and inciting perjury. The case involved his

---

37. The *Mofussilite* approved of "the report of the Local paper—the *Agra Messenger*—which we are informed is correct and highly creditable to the Reporter" (1 April). For it, there was a benefit to the arrangement: as the barrister arguing the case was also the newspaper's owner, the *Mofussilite* had to tread carefully, and reprinting from the *Agra Messenger* protected it from accusations of conflict.

allegedly overcharging the government for approximately 5,000 bullocks that were never delivered during the second Punjab campaign of 1848–49. The overcharge was claimed to be approximately 40,000 rupees out of a bill of approximately Rs. 1 million.[38] The prosecutor, E. Wylly, called members of the Commissariat Department who had engaged Prasad and worked with him, as well as several of Prasad's subordinates. Newspapers commented that the picture of the commissariat that emerged from the testimony of its officers was of a department in disarray with a negligible system of accounting and oversight. On the fifth day of the trial, Captain Newbolt, a veteran officer of the commissariat called to the stand by the prosecution, admitted to Lang in cross examination that "If every Commissariat Gomashta [agent] were brought up for fraud for overcharges . . . the Commissariat system would certainly be paralysed."[39] The *Hurkaru* dryly commented that the testimony of the commissariat officers "seem to make rather in favour of the accused."[40]

Even more damning to the case of the prosecution was the testimony of Prasad's subordinates, men who had previously perjured themselves but, following a pardon, turned state's witnesses. Almost every newspaper was withering in its condemnation of these witnesses; the *Hurkaru* declared in disgust, "The evidence of the native witnesses will hardly pay in interest the labour of perusal" (23 April). Nevertheless, the newspaper evidently

---

38. The overdue bill was said to be 10–11 lakh rupees or roughly Rs. 1,000,000 (one lakh equals 100,000). The outstanding sum was from one campaign only (and was cited by Newbolt, whose testimony appears on the fifth day of the trial). Lang claimed that Prasad's unpaid bills over the course of several campaigns amounted to 57 lakh rupees (or Rs. 5.7 million). The *Times* echoed this number, translated into British pounds: "Jotee Persaud's claims against the Indian Government reached the very considerable sum of 570,000*l*." (6 June), and Broughton, the president of the Company's board of control, confirmed it in the Lords, adding sarcastically that Prasad had presented the government a bill for "the small sum of 570,000*l*." (*Times*, 25 June).

39. *Bengal Hurkaru*, 23 April. The *Times*'s correspondent in Bombay corroborated this claim: "These proceedings against [Jotee Persand] were founded on what is an every day occurrence in Indian commissariat accounts" (2 June). Shortly after the conclusion of the trial, Dalhousie, the governor general, appointed a Commissariat Commission to investigate the department's practices (see *Mofussilite*, 25 April, and Trotter 84–85).

40. Even the pro-government *Delhi Gazette* noted that the British officers brought by the prosecution "gave very decided testimony to the extraordinary ability and services of Jotee Persaud, as contractor for the commissariat supplies of the British army in different campaigns, and at periods of great emergency" (*Bengal Hurkaru*, 18 April).

did peruse the testimony of these witnesses, and on four separate occasions wrote sharp editorials condemning the government for "offering the bribe of pardon to declared perjurers who would support [the Government's] prosecution with the required evidence."[41] The charge that the government prompted its witnesses echoed for several months in numerous newspapers. In regard to the witnesses themselves, even the judge, S. S. Brown, on the sixth day of the trial, interrupted a witness and objected to hearing the testimony of a man who had admitted to perjury. When Wylly, the prosecutor, responded that the governor general had pardoned the witness for his perjury, the judge, in a comment that many papers repeated, responded, "The Governor General's pardon has given the man freedom from the consequences of his crime, but the Governor General's power cannot make the man a good witness."[42]

Although *Allen's Indian Mail*, the unabashedly pro-government, fortnightly digest of colonial news for resettled Britons, went so far as to blame the acquittal of Prasad "principally to the gross misconduct of some of the native witnesses, who proved themselves utterly unworthy of credit" (3 June, 313), most Anglo-Indian newspapers laid the responsibility squarely on the shoulders of the government that had brought such a "shabby" case to trial.[43] Many in the press made much of the fact that Prasad had supplied the military not only in the Punjab, but also in Afghanistan, "Guzerat," and Gwalior, and that in all these campaigns he had served on the field with the military "during its hour of need."[44] Several writers reached for metaphors of pollution to describe the outcome: the case was a "blot" or "stain" on the British, or it had tainted the "character" of the government.[45] Perhaps the most incriminating commentary came from a widely recirculated editorial in the *Bombay Times*, a newspaper the London *Times* characterized as "usually a stanch supporter of the Indian Government" (2 June). The *Bombay Times*'s commentary of 28 April situates the Jyoti Prasad trial in historical context and is a powerful indictment of the government. The piece speaks of the government's "long career of past

---

41. *Bengal Hurkaru*, 17 April; see also their commentaries on 11, 15, and 18 April.

42. *Bengal Hurkaru*, 26 April.

43. *Bengal Hurkaru*, 23 April. The *Bombay Times* on 28 April also uses this word to describe the government's management of the case (see *Bengal Hurkaru*, 8 May).

44. *Bengal Hurkaru*, 17 April. See also the *Times*, 2 June, and Ellenborough in the House of Lords as reported in the *Times*, 25 June.

45. *Bengal Hurkaru*, 17 April; *Times*, 2 and 6 June.

misconduct" and "dishonest dealing," its acquisition of "territory, power, or wealth . . . by dishonest means," the "frauds" it practiced in order to take possession of lands.[46] It draws a direct line from this history of malfeasance to the Jyoti Prasad case, which it considers a "natural punishment." The editorial concludes, "The trial of Jotee Pershad will inflict an injury on our character which half a century of good government will scarcely repair, perfectly convinced, as the natives will be, that our intention was to perpetrate a stupendous fraud by form of law."

"To perpetrate a stupendous fraud by form of law": the ghost of Burke rears its head. (He had charged that "in order to cover our participation in guilt, and our common interest in the plunder of the East, we have invented a set of scholastic distinctions" [274].) The *Bombay Times* was not alone in invoking Burke: the credit for that reference goes to Lang who, in his closing arguments on 8 April, invoked that "celebrated statesman and philosopher" (*Trial* 125). Echoing Burke's remarks from February 1788 in the impeachment of Warren Hastings, Lang, with his customary rhetorical flair, declared that were Burke to have appeared in this court "he would have discovered that the Governor General of India has arbitrary power—that Mr. Thomason, the Lieutenant Governor, has arbitrary power—that the Sudder [mofussil court] has arbitrary power—that you, Sir, have arbitrary power—that Mr. Gubbins, the officiating Magistrate of Agra, has arbitrary power—aye, that the Nazir—(with whose name I do not happen to be acquainted) has arbitrary power!"[47] The reference to Burke's "arbitrary power" was deployed to expose the failures of the mofussil legal system and its incestuous relation to the Company. Aside from Lang and the *Bombay Times*, however, no other Anglo-India newspaper was willing to "Burkenize" the case, much less draw a line between this trial and the colonial venture itself.

Even the more diffident newspapers, however, agreed that the Jyoti Prasad case had revealed the many flaws of the courts and legal system in India. As early as 3 February, before the trial had even begun, the London *Times* reported that it had it from "official documents of unquestioned authenticity" that "evidence against Jotee Persaud has been extorted by intimidation."[48] The *Times* continued that such practices are "very general

---

46. Qtd. in *Bengal Hurkaru*, 8 May.

47. *Bengal Hurkaru*, 25 April 1851.

48. The *Bengal* Hurkaru echoed a version of this charge during the trial when it accused the government of "bribing" witnesses with pardons.

in the company's Courts in India," but not "experienced in Her Majesty's Supreme Courts." The distinction between the Company's and Her Majesty's courts requires explanation. Prior to 1861, two parallel legal systems operated in British India: Crown courts and Company courts. Crown courts had jurisdiction over residents of the presidency towns (Calcutta, Bombay, and Madras) and British subjects throughout the mofussil; they operated on English legal principles and precepts and administered English law in India. Company courts, known as the *sadr* (or sudder in Anglicized spelling) *adalats*, on the other hand, had authority over Indians in the mofussil. In short, British law governed British subjects and Indians in the presidency capitals, but Company laws governed Indians in the remainder of the country. The *sadr adalats*, as the legal scholar Nasser Hussain writes, were "a mixture of precolonial institutions upon which the Company had grafted new offices and jurisdictions" (79). The split between the two systems, Hussain argues,

> institutionalized two distinct sources of authority in the colony and two distinct sources of law . . . [B]oth the governor-general and council, as well as the Supreme Court, were in the position to supply laws [to the *sadr* courts] as needed. The governor-general and council were vested with all political and executive political power, [and] capable of making . . . Company regulations enforceable in Company courts . . . On the other hand, the Supreme Court . . . became the instrument for the extension of not only specific English laws into India, but also the fundamental "principles" of the king's justice. (80)

In short, Company courts, which regulated the lives of Indians, could rely on the Company's apparatus, including the governor general and the Council of India, to develop laws that suited its purposes. The result, in the words of the *Bombay Times*, was that "Heretofore the Company, or . . . their officers, have had it all their own way in judicial processes out of the Queen's jurisdiction."[49] Almost every Anglo-Indian newspaper chafed at what Hussain in our century calls a "foundational schism in the conceptualization of authority" (80).

Two themes recur in Anglo-Indian newspapers' coverage and commentary of the Jyoti Prasad trial: (1) that the Company was cowardly

---

49. Qtd. in *Allen's Indian Mail*, 3 June, 314.

in trying Prasad in the Company's mofussil or *sadr* courts rather than a Crown court; and (2) that despite the Company's effort to stack the decks, principle had prevailed and Prasad was acquitted. The Anglo-Indian media presented mofussil courts as the instrument of the Company and government, politicized rather than judicial bodies, with incompetence if not outright chicanery ruling the day.[50] A poem in the *Englishman* about the judge, S. S. Brown, presiding over the case included these lines:

> High on the Huzoor's Chair sat Mr. Brown
> With fiery eyes and harsh contracted frown, . . .
> He sat, the incarnate image of a Judge,
> A Tool to pay off old John Comp'ny's grudge.[51]

Such sentiments were common in the Anglo-Indian press that was dismissive of the Company's mofussil courts and of an Indian's chances of getting justice in them. The assumption was that the Company's British officers presiding in these courts would serve the Company's interests. As the *Mofussilite* wrote on 11 March before the trial started, "Under the present construction of the Mofussil Courts it is unreasonable to expect an honest or independent bar, and this has been shown so often . . . [that the day] until the tribunals are reformed . . . is very distant indeed" (156). Lang no doubt considered his agreeing to represent Prasad in a *sadr adalat* as a first step in such a reform.

While one newspaper, the *Calcutta Gazette*, was perturbed by the racial dynamic of an English-trained barrister defending a "native" against charges brought by the Company in a mofussil court, it was alone in its consternation.[52] Most newspapers welcomed the presence of Lang in a "Sudder" court, an appearance made possible by the passage of Act XXXVIII in 1850, just months earlier. The act had extended to Company courts the "right of counsel to all persons on the trial of all offenses."[53] Innocuous in

---

50. At the trial, Lang made much of the fact that the depositions of witnesses were taken by a magistrate with no representative of the defendant present.

51. Qtd. in *Mofussilite*, 25 April. The *Times* called the trial "this prostitution [by the Government] of their own law courts to official convenience" (6 June 1851).

52. The *Calcutta Gazette* found Lang's decision to represent Prasad "obscure and perplexing" and sought an explanation for "why Jotee Pershaud is defended"; its only explanation was Lang's choleric and irascible personality. The *Mofussilite*, in evident relish, cited the lengthy piece in full on the last day of Lang's editorship, 7 January.

53. United Kingdom, House of Commons, *East India* 42.

itself, the act's relevance to this case lay in its third clause, which declared that those "authorized" to serve as counsel in mofussil courts included "advocates of one of the Supreme Courts of Justice." This clause permitted Lang, who had argued cases before the Calcutta Supreme Court shortly after he first arrived in India in 1842, to represent and defend Jyoti Prasad in a *sadr nizamut adalat*, or Company's criminal court. In the words of the *Mofussilite*'s editor, "this was the first apparition of an independent barister [sic] in a Company's Court" (25 April).[54]

That Lang's presence was seen to make a difference is evident in the following remark by the reporter of the *Agra Messenger*, the only press agent at the hearing: "Here we have a Mofussil Court suddenly transformed into the semblance of the Courts,—English pleadings,—a gowned Barrister,—and the Press represented by an experienced Reporter; all contributing to the novelty."[55] According to the *Messenger*, the "old Company's Judge" needed "Mr. Lang [to explain] the proper position of a Reporter." Part of the case's "novelty" lay in this crossover between the parallel legal systems whereby a barrister trained in the English judicial system brought his legal tools to a hybrid and allegedly politically driven judiciary. It bears noting that for the Anglo-Indian press, the adversaries here were not a British judicial system versus, say, a Mughal system; the opposed parties were an English judicial system versus the Company's judiciary, which much of the Anglo-Indian press considered a kangaroo court. At the conclusion of the trial, a letter to the editor in the *Mofussilite* predicted that Company officials would venture that "our Mofussil Courts are not sufficiently ripe for English Barristers"; to this the writer retorted: "THEY ARE MUCH TOO ROTTEN!" (25 April). Act XXXVIII and Lang's presence in a mofussil court were viewed as a first step towards repairing the rot that many Anglo-Indians identified as endemic to Company courts.

Newspapers lauded the fact that despite the "miserly bad grace" of the Government in pursuing the case in its courts, justice had prevailed.[56] The *Bengal Hurkaru*, in a commentary it said it wrote "more in sorrow than in anger," maintained that the only good to come out of the "unfor-

---

54. One might argue that Act XXXVIII and Lang's representation of Jyoti Prasad serve as a reverse image of the controversial Ilbert Bill of 1883 that would have allowed Indian magistrates to preside over cases featuring British subjects.

55. *Bengal Hurkaru*, 11 April.

56. *Bengal Hurkaru*, 17 April.

tunate proceeding" is that "even in a Company's court bad as it is, even in a Company's judge, even in a jury dependent on our Governors in a case in which they are the prosecutors, freedom and justice are sometimes triumphant" (17 April). Implicit in such remarks is the assumption that the Crown courts would have been a safer place for an Indian to find justice. Whether this was true—the civil suit Prasad brought in Calcutta's Supreme Court indicated that he (or his counsel) believed it was—we will never know. Historically, it had not been so.

I noted earlier that few in the press were willing to take up the history lesson Lang doled out in his closing remarks. Consequently, while the apparition of Burke hovered, it never landed. Rather than the trial of Warren Hastings—which the political theorist Jennifer Pitts writes "delineated the crimes of Hastings as an individual, the structural vices of the East India Company, and the failings of British rule in India generally" (65)—Anglo-Indian newspapers in 1851 looked to another trial from the past. This trial occurred in 1775 and had a cameo in the Hastings impeachment hearings. Shortly after Hastings was appointed governor general in 1773, Nandakumar (or Nuncomar in Anglicized spelling), a Company revenue collector, accused Hastings of bribery, and Hastings counter-charged him with conspiracy. The case came before the newly created Supreme Court, where Elijah Impey, a school friend of Hastings, presided. Nandakumar was tried, found guilty, and executed in August 1775.[57] A decade later, in 1787, as Parliament was drawing up charges against Hastings, Impey was charged with the "judicial murder" of Nandakumar. Though Impey was acquitted in 1788, Burke nevertheless, in an April 1789 speech, charged both Hastings and Impey with murder.[58] The similarities between the cases of Nandakumar and Jyoti Prasad are striking: in each, an Indian in the hire of the Company brought a charge against a superior or the government, and in each the government brought charges against him in turn. One man was tried in the newly established Supreme Court in Calcutta—a Crown court—the other in a mofussil or Company court in Agra. Though in 1851 the Supreme Court may have looked like the more judicious body, this was not so three-quarters of a century earlier, not to Burke, who charged Hastings and his cronies with the murder of Nandakumar.

---

57. See Carter and Harlow (132–33).
58. See Rodensky (189–92).

The earliest reference to the Nandakumar trial in relation to Prasad's case comes from a discussion on the floor of the House of Commons on 3 April. Gearing up for the next charter renewal (slated for 1853), the MP Thomas Chisholm Anstey stated that in India "frightful abuses . . . still existed." His key example was that when Prasad brought suit against the Company for outstanding payments, the Company retaliated by charging Prasad with fraud; Prasad, Anstey claimed, would "in all probability be tried, convicted, and condemned to death—as Nuncomar had been—before his action could come on."[59] In a striking coincidence, two days later and six thousand miles away, the *Agra Messenger* cited this historical precedent as well. Bitter about the judge's prohibition on publishing witnesses' testimony until the conclusion of the trial, the *Messenger* on 5 April complained that "from the time of Nuncomar to the present, no Indian State trial has possessed such extensive interest as this one."[60] In London, the *Bengal Hurkaru*'s correspondent noted, "public writers are beginning to allude to the old case of Nuncomar, and to hint that Lord Dalhousie [the governor general in 1851] is another Hastings."[61]

The *Times* devoted a lengthy editorial to probing the analogy. Citing Macaulay and Burke before summarizing the Jyoti Prasad case, it concluded, "Such was the trial of JOTEE PERSAUD, which has been regarded, not unnaturally, by those on the spot as a prosecution only second in interest to the famous arraignment of NUNCOMAR. The distinctions, however, between the two cases are both singular and instructive. NUNCOMAR, if unfairly prosecuted, was fairly attacked; he was found guilty and was executed. JOTEE PERSAUD was neither fairly prosecuted nor fairly attacked; but he was acquitted."[62] Despite its acknowledgement that Prasad "was neither fairly prosecuted nor fairly attacked," the newspaper, leaning heavily on his acquittal, concluded that "as far as the administration of justice is concerned, we have no reason to be ashamed at the results of the contrast before us." While Anstey in April read the echoes between the cases as a sign of the continuation of abuses—he was speculating on

---

59. *Times*, 4 April.

60. Qtd. in the *Bengal Hurkaru*, 11 April, 1851.

61. *Bengal Hurkaru*, 14 July. Perhaps Anstey, the *Messenger*'s writer, and the *Hurkaru*'s correspondent had all been reading Macaulay's essay on Hastings that appeared in the *Edinburgh Review* in 1841 and that discussed the Nandakumar episode at length.

62. *Times*, 6 June.

the outcome—the *Times*, homing in on the different outcomes, used the analogy to mark the maturity of Indian jurisprudence. The history lesson was over; the English judiciary and its putative maturity had saved the day and the imperial project. Following this commentary, both Burke and Nandakumar were set aside in the print media.

The matter that aroused the greatest debate in the newspapers instead was a narrower question: did the Government of India bring criminal charges against Jyoti Prasad in order to avoid settling its bill? Did the government bring their criminal suit in retaliation when Prasad brought a civil suit against the government in the Calcutta Supreme Court for outstanding payments due? These questions were hotly debated, both on the floor of Lords and in the newspapers. The *Friend of India*, which had remained strikingly mute on the case itself throughout the trial, took up the question of timing with gusto. In the eight months following Prasad's acquittal, the *Friend* published twelve articles on the Jyoti Prasad case, almost all concerned with the question of whether the government undertook its case vengefully and/or to avoid paying its bills (the *Friend* strenuously denied both charges). The *Times* as well devoted a considerable number of column inches to the topic, first publishing a letter to the editor from an "Indian Magistrate" on 10 June, then transcripts of the debate between Ellenborough and Broughton in the House of Lords that are numbingly detailed about the dates of missives between the military board and magistrate, magistrate and secretary of the council, secretary and governor general, and so on (see 25 June). According to the debates, the record indicated that the authorities began investigating Prasad's invoices from the second Sikh campaign in the spring of 1849 and decided to bring charges in July 1850; Prasad, on the other hand, brought his civil suit for back payment on 4 October 1850.

None of the deliberations concerns itself with the question of why Prasad was not paid for services going back more than a decade. (Indeed, most repeatedly cite Prasad's immense wealth as if that obviated the obligation to pay him.) In light of the discussion in the Lords only a month earlier about prize money "owed" to soldiers, the absence of attention to payment owed Prasad is glaring.[63] Accounts of the case proliferated and

---

63. Ellenborough was fulsome in his praise of Prasad's character, referring to him as a "gentleman" (*Times*, 24 June) and to the family as "very trustworthy individuals" who had "rendered very valuable services to the Government" (*Times*, 25 June); but he did not make a case for payment on principle or debt owed.

circulated—but they revolved around a narrow question. Pitts has argued that the difference between the Burkean vision of imperial relations and the views that flourished in the nineteenth century under the guidance of James and John Stuart Mill pivoted on the difference between Burke's insistence that the "source of colonial injustice [lay] in the British failure to sympathize with their Indian subjects" (68), while the Mills subscribed to a notion of British superiority and Asiatic "backwardness" (131–62). In practical terms, the distinction made by the Mills translated into the younger's infamous declaration that the rule of law applied to Britons, but "despotism" was appropriate for Indians. On the one hand, the Anglo-Indian press's dressing down of Company courts and their calls to reform that system by extending English law to Indians in the mofussil looks like the Burkean vision of extending sympathy, reignited in the mid-nineteenth century. On the other hand, the myopia of the discussion—the press's silence on the monies owed Prasad and bickering over the "municipal" question of dates and who went first—marks the outer limits of their critique.

On the other side of that line in the sand lay a reckoning with colonialism itself. The Jyoti Prasad case, with the government's non-payment for services at its core, was an individuated version of the very thing that was occurring at a macro level in principalities large and small over the subcontinent. In case after case, the Company refused to repay loans provided by rajas to finance its wars of conquest and followed up those refusals by annexing the troublesome rajas' principalities. In the case of the individual, the matter went to court and was settled; there was no court to settle the matter of imperial conquest. In a reading of Burke's impeachment charges against Hastings, Sara Suleri argues that in charging Hastings and his associates with financial extortion, brutality, deception, and more, Burke failed to comprehend that "[t]he exercise of 'arbitrary power' for which he sought to impeach Hastings could not be so easily expunged from the history of colonialism" (51). Though Burke had inklings—Suleri calls it "a subterranean admission" (51)—that "it was indeed too facile to assume that Hastings alone could be held responsible for the exigencies of what it means to colonize" (51), Burke could not grasp that "Hastings's misdeeds were merely synecdochical of the colonial operation" (52). Of Burke's hesitation to indict colonialism itself, Suleri writes that this was a crime "for which no language was ready" (55). It is debatable whether more than half a century later the language was still not ready—but the Anglo-Indian press certainly was not. The many leaders and opinion pieces insistently focused on the flaws of the Company and on legalisms. Such minute legal matters and legalese allowed them not only to evade the question of the British imperial presence in India, but to pat themselves on the back for upholding the rule of law.

The Trial in Many Mirrors

The trial of Jyoti Prasad spawned a number of cases, each serving to confirm a belief in British "fairness" and principled legal commitment. The first challenged the right of the magistrate of Agra, Martin Gubbins, to "estreat" or confiscate Lang's property when he and his client did not arrive in Agra in time to meet the court order. The case was tried in the Calcutta Supreme Court and decided in early August 1851, and Gubbins was found to have overstepped his authority and was fined Rs. 50.[64] The second case pertained to Lang's closing remarks on the final day of the trial; in the published version of his remarks—but not in the version he delivered orally in court[65]—Lang inserted a comment about one member of the military board, Colonel William Mactier, who had ruled that the allegation of fraud against Prasad should be forwarded to the magistrate. (Had Mactier ruled otherwise, the judgment of the other two board members who believed the charges did not merit attention would have prevailed and the case died there.) In the version published in the *Agra Messenger*, Lang inserted a clause about Mactier's "cowardice" on the battlefield in 1821, and Mactier's lawyers charged Lang with libel. The case was tried in the Supreme Court as well (*The Queen v. John Lang*) and in August 1851 Lang was sentenced to two months in prison and a fine.[66] Finally, Prasad pursued his case for payment on past bills, also in the Calcutta Supreme Court, and won in April 1852, though he was not paid in full until March 1853.[67]

---

64. See *Bengal Hurkaru*, 7 August, and *Friend of India*, 14 August.
65. See *Bengal Hurkaru*, 29 and 30 April, for the account of Lang inserting the remark in the *Agra Messenger*'s published version over the protests of the *Messenger*'s editor. *The Trial of Lalla Jotee Pershad and Others*, which appeared in late 1851, does not include the aside.
66. For a full account of the case, see *Friend of India*, 28 August, and *Allen's Indian Mail*, 18 October, which carried a transcript of the trial.
67. See *Friend of India*, 8 April 1852 and 17 March 1853.

In addition to its legal offspring, the trial made John Lang a minor celebrity, if not notorious. While some newspapers relished his spirit and the competence with which he defended his client, others faulted him for his irreverence. The *Times* wrote that "Mr. Lang in his speech in defence overwhelmed the Company's judicial system with ridicule" and addressed the court "in [Prasad's] favour with superfluous energy."[68] Lord Broughton, the president of the Board of Control, described the speech as "a defence which was not conceived in any moderate spirit, or in any very measured language."[69] By contrast, the *Bengal Hurkaru* declared the remarks both "able and brilliant" and "a splendid piece of forensic eloquence."[70] The *Bombay Times*, taking a broader perspective, wrote,

> So accustomed were the natives to persuade themselves Government could not be struggled with where its wish was once understood—and in Jotee Pershaud's case it was understood—that they habitually shrank from competition; but Mr. Lang has pointed to a new leaf in the volume, where they may all read, as plain as language can make it, that memorable fact, that the state, with its officials to back it, is not invincible.[71]

Though the *Bombay Times* shifted attention from the man to the infrastructure and institutional norms—and was notably congratulatory about British "fairness"—two decades later it was Lang's performance that was remembered. In its 1870 obituary of Prasad, the *Englishman*, recalling the case that made Jyoti Prasad a household name, wrote of Lang's "bold defiance of [the] Government."[72] The remark serves as an uncanny echo

---

68. 2 and 6 June 1851.

69. 8 July 1851.

70. 29 and 24 April 1851.

71. Qtd. in *Allen's Indian Mail*, 3 June, 314. The London *Times*'s Bombay correspondent came to a similar conclusion, though his language was laced with racial condescension: "Throughout the proceedings the population of the whole city of Agra were crowding in and about the court. The natives, who have been so long accustomed to the sycophantic style of pleading which Vakeels [public pleaders in the *sadr* courts] deem it prudent to adopt, were astounded when they beheld Mr. Lang frequently in fierce debate with the 'huzoor,' [judge] and not yielding a single point without a contest and a struggle" (2 June).

72. Qtd. in *Allen's Indian Mail*, 29 March 1870, 290.

of the substitution this chapter has highlighted: while the Great Exhibition was displaced by the Jyoti Prasad trial, two decades later another reversal took place with the Indian man subsumed by his colonial defender.

In its obituary of Prasad, the *Englishman* recalled Lang's "famous simile of the . . . menu of a passenger ship" that "took the court by storm." The moment referred to is from Lang's closing remarks at the 1851 trial, in which he intoned,

> The further I proceed, the more am I reminded of the peculiarities of my present position. I am addressing a Company's Judge, in a Company's Court, with a Company's "Jury," the Prosecutor a Company's Covenanted Officer—acting for the Company itself. I never beheld such a spectacle before. It most reminds me of an impression a person receives at sea—when on Saturday evening they kill a pig, and on Sunday you behold the Cuddy table a perfect grove of Pork. There is roast loin at one end—boiled leg at the other—while the side dishes consist of Pork Chops, Pork Pie, Chitlings, and Cheek. The whole affair is Pork—and so is this—Nothing *but* Pork.[73]

The remarks provide a flavor of Lang's oratorical style: the drum-beat of "Company" dramatizes the voracious machinery of the state and is rhetorically skillful. But the force of his argument—about the impossibility of justice when the deck is stacked—is undercut by Lang's conclusion that the case is "but Pork." To claim that the trial was merely padding or waste was to limit the charge, to redirect it from a structural critique to an amusing triviality. Lang's verbal cleverness prevented him from making a stronger attack on a matter that he and his newspaper had written about for years: the ills of the mofussil judiciary.

The reference to pork was in fact an inside joke. More than half a century after the trial concluded, William Forbes-Mitchell wrote a memoir of the 1857 Uprising in which he offered the backstory to Lang's dramatic closing:

> Mr. Lang, who appeared in court every day in his wig and gown, soon became a noted character in Meerut [sic], and

---

73. *Mofussilite*, 18 April and 8 April in the trial testimony.

> the night before he was to sum up the case for the defence, some officers in the Artillery mess asked him his opinion of the members of the commission [trying the case]. Not being a teetotaler, Mr. Lang . . . replied that the whole batch, president and members, including the judge-advocate-general, were a parcel of "d—d *soors*" [which a note translates as pigs]. Immediately several officers present offered to lay a bet of a thousand rupees with Mr. Lang that he was not game to tell them so to their faces in open court the following day. Lang accepted the bet. (155–56)

In requoting Lang's remarks, Forbes-Mitchell inserts parentheses indicating that each time Lang mentioned a dish of pork, he gestured towards one or another of the court's officials. Lang won his thousand rupees. The story makes for an entertaining narrative and provides insight into the unpopularity of the Company and especially its mofussil courts. The anecdote, however, also reveals the shift in focus from the Indian who lay at the heart of this case to an Anglo-Indian and his prankish defiance of the government.

As the anecdote underscores, the figure at the center of the narrative, Jyoti Prasad, remains elusive. The slippages and many variations of his name are, in some measure, emblematic of the lack of certainty about—even disregard of—the man. Despite bestowing his name on—and paying handsomely for—a trial that was one of the most significant cases to precede the anti-colonial movement, a case that pitted the Government of India against an Indian, Prasad himself remains a cipher. He was never called to the stand, so we literally do not hear his voice either in the press or in the trial transcripts. And after 1851, he virtually drops out of the public record until his death in 1870.[74] The "great contractor," as he was known in 1851, reappears in the newsprints in only one other significant historical moment, one that offers insight into the Anglo-Indian conception of the "good Indian."[75] On 23 June 1857, six weeks after the start of what Britons called the "Mutiny," the *Mofussilite*, now headquartered in Agra,

---

74. *Allen's Indian Mail* unkindly if candidly noted in Prasad's obituary that the man "long dead to the world, is now announced as having died his natural death" (29 March 1870).

75. An early reference to this manner of referring to Jyoti Prasad appears in the *Friend of India*, 14 November 1850.

reported that during the siege of the city, Prasad did what he had been doing for almost two decades: he provisioned his British masters who had retreated to the Agra Fort. The newspaper wrote, "Our old friend Jotee Pershad has again shown himself the best Commissariat Officer in the world, by laying in, with-in thirty hours of receiving the order, stores and provisions to last 10,000 men for a month . . . [and] accommodation for upwards of 3000 inhabitants." Ten months later, as the British regained control of the towns and cities of the plains, a letter to the editor appeared in the London *Times*. Signed by "One of the Late Garrison at Agra," the writer offered an account he believed would be "as gratifying to the public generally as to the Lalah's old friend and advocate, Mr. John Laing [sic]."[76] As Agra prepared itself for the siege in May 1857, the writer related, the magistrate of Agra and commissariat officials squabbled and were unable to secure provisions. Authorities turned to "Jotee Persaud, who in five or six days laid into the fort provisions for 3,000 men for six weeks." In addition, Prasad provided another key provision—intelligence: he "kept up a regular communication of his own with Delhi and Gwalior, and used to inform the authorities at Agra of all that he heard." The writer concludes, "He stood almost alone, loyal and friendly, in the midst of the large traitorous and blood-stained populace at Agra . . . act[ing] as none of the highly paid, pampered native officials acted."[77]

This was Indians as the British wanted them: attentive, devoted, and above all loyal. The *Friend of India*, in its obituary of Jyoti Prasad, rehearsed the sensational trial and concluded, "The name of Jotee Pershad is more pleasantly associated with assistance rendered to our countrymen when shut up in the Agra Fort, an act for which he was subsequently created Rai Bhadhur."[78] In 1851, Prasad had challenged the Company and state, and much of the Anglo-Indian press (with the notable exception of the *Friend of India*) had supported him. In 1857, he returned to his "place" and supplied the masters who in 1853 had finally paid him his

---

76. *Times*, 9 April 1858.

77. *Times*, 9 April 1858. In its obituary, the *Englishman* added a melodramatic flip to the story: it stated that in 1857 Prasad "had a glorious opportunity of avenging himself during the Mutinies. The civilians of Agra took refuge in the Fort, and amongst them were his actual prosecutors. The revenge he took was noble. He supplied the Fort with all sort of food, as he had hitherto supplied the army" (qtd. in *Allen's Indian Mail*, 29 March 1870, 290).

78. *Friend of India*, 24 February 1870.

outstanding bills. His loyalty to these masters is one reason Prasad has been unpalatable to proto-nationalists and nationalists in the second half of the nineteenth century as the events of 1857 created a line in the sand. The next chapter examines those events, but before we turn to 1857, a final note on Prasad. In May 1863, the *Mofussilite* carried a small notice about the ruins of British buildings in Meerut, where the uprising had begun. The newspaper reported that "these monuments are looked upon with pleasurable eyes by all those who are inimical to our rule in the East, and by many Natives in this station who aided and abetted in the destruction of these edifices which sheltered Christian men, women and children. Europeans of all classes view them in an entirely different light, and, gazing on them, the hottest feelings of revenge are inspired."[79] These ruins, the *Friend* continued, had been purchased by Jyoti Prasad for three lakh rupees. No explanation for why Prasad purchased the ruins is offered. Was it as a gesture of solidarity with Indians who looked "pleasurably" upon the Uprising of 1857? In homage to Europeans killed there? We can only speculate. And acknowledge that within this archive, Prasad remains a cipher. The faint outlines that emerge suggest an Indian who, like many others of his caste and class, straddled two worlds.

I return to the questions I posed at the start: Why did the trial of Jyoti Prasad come to dominate the pages of Anglo-Indian newspapers? What does the displacement of the Great Exhibition by the trial of Jyoti Prasad signal? Why has the case been largely neglected and what is its relevance today? The substitution of the trial for the Great Exhibition is the local asserting itself. The trial of Jyoti Prasad was close at hand and revolved around issues that were near to the interests of Anglo-Indians: the "character" of British rule, the Company's governance, the perversion of justice in mofussil courts, and Anglo-Indians' relationship to Indians whom they relied on and sometimes worked with. That the local dominated their sightline is unsurprising and only noteworthy because Anglo-Indians have been characterized as taking their cues from Britain and British politics. In the *Victorian Periodical Studies* issue on *The Nineteenth-Century Press in India*, Julie Codell writes that "[t]he Indian press reflected much of the reformism, belief in progress and democratization of public life and of the press in Britain" (106). Indian newspapers excerpting news from English newspapers is frequently referenced as a sign of their reliance on "home news" and detachment

---

79. Reprinted in the *Friend of India*, 21 May 1863.

from the local. A focus on the Anglo-Indian newspaper archive suggests that their world was distinct from—though it intersected with—Britain and Britons' concerns. Anglo-Indian newspapers' turn to the Jyoti Prasad story is an instantiation of their engagement with the local and a correction to the claim that Anglo-Indians simply mirrored British views and politics.

David Finkelstein and Douglas Peers, in their introduction to a volume of essays about India in the nineteenth-century media, write, "Anglo-Indian newspapers rarely challenged the status quo . . . Submission to the status quo was . . . predicated on a sense of beleaguerment that pervaded the Anglo-Indian community. As a result of this anxiety, ideological divisions within the Anglo-Indian community were subordinated to the need to demonstrate political and cultural unity" (9).[80] As this chapter has argued, such was not the case in 1851 when Anglo-Indian papers clamored to critique the Government of India. In fact, their critiques were so loud and sharp that the *Friend of India* complained, "All papers in India attack the Government . . . [T]he Press of India, generally speaking, is in a state of opposition to the Company's Government. With some, the opposition is more virulent, with others, less so."[81] The remark comes from a staunchly pro-government source, so it is tempting to dismiss it as paranoia, but this chapter has illustrated that the remark is not off the mark. In addition to their independence from the government on the Jyoti Prasad case, newspapers of the time also did not hesitate to dispute and debate one another's assessment of the news. (Reading multiple Anglo-Indian newspapers often feels like an exhausting exercise of witnessing an unending squabble.) With the exception of the *Friend of India*, all the newspapers in my sample wrote critically of the government's suit against Jyoti Prasad. Within that broad agreement, there were differences of degree: the *Bengal Hurkaru* believed that the government had overreached, the Bombay *Times* that this case was emblematic of a broader array of injustices; the *Delhi Gazette* believed that the mofussil courts could be reformed, the *Mofussilite* that they must be abolished. Anglo-Indian newspapers at this specific moment were deeply engaged in local affairs—and this included challenging the status quo. It

---

80. In his essay on J. M. Kaye, Peers writes about the distance between Anglo-Indian and British society: "Anglo-Indian society was not simply an offshoot of British society. The two worlds had much in common, yet Anglo-Indian society had acquired certain distinctive traits, such as a very militarized view of the world and a propensity to identify itself in terms of its Indian surroundings" (274).

81. *Friend of India*, 12 September 1852.

did not include challenging or questioning the imperial project. While much of the press in my sample raised uncomfortable questions about the Company, those questions were severely limited by their reliance on a narrowly judicial framework to assess their government's actions.

Scholarship since 2000 has emphasized that empire was not monolithic but a complex, multifarious, even contested and fractured formation. Ann Stoler and Fredrick Cooper write eloquently about what they characterize as "tensions of empire": "As we engage colonial archives, we see much protracted debate," debate that "puts contradiction at the center of the colonial state's operative mode, rather than as an episodic manifestation of its reaction to crisis" (9, 20). Rather than "assuming coherence" among colonists, scholars should attend "to dissonant voices" that allow us to "see beyond an omniscient colonial apparatus to one shot through with conflicts" (21). In a similar vein, Martin Wiener argues that "imperialism" is not a "single project" and that "the nearer one looks . . . the more this supposed monolith dissolves into a multitude of often incompatible projects and actors" (4). Acknowledging such tensions or "dissonance" does not imply that we deny the power of empire. John Comaroff writes, "the historical fact that there were these 'tensions of empire' did not make imperialism any less exploitative. Or coercive. Nor did it soften the inequalities that saturated colonial societies everywhere; if anything, it sharpened them. But, for the colonized conflict among colonizers sometimes opened up fissures through which the contradictions inherent in colonialism became visible" (qtd. in M. Wiener 4n11). Attending to conflicts among colonizers means, as well, that we focus less on the broad fact of empire and more on what Homi Bhabha calls the "perplexities of living" (167). In the South Asian context, grappling with the dissonances in the Anglo-Indian press provides insight into some of the reasons the British colonial project in India was both successful and of such longevity. This chapter's focus on an alternative archive has punctured the notion that the Anglo-Indian press simply mirrored the British press or that the workings of colonialism in India were monolithic. While almost all Britons in India subscribed to the imperial mission, their notions of what empire meant, how the colony ought to be governed, and how to engage Indians were diverse. In terms of the Jyoti Prasad case, some commentators were driven by the need to reform the mofussil courts, others to undermine the authority of the Company; some to safeguard British interests, others to preserve British legal integrity. Anglo-Indian press responses to the trial and governance of India thicken our understanding of the day-to-day functioning of empire.

Finally, the newspapers' substitution of the Jyoti Prasad trial for the Great Exhibition makes an inadvertent link between the two events. The Great Exhibition, though by no means only a paean to British ascendency, celebrated the global reach and scope of the nation.[82] The case of Jyoti Prasad tells an alternative story about the "booty" that lay carefully tucked away in the glass palace, outside the India Court. That the goods on show were not all acquired by legitimate means is a story few in the nineteenth century were willing to entertain. The Kohinoor, dismissed or relegated to barbaric splendor though it might have been by organizers and commentators such as the *Times*, was a reminder of the violence of empire. Like the rock whose light metropolitan commentators wished to put out, the Jyoti Prasad trial captured the cost of empire, the price that must be paid both for something as mundane as bullocks and for British prestige.

Although the *Times* briefly linked the diamond to the annexation of Punjab, it did so in amusement. The only other news outlet that made a connection between the Great Exhibition and Britain's wars of expansion was the *Mofussilite* on the anniversary of the Jyoti Prasad trial. In an extended commentary, Lang (he self-identified) wrote,

> If the Government were to act with only decent liberality, they would pay Lallah Jottee Persuad 59 Lacs of rupees for that is about the sum that he ought in fairness to receive. Yet gentlemen who wear their medals and ribbons on their breasts, awarded unto you for your valour in the campaign against the Sikhs, we desire to tell you that the man who supplied you with food is to this very hour a creditor to the Government, to the extent of upwards of half a million sterling. Batta [a form of prize money] has been distributed, the Punjab has been annexed, the jewels of Runjeet Singh and his golden insignia of office have been appraised and sold by auction, by a Calcutta jeweller; the Koh-i-noor has been exhibited [at] 'the greatest exhibition of all nations'; and yet the man on whose exertions . . . our operations much depended on, is 'fobbed off' and 'fobbed off' and paid in driblets. (6 April 1852)

---

82. Auerbach writes that "while Britain performed well at the exhibition, premonitions of its decline appeared almost as often as proclamations of victory" (1).

The *Mofussilite* insisted, long after others had moved on to the next item, that there was a price to pay for empire. That the newspaper was secure in its belief that the British presence in India was desirable does not take away from the argument that colonials came in many stripes.

Despite the sensation that Jyoti Prasad's case aroused for a short moment in India and for its challenge to the government, it never ignited the imagination of Indian proto-nationalists or nationalists. The reasons are not difficult to grasp: Prasad serviced the empire, both prior to and following his trial. By no means a subaltern, he deserves attention, nevertheless, because his story requires us to grapple with the many Indians who did not resist the British. Narratives of resistance make for compelling—and uplifting—reading. But they tell a partial tale. If the archive of Anglo-Indian newspapers helps displace a metropolitan-focused narrative, it also pokes holes in a narrative of colonial resistance. In Vinay Dharwadker's typography of "subject-positions" birthed by print culture in British India, Prasad would belong to the category of "voluntary Indian collaborators," "professionals who mediate between the colonial state and a colonized people" (117–18). Prasad was both a collaborator and a mediator—but, unlike the collaborators Dharwadker speaks of who "frequently became the scribe and scribal repository or archive of the empire" (119), Prasad never appears in the print archive of his day. The sign "Jotee Pershuad" survives in the trial that bears his name and in the archive of Anglo-Indian newspapers, but the man does not appear. The trial looked backwards—to Burke's challenge—and also forward, a harbinger of the future and demise of the Company that came to a head in 1857. But the man at its center remains a blank in this archive.

Chapter 3

The Uprising in the Anglo-Indian Press

The year 1857 began innocuously enough in the pages of Anglo-Indian newspapers. On 31 January 1857, a five-line notice in the *Bengal Hurkaru* announced the death of Mr. G. R. Wilby, "one time Sub-Editor of the *Hurkaru*." Wilby, readers might recall, was the man who replaced John Lang at the helm of the *Mofussilite* in 1851 when Lang stepped down to represent Jyoti Prasad in the trial discussed in the previous chapter. The *Hurkaru*'s small announcement fails to mention Wilby's stint at the *Mofussilite*, but notes that he worked at the *Delhi Gazette*, the *Lahore Chronicle*, and the *Friend of India*; a few days later, the first of these journals published an extended obituary of the man who had lately served as its editor.[1] A native of Nova Scotia, Wilby headed to India for his health. Landing in Calcutta at the age of 20, he became a journalist and moved through the ranks at various newspapers: starting as a freelance writer at the *Englishman*, he was picked up by the short-lived *Economist*; next came a stint as temporary "chair" of the *Calcutta Star*, a position he was obliged to leave due to a libel case. The *Hurkaru* hired him, but a "breach ultimately occurred," and Wilby moved on to the *Citizen*. From here, Lang picked him up, and Wilby moved up the ranks and to the mofussil, where, according to the obituary, his work "has been familiar to our readers." From the *Mofussilite* he moved to the *Delhi Gazette*, then to the *Lahore Chronicle*, and finally to the *Friend of India*. Wilby was just thirty-one years old when he died.

---

1. The *Delhi Gazette*'s obituary appeared on February 5 and was reprinted in the *Bengal Hurkaru*, 10 February 1857.

In his time in India, Wilby embodied the defining feature of his trade: circulation. In the space of ten years, Wilby worked at nine different newspapers, among them some of the oldest and most reputable Anglo-Indian journals—the *Englishman*, the *Bengal Hurkaru*, and the *Friend of India*—as well as a paper that was in equal parts admired and denounced, the *Mofussilite*. Journalism has always been a fast-evolving enterprise. In mid-nineteenth-century India, dozens of periodicals appeared and disappeared—the weekly *Indian Sun*, for example, lasted but one week in 1846[2]—and staff moved with considerable speed from one enterprise to another. Wilby's itinerant existence and experience at such a large number of metropolitan and mofussil, lasting and fleeting, small and large newspapers serves as an apt entry into the turbulence of 1857 and the Uprising that shook northern India. Much has been written about the Uprising. This chapter does not rehearse that history; instead, it approaches the Uprising through the prism of Anglo-Indian newspapers and their coverage of the events that roiled the central plains of the subcontinent. Integral to this coverage are the editorial circulations and realignments that took place in the newspaper business in 1857–58.

In his model for the holistic study of print culture, Robert Darnton offers the elegance of the "communications circuit." Its nodal points are not discrete: the very reader "who completes the circuit" is also sometimes an author whose reading shapes his writing. At the center of Darnton's blueprint lies a Venn diagram of the forces that shape print and that suggest a web or network of relations. Laurel Brake has urged us to think about networks as "part of the *structure* of journalism" ("'Time's Turbulence'" 117). She sketches several approaches a focus on networks might take, including "cross-referencing to fellow writers, [to] issues past and to come, to correspondents, to rivals" (121), as well as the relations between serials exemplified in their borrowing from one another (117–19). Drawing on Brake's suggestions, this chapter examines a network of relations between Anglo-India media in 1857–58. It will begin with the circulation of personnel between and within outlets in my sample, exchanges that echo Wilby's peripatetic journey through the ecosphere of Anglo-Indian newspapers. The circulation of personnel and copy, however, all but ground to a halt as the disturbances of 1857 spread across the Gangetic Plain and the flow of goods and people was disrupted. For newspapers, congested, sometimes

---

2. Chanda (*History* [1987] 267). Between 1780 and 1857, more than two hundred new English-language newspapers and periodicals appeared; most languished within a short time (xix).

impassable, roads and the delayed *dâk*, or mailbag, were the preeminent material factors that shaped their reporting of events in 1857–58.[3] These impediments transformed newspapers' access to information and led, paradoxically, to an expansion of views and voices; the result was a chaotic free market of ideas and considerable inconsistency.

My core sample remains the *Mofussilite* (biweekly from Agra), the *Bengal Hurkaru* and *Englishman* (dailies from Calcutta), and the *Friend of India* (weekly from Srirampur, outside Calcutta). The chapter introduces a new paper, the *Hindoo Patriot*, an Indian-owned and -edited English-language weekly that began publication in 1853 in Calcutta. The relations between these newspapers were both long-standing and evolving; with the exception of the *Hindoo Patriot*, all traded personnel. Yet these exchanges did not produce accord. In the previous chapter, we saw that, with the exception of the *Friend of India*, all our papers were critical of the East India Company (though they had differing views of its problems and emphasized different solutions). The story of 1857, contrary to the view of many historians, is less tidy. As this chapter demonstrates, the Anglo-Indian press did not speak in one voice; chaos and inconsistency reigned, not only between organs, but *within* individual newspapers' columns.

Editorial Turbulence

The year 1857, in the history of the *Mofussilite*, is marked by a series of absences. As I sketched in the first chapter, by 1847, the *Mofussilite* was settled in Meerut; for reasons that are not clear, in 1853 the paper moved to Agra, then the capital of the North-Western Provinces. Consequently, when, on the evening of 10 May 1857, the mutiny in Meerut morphed into a rebellion, the *Mofussilite* was publishing from a hundred and fifty miles south in a town that played a relatively minor role in the uprisings that swept through the central plains of the subcontinent. For Lang personally, matters were doubly unfortunate: in 1857 he was in London. For

---

3. As transportation through the North-Western Provinces was often blocked or impassable in the second half of 1857, fears of alternate forms of circulation proliferated among Anglo-Indians. To wit, the many accounts of the circulation of *chapatis*—unleavened bread—that supposedly carried word of the uprisings from village to village in the months prior to the disturbances. Rumors of *chapatis* carrying news telegraph the British fear of a system of news circulation that pre-dated their print forms. For a discussion of *chapatis* and rumors, see Chaudhary (61–63).

a journalist to be away when the biggest story of his career breaks in a town he lived in for almost a decade is a missed opportunity of colossal proportions. For a researcher, more gaps follow: not only had the offices of the *Mofussilite* relocated with its well-connected editor missing, but all copies of a full four months of the newspaper are missing as well. In the archive of the *Mofussilite* no copies between 30 June and 27 October 1857 exist.[4]

The popular explanation for the missing numbers is that the newspaper's provocative stances elicited government censorship. This claim appears to have been first promulgated by AustLit, a site established and run by Australian archivists and scholars, which writes that "[a]s [the *Mofussilite*] carried anti-government reports, its file copies were destroyed."[5] Crittenden repeats the charge in his 2005 biography of Lang, and the claim has been offered to me by an archivist at the British Library as a possible explanation for the missing numbers. Whereas Book History scholars cite quotidian factors such as disintegrating paper or hasty preservation as the culprits of a lost or disappearing archive, the AustLit explanation tells a more riveting tale of political resistance to colonial authority. The basis for the claim that the missing numbers indicate censorship lies in the notion, disseminated by Crittenden and others, that Lang was a firm "friend of Indians" and staunchly anti-government. As I have argued in previous chapters, Lang's critiques of the government, though caustic, were firmly anchored in an imperial discourse of civilizational superiority and certitude. I shall turn shortly to examine the *Mofussilite*'s coverage of events in the extant 1857 copy to determine whether it was "anti-government," but will first attend to its editorial leadership in the absence of Lang.

Lang continued to own the *Mofussilite*, but was not its editor in 1857. As far as I have been able to reconstruct, aside from a short period in early 1854, Lang had not edited the paper since he stepped down from the helm in 1851 to represent Jyoti Prasad. (See figure 1.7 in chapter 1 for the paper's editors between 1845 and 1860.) Following the trial, Lang was charged with libel and relocated to Calcutta to await his trial; there, in June 1851, he started a biweekly called the *Optimist*, which folded three

---

4. In addition to the missing numbers from July to October, a number of weeks in the middle of June are missing as well.

5. http://www.austlit.edu.au/austlit/page/A7038. Accessed 14 December 2014.

months later when he was sentenced to two months in prison.[6] Crittenden reports that following his prison term, Lang returned to Meerut in 1852 and arranged for the *Mofussilite*'s offices to be relocated to Agra (129). In September 1852, Lang departed for London and did not return to India until February 1854, when he briefly resumed editorship of the *Mofussilite*, only to leave again, this time summoned by Laxmibai, the rani of Jhansi, whose principality had recently been annexed by the Company (I shall turn to this episode in the next chapter). Shortly after his meeting with the rani, Lang left India once again in July 1854 and did not return until March 1858. In short, during much of the 1850s, Lang was the newspaper's absentee proprietor. While in London, he served as the *Mofussilite*'s London correspondent, but he was neither loyal to the newspaper he owned nor had any say in its daily management or content.[7] The scholars who write about the *Mofussilite*—Crittenden and Douglas Peers—treat the paper as Lang's instrument, but nothing could be further from the case in the 1850s. Indeed, contemporaries commented on the *Mofussilite*'s lackluster quality when Lang is not in the editorial seat.

Who, then, was the editor of the *Mofussilite* in the 1850s, when Lang was away, and particularly during the Uprising? Wilby served in the editorial chair for a year in 1851, but departed for the *Delhi Gazette* in early 1852.[8] I have been unable to determine who replaced Wilby at the *Mofussilite*, and the two years between 1852 and Lang's brief return in February 1854 remain a blank. When Lang left once again in May 1854 to consult with the rani of Jhansi, he handed over the reins of his newspaper to Sidney Laman Blanchard. Blanchard was from London and acquainted with Dickens, who had published a number of Blanchard's essays in *Household Words* in 1851–52. There is every reason to believe that Lang

---

6. On the journal's start, see *Bengal Hurkaru*, 18 June 1851, and *Friend of India*, 19 June 1851. The *Hurkaru* reported the paper's demise on 10 October 1851. See also Chanda (*History* [1987] 316).

7. The *Mofussilite*'s editor in early 1857 was unhappy when he learned that Lang was moonlighting for *Thacker's Overland Mail*, a steamship journal published in London (see *Mofussilite*, 13 and 27 February 1857).

8. The *Mofussilite*'s 6 February 1857 notice of Wilby's death is relatively terse and notes only that "he was for a short time Editor of the *Mofussilite*." How short is up for debate: Crittenden writes that Wilby served as editor from January 1851 to January 1854 (see 117, 132, and 158), but Ram Gopal Sanyal writes that by early 1852 Wilby was editor of the *Delhi Gazette* (179). My investigations support Sanyal's dates over Crittenden's.

and Blanchard met in London in 1852–53, as both men passed through that busy portal called *Household Words*. It seems more than plausible that Lang directed Blanchard towards India and Indian journalism; the accepted narrative in India was that Blanchard was Lang's protégé.[9] In 1853, Blanchard landed in Calcutta and within the year took over the editorial position at Lang's mofussil newspaper, where he served from May 1854 until January 1857.[10] Their acquaintance in London would explain why Lang was willing to entrust his ailing newspaper—the *Mofussilite* had lost much of its sting since Lang's departure in 1851—to Blanchard in 1854. A fresh and opinionated writer from London seemed an ideal choice to edit the languishing *Mofussilite*. Lang and Blanchard's London acquaintance and the latter's appointment to edit the *Mofussilite* indicates that a network of journalistic exchanges existed not only among Anglo-Indian newspapers—to wit, Wilby—but between British and Indian newspapers and journals as well.[11]

Lang's protégé left the paper in January 1857, and by early March 1857 Blanchard was settled into the editorial chair at the *Hurkaru*. With his departure, the *Mofussilite*'s editorial trail goes a bit cold. A few months after Blanchard had vacated his post at the *Mofussilite*, the *Hurkaru* published a lengthy piece by a correspondent in Agra who wrote, "People up here heard that John Lang was coming out last January to look after the

---

9. See "The Meerut Muff," dated 29 May 1858, in the *Indian Field*, a Calcutta weekly, reprinted in the *Mofussilite*, 8 June 1858.

10. Chanda reports that Blanchard left the *Mofussilite* in January 1856 to take over as editor of the *Bengal Hurkaru*. The date is clearly a typo by the otherwise meticulous Chanda. The *Friend of India* reported on 5 March 1857 that Blanchard had left the *Mofussilite* for the chair of the *Hurkaru*, and the *Hurkaru* announced that Blanchard became its editor on 10 March 1857 (*Hurkaru*, 6 April 1857). Other evidence indicates that Blanchard left the *Mofussilite* in a hurry in January 1857 to assume his new position at the *Hurkaru* (see Blanchard's statement in the *Mofussilite*, 9 April 1858). Blanchard's 1867 *Yesterday and To-Day in India* fails to mention his editorial leadership at either the *Mofussilite* or the *Hurkaru*; both papers are breezily dismissed.

11. The traffic between Indian and British journalists deserves a volume of its own. In the early days, when the Indian government punished erring newsmen with deportation, several (such as Buckingham) continued their truncated journalistic careers in Britain. Even as press restrictions relaxed, the journalistic traffic between India and Britain continued. For instance, Meredith Townsend, after a long career in Calcutta at the helm of the *Friend of India*, returned to London and became owner and co-editor of the *Spectator* in 1861, a post he remained in for twenty-five years.

Moff., and re-seat himself in the chair you abandoned; but that erratic individual is [elsewhere]. Some one should look after the paper and that soon. Something ails it. The present Editor is too fond of flowers of poetry and elegant extracts to last long."[12] The interpolated "you" is Blanchard, of course, now at the helm of the *Hurkaru*. His correspondent offers no further details on the *Mofussilite*'s flowery editor. In an essay in *Household Words* in early 1858, Lang, in London at the time, wrote that "the late Major Thomas was virtually the editor of the Mofussilite at Agra at the time he received his death wound in the field of battle."[13] George Powell Thomas was an India hand: born in the country in 1808 and the son of a major general in the Company's army, he was a seasoned officer who served in the 64th Bengal Native Infantry and the 3rd Bengal European Regiment stationed in Agra (Stanley 53). Was Major Thomas the poetically inclined editor the *Hurkaru*'s Agra correspondent is so dismissive of? Details on Thomas are hard to come by; the only record of him in the media is of a dismissed court-martial case from 1852 in which he was charged with writing libelous letters in the *Agra Messenger* and *Mofussilite*.[14] If the charges have any merit, Thomas certainly fit the *Mofussilite*'s profile. If it were Thomas who stepped in as "virtually editor" upon Blanchard's abrupt departure in January 1857, he did so for only six months as he was wounded on 5 July 1857, in the battle of Sussia, the one skirmish Agra experienced during the Uprising, and died of his wounds a month later on 4 August.

Assuming Lang was correct and Thomas was editor in the early days of the Uprising, his replacement between July 1857 and April 1858, when Blanchard returned to the *Mofussilite*, is a blank too.[15] The trail goes even colder for this period, but one report suggests an intriguing possibility. On 4 July 1857, the European inhabitants of Agra moved into the fort, where they remained for some four months (provisioned by Jyoti Prasad). In early September, the *Hurkaru* printed a letter it had received from Agra dated 1 August—around the time Thomas died of his wounds. The letter includes this unexpected bit: "Mr. Gibbons of the *Moff.* who brought in a portion of his Press materials with him publishes a paper

---

12. *Hurkaru*, 11 May 1857.
13. "Wanderings in India," *Household Words*, 16 January 1858, 114.
14. See *Allen's Indian Mail*, 1 September 1852, 479–80, and Stanley (53).
15. On Blanchard's return, see *Mofussilite*, 6 and 9 April 1858.

now pretty regularly."[16] Gibbons, readers might recall from chapter 1, was the *Mofussilite*'s printer, publisher, and, during Lang's frequent absences, trusted manager. The report that Gibbons published the paper regularly indicates that contrary to the supposition that the *Mofussilite* was censored and ceased publication, it in fact continued to appear during the Uprising. Though the letter does not mention an editor, it strongly suggests that the enterprising Gibbons had now added "editor" to his many roles.

Though gaps remain in my reconstruction of the *Mofussilite*'s editor, and my account of the critical months of the Uprising is speculative, the details are suggestive. The editorial shifts in the period between January 1857 and April 1858—Blanchard to Major Thomas to Gibbons back to Blanchard—are more turbulent than was generally the case at the *Mofussilite*. These shifts mirror the turbulence occurring in the political and social landscape. The changes also underscore the traffic of personnel between Anglo-Indian newspapers. Blanchard is the key figure here, moving from the *Mofussilite* to the *Hurkaru* then back to the *Mofussilite* in the space of eighteen months. (Lang, too, was a journalistic sojourner: he was no longer editing the *Mofussilite*, but made good in London where Dickens published his twelve-part "Wanderings in India" in *Household Words*, beginning in November 1857, which I discuss in the next chapter.) Only Gibbons did not flit from outlet to outlet and remained at the newspaper where he appears to have spent his entire career, longer than Lang himself. The *Mofussilite* was consistently identified with Lang and viewed as an outlier and voice of opposition. My reconstruction indicates both that the newspaper's editorial direction was less stable than believed and that, throughout the 1850s, it was firmly looped into the Anglo-Indian publication business by the circulation of personnel.

If the traffic between Anglo-Indian print outlets, embodied in Wilby and Blanchard, telescopes the network of relations between newspapers, the textual networks they relied on helps solve the *Mofussilite*'s archival aporia. The letter cited above is the first clue that the paper continued printing throughout the Uprising. The practice of scissors-and-paste offers definitive evidence that the *Mofussilite* was never shut down or censored, nor went dark, but appeared continually during the months of the archival gap. The *Bengal Hurkaru* repeatedly carried excerpts from the July, August, September, and October numbers of the *Mofussilite*. For instance, on 10

---

16. *Hurkaru*, 8 September 1857. The *Mofussilite*'s masthead on the extant 27 October to November numbers identifies the place of publication as "Fort Agra."

August, the *Hurkaru*, published a portion of the *Mofussilite*'s 15 July account of the Europeans' retreat to the fort and the battle of Sussia at which Major Thomas was wounded. This account, to use a twenty-first-century term, went "viral" and portions of it appeared in dozens of British newspapers, including the *Stirling Observer* on 3 September 1857.[17] (Only the *Dublin Evening Mail* of 31 August 1857 published the *Mofussilite*'s lengthy account in its entirety. The irony of learning about the fate of Britons in Agra, the former capital of the Mughals, via Dublin is rich).

These reprints confirm that the *Mofussilite* continued to publish and, moreover, that its content was neither inflammatory nor worth censoring. On the contrary, the newspaper—at least in the excerpts reprinted in the *Hurkaru* and other sources—was steadfastly pro-British. In regards to the missing numbers of the *Mofussilite*, we can lay to rest the misperception that it was censored due to "anti-government" views. The gap in the archive—the last extant number is June 30 and first on resumption October 27—coincides almost exactly with the dates the Europeans retreated into and reemerged from the Agra Fort: 4 July to mid-October.[18] The more likely explanation for the missing numbers of the paper is that though it continued to publish and its copies sporadically arrived at the offices of rival papers in Calcutta and Bombay—from where they were disseminated throughout Britain—none were delivered to authorities for deposit purposes during the period the paper published from the fort. Perhaps disintegrating copies survive in some corner in Agra; given the brisk trade in old newspapers that were recycled for any number of daily and household tasks, however, this is doubtful.[19]

---

17. See Cordell ("Viral Textuality" 31–32) for a nuanced theorization of "virality" as a framework for reprints and networks. For an account of the network of transnational papers that published the *Mofussilite*'s 5 July Battle of Agra story, see Priti Joshi ("Scissors-and-Paste").

18. The Europeans and Christians of Agra took refuge in the fort on 4 July 1857 and remained there until Colonel Edward Greathed relieved the city on 10 October. A month prior to the relief, numerous Europeans made sojourns outside the fort as conditions inside were crowded and unhealthy (*Hurkaru*, 9 October 1857, citing a letter dated 9 September). By 23 October, a writer from Agra reported that order had been restored and conditions returned to normal in the city (*Hurkaru*, 6 November 1857). Nevertheless, many lingered in the fort: Mrs. Coopland, a refugee from Gwalior, did not leave until 12 December 1857 (Coopland 247).

19. In *How to Do Things with Books in Victorian Britain*, Leah Price discusses the many non-reading uses to which books and paper were put and their afterlives as they continued to circulate in realms beyond print.

The *Mofussilite* was not unique in its editorial transitions and busy exchanges during this period. Anglo-Indian newspapers from Bengal also experienced considerable turnover during the tumultuous days of the Uprising, when many had a "temporary manager."[20] The *Bengal Hurkaru*, the leading Calcutta daily, got a new editor on 1 January 1856, Patterson Saunders.[21] Sometime in 1856, Saunders left the *Hurkaru* to take up as editor at its rival newspaper, the *Englishman*. Blanchard, coming from the *Mofussilite*, stepped in as editor of the *Hurkaru* in March 1857. He did not, however, bring stability to the journal: having violated the government's "Gagging Act"—which we shall turn to shortly—Blanchard left the *Hurkaru* in September 1857 and was replaced by E. P. Moore, a former editor of the *Phoenix*. Moore remained at the *Hurkaru* post for only six months, until March 1858 (Chanda, *History* [2008] 1, 250–51). With the Uprising still smoldering, the proprietor brought Patterson Saunders back as editor of the *Hurkaru* (Chanda, *History* [2008] 1–4). In short, in the space of two years, the *Bengal Hurkaru* saw four different editors. Each man moved easily between rival papers. Despite the heavy traffic and shared personnel, the rivalry between the papers did not diminish, though the tone of the *Hurkaru* changed discernably with each new editor.

The *Friend of India* was a more stable newspaper, generally, yet it too saw its share of upheavals in this period. Founded in 1835 by John Marshman, the weekly was printed at the Serampore/Baptist Mission Press and had the largest share of British and Indian subscribers (Chanda, *History* [1987] 48–50). In 1857, Marshman was in England and the paper was edited by Meredith Townsend; at some point during the year, Townsend placed Henry Mead in the editor's chair. Like Saunders, Blanchard, Moore, and Wilby, Mead had also moved easily through the Anglo-Indian media landscape, having previously served as editor at the *Madras Athenaeum* and *Delhi Gazette* (Chanda, *History* [2008] 258–60). At the *Friend* that summer of 1857, Mead published articles that brought the government's censure on the newspaper; only Marshman's intervention from England and Mead's departure kept the newspaper's license from being revoked (258–60). Townsend resumed his post, but departed soon thereafter, leaving

---

20. *Mofussilite*, 27 October 1857.

21. See *Bengal Hurkaru*: "The Proprietor of the *Hurkaru* has appointed Mr. P. Saunders, Sr., Editor from this date. Calcutta, January 1, 1856" (15 January 1856, 50). See also Chanda (*History* [1987] 35) and Chanda (*History* [2008] 255–57). Despite the newspaper's own spelling on its masthead, Chanda spells the name *Harkaru*.

a Mr. Browning in charge; he too departed and in March 1858, the *Friend of India*'s new—and more stable—editor was George Smith, who stayed in the post until December 1863 (5–7). Although the *Friend*'s editorial changes were not as extensive as the *Hurkaru*'s or the *Mofussilite*'s, they are more dramatic both because of the stature of the paper and because some of the changes were occasioned by government restrictions.

The *Hindoo Patriot* is the final newspaper I take up here. It was established in 1853 with Harish Chandra Mukherjee as editor and, from 1855, owner, roles he remained in until his death in 1861 (Nakazato 249).[22] Mukherjee began his journalistic career under the tutelage of William Cobb Hurry at the *Englishman* before honing his skills at the *Hindu Intelligencer* (Chanda, *History* [1987] xxiii, 171, 277). The *Patriot* did not experience the editorial shifts its Anglo-Indian contemporaries did in 1857–58, a stability manifest in the consistency of its views throughout 1857. A small, Calcutta-based weekly owned and edited by a Bengali, the *Patriot* in 1857 had thirty-six subscribers.[23] It remained afloat because Mukherjee subsidized it with his salary from the office of the military auditor general. Mukherjee had started there as a clerk with a salary of Rs. 25 a month; by 1857, he had risen through the ranks to earn a monthly salary of Rs. 400 (Ghose, *Selections* [vol. IV] xii). The *Patriot* has not always received favorable treatment from the handful of scholars who have written about it in part because of Mukherjee's job in a military department of the Company, but also because during the Uprising the paper consistently supported Canning, the governor general, even as it criticized the Anglo-Indian press. Benoy Ghose is especially caustic about Mukherjee, charging that he "was more a vociferous 'Canningite' than even a whispering sympathizer of the mutineers" ([vol. IV] ix). Ram Gopal Sanyal, one of the earliest chroniclers of the Indian press, is more sympathetic. In his 1894 *Reminiscences and Anecdotes of Great Men of India*, Sanyal wrote, "[Mukherjea] made a tremendous sacrifice of his time and money for maintaining and editing that newspaper, and

---

22. Mukherjee's name is transliterated in a number of ways: Chanda spells it "Hurish Chunder Mookerjee"; Sen-Gupta spells it "Hurrish Chunder Mookerji"; Ghose spells his last name "Mukherjea"; Debapriya Paul spells it "Mookherjea."

23. Paul writes that the newspaper's "circulation was barely 100" (163); Nakazato provides similar numbers with a rise to 250 subscribers by the early 1860s (255–56). Chanda's number is far lower and is supported by the *Patriot*'s 1857 list of 36 subscribers (*History* [1987] 227–337).

died a pauper for the cause of his country. No other native of India, since his time has been able to show that amount of self-sacrifice for the good of his native land" (34). Nariaki Nakazato provides a more nuanced reading of Mukherjee, placing him at the intersection of colliding forces, a reading compatible with the approach I take in the final section of this chapter.

Extracting News: Improvisation and Chaos

The circulation of editors is one dimension of the 1857 Anglo-Indian press. Sources—in particular their shrinkage and, as I will argue, also unanticipated proliferation—is the other press story of that year, one directly impacted by the events of what is inaccurately referred to as "the Mutiny." In 1857, scores of Indians rose in rebellion against the British military, the government, and Europeans in their midst. The disturbances started in military cantonments. The 10th of May is generally marked as the start date, but it was preceded by a series of warning shots. On 26 February 1857, the *sipahis* (sepoys, in the Anglicized version) of the 19th Native Infantry (N. I.) at Berhampur refused to use the new Enfield rifle cartridges and the unit was disbanded. A month later, on 29 March, a sepoy of the 34th N. I. in Barrackpur, Mangal Pande, shot at officers of his regiment while his comrades looked on. Pande was hanged and this regiment disbanded too. On 10 May in Meerut, one of North India's largest garrisons, one cavalry and two infantry units mutinied in response to the court-martial of eighty-five of their comrades for refusing to use the suspect cartridges. This time events took a turn: the mutinying sepoys marched into the town and broke open the jail, releasing their comrades. They were joined by townspeople and together they looted the revenue office, burned the houses of Europeans and moneylenders, and cut telegraph wires. When the *sipahis*, *sowars* (cavalry), and townspeople marched to Delhi and demanded that Bahadur Shan Zafar, the aged Mughal emperor, assume leadership of the insurgency, the military mutinies that had been erupting since the start of the year took on a different color. The alliance of barrack and bazaar and the turn to a recognized ruling figure signaled that the military mutinies had morphed into a broader uprising.

Throughout the summer of 1857, *sipahis* of the Bengal army mutinied and merged with civilians; large numbers of Indians of many classes, backgrounds, castes, and religions challenged the ruling authorities, their governing infrastructure, and the European presence in India.[24] Historians have struggled to approximate the extent and breadth of the Uprising. While over 100,000 of the 139,000 sepoys of the Company's Bengal Army mutinied, sepoys in the Bombay and Madras Armies remained largely on the job.[25] In regards to civilians, it is more difficult to ascertain what proportion of the population resisted, largely because some resistance was active, others more passive. Though the number was large enough to rattle the government and British authorities and to register the disturbances as a substantial rebellion, if not an embryonic national uprising, it bears underscoring that geographically the rebellion was fairly contained, clustered along the Ganges river or Grand Trunk Road from Punjab to present-day Bihar. Even in the geographical space of the central plains, for every report of a *sipahi* or a peasant burning a revenue office, jail, or European house, there was an account of an individual, community, or leader shielding, protecting, and aiding Europeans. The historian Rudrangshu Mukherjee's insistence is germane: the "Indian Mutiny" was never one thing, but various and shifting ("Sepoy Mutinies").[26]

This variety is mirrored in Anglo-Indian press coverage of 1857–58. Because no detailed study of the Anglo-Indian press of this time exists, the general view of it—derived from officials' reactions or the writings of W. H. Russell, the *Times*'s special correspondent—is that the Calcutta press spoke in one voice: vengeful, inflammatory, hyperbolic.[27] In what follows, I offer a granular view of the coverage in my sample of Anglo-Indian newspapers. The discussion identifies material factors—cut telegraph wires, impassable roads, delayed mailbags—that affected newspapers' access to sources and material. Under the circumstances, editors improvised, with the result that the types of sources newspapers drew on altered; from famine, newspapers engineered, if not feast, at least something like a regular prod-

---

24. In the months following the Meerut mutiny, another forty-seven units in twenty-six locations mutinied; for a list of regiments that mutinied, see R. Mukherjee (*Awadh* 184–86). For an overview of the Uprising, see Priti Joshi ("1857").

25. For numbers, see Habib (8) and Bandyopadhyay (5).

26. On the evolution of the mutinies, see Roy ("Vision").

27. Chandrika Kaul's essay on Russell in India draws its remarks about the Anglo-Indian media from Canning's and Russell's papers ("You" 24–32); Gautam Chakravarty writes of the "shrill" and "hysterical" popular mood of Britons and Anglo-Indians, but his data is drawn from the writings of those in Britain (40, 94).

uct. From material factors, the discussion will turn to an analysis of the coverage itself, which registers a striking multiplicity and lack of internal consistency. While the Anglo-Indian press responses emerge from within an imperial vision, they present a portrait of instability and turbulence.

As regiment after regiment mutinied, as *sipahis* shed uniforms and returned to their villages or joined comrades in other mutinying regiments, as civilians in towns and peasants in villages joined *sipahis*, and as the military began its offensive, the roads in the central plains became increasingly congested and unsafe. A letter from Meerut dated 12 May—two days after the regiments there mutinied—began, "I wrote a long letter to you yesterday regarding the present state of affairs in Meerut, but am sorry to say the Mail was plundered a few miles out of the Station, and the horse and mail-cart both made away with."[28] Before the disturbances, the *dâk*, or mail, between Agra and Calcutta took approximately four days. Once the disturbances began, this transport time extended to three weeks or more; the *Mofussilite* of 16 June, for instance, did not arrive in Calcutta until 7 July.[29] Many towns in the central plains, previously oriented towards Calcutta, now turned westward, towards Bombay; in October, the *Mofussilite* announced that "the Bombay dak now reaches Agra pretty regularly in eleven or twelve days."[30]

For the *Mofussilite* and other up-country newspapers, postal interference caused a genuine crisis. Less than two months after the Meerut uprisings, the *Mofussilite*'s editor wrote, "we are in a manner regularly blockaded in Agra, being deprived of all postal or other communication with the outer world, beyond Mynpooree on one side, and Gwalior on the other—it is consequently a matter of extreme difficulty to write articles, seeing that we possess no text upon which to dilate; and therefore under the circumstances we must solicit the readers' indulgence for short-comings in this respect."[31] Eight months later, as the situation began to settle and the *dâk* from Calcutta improved, the *Mofussilite*'s editor wrote optimisti-

---

28. *Mofussilite*, 15 May 1857.

29. *Hurkaru*, 8 July 1857. Within the affected region, news traveled haphazardly: word of the Satichaura massacre that occurred on 27 June in Kanpur arrived at the Agra Fort, 170 miles away, on 20 July, over three weeks later (see Coopland 191).

30. *Mofussilite*, 27 October 1857.

31. *Mofussilite*, 26 June 1857. Bayly writes that the British in Agra were "totally starved of information" during the first two months of the uprising (324).

cally, "we shall [soon] be able to bring out the *Mofussilite* [in] its proper dimensions, which is impracticable at present in consequence of the difficulty of finding matter to fill a double sheet, seeing that sometimes for days together we receive no papers from any part of the world."[32]

Both lament and relief are preoccupied with sourcing: "the difficulty of finding matter" and the consequent shrunk "dimensions" of the published product. The lack of source material affected newspapers materially and editorially. The *Mofussilite*'s 30 June and 27 October papers—the extant numbers immediately before and after the missing copies—were each only four pages long, half its customary length.[33] The dearth of material—"text upon which to dilate"—meant that editors were forced to adjust practices. While culling and reprinting from other news outlets continued, the delayed or plundered mailbag altered the reliance on a network of other print media. Increasingly, editors opened their pages to a wider array of sources, publishing any copy they could lay hands on, whether it reflected the paper's views or not, and offered such material without editorial commentary. The infusion of sources and editorial restraint introduced a cacophony of voices and traded consistency for copy.

Newspapers based in Calcutta and its vicinity could draw on material from one another or from Madras, Bombay, or British papers (sea travel was unaffected); but what they needed were reports from the center of the country, from the towns where Europeans had retreated for safety (Agra or Kanpur) or where rebels held territory (Delhi). As the editor of the Bengali-language *Bhaskar* complained on 9 June, the "Outbreak . . . has been felt rather severely by Editors and Proprietors of newspapers in particular. For the last two weeks we have neither received any letters from, nor been able to despatch our papers to the North Western Provinces"[34] Compounding an irregular *dâk* was the danger media outlets have always faced during strife: they are a target of warring forces seeking to control them and manage the dissemination of ideas. I will turn to the British state's embargo on the press shortly, but note that insurgents too tried

---

32. *Mofussilite*, 1 January 1858. In his account of 1857, William Muir, head of the intelligence department in Agra, cites January 1858 as the date when the mail and local papers were re-established (17).

33. The reference above to the challenges of filling a "double sheet" implies that the editions published from the fort between July and October—missing in the archives—were likely truncated as well, only four pages long.

34. Translated by and qtd. in *Hurkaru*, 12 June 1857.

to control the media in 1857: the equipment of at least one publication, the *Delhi Gazette*, was impounded by rebels, who, the *Hurkaru* reported, "made use of some of the presses to print their proclamations and other important documents."[35] In sum, while metropolitan newspapers were cut off from the scenes of action, mofussil newspapers were blockaded, isolated, or repurposed. In 1857, as the means of circulation became increasingly constrained, newspapers in India faced a crisis of access to copy.

Editors found alternative sources for copy in unexpected places. They increasingly carried reports by individuals who were not the papers' customary correspondents. Whereas earlier, newspapers had published reports from a select number of (unnamed) correspondents, now the correspondents they published rose dramatically. Anxious to provide readers with news—and for copy to fill their columns—editors included series upon series of short items that begin, "We have received a communication from [place name] . . ." or "A letter from [name of a town] informs us . . ." or "The following is from a correspondent at . . ." or "A friend writes us as follows . . ." or "From the pen of an eye-witness . . ." Unable to count on their customary sources, whether other newspapers or trusted correspondents, editors turned to correspondents—literally, letter writers—for reports. Headnotes such as this one indicate that editors published letters from persons unknown: "The following narrative has been sent to us by a correspondent, who signs himself A SOLDIER OF ARRAH."[36] Just as often, letters written to a friend or relative and consigned to the *dâk* made their circuitous way into the hands of an editor, where they were treated unquestionably as a source of information.[37]

---

35. *Hurkaru*, 25 November 1857. After its presses in Delhi were seized and its editor S. G. T. Heatley killed, the *Delhi Gazette* published from its Agra offices (*Hurkaru*, 25 May 1857). When Agra's Europeans retreated into the fort, both Gibbons of the *Mofussilite* and the *Gazette*'s Agra printer brought their presses into the fort and put out newspapers (*Hurkaru*, 19 August and 8 September 1857). For the fate of the *Delhi Gazette*, see Dalrymple.

36. *Hurkaru*, 13 October 1857.

37. A message of this nature spread word of the Meerut mutiny beyond the city. On the evening of Sunday, 10 May, an English woman in Meerut telegraphed her aunt in Agra suggesting that she postpone her planned trip to Meerut due to disturbances in the barracks. The aunt carried the telegraph to the offices of the *Mofussilite*, which published the notice and conveyed word to the lieutenant governor, John Colvin, stationed in Agra. Shortly after the telegraph was sent, rebels cut the wires. See *Mofussilite*, 2 February 1858.

A striking number of these unsolicited letters were not shunted to the Letters—or, as they were termed, "Correspondence"—columns, but made their way into the letterpress section of the newspaper, appearing under the sign of the newspaper's editorial stamp. In incorporating letters that contained an eyewitness or orally transmitted account and elevating them to reports, newspapers broke with their past practice and promoted private correspondents—i.e., letter writers—into correspondents or reporters. This expansion in the number of sources is the print parallel of the revolving door of editors discussed earlier.

Reading the *Mofussilite* and *Hurkaru*, it is evident that their editors were improvising. In publishing the private letters of so many individuals, Anglo-Indian editors inadvertently remade their newspapers into something resembling the Mughal court's *akhbarat*, or newsletter, scribal reports that preceded print media in the subcontinent and that Christopher Bayly describes as focused on affective rather than institutional knowledge (144, 337). (The analogy is inexact and partial as the *akhbarats'* news writers were court-sponsored, whereas these writers were not officially assigned roles by anyone; the scribal and affective is the analogue.) Moreover, because the sources were so various and ad hoc—whatever mail slipped past the warring sides or streams of displaced soldiers and made it to an editor's desk—they offer a striking contrast to the editorial curbs that had prevailed prior to the Uprising. Counterintuitively, the blockage of roads and circulating newsprint led to an amplification of types of sources and voices.

Publishing items from so many correspondents was a boon—it filled copy and provided anxious readers information about relatives and friends—but also carried perils. As the tumult of the Uprising abated, editors attempted to rein in writers they had relied on a few months previously. On 31 October 1857, the *Dacca News* carried a lengthy piece entitled "A Few Words to Our Correspondents." The *Hurkaru* approvingly reprinted the entire notice, which asked correspondents "always to authenticate their letters."[38] This, the *Dacca News* clarified, meant "confiding to us his name." Even with such "authentication," the notice confessed that the best correspondents are those "who are intimately acquainted with us."[39] Similarly, almost a year after the disturbances started, with the country

---

38. *Hurkaru*, 4 November 1857.

39. In early August 1857, the *Dacca News* had been warned for violating the press restrictions imposed on print media; this notice to correspondents follows the threat that their license could be revoked.

returning to business, the *Mofussilite* warned a correspondent: "'FELIX' should authenticate his communications, and make a more definite charge. We cannot allow anonymous correspondents to insinuate away any gentleman's character."[40] What had been a necessity a few months prior had now become a burden. The *Mofussilite* even went so far as to counsel a rival newspaper to require correspondents to send in their letters "written on stamped paper and an affidavit of the truth of their contents be sworn to before a Magistrate."[41] A year after the Uprising began, the expediency of relying on individuals as reporters ended. Its demise brought to a close the profusion of voices that animated Anglo-Indian newspapers and a return to a more cohesive editorial stance.

If material impediments to circulation forced editors to improvise and led to a plethora of voices, the effects of these numerous sources—and editorial efforts to restrain them and regain control—on Anglo-Indian newspapers' coverage of the Uprising are striking. In the letterpress section of each newspaper, the number of both short reports and leaders rose dramatically, and these often came from diametrically different pens. In the leaders themselves and in the relation among leaders, letters, and correspondents' reports, multiplicity and chaos reigned. In the previous chapter, we saw editors stepping into the rupture created by the Jyoti Prasad case and offering what Dallas Liddle calls the "long, authoritative" opinion essay (7), with ready-made opinions for readers. In 1857, the opposite occurred: not only did leaders fail to offer ready-made views for consumption and dissemination; they offered a product with little consistency or clarity. These leaders served as neither the "Voice of Public Opinion" nor the "press as public instructor" (Liddle 12). The crisis of this moment produced print chaos.

In early February, a *Bengal Hurkaru* commentary took a stern stance on the growing disturbances in the army. Upon learning of the "disaffection" among sepoys at Barrackpur, the paper dismissed the stated cause—the grease used in the new cartridges of Enfield rifles—as "mere pretense" and urged the government to "put its heel upon the neck of the embryo mutiny and crush it in the womb."[42] Throughout the spring, the paper maintained this implacable stance: on 16 March—by which point

---

40. *Mofussilite*, 4 May 1858.

41. *Mofussilite*, 12 March 1858.

42. *Hurkaru*, 9 February 1857.

the 19th N. I. at Berhampur had mutinied and the 34th in Barrackpur was rumbling—the *Hurkaru* insisted that any leniency would be "mistaken."[43] Eight days later, it reprimanded the government for its "policy of concessions," and again called for a "strong hand" and "severity" in dealing with the *sipahi*'s "contempt for the authority of their officers."[44] By April, the newspaper was expressing these views in its Overland Summary, a fortnightly compilation of news and views for British subscribers. Noting that the *Friend of India* "suggests cannon instead of 'compliance' as a check upon mutiny," the *Hurkaru* declared, "The *Friend of India* is right."[45] The *Hurkaru*'s leader dilated that cannon is the only response to a "hostile race" and asserted that "an example or two will have to be made" before it is time for "humanity and enlightenment." The *Hurkaru*—a liberal organ in the 1820s, favorite of Young Bengals, and owned by Dwarkanath Tagore from 1834 to 1846—adopted a strong disciplinary stance and rejected explanations of low pay and cartridges as "merely pretences."[46]

But the paper also aired a number of contrary views, consigned though they were to the letters section. In April, before the mutinies had evolved into a broader rebellion, two military men offered analyses. The first stated that sepoys are "shamefully neglected by their European officers" who are "bigots" and that the annexation of "Oude" (Awadh) was a "blunder."[47] In time, sepoy–officer relations and Awadh became frequently cited explanations for the discontent, but this letter marks one of the early expression of those views. The second letter, signed "military correspondent," noted that the cartridges were merely a "straw," but the deployment of *sipahis* to Burma, Canton, and Bushire, where they were far from home and sent for longer than promised, was a genuine grievance. The writer concluded that "[t]he real cause . . . [is] a feeling [that] has been gradually spreading throughout the Native Army that they can no longer

---

43. *Hurkaru*, 16 March 1857.
44. *Hurkaru*, 24 March 1857.
45. *Hurkaru Overland Summary*, 8 April 1857. The *Hurkaru*'s reference to the *Friend* was almost certainly strategic: the *Friend* not only had the largest circulation among Indian newspapers, but was also, largely due to Marshman's stature, respected in Britain and well regarded by Bengal's young elite (see Chanda, *History* [1987] 50).
46. *Hurkaru*, 17 April 1857.
47. *Hurkaru*, 6 April 1857.

trust the promises of Government."⁴⁸ Neither writer suggested cannon or crushing and both sought causes. The historian Salahuddin Malik has argued that narratives of sepoy grievances were deployed by those who wished to diminish the civilian element of the insurgency.⁴⁹ Like much of the historiography, Malik's argument is derived from and describing "British public reactions"—the subtitle of his book—not Anglo-Indian views or prints. In India, in April 1857, and in the context of the *Hurkaru*'s belligerent editorial stance, these writers' attention to structural over racial factors is salient. It alerts us to the tensions between leaders and letters—or editors and readers—a tension that served to open a space for conflicting views for a brief moment in 1857.

In contrast to the *Hurkaru*, the *Mofussilite* hardly registered the growing turmoil in the military units, and when it eventually did, its commentary was haphazard. Its reports on the Berhampur and Barrackpur mutinies were drawn from the *Hurkaru* (whose editor from 10 March was Blanchard, the *Mofussilite*'s recently departed editor). Surprisingly, despite the *Mofussilite*'s location in Agra, which had a sizeable cantonment, and its possible military editor (Major Thomas), it offered no independent commentary on these reports. Not until early April—two months after the *Hurkaru* had taken notice of the "disaffection" and offered its "heel upon the neck" response—did the *Mofussilite* take note of the mutinies. Its first leader on the subject declared that because "Hindoo sepoys have too much love of money," and "Moohummadans . . . [are] a body of disappointed zealots," the two "can never make common cause for any length of time, or to any vast extent."⁵⁰ The next week, the *Mofussilite* reprinted an article from the 6 May edition of the Lucknow-based *Central Star* on the disbanding of the 7th Oude Irregular Infantry. It reported that "many [sepoys] displayed that loyalty and gallantry, which, it is a libel to say the sepoy does not possess to a certain degree, rallying round the officers and protecting them with drawn swords against the fury of the more violent."⁵¹ Avaricious Hindus, Muslim zealots, loyal sepoys all appear in the

---

48. *Hurkaru*, 18 April 1857.

49. See Malik ("Popular" 26–30) and Malik (*1857* 16–60).

50. *Mofussilite*, 3 April 1857.

51. *Mofussilite*, 12 May 1857. The *Central Star* does not appear to have been particularly consistent; in the *Hurkaru*'s words, the *Star* "earnestly hopes that the next overt act of mutiny may be marked by the prompt discharge of a few rounds of grape

same paper within the span of a week and mark the poles of the playing field *sipahis* were judged on: racist slurs and loyalty. This small example captures the unevenness of coverage, which intensified as sources shrank and editors leaned on irregular correspondents.

Until mid-May, the *Mofussilite* devoted the bulk of its space, not to the mutinies, but to a debate it incited that caused a mutiny of sorts among Anglo-Indian newspapers. On 17 March 1857, the *Mofussilite* proposed that the "native press"—both vernacular and English-language—be censored because it incited sepoys and civilians and for its "wanton attacks on our policy, and our Government."[52] It is worth underscoring that this opinion appeared as a leader in the *Mofussilite*, "John Lang's paper." With the exception of the *Hurkaru*, the majority of the Anglo-Indian press—the *Bombay Gazette*, the *Englishman*, the *Bombay Times*, the *Friend of India*—objected, and a furious controversy erupted that consumed the *Mofussilite* for six weeks.[53] In response to objections, the *Mofussilite* clarified that it was not proposing to shut down or suppress the Indian press, only "confining the range of newspapers to social and educational subjects."[54] It continued that treating the Indian and Anglo-Indian presses differently is not "unfair" as a free press requires "truth, self-reliance, and patriotism . . . qualities in which the anglo-saxon [sic] race is pre-eminent, and in which the Hindoo races are especially deficient." "In India," the *Mofussilite* concluded, "a Free Press is an exotic on extremely unfavorable soil."[55] As with its editorial on covetous Hindus and zealous Muslims, this one is saturated in racist discourse.

The *Friend of India*—mirroring the Rev. James Long's view on a free press—objected that "no suppression could remove discontent" and that

---

and canister among the mutineers, and *no questions asked*" (*Hurkaru*, 15 May 1857; emphasis in original).

52. *Mofussilite*, 10 April 1857.

53. The *Mofussilite* offered an overview of its rivals' support and objections on 25 June 1858. For "live" commentary on the controversy, see the *Mofussilite*, 17, 27, 31 March; 3, 10, 17, 21 April; and 1 May 1857. Only the *Hurkaru* supported the *Mofussilite*'s position, declaring that the vernacular press "is notoriously opposed to Government," takes every opportunity to "speak disparagingly of its acts," and spreads "malignant lies . . . among an ignorant people"; it concluded that this press "should be suppressed at once" (*Hurkaru*, 4 April 1857).

54. *Mofussilite*, 17 April 1857.

55. See also: "a free Press [is] not appreciated by the Natives" (*Mofussilite*, 10 April 1857).

"it is wiser to keep the cork out of the bottle, to let the mixture effervesce without exploding."[56] Sidestepping the *Friend*'s suggestion about managing dissent, the *Mofussilite* doggedly reiterated that "[t]he Natives and the British public are as different as their colours." Protecting its flank, it added, "The articles of the *Englishman*, however anti-governmental, are always patriotic."[57] If loyalty was demanded of Indian subjects, patriotism was the self-regulating test Anglo-Indian newspapers imposed on one another. Consequently, establishing patriotism was of the utmost urgency. The *Bombay Telegraph*, conceding that "now and then journalists may have been momentarily misled by their correspondents," insisted too that "the European press has exhibited nought but the purest patriotism."[58] The distinction between "patriotism"—a quality these writers claimed was innate to Britons—and "loyalty," which they demanded of Indians, was the linchpin upon which the Anglo-Indian press sought to preserve its freedom from constraint. The contrast to 1851, when almost all the Anglo-Indian press flexed its fourth-estate muscle as it pummeled the Company, could not be starker. In 1851, the fortunes and future of the Company was at stake; at this stage in 1857, Anglo-Indian newspapers saw another future—and freedom—at stake: their own.

For the freedom of the press was under attack. As the mutinies spread and took on the flavor of a broader uprising, the Government of India passed Act XV on 13 June 1857. The act required all printing presses to obtain a license which could be revoked if papers published material that "excite[d] disaffection or unlawful resistance to [Government] orders," created "alarm or suspicion among the Native population," or "weaken[ed] the friendship . . . of Native Princes, Chiefs or States" towards the Government.[59] The Anglo-Indian press dubbed Act XV the "Gagging Act" and militated against its censorship. Government allies responded that the act did not censor material prior to publication, it merely threatened revocation of license should a paper publish something the government deemed inflammatory. As the *Bombay Gazette* of 25 June pointedly retorted, "censorship is a direct check on the publication of objectionable matter;

---

56. *Friend of India*, 9 April 1857.

57. *Mofussilite*, 21 April 1857. Recall that in 1851 the *Mofussilite* was unabashedly "anti-government," while the *Englishman* avoided critiquing the government too explicitly in the Jyoti Prasad case.

58. Qtd. in *Bengal Hurkaru*, 8 July 1857.

59. See United Kingdom, House of Commons ("Papers" 37–38).

the license revocable at will is an indirect one."[60] Crucially, in contrast to the *Mofussilite*'s suggestions in March and April, the Press Act treated the Indian and Anglo-Indian press equally and imposed the constraint on both, much to the latter's outrage and chagrin.

On first learning of the act, the *Hurkaru* registered a "SOLEMN PROTEST against such an insidious attempt to choke public opinion."[61] Drawing on the language of patriotism that the *Mofussilite* had deployed just weeks earlier, the *Hurkaru* acknowledged "we have been compelled occasionally to comment severely but not unjustly on . . . instances of official ignorance or want of energy," but insisted that "we have done our best *to support the Government through the present crisis*."[62] Claiming to have resisted publishing "one tithe of the information given to us relating to the murders, massacres and abominations which have been perpetrated, or . . . one-half the instances of official blundering," they echo the *Mofussilite*'s call to suppress the Indian press but leave "English journals" alone. Hardly a day passed when the *Hurkaru* did not renew its attacks on the Press Act, one day claiming that in the early days it had "created a public feeling in favour of Lord Canning, which we are sorry to say his Lordship valued so little";[63] another day excerpting critiques of the act from journals such as the *Examiner* or *Singapore Free Press*;[64] and yet another informing readers that it is "casting lots of admirable articles into the waste paper basket, as being too dangerous to appear in print."[65]

In the early days of the act's proclamation, Anglo-Indian newspapers wondered whether the legislation had been prompted by the Indian or Anglo-Indian press. Much finger pointing ensued, and on multiple occasions, the *Hurkaru* defended itself from the charge that the act was prompted by its publication of what was referred to as the Rebel or Delhi Proclamation.[66] On 13 June, under the title "A Seditious Proclamation," the *Hurkaru* had published a letter to the editor from "H." that directed attention to the insurgents' proclamation which had appeared in two vernacular-language newspapers, the *Doorbeen* (or *Durbin*) and

---

60. Qtd. in *Bengal Hurkaru*, 6 July 1857.
61. *Hurkaru*, 15 June 1857; caps in original.
62. *Hurkaru*, 15 June 1857; emphasis in original.
63. *Hurkaru*, 27 June 1857.
64. *Hurkaru*, 13 July and 20 August (Supplemental Sheet) 1857, respectively.
65. *Hurkaru*, 17 July 1857.
66. *Hurkaru*, 1 July 1857.

the *Sultan-ul-Akbari*. H. includes a translation of the proclamation "in order that the Government and the European public may be apprised of the existence of such a document, and of the mode adopted in giving it publicity."[67] The *Englishman*, one of the *Hurkaru*'s oldest rivals, appears to have led the charge that the *Hurkaru*'s publication of this document prompted the government to impose press restrictions; but as the *Hurkaru* repeatedly pointed out, its publication of the Rebel Proclamation could hardly have prompted the government to impose press restrictions as the proclamation appeared in its pages on 13 June, the very day the Legislative Council passed the act.[68] As the proclamation had first appeared in two Indian newspapers, the *Hurkaru* repeated that it was these papers—and by extension the Indian press—not the Anglo-Indian press that ought to be gagged. For our purposes, the significance of the debate about the original provocation lies in the detail that "dangerous" material appeared in the *Hurkaru*'s letters, not letterpress, section. Whether the *Hurkaru* moved it there for deniability and "H." stands for its own name can only remain speculative.

Historians have argued that the government's primary concern was the indigenous press. Chandrika Kaul references a letter in which Canning wrote that the "Native Press" does much "mischief . . . amongst the ignorant and childish, but excitable, Sepoys and the fanatical Mahomeddans of every class" (" 'You' " 25). But the government was equally uneasy about the Anglo-Indian press because it believed that material from this press could, in the hands of "mischievous" Indians, become a dangerous instrument. In the same letter, Canning continued, "As to the English press it has no claim to exemption . . . [T]he Articles of the English newspapers are translated into Native Languages and are read by all" (C. Kaul, " 'You' " 26). Canning did not share such views in private correspondence only; the *Madras Athenaeum* cited him in a speech: "I have seen articles appear from time to time, which, however innocuous to European readers, might prove very injurious when dressed up for the native ear by designing per-

---

67. *Hurkaru*, 13 June 1857.

68. See *Hurkaru*, 1 and 3 July, 5 November 1857; the *Hurkaru*'s direct responses to the *Englishman*'s charges appear on 3 and 8 July. Act XV was passed on 13 June, but the document spelling out the conditions under which a license could be revoked was not published until 18 June (see "Resolution, Home Department, 18 June 1857" in United Kingdom, House of Commons ["Papers" 37–38]).

sons."[69] Canning shared the *Mofussilite*'s and *Hurkaru*'s view of Indians as intellectually inferior ("childish, but excitable"), but drew from that racist view a different policy conclusion: all outlets, Indian or Anglo-Indian, English or vernacular-language, would be embargoed.

While Canning's remarks indicate that he was concerned about misappropriation by "designing persons," the clause in Act XV against creating "alarm or suspicion among the Native population" suggests that the government viewed Anglo-Indian press copy as provocation and damaging on its own merits as well. The government's enforcement of the act confirms this. The first charges under the act were brought against three indigenous newspapers, the *Doorbeen*, *Sultan-ul-Akbari*, and *Samachar Sudhabarsan*, for publishing "seditious libel."[70] But shortly thereafter, to the surprise of many, the government "warned" the respected *Friend of India* for its leader "The Centenary of Plassey." An analysis of this editorial provides insight into the nature of the government's thinking. The leader contrasts the early period of British rule—from the Battle of Plassey (or Palashi) in 1757, when the Company gained the right to collect Bengal's *diwani*, or revenue, and became the ascendant player on the subcontinent—with the present. India was won, the editorial states, by the "greediness of traders" who "made and broke treaties, planned and fought battles for the mere love of gain"; wealth was their "deity" and they cared nothing for the "welfare of Asiatic souls, or the social interests of the great body of Englishmen."[71] Today, by contrast, "[w]e have swept away all the obstacles . . . We spread out before the dormant Asiatic soul, all the mental treasures of the West, and feel only too happy in being allowed to distribute them."

Notwithstanding the self-extolling, evangelical ethnocentrism, this is hardly the stuff to attract the censor's ax. What made the *Friend*'s "Centenary of Plassey" objectionable? Its final paragraph:

> [W]eigh the broken pledges, the ruined families, the impoverished ryots, the imperfect justice, against the missionary and

---

69. Qtd. in *Hurkaru*, 13 July 1857.

70. See Chakraborti (128). For the government's account and English translation of text that appeared in the Urdu-language *Doorbeen* on 8 June, the *Sultan-ul-Akbari* on 10 June, and the Bengali-language *Samachar Sudhabarsan* on 10 June, see United Kingdom, House of Commons ("Papers" 34–36).

71. *Friend of India*, 25 June 1857.

the schoolmaster, the railway and the steam engine, the abolition of Suttee, and the destruction of the Thugs and declare in which scale the balance lies!

The soaring language of the civilizing mission was unexceptional for its time—but the reference to missionaries was playing with fire. That fire exploded in the final sentence which sealed the leader's fate: "The first centenary of Plassey was ushered in by the revolt of the native army, the second may be celebrated in Bengal by a respected Government, and a Christian population." The reference to "a Christian population" was the rub.

Many Anglo-Indian newspapers had reported—and some dismissed—concerns among Indians about the Christianization of India. As early as March 1857, the *Hurkaru* had noted "an extravagant idea which is said to be taking possession of the minds of the natives . . . that Lord Canning came to India to convert the native population to Christianity . . . in three years."[72] By the end of the month when the Barrackpur regiment mutinied, the *Hurkaru* was less dismissive and reported that the commander of the regiment was a "Christian Officer of proselyting [sic] propensities."[73] The "Centenary of Plassey's" celebration of the Christianization of India would have confirmed the fears of Indians and provoked, in the language of the act, "alarm or suspicion among the Native population." The *Hurkaru* protested that it could not see how the editorial violated the Press Act.[74] Its defense underscores that the Christianizing vision the *Friend* espoused was invisible: by 1857, even a non-missionary, once-liberal journal like the *Hurkaru* had assimilated the evangelical rhetoric of Britain's imperial mission. The missionary had become the hegemon, the evangelical mission secularized into the civilizing mission.

The government did not revoke the *Friend*'s license, but merely warned the newspaper. The editor of the *Friend*—and author of the "Centenary

---

72. *Hurkaru*, 16 March 1857.

73. *Hurkaru*, Overland Summary of News, 8 April 1857. The commander was S. G. Wheeler (not to be confused with Hugh Wheeler, commander at Kanpur, and reputed to be much loved by those who served under him; see Taylor 345).

74. The *Hurkaru*, which spent much of the first part of 1857 carping with and attacking the *Friend*, now came to its defense: "We have carefully perused the article in question and cannot see that it violates any one of the conditions upon which licenses are to be granted to the Press. The Government, however, is of opinion that it violates all of the conditions" (2 July 1857).

of Plassey"—was Henry Mead. On 2 July, in a spirited rejoinder, Mead not only published the government's warning letter, but also defended his essay.[75] In his rejoinder, Mead refused to recant his fantasy, "the pleasing vision that in 1957, a Christian people may live happily under a respected Government," and insisted that he was only expressing that which was "in the interest of England," whereas "high officials" cared only for their own reputations. Rehashing the parsing of anti-government versus patriotic the *Mofussilite* had deployed just months earlier, Mead equated an anti-government stance with a pro-imperial one. The imperial nation lay on one side with true patriots, the Company on the other. The *Friend* survived—with Meredith Townsend reinstated as editor[76]—but the *Hurkaru* soon came under the chopping block. On 18 September 1857, the *Hurkaru*'s license was revoked and the paper went dark for five days. When it returned on 24 September, the *Hurkaru* was without Blanchard in the editor's seat (Sanial, "History" [IV] 202).[77]

The direct cause of the *Hurkaru*'s revocation is unclear. The historian Deep Choudhury identifies letters by a "Militaire" as the provocation (78), while Chanda also fingers a letter that called the government's policy towards rebels "cowardly imbecility."[78] Militaire's letters—one was titled

---

75. According to the government's warning, Canning objected to the final paragraphs of the leader for inciting "disaffection" against the government, spreading alarm among Hindus and Muslims about their religion, and undermining relations with independent princes (*Friend of India*, 2 July 1857, 626).

76. In response to Mead's second leader, Canning ordered the *Friend*'s license revoked; only the intervention of Marshman's agents and Mead's agreeing to vacate the editorial chair prevented the paper from going under (see *Friend of India*, 9 July 1857, 653 and Chanda, *History* [2008] 258–59).

77. The newspaper did not refer to its absence in its daily editions, but the leading article in its Overland edition—which the governor general of India had no jurisdiction over—noted indignantly, "It is a curious fact that the two papers which . . . were always supposed to represent more or less the views and wishes of the Government, the *Friend of India* and the *Hurkaru*, have been the first to feel the iron heel of despotic and irresponsible authority" (*Hurkaru*, Overland Summary of News, 24 September 1857). The *Hurkaru*'s tussles with the government were not over: in October, it received a warning for publishing material from the London-based *Press* (see *Hurkaru*, Overland Summary of News, 22 October 1857).

78. Chanda writes that following the 5 September letter, the *Hurkaru* was warned; it defied the warning and published another objectionable letter and an editorial on 14 and 15 September, leading to the cancellation (*History* [2008] 247).

"How to Crush the Rebellion"[79]—are noxious in tone and substance but not exceptional; leaders and commentaries calling for "instantaneous retribution" or to "exterminate the mutineers" had, as we have seen, appeared in the *Hurkaru*'s pages in the spring of 1857, so advocating harsh measures against rebels was clearly not reason enough to cross the censor.[80] Neither was abusing the government—almost every Anglo-Indian newspaper did it, though in increasingly muted tones. While the immediate cause of revocation is unknown, that it possibly lay in letters that appeared in the pages of newspapers suggests that editors may have been using this section for charged material—and for deniability.

Letters were by no means the only location for belligerent views—on the contrary, bellicose comments appear in the leaders of the *Hurkaru* and *Mofussilite* as well. But these were interspersed with commentaries that were more measured and also divergent in their views. The experience of reading each paper end to end and serially is to encounter inconsistency and chaos over stability or coherence. (The *Friend*, a weekly consisting entirely of editorial content, absorbed and managed its sources more seamlessly and maintained a more consistent editorial stance.) The swift and frequent editorial turnover accounts for some of the inconsistencies and uneven tenor. (Recall that in this period, the *Mofussilite* was edited by Blanchard, then possibly Thomas and speculatively Gibbons, and then Blanchard again; the *Hurkaru* was led by Patterson Saunders, then Blanchard, then E. P. Moore, then Saunders again.) The inclusion of an array of correspondents also plays a role in the inconsistency. And finally, the Gagging Act and newspapers' self-censorship after government warnings or suspensions surely accounts for some of the lack of consistency we encounter in Anglo-Indian newspapers of 1857.

A few examples will convey the contradictory views appearing in these newspapers. A week after the mutiny at Meerut extended into the countryside and to Delhi, a leading article in the *Hurkaru* declared, "the severest and most prompt measures ought now to be adopted, . . . the resolute extermination of the mutineers on the spot."[81] Less than a week

---

79. *Hurkaru*, Overland Summary of News, 9 September 1857.

80. *Hurkaru*, 21 April and 19 May 1857. Nor was the *Hurkaru* alone: on 29 December 1857, the *Delhi Gazette* wrote that "the paramount duty of the British Government is now retribution—a duty to the dead and living." (qtd. in Streets 43).

81. *Hurkaru*, 19 May 1857.

later, however, the *Hurkaru* chastised the *Friend* for its "exterminating theory," which it considered "mischievous"; evidently forgetting its own call for extermination, the *Hurkaru* insisted "there is still good material in the Bengal Army."[82] Such about-faces could be the outcome of a rapidly shifting political landscape. But the series of letters that appeared in the *Hurkaru* over the next three days underscore both that a species of confusion reigned and that the newspaper was willing to publish virtually any copy, regardless of whether or not it subscribed to the newspaper's (uncertain) editorial position. First, it reprinted a leader from the *Bombay Times* that included a letter from Olim Soriua who asked those who dismissed Muslim's or Hindu's reactions to pig or cow to consider how they would feel "if you were made to dance at a Ball on a Sunday evening?"[83] The following day, the *Hurkaru* printed two letters, both signed only "X": one dismissed the cartridges, calling them a *bahana*, or excuse, and defended "Wheler" by arguing that his tracts were not forced on sepoys but "optional." This X joined the chorus urging the government to "quell the mutiny, to crush it with a strong hand" because "a barbarous people . . . with true animal propensity have turned on the hand stretched to feed them."[84] The next X wrote that a young officer, instead of "being required to devote [his] first two or three years to the study of the language and character of the people he has to deal with, spends his time in *ennui* and ridiculing everything native."[85] Claiming that "officers are highly responsible for having such a state of feeling smouldering in their regiments," the writer proposed that "young Cadets [be] sent back to their mothers to learn civility and proper treatment of natives." Both writers speak from within an ethnological perspective of the distinct national and native characteristics of peoples to arrive at differing explanations for the rebellions. Both are given airtime in the *Hurkaru*.

The next day brought a letter by "Aliquis" who offered that it was not the fear of conversion to Christianity that perturbed sepoys, but concerns about the diminution of their pay and pension.[86] The letter offers details on the situation of sepoys, and the editor of the *Hurkaru*, again display-

---

82. *Hurkaru*, 25 May 1857.
83. *Hurkaru*, 26 May 1857.
84. *Hurkaru*, 27 May 1857.
85. *Hurkaru*, 27 May 1857.
86. *Hurkaru*, 28 May 1857.

ing editorial uncertainty, promptly adopted this position. A leader in the same number mocked the *Friend of India* for believing that cartridges were the cause and argued that the shrinking value of sepoys' monthly salary of Rs. 7 was the true grievance. The following day brought a letter by a "Hooghley," who, in particularly aggressive prose, needled "the native gentlemen of Calcutta" for their "want of manly courage."[87] Declaring that "the Briton can never look upon the Hindoo as an equal," Hooghley explained that while "the Briton has almost a veneration for women," "Hindoo gentlemen" have not emancipated or educated their daughters. Letters to the editor can constitute a section of divergent opinions, but also, as we saw in chapter 1, a space editors exercised some control over. The range of opinions on display here suggests editorial abandon. And it indicates that the *Hurkaru*'s readers represented a wide range of Anglo-Indians, some more analytic than the newspaper's editors, others blustering, yet others blatantly racist.

In the *Mofussilite*, variations and fluctuations were generally expressed in leaders that were strikingly inconsistent. On 30 October 1857, shortly after Colonel Greathed's relief of Agra, the *Mofussilite* published a leading piece in which it boasted that "[e]xecutions are almost every-day occurrences here . . . We make very short work of it. A fellow is caught in the morning, tried at noon, and hanged at sunset."[88] One trial, the paper approvingly reported, "occupied nearly three minutes and a quarter," during which time an official was fastening a rope to the tree over the prisoner's head, thus efficiently accomplishing "speedy justice." The leader's ugly tone and approval of such "trials" is at odds with the many stories that appeared in the pages of the *Mofussilite* about Indians assisting Europeans, including the Greatheds at Meerut.[89] In fact, if there is one consistent thread in items that appeared in the *Mofussilite*'s pages since the start of the disturbances, it is of the many Indians who rescued or aided Europeans and British forces, many at some cost to their own safety. The ferocious editorial about swift executions of suspected insur-

---

87. *Hurkaru*, 29 May 1857.

88. *Mofussilite*, 30 October 1857.

89. The rescue of the family of Harvey Greathed—erroneously identified as the brother of Col. Edward Greathed, who relieved Agra—by their servants appears in the *Mofussilite*, 15 May 1857. Other reports of Indians, including Man Singh, rescuing or aiding individuals or British forces appear on 29 May, 19 June, 30 October 1857, and 12 and 16 February 1858.

gents appears in the same newspaper; it is almost as if newspapers are not reading themselves.

Just ten days following the boastful "speedy justice" report, the newspaper ran two back-to-back leaders. The first is a defense of Canning, who was under attack by Anglo-Indians for his putative leniency towards sepoys. The governor general's calls for a more measured response to insurgents, along with his policy applying press restrictions on both Anglo-Indian and Indian presses, had earned him the nickname "Clemency Canning."[90] In contrast to its Calcutta contemporaries, the *Mofussilite*'s leader countered that "severity not leniency has ever been the characteristic of a weak and inefficient Governor."[91] Arguing that "indiscriminate plunder and burning of villages and hanging of villagers [has] done us and our cause no little harm," the leader declared that "a tendency to forgive is rather an indication of strength than the reverse." The passage of ten days can hardly explain the discrepancy between the approving report on daily executions and this rejection of wholesale violence and retribution. The writer of this leader reads as manifestly different from the one who wrote the earlier one, suggesting that editorial control or consistency had become a fantasy.

Following this commentary on discretion in punishments and separated from it by only a French dash is another that could not be more different. The second leader reports that the Aborigines Protection Society has written the Board of Control, the parliamentary body appointed to oversee the Company's court of directors, appealing for mercy towards rebels who are "A Man and a Brother." The editorial vehemently denies that Hindus and Muslims "who slaughtered tender women and innocent children" have "any of the humanizing instincts of man's nature"; they are "no more men than is the Ooorang-ootang."[92] It continues, "There is nothing else in common between us, excepting that both are endowed with reasoning faculties, which only render the savage cruelty of the loathsome Sepoy still more hideous and dangerous to mankind than that of the ordinary beast of prey, and renders it our more imperative duty to

---

90. This alliterative sobriquet was abandoned in the course of the year in favor of a more racially ugly one: on 11 November 1857, the *Bombay Times* spoke of the government as a "Pandy administration," a reference to Mangal Pande of the Barrackpur unit (qtd. in *Hurkaru*, 1 December 1857).

91. *Mofussilite*, 10 November 1857.

92. *Mofussilite*, 10 November 1857.

exterminate him from off the face of the earth." Having worked himself up into a passionate frenzy, the writer angrily asks the society not to "interfere between us and our just revenge." The forgiveness extolled in the leader just above is absent here. The writers of these leaders—celebrating daily executions, preventing burning and hanging, and demanding revenge—all find a home in the columns of the *Mofussilite*.

Not three months later—by which point much of the rebellion had been crushed and towns retaken—the *Mofussilite* took yet another tack: it reprinted a small excerpt from the *Atlas for India*, a bimonthly steamship journal, reporting that sepoys had cut off the tongue of a young woman, the daughter of a clergyman. The excerpt was prefaced by the *Mofussilite*'s withering comment that "[i]t bears the stamp of falsehood . . . for if Sepoys had cut out the lady's tongue, they would have cut off her head too! Why will people invent such fictions[?]"[93] And in mid-March, the *Mofussilite* ran a lengthy leader that expressed views that had thus far only appeared in traces in the occasional letter to the editor. The commentary begins with the assertive declaration that "the natives of India were happier, not merely under their good princes, but happier under the average of their native sovereigns, than they have been under our rule."[94] About India's erstwhile rulers, the Mughals, whom the British consistently presented as corrupt and ineffectual, the leader stated,

> The Mahomedan conquerors of India had settled in the country and identified themselves with the interests and sympathies of its inhabitants—they respected the customs and the private landed property of the people; they preserved the municipal institutions and arbitration system—they never burdened the country with a nation debt—they spent large sums on public works—they did not destroy the native aristocracy whose capital was the support of the labourers, manufactures, and merchants of India—finally they did not treat the people as an inferior race of beings, but on the contrary they maintained free social intercourse with them—in short, they did not by dividing the community into two distinct bodies of privileged foreigners and native serfs, systematically degrade a whole nation.[95]

---

93. *Mofussilite*, 2 February 1858.
94. *Mofussilite*, 19 March 1858.
95. *Mofussilite*, 19 March 1858.

The English in India, by contrast, are "foreigners, constantly shifting their quarters, having no permanent connexion, always looking forward to the day when they shall return to England with a fortune."

The commentary presents a laundry list of Britain's faults in India. It has "made the world believe our wars to have been defensive"; obtained territory, "not by conquest, but by cessions extorted from our unfortunate allies"; confiscated the estates of the landed aristocracy; introduced revenues and transit duties; destroyed municipal institutions; "set up an exotic English law, which has . . . deprived the people of security, besides corrupting their morals"; "levied taxation on the people and drained off one-seventh of their nett [sic] revenue to England at the same time burdening them with a nation debt"; introduced no public works or education; destroyed their aristocracy who were patrons of the arts and promoted agricultural improvements; threatened princes with absorption which made them reluctant to introduce improvements; and "have regarded the natives as vassals and servants, more than as the ancient owners and masters of the country." For those who wonder why Indians have preferred to live under "effete native governments," the writer responds that under them Indians "did not feel themselves degraded for it is not the arbitrary power of a national sovereign, but subjugation to a foreign one that extinguishes national spirit."[96]

This leader would not have been out of place in an anti-colonial newspaper and reads virtually like a historian's account of the ills of British colonialism in India. In its grasp both of the structural conditions and the social disruption the British wreaked in India, it echoes the historian Rudrangshu Mukherjee's argument that the etiology of the insurgency was not just material factors such as sepoys' pay or a new revenue system or the loss of livelihoods or zamindars' deflated prestige. The reason so many Indians with disparate interests came together and rebelled in 1857 was, Mukherjee writes, because "[t]he Raj assaulted the traditional view of social norms and obligations, the realms of mutual interdependence between the raja and the peasant that constituted its moral economy" ("Awadh" 230). The Uprising, Mukherjee argues, coalesced around concerns about the disintegration of social relations and a way of life.

My interest lies less in this fairly singular editorial per se, as in the inconsistent coverage that appeared in Anglo-Indian newspapers in the first year of the Uprising. The multiplicity of voices that appeared—or

---

96. *Mofussilite*, 19 March 1858.

slipped into—the columns of newspapers, taken as a whole, express almost every analysis of the causes of the rebellion that the historiography of 1857 in our own time has offered. An April 1857 letter in the *Hurkaru* identified the "real cause" of the mutinies as the "feeling [that] has been gradually spreading throughout the Native Army that they can no longer trust the promises of Government."[97] The government's reneged promises, particularly in regard to Awadh, were identified early on as a cause of the discontent. Though the *Hurkaru* initially dismissed this "thoroughly preposterous" idea, it shortly accepted the notion that the Company's policy of annexation was a cause of the uprisings, and in June it published a letter that argued that sepoys and their families had lost both income and prestige when the British annexed Awadh.[98] Numerous publications referred to the fractured relations between sepoys and officers, particularly the latter's lack of interest in or knowledge about soldiers; others wrote of the shrinking value of sepoys' pay and the disparity between the tasks of Indian soldiers and their European counterparts.[99] Yet others pointed to the crushing revenue structure that "has tended to destroy the landed aristocracy of this country" and deprived peasants of pasturage they had depended on.[100] Many wrote of the fear of conversion, and while some rushed to dismiss the concern as unfounded, most publications considered it seriously. Early on, an editorial in the *Mofussilite* argued that Indians were drawn to rebel "because they really thought their feelings of religion and honor injured by measures of Government"[101]; while another writer linked religion to modernity more broadly, observing that steamers and railways add to the fears of the sepoy that the "white man in going to bring in his religion."[102]

Broken promises, annexations, Awadh, religion, taxation, modernity: every standard historical account of 1857—from the Metcalfs to Wolpert—cites these as the array of causes that ignited discontent into

---

97. *Hurkaru*, 18 April 1857.

98. *Hurkaru*, 7 March 1857; the *Hurkaru* reprinted a 19 May editorial from the *Madras Athenaeum* that stated that the annexations were "a cruel breach of . . . fundamental principles of justice" (*Hurkaru*, 2 June 1857); *Hurkaru*, 9 June 1857.

99. *Hurkaru*, 28 May 1857, and 1 July 1857.

100. *Mofussilite*, 30 and 5 March 1858, respectively.

101. *Mofussilite*, 29 May 1857.

102. *Hurkaru*, 26 May 1857.

rebellion. Detailed studies might highlight one constellation of causes over others—Eric Stokes highlights revenue and sepoys' livelihoods, Rudrangshu Mukherjee focuses on cultural and social disruption—or elaborate on the manner in which dissatisfaction unfolded in a particular region (*viz.*, Tapti Roy, Iqtidar Alam Khan, and E. I. Brodkin). But the causes discussed by scholars today all appeared, albeit in attenuated form, in the pages of the *Bengal Hurkaru*, the *Mofussilite*, and to a lesser extent the *Friend of India*. These explanations were often embedded in an ethnological framework and surrounded by reports and leaders that can only be characterized as bloodthirsty. Yet, as I have endeavored to demonstrate, the explanations were neither isolated nor sporadic: they appear continually, often beside opposing views. Those expressing such views lack the anti-imperial framework of today's scholars, but they contain, if in embryonic form, the range of historical explanations available today (the *Hurkaru* even considered the Uprising a national movement at one point[103]).

Rebecca Merrit and Salahuddin Malik, in separate essays, refer to debates about the causes of the Uprising that appeared in British periodicals as political tussles, the "fissures between different interest groups" (Merrit 6). Their dismissal feels pat, unwilling to address in these "fissures" the "tensions of empire," its contingencies, or the "plurality of competing visions by which Europeans in the colonies fashioned their distinctions" (Stoler and Cooper 16). This chapter brings detailed attention to the archive of Anglo-Indian newspapers to illustrate that journals in 1857 were neither consistent nor stable. A leader about the "antagonism of race" and expressing the belief that "a large portion of the population have been always Rebels"[104] might appear in the same paper that only months previously condemned the "fanaticism of Colonel Wheeler."[105] Or a criticism of the government as "buttering the black and snubbing the Saxon"[106] appears only a few weeks after a leader that declared of the British in India that "[w]e have regarded the natives as vassals and servants, more than as the

---

103. In contrast to many accounts that sought to downplay the extent of discontent, this leader stated that "the Rebellion is a national one" (*Hurkaru*, 16 November 1857). It also referred to the events as "the great Indian Rebellion of 1857 and 1858" (*Hurkaru*, Overland Summary of News, 8 October 1858).

104. *Hurkaru*, 16 November 1857.

105. *Hurkaru*, 29 May 1857.

106. *Mofussilite*, 7 May 1858.

ancient owners and masters of the country."[107] Such commentaries—both analytic and belligerent—jockeyed for space with one another.

One explanation for the many contradictory strands weaving through the prints is that they reflect the uncertainty and ignorance of Anglo-Indians as they sought to grasp the enormity of the eruptions they were entirely unprepared for due to their isolation and oblivion about the discontent that flowed like a powerful river through the country. This is indisputable. The profusion and confusion in Anglo-Indian newspapers also tells another story, this one about the eruption onto the page of views and voices that had not made it into print prior to the crisis and would not continue after it. The blockage that interrupted the official circulation of texts and routes required editors to permit alternative pathways of information. And into these flooded, counterintuitively, a plethora of accounts, some analytic, others blustering, yet others bluntly racist. My goal in drawing out such stories is not to sanitize the Anglo-Indian press. That they were "shrill" and bloodthirsty is not inaccurate—the *Bengal Hurkaru* maintained its unyielding stance on reprisals. But that shrillness did not dominate and was in fact often subsumed by different strands. My purpose has been to dwell on the granular in a moment when circulation broke down, when blocked pathways and a collapsed circulatory system necessitated new routes which were dead-ended by 1858 as "order" was restored. Anglo-Indian newspapers expressed a wider range of views on the Uprising, its causes, and responses to it than historians have allowed, a range precipitated by the interrupted networks of personnel, routes, and mail in Central India. Like newspapers themselves and the newspaper archive, many of the views expressed in Anglo-Indian prints in 1857 were transitory—both fleeting and in transition.

The *Hindoo Patriot* in the Balance

On 26 November 1857, there appeared in the *Hindoo Patriot* a threnody of sorts: "For some time past the relations of this journal with the local community of Europeans have assumed a form which we for our part cannot contemplate without real pain."[108] Lamenting "[t]he ill grace into

---

107. *Mofussilite*, 19 March 1858.
108. Qtd. in Ghose, *Selections* [vol. IV] 202.

which we have fallen with the European community" and the resulting "sacrifices of personal friendships," the writer is also clear: "Not that upon the closest examination we find any thing that duty and justice seriously call upon us to retract or to apologise for."[109] In a chapter that traces the network of relations between Anglo-Indian newspapers, personnel, and their correspondents, I close with a section that highlights the *severing* of relations. Harish Chandra Mukherjee, the *Patriot*'s editor in 1857, was typical of Calcutta's English-speaking Bengalis who served as intermediaries between the establishment and Indians. Mukherjee's journalistic apprenticeship occurred under William Cobb Hurry at the *Englishman* and his day job was at the office of the military auditor general. Thus, he was well acquainted with civilian and bureaucratic Anglo-Indian society; 1857 strained those relations. This section examines the *Patriot*'s coverage of the Uprising and Mukherjee's attempt to forge a response that balanced a number of irreconcilable differences at once.

I have reserved discussion of the *Hindoo Patriot* for a separate section for two reasons. The first pertains to access and archives: unlike the *Bengal Hurkaru*, the *Englishman*, the *Friend of India*, and the *Mofussilite*, all of which are preserved and relatively accessible to the researcher, the *Patriot*'s 1857 holdings are only available in edited volumes of selections. Benoy Ghose's *Selections from English Periodicals of 19th Century Bengal* dedicates more than three-quarters of its fourth volume to the *Hindoo Patriot*'s writings on the Uprising, and Nares Chandra Sen-Gupta's 1910 *Selections from the Writings of Hurrish Chunder Mookerji Compiled from the Hindoo Patriot* devotes roughly half of the volume to commentaries from 1857–58. Neither identifies the archive used to access the newspaper—Sen-Gupta writes cryptically that "only two volumes of the *Hindoo Patriot* of [Mukherjee's] day are all that we have been able to hunt down" (G)—and the libraries I have consulted carry copies only from December 1857 forward.[110] Although Ghose's and Sen-Gupta's selections are substantial, they are excerpts culled by an editor. Excerpting and reprinting were a central feature of the nineteenth-century press, and this book has dwelt at some length on the meaning-making embedded in these practices. Given my effort to establish the context and ecosystem of excerpts, I have

---

109. Qtd. in Ghose, *Selections* [vol. IV] 202–03.

110. For his excellent article on Mukherjee and the *Hindoo Patriot*, Nakazato relies on Sen-Gupta's 1910 edited collection.

elected, in the face of this archival limit, to proceed modestly with the decontextualized archive of the *Hindoo Patriot* at my disposal.

I have also placed discussion of the *Patriot* in a separate section because its increasingly frosty relations with its Anglo-Indian contemporaries mark a turn in the relation between Anglo-Indian and Bengali journalists. Since the beginning of the century, Bengali pressmen had worked alongside Anglo-Indians. In Calcutta especially, as Indians started their own newspapers, they did so in engagement with their Anglo-Indian parallels. Rammohan Roy is the most prominent example of this interaction: his long association with William Carey of the Serampore Press served as a spur to Roy's founding the Bengali-language newspaper the *Sambad Kaumudi* (est. 1821). Roy's spirited protest against the 1823 press regulations, which placed severe restrictions on both Anglo-Indian and Indian, English- and vernacular-language presses, was heralded by Anglo-Indian pressmen and is an example of the collaboration between the British and Bengali presses in Calcutta.[111] Even after Roy ceased publication of his newspaper in protest against the censorship, he continued his involvement with Anglo-Indian newspapers such as the *Unitarian Repository* (est. 1823) and the *Bengal Herald* (est. 1829).[112] Roy was not alone: the first Bengali publisher, Gangakishore Bhattacharya, was a former employee at the Serampore Press, and founded his own press, where he published the weekly Bengali-language newspaper the *Bengali Gazette* (est. 1816).[113] The *Bengali Gazette* is often referred to in conjunction with the *Samachar Darpan* (est. 1818), another Bengali-language weekly published by the Serampore Press and edited by John Marshman (later of the *Friend of India*), who was assisted by a number of Bengali writers (Bhatnagar 24). Behind several of these endeavors was Dwarkanath Tagore, the wealthy zamindar and businessman, who put his financial weight behind a number of notable Bengali and Anglo-Indian newspapers. In 1834, Tagore purchased the *India Gazette*—the subcontinent's second newspaper after *Hicky's Bengal Gazette*—and merged it with the *Bengal Hurkaru* (Chanda, *History* [1987] 35).

Such cooperation was at its pinnacle in the 1820s and 1830s, but on the wane by the 1840s; the Uprising was the breaking point, and the

---

111. See Chanda (*History* [1987] 428).

112. Chanda (*History* [1987] 84, 115–16).

113. Roy ("Disciplining" 31); Ahmed (85).

Hindoo Patriot's "pain" at finding itself at variance with its Anglo-Indian contemporaries captures Mukherjee's attempts to manage relations that were turning from sour to toxic. Charged with "'insolence' . . . towards the European community," the *Patriot* responds: "[W]e hold the position of this journal to be, that it is representative of the great mass of people," while the Europeans in India are "extremely limited in number, and hav[e] the least possible interest in the welfare of the country they sojourn in."[114] As almost every newspaper does, the *Patriot* claimed to represent a "great mass of people" whose interests other organs ignored. Its claim was manifested in the colonial situation, the supremacy of Europeans disinterested in the "welfare of the country they sojourn in." Mukherjee, in Vinay Dharwadker's typology, "fashioned himself . . . and acted as an agent of historical change, even when the colonizer seemed to control or dominate the medium and its culture" (120).

Challenging Anglo-Indians and their dominance of the print public sphere, the paper presented itself as "the organ of those amongst [the people] *who have a right to take* and habitually do take a lead in public affairs."[115] For the *Patriot*, the English-educated Bengali—many had been part of the movement called Young Bengal—was "the interpreter between his rulers and his countrymen."[116] To illustrate both the responsibility and burden that came with its intermediary position, the newspaper provided an example that is suggestive, particularly in light of charges that Indian newspapers incited the Uprising:

> There was issued for some months under the same editorial management with this journal a Bengallee newspaper. While the articles in the English weekly breathed hot opposition to the measures of Government, those in the vernacular journal were framed with the chief object of convincing our countrymen, how infinitely superior to any thing known in our past history were the acts and principles of the British Government in India. This dualism in the political language and conduct of Young Bengal exposes him to considerable misrepresentation.

---

114. *Hindoo Patriot*, 26 November 1857 (qtd. in Ghose, *Selections* [vol. IV] 204).

115. *Hindoo Patriot*, 26 November 1857 (qtd. in Ghose, *Selections* [vol. IV] 204); emphasis added.

116. *Hindoo Patriot*, 11 June 1857 (qtd. in Ghose, *Selections* [vol. IV] 91).

His countrymen deny his patriotism; his rulers' countrymen deny his loyalty.[117]

In the previous section, we saw the language of patriotism and loyalty wielded by the Anglo-India press: Indians lacked—or had to prove—loyalty, while Anglo-Indian prints had patriotism to spare. The *Patriot* draws on the same language of patriotism, though for it the stakes required it to also prove its "loyalty"—to the idea of Britain and to Britons in India. But this was a doomed enterprise: as intermediary between Indians and Anglo-Indians, it was bound to be not "Indian" enough for some, "too Indian" for others. (Benoy Ghose's dismissal of the *Hindoo Patriot* for its "Canningite" leanings suggests the danger exists even from a historical distance.)

What particularly earned the *Patriot* the wrath of its Anglo-Indian contemporaries was that—unlike Rammohan Roy, who was at the forefront of the protest against the 1823 press restrictions—Mukherjee supported the 1857 Press Act. The paper's November 1857 response to contemporaries who attacked it reads,

> We have of late been honored with a slight suspicion of being a 'Government organ.' We decline the dignity not so much from modesty as from prudence. . . . There was a time when the Patriot was not much behind the front rank of those who opposed an unprincipled and short-sighted administration. It is no dread of press laws that makes it support a newer and better minded one . . . When, as during Charter discussions, the interests of the native community coincided with those of non-official Europeans, we fought by their side . . . And when, as now, we find our national interests bound up with those of the administration of the day, our duty is to render it our humble support.[118]

Although it pointed to the "many evil deeds committed by the [past] British Government in India,"[119] the *Patriot* supported *this* government

---

117. *Hindoo Patriot*, 11 June 1857 (qtd. in Ghose, *Selections* [vol. IV] 91).

118. *Hindoo Patriot*, 26 November 1857 (qtd. in Ghose, *Selections* [vol. IV] 205–06).

119. *Hindoo Patriot*, 11 June 1857 (qtd. in Ghose, *Selections* [vol. IV] 89).

because it believed that "[t]he measures which the Government of India has adopted to reassure the public mind in the present agitated state of the country have all been marked by wisdom, firmness and moderation."[120] Its support for a government despised by much of the Anglo-Indian press made the *Patriot* highly unpopular among its contemporaries.[121]

Notwithstanding its support of the Canning administration, the *Patriot* understood that the mutinies were the tip of the putative iceberg. Following the Berhampur and Barrackpur mutinies in early 1857, it wrote that "[i]t was neither the fat of oxen nor the dread of proselytism, but a deep-rooted cause of estrangement that led to these mutinous outbreaks."[122] And though dismayed by events in Meerut—it described them as "the horrible details of mutiny and massacre"[123]—the newspaper intuited that the disturbances were "no longer a mutiny, but a rebellion."[124] Its earliest analysis highlighted social factors:

> How slight is the hold the British government has acquired upon the affections of its Indian subjects has been made painfully evident by the events of the last few weeks. . . . There is not a single native of India who does not feel the full weight of the grievances imposed upon him by the very existence of the

---

120. *Hindoo Patriot*, 4 June 1857 (qtd. in Ghose, *Selections* [vol. IV] 77).

121. The Anglo-Indian press was on the warpath against Canning and his council; in the autumn of 1857, almost 1,000 Calcutta Anglo-Indians sent a petition to the Queen calling for Canning's recall. See *Bengal Hurkaru*, 14 October 1857; *Hindoo Patriot*, 13 August 1857 (qtd. in Ghose, *Selections* [vol. IV] 145); and the government's annotated copy of the petition to London in United Kingdom, House of Commons ("Petition"). The *Patriot*'s support of Canning provoked a venomous attack from the *Hurkaru*, which called the *Patriot* a "third rate" journal (*Bengal Hurkaru*, 28 August 1857; see also *Hurkaru*, 24 April 1857).

122. *Hindoo Patriot*, 2 April 1857 (qtd. in Ghose, *Selections* [vol. IV] 19–20).

123. *Hindoo Patriot*, 21 May 1857 (qtd. in Ghose, *Selections* [vol. IV] 57–66).

124. *Hindoo Patriot*, 21 May 1857 (qtd. in Ghose, *Selections* [vol. IV] 57–66). By December, the paper had modified its stance: "As yet the revolt appears to us to be a sepoy revolt, originating in a panic and in military disorganization, led by ambitions eager to carve out a path of glory for themselves, and fostered by the legitimist feeling which the British Government has done nothing to eradicate from the breasts of the people and much to strengthen by a careful prescription of 'English ideas' in its scheme of Indian rule" (*Hindoo Patriot*, 3 December 1857, qtd. in Ghose, *Selections* [vol. IV] 212).

British rule in India—grievances inseparable from subjection to a foreign rule. There is not one among the educated classes who does not feel his prospects circumscribed and his ambition restricted by the supremacy of that power.[125]

On the one hand "grievances inseparable from subjection to a foreign rule"—an indictment of colonialism; on the other, circumscribed prospects and restricted ambitions—an appeal to reform particular colonial practices. In the excerpts of 1857, the *Patriot* repeatedly turns to race relations and racial wounds: "So long as we are treated by Englishmen as an inferior race, and feel that in some respects we deserve to be so treated, much of warmth and ardour cannot be expected to enter into the composition of our loyalty"[126]; on at least three occasions, the *Patriot*, mirroring language that appeared in the Anglo-Indian press, wrote of the "antagonism of races"[127]; and it concluded the year on a pessimistic note: "For the time, the estrangement between the native races and the mass of the English people has become complete."[128]

And yet the *Patriot* not only supported the Canning government, but, like its Anglo-Indian contemporaries, was a confirmed imperial organ. In the excerpts Ghose provides, numerous commentaries elaborate on the benefits of British rule. In June, the newspaper wrote that educated Bengalis "have a splendid future before them, . . . which can be realized only by the existence of the British rule."[129] That future consisted of shared governance between imperial elites and the nation's western-educated men:

> [Bengallees] are in hopes that by lawful and constitutional appeals to the good sense and justice of the English people sitting by representatives in a sovereign council or Parliament, they, when the fitting moment arrives, will rise yet further in the scale of equality with their foreign rulers and divide with

---

125. *Hindoo Patriot*, 21 May 1857 (qtd. in Ghose, *Selections* [vol. IV] 57–66).

126. *Hindoo Patriot*, 11 June 1857 (qtd. in Ghose, *Selections* [vol. IV] 90).

127. See *Hindoo Patriot*, 18 June, 3 and 31 December 1857 (qtd. in Ghose, *Selections* [vol. IV] 95, 211, 228).

128. *Hindoo Patriot*, 31 December 1857 (qtd. in Ghose, *Selections* [vol. IV] 224).

129. *Hindoo Patriot*, 11 June 1857 (qtd. in Ghose, *Selections* [vol. IV] 90).

them the honour and the responsibility of administering the affairs of the largest and the most well-established empire in Asia.[130]

For the *Patriot*, the period of tutelage had been thrown into turmoil by the events of 1857. It found a glimmer of hope in the British elite: "It is one consolation to find amidst this outburst of vengeful feelings that the sentiments of the upper classes of Englishmen still continue untainted by them—and the British empire is still governed by the upper classes."[131] Mukherjee, in short, reached over Anglo-Indians to align with the imperial metropole. As Nakazato puts it, "[Mukherjee's] ideological stance was mainly conditioned by his position at the intersection of social networks formed by the [Bengali] landed aristocracy and rising elites from the legal profession" (257–58). Two sets of elites finding common cause.

Finally, despite its insistence that the rebellion expressed deep and justified dissatisfaction with British rule and treatment of Indians—the "grievous oppression" of sepoys[132]—the *Patriot* also condemned the violence. The insurgents' actions in Delhi disturbed the newspaper and were a turning point: "The tales of horror to which the acts of mutineers have given birth, as they rise in one's memory, obliterate all the feelings of commiseration that their desperate situation might otherwise excite . . . The people of Delhi, among whom we doubt not there are many innocent and loyal, will to a great extent have to share in the punishment due to the guilty rebels."[133] As for so many observers that summer, the events at Kanpur were the final straw. When the newspaper learned of Satichaura Ghat—where Nana Sahib's men fired on the Europeans whose safe passage had been negotiated—it wrote, "The tale of mutiny and rebellion this week has been varied by accounts of a catastrophe even more horrible in its details than the massacres with which the revolt was inaugurated. . . . For treachery so base, so vile and so appalling in its consequences punishment

---

130. *Hindoo Patriot*, 4 June 1857 (qtd. in Ghose, *Selections* [vol. IV] 80).

131. *Hindoo Patriot*, 17 December 1857 (qtd. in Ghose, *Selections* [vol. IV] 219–20).

132. *Hindoo Patriot*, 2 April 1857 (qtd. in Ghose, *Selections* [vol. IV] 20).

133. *Hindoo Patriot*, 29 May 1857 (qtd. in Ghose, *Selections* [vol. IV] 68). Farooqui's cache of documents indicates that ordinary Delhiites suffered considerably during the Uprising, at the hands of both insurgents and the British.

no doubt will be meted out. We only hope that punishment may not be dealt out too late."[134]

If the seemingly indiscriminate violence of the rebels horrified the *Patriot*, so did the brutal response of the relief forces. In August, the paper wrote, "The pillage of the town of Allahabad, to which a contemporary has traced, with some show of reason, the subsequent catastrophe at Cawnpore, was committed both by European and Seikh [sic] soldiers. . . . Our military commanders ought to remember that after the rebellion is over, the country will have to be reoccupied and regoverned."[135] The comment is striking, both for its understanding that the events at Kanpur were not simple treachery but *in response* to British actions and for its belief that a government that perpetrated such "pillage" ought to endure. Less than a month later, the paper noted, "It is impossible to deny that immediately after the first successes over the rebels the work of retribution was carried a little too far, and that too in a manner not to be expected from the agents of a civilized Government. At the town of Allahabad only, nearly eight hundred men were hanged between the 6th June and 16th July. The Seikhs [sic] were let loose upon the townspeople to wreak summary vengeance for the murder of a comrade. Brigadier Neill's course from Benares to Allahabad was marked by corpses of villagers all of whom did not approach his force with hostile intentions."[136] Notwithstanding these atrocities, the paper persisted in believing in the government, and the leader ended on this note: "The European soldiers in India should have explained to them that marauding is unsoldierly and murder a cowardly offense, and if any of them should commit either offense let no consideration interpose to save him from adequate punishment."[137]

What are we to make of the *Hindoo Patriot*? Nakazato writes that Mukherjee's thinking was an "uneasy combination of [John] Bright's liberalism and [Mukherjee's] own conservatism" (263). In its self-appointed role as intermediary between Britons and Indians, the *Patriot* indicted the British for their arrogance and disregard of Indian ways of life, which it pronounced as the root cause of the widespread rebellion. The newspaper also celebrated the political and intellectual revival the British had ush-

---

134. *Hindoo Patriot*, 9 July 1857 (qtd. in Ghose, *Selections* [vol. IV] 108–09).
135. *Hindoo Patriot*, 13 August 1857 (qtd. in Ghose, *Selections* [vol. IV] 148–49).
136. *Hindoo Patriot*, 10 September 1857 (qtd. in Ghose, *Selections* [vol. IV] 165–66).
137. *Hindoo Patriot*, 10 September 1857 (qtd. in Ghose, *Selections* [vol. IV] 170).

ered into Bengal and subscribed to a gradual system of power sharing. It recoiled from the massacres and excesses of violence perpetrated by insurgents, and it criticized the corresponding violence of the British response. During the charged days of 1857, the *Hindoo Patriot* was never warned, its license never revoked. Canning is rumored to have forwarded copies of the *Patriot* to London to demonstrate the sentiments of loyal Indians.[138] Its Anglo-Indian rivals disdained it and nationalist scholars have ignored or dismissed it.[139] For our purposes, the *Hindoo Patriot* is relevant because at a moment of severed relations and the "antagonism of races," the newspaper expresses what Dharwadker refers to as the "burdens of incompletely translated and substantially hybridized Enlightenment activism, quasi-civil society protocols, and protopublic-sphere conventions" (120).[140] With its relations to its Anglo-Indian contemporaries in shreds, it reached halfway across the planet to forge an alliance and network with Britain's ruling classes whose imperial vision it shared.

---

138. See Chanda (*History* [2008] 17).

139. The newspaper redeemed itself in the 1860s by its "historic role against the tyranny of the indigo planters" in the 1860s (Chanda, *History* [1987] 331).

140. Rosinka Chaudhuri's description of Iswarchandra Gupta, the poet and editor of the first Bengali daily, *Sambād Prabhākar*, as living a life "fluidly contradictory in its politics" offers an apt parallel: "Gupta belonged to a class of administrators and professionals created in Calcutta by the exigencies of colonialism, whose life story could only have been thrown up by the paradoxical modernities" (33). Like Mukherjee, Gupta supported the British in 1857 and was "contemptuous" of Nana Sahib, the rani of Jhansi, and Muslims in general (R. Chaudhuri 71–72).

Chapter 4

Wanderings and Textual Travels

On 16 January 1858, *Household Words* published the sixth installment of "Wanderings in India," a series that had been appearing in its pages, on and off, since mid-November 1857. "Wanderings" is the lengthiest entry in this issue, clocking in at almost thirteen full columns;[1] at its heart is an account of the narrator's six-week visit to Meerut, where he was the guest of a newspaper editor whom he assists in running the local newspaper. Our narrator relates that several Indians who worked at his friend's press started to publish an Urdu-language newspaper called "Jam-i-Jumsheed" on the side. "Unknown to the conductor of the [English-language] Meerut paper," our traveler writes, the editor of the Urdu paper "published quantities of matter which the conductor of the Meerut paper thought proper to suppress."[2] To illustrate the "evil" and "mischief" the Urdu-language newspaper was up to, our narrator reproduces a leading article that the English-language newspaper editor had "kept out of the columns of [his own] Meerut paper," but that appeared in the Urdu paper (114). The article tells the story of a British magistrate who, seeking an escaped convict and based on only a suspicion, summarily burns down an entire village in the dead of night, killing thirteen villagers and rendering six hundred homeless. The selection, reproduced from the Urdu-language newspaper,

---

1. *Dickens Journal Online* (djo.org.uk) has made high-quality, searchable digital editions of Dickens's journals available for free, and integrates into the site essential information on contributors and payments drawn from Anne Lohrli's painstaking work with the office books of *Household Words*.

2. *Household Words*, 16 January 1858, 114.

concludes on the withering note that such are the "manifest blessings that arise out of British rule in India" (115).

From Meerut to London, Urdu to English, the *Jam-e-Jamshed*[3] to *Household Words*, colony to metropole: this densely textual episode weaves a multiplicity of locations, languages, print media, and positions into a web of intertwined relations. Its appearance captures the complexities of newsprint as it travels between colony and metropole. Recounting, in a London periodical, this very colonial story of intimacy and tutelage, independence and betrayal, pillage and exposé, and the role of the news media in mediating relations between colonizer and colonized, the episode serves as an apt gateway to the questions this chapter takes up. The previous chapter explored the traffic between personnel in the Anglo-Indian media and the circulation—often stalled—of reports within India during the Uprising. This chapter considers the circulation of news, text, and personnel from colony to metropole. What happens when the colony returns "home"? How do colonial stories travel or translate? Who has the authority to carry them and how do they settle in their new home?

At the time the story of the *Jam-e-Jamshed*'s printing the item about the magistrate's crime appeared in *Household Words*, Britons were shaken by what they had learned about the military mutinies and unrest that was sweeping across the Gangetic Plain of India. Though Delhi, the seat of the Mughals, had been retaken by September 1857, the Uprising was far from over. As news of atrocities, such as the massacres at Kanpur, and reports of Europeans retreating into and trapped in forts and garrisons filtered into London, Britons reacted with betrayed outrage and unbridled fury.[4] The *Jam-e-Jamshed* narrative appeared in *Household Words* in the midst of this fevered climate. In "Wanderings in India," the narrator shares this story of an Urdu newspaper "filching" news "intended only for European eyes" in order to convey the "danger of permitting native newspapers to be published without any sort of supervision" (115, 114). Yet not just any supervision would do: the narrator believes that governing authorities in

---

3. For the newspaper's name in English, I have opted for the spelling used by Nadir Ali Khan, whose history of nineteenth-century Urdu journalism is indispensable.

4. Gautam Chakravarty writes that the public outcry in Britain and Anglo-India "with its xenophobia and shrill call for revenge" was "more hysterical, more intolerant generally of the rebel cause" than policy makers in London and Calcutta (32, 94).

India are incapable of reading the sarcasm of "Asiatics" who "wrap up the most bitter irony in the most complimentary phrases" (115). Our seasoned traveler, by contrast, has "wandered" in India a good many years and is not deceived by superficial compliments; his story serves as a cautionary tale about trusting "Asiatics."[5] It belongs to and fuels what Salahuddin Malik characterizes as the "atmosphere of nervousness, tension, gossip, fabrication, absence of any familiarity with the people of India and, above all, claimed racial superiority over the natives" (*1857* 9).

Yet something about this narrative intrigues. Under the guise of exposing the deceit of Indian newsmen who are textual thieves and artful wordsmiths, the writer shares a scathing story of arbitrary *British* power and absence of the rule of law. Appearing in London in January 1858, when fury over the treatment of British women, children, and men was running high, this vignette of British atrocity and its Indian victims flips roles. The British atrocities are not denied in "Wanderings in India"; moreover, we are informed that the story was *written* by the editor-friend who, we are told, withdrew the article from his English-language newspaper just before it went to press "at the instance of the friends of the gentleman who was guilty of the indiscretion" (114). Thus, compounding the colonial official's crime is the complicity of the family and editor in covering up the crime. The incident is not a matter of "a few bad apples," but of a system rotten from magisterial top to editorial bottom. At a moment when predation, despotism, and tyranny were laid at the feet of Indians, and victimhood the mantle many Britons wrapped themselves in, this account forces readers to recalibrate.

In "Wanderings," the report of the magistrate's rampage is reprinted from the *Jam-e-Jamshed*. Quoting from the Urdu-language newspaper allows the author of "Wanderings" to distance himself from the anti-colonial views of the Urdu-language newspaper. Yet the account of magisterial malfeasance appears in *Household Words* in English, though in *Jam-e-Jamshed* it had appeared in Urdu. In other words, the "Hindoostanee"-speaking author of "Wanderings in India" had to translate the story from Urdu into English

---

5. In fact, the authorities were perfectly "capable" and shared this writer's disparaging view of "natives": in a July 1857 speech, Canning said, "I have seen articles appear from time to time, which, however innocuous to European readers, might prove very injurious when dressed up for the native ear by designing persons" (qtd. in *Hurkaru*, 13 July 1857).

for his metropolitan readers.[6] Of course, the item that appeared in the *Jam-e-Jamshed* was itself a translation of a story initially written in English by the narrator's editor-friend. In short, the linguistic transmutations of this narrative chart a complex tale of multiple "authors" and myriad readers: a text originally written in English and meant only for Anglo-Indian eyes is suppressed and does not see the light of print; it surfaces translated into Urdu for consumption by Meerut's Hindustani-speaking audiences; once aired, the text is *re-translated* into English for consumption by Dickens's British readership.

Adding to the linguistic metamorphoses of the text is the spatial and temporal distance it traveled. From Meerut where the magisterial crime occurred in the late 1840s[7] to London a decade later, this report's appearance in Dickens's *Household Words* captures the displacement, migration, and journey of news accounts as they circulated between India and Britain (see figure 4.1). This story of movement across space, time, and linguistic registers, of circulation and circuits, of networks and connections between India and Britain complements the previous chapter's account of circulation within the colonial sphere and among the Anglo-Indian press. While that chapter traced the incoherence and confusion that arose from the multiauthored and polyvocal coverage that resulted from the stalled circulation of print and mailbags during the Uprising, this one examines the effect introduced when a single author and his work travel from colony to metropole. The instability of the *Jam-e-Jamshed* story as it appeared in *Household Words*—is it about Indians as deceptive or Britons as tyrannical?—is a preview of the slipperiness and multiple valences that emerge from such travels.

---

6. In the first installment of "Wanderings," the narrator informs us that shortly upon arriving in India he undertook the study of "Hindoostanee and Persian" and soon "I found myself capable, not only of holding a conversation, but of arguing a point in either of these languages" (*Household Words*, 14 November 1857, 399). In the mid-nineteenth century, the word "Hindustani" was used interchangeably with "Urdu" and denoted a hybrid language that combined elements of the local Khariboli dialect of Delhi with Persian, Arabic, and Turkic words.

7. Though the account in "Wanderings" provides no dates, bibliographic details narrow the range to between 1847 and 1851. The weekly *Jam-e-Jamshed*, owned by Babu Shiv Chandra Nath and edited by Munshi Har Sukh Rai, started in Meerut in 1847. The newspaper lost one of its editors when Rai founded the *Akbar Koh-e-Nur* in Lahore on 14 January 1850; Nath moved the *Jam-e-Jamshed* to Agra in 1851 (N. A. Khan 227–28, 243).

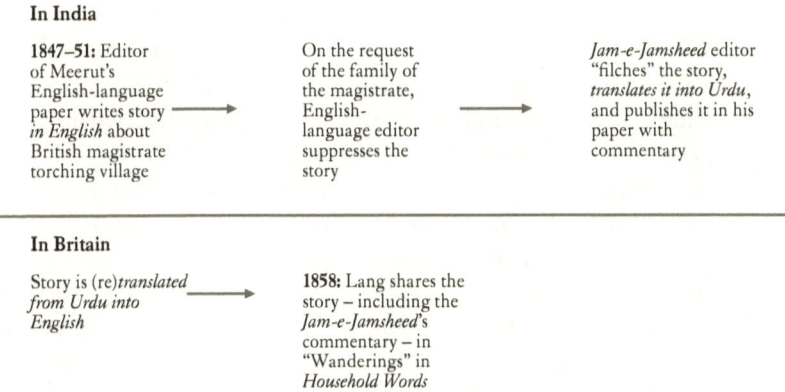

Figure 4.1. The Geographic and Linguistic Journey of the Magistrate's Tale of Pillage.

Thus far I have referred to the author of "Wanderings in India" as "narrator" or "author" because, in keeping with house policy, all essays in *Household Words* appeared without attribution.[8] Yet the author was not unknown for very long: on 5 August 1859, a volume entitled *Wanderings in India and Other Sketches of Life in Hindostan* appeared in London. Its author was John Lang and the volume's preface reads, "The greater part of the Papers which form this Volume have appeared in 'Household Words;' and the Author has to acknowledge his thanks to Mr. DICKENS for sanctioning a reprint of them." Lang was, of course, the owner and on-again, off-again, editor of the *Mofussilite*, the Meerut-based English-language newspaper at the center of my study. He was a significant, if not notorious, figure in the Anglo-Indian press scene, due in part to his defense of Jyoti Prasad in 1851. Lang was in London when the Meerut regiment mutinied and disaffection spread through the North-Western Provinces. But the reporter's bad luck in missing the day's big story was the editor's good fortune: Dickens needed material on India and turned to the Australian barrister who had lived more than a decade in India, was fortuitously resident in London at the moment, and had already published some dozen pieces in *Household Words*. Thus was born the twelve-part "Wanderings in India," appearing as the periodical's lead on 14 November 1857 and continuing

---

8. In imposing anonymity on contributors, *Household Words* was out of step with journals of its kind that were publishing either author's names or initials (Drew 117–18).

until 27 February 1858.⁹ Eighteen months after its last installment, a volume of the collected essays—with additions—appeared in London.

As the serially published "Wanderings in India" morphed into the single-volume *Wanderings in India*, we encounter yet another journey, here across print media. This chapter will delve into the mutations of a text about the colonies in the metropolis by first examining "Wanderings" in the context of *Household Words* before turning to analyze its transformation into *Wanderings*. The questions framing this inquiry are focused on the circulation and exchange of ideas and technologies; the transformations wrought as stories move from India to Britain and back, from newspaper to periodical to book, from English to Urdu and back, from Indians to colonial recorders and metropolitan readers. This analysis of "Wanderings"/ *Wanderings* is a fitting close to *Empire News* as it is with these publications that residue from Anglo-India newspapers circulate back to the metropole, where the animating idea of print newspapers originated.

House Rules

Although one critic has claimed that "Most of the chapters in *Wanderings in India* first appeared in Lang's English-language newspaper *Mofussilite* in the mid- to late-1840s in India," no evidence for this claim has surfaced in the newspaper itself (Hosking 89). The twelve essays that appeared in *Household Words* as "Wanderings in India" were, as Lang's earliest biographers Colin Roderick and John Earnshaw contend, "written for Dickens, who no doubt believed that the Indian Mutiny of 1857–8 would have created a desire in many minds to know more of the country in which it had occurred" (128).¹⁰ Once word of the mutinies started to arrive in Britain, the British press, "short on up-to-date information on Indian events, took the opportunity to print background information about India's cities, religions, and peoples" (Merrit 3). As the disturbances spread and their extent registered, news and analysis of the Indian situation became

---

9. Only the first two installments of "Wanderings in India" appeared in the periodical's lead position; subsequent parts were in fourth or fifth place in the lineup.

10. Crittenden concurs, writing that Lang transformed his "earlier travels through India" into a travelogue when copy on India was in demand (186).

a precious commodity. Yet, despite the growing sense of urgency and increasing outrage over the news from India, *Household Words'* coverage and commentary on events in India got off to a slow start. John Drew, speaking of the journal's coverage of current affairs more generally, writes that "in its response to public events, *Household Words* was not pre-emotive, and followed in the wake of the daily press" (22). Even so, the periodical's exploration of the events in India was tardy, even for a weekly periodical.[11]

Household Words' first reference to the disturbances in India did not appear until 15 August 1857, two months after news of the Meerut mutiny and the rebels' capture of Delhi appeared in the London print media.[12] "A Mutiny in India," written by the major of a brigade of irregulars, is an account of a mutiny that occurred "years ago" when Indian soldiers killed their tyrannical and "feudal" brigadier.[13] Largely sympathetic to the men and disapproving of the Company's decision to hush up the mutiny, the major concludes, "Surely, we may make some use of the follies of the past, to serve as beacons for the future; and surely those have much to answer for, who are prevented by a foolish punctilio from exposing the true causes of the rottenness of our Indian civil and military system" (156). Whether the "follies" he refers to are the "rottenness" of the Company or its cover-up is unclear. A month later, on 12 September, an essay entitled

---

11. Though it may be tempting to suppose that *Household Words* steered away from "hard news" in order to avoid the stamp tax imposed on newspapers or news, that duty was lifted in 1855. Even prior to its abolition, as Martin Hewitt has demonstrated, the Revenue Board applied the law unevenly, allowing some monthlies and weeklies to publish news and sanctioning others (49). Additionally, *Household Words* had registered as a newspaper so it could stamp a portion of each issue and take advantage of free postal transmission (Hewitt 49). Following the repeal of the newspaper stamp tax but before the repeal of duties on paper in 1861, every issue of *Household Words* from 14 July 1855 forward lists two prices: 2*d.* or "Stamped 3*d.*"

12. The earliest notice of the 10 May mutiny at Meerut appeared in the *Times* on 8 June 1857. The military disturbances of the early spring—Berhampur in late February, Barrackpur in late March, and the disbanding of the 19th Native Infantry—were reported in the *Times* through April and May, with a lengthy leader on cartridge-inspired disobediences appearing on 29 April 1857.

13. "A Mutiny in India," *Household Words*, 15 August 1857, 154–56. The journal's office books identify the author as E. Townsend.

"Indian Irregulars," clearly by the same hand, explains the difference between irregulars and the standard units of the Company's army. The author is expansive in his praise of irregulars, whom he considers a superior and more reliable force.[14] The essay concludes, "If they [irregulars] mutiny, depend upon it there is some flaw in the personnel of their officers" (245). Between them, the two articles are a striking endorsement of military insurgency, even if only among some units.[15] Written by a military man who spoke with knowledge of the British-Indian military—if of past events—the essays offer somewhat oblique commentary on the current events.

By contrast, *Household Word*'s second foray into the Uprising hints at a measure of editorial desperation. On 5 September 1857, the "Sepoy Symbols of Mutiny" took up the rumor that the insurgencies were premeditated and organized: "The conspiracy which broke out in British India, by the mutinies of Sepoys, in the month of June, eighteen hundred and fifty-seven, was first shown by the circulation of symbols in the forms of cakes and lotus-flowers."[16] The putative passing of *chapatis* (here transmuted into "cakes") and flowers from village to village leads the author into a lengthy disquisition that begins, "Herodotus described the lotus under the name of the lily of the Nile, and Theophrastus portrayed it as the Egyptian bean" (228). Over the next five and a half columns, we learn everything there is to be known about the lotus . . . *in Egypt*. The faux-learned treatise concludes in this tautological vein: "The [lotus] flower was circulated [in India] to rally the votaries of the goddess of the lotus" (231). One is not sure whether to sympathize with the author as he stretches to fill a blank sheet or commiserate with the editors who were swindled out of four guineas for such a dubious piece of writing.[17] (The Anglo-Indian press, always ready to pounce on London's ignorance about Indian matters, had

---

14. "Indian Irregulars," *Household Words*, 12 September 1857, 244–46. Townsend is listed as the author of this piece as well in the *Household Words* office books.

15. For *sipahis* this author has nothing but contempt and derision and he considers "native commissioned officers a set of worn-out, puffy, ghee-bloated cripples" ("Indian Irregulars," 244).

16. "Sepoy Symbols of Mutiny," *Household Words*, 25 September 1857, 228. Office books identify the author as John Robertson. For rumors about the circulation of *chapatis* in the months prior to the disturbances, see Chaudhary (61–63).

17. For Robertson's payment, see http://www.djo.org.uk/household-words/volume-xvi/page-228.html.

a field day with this piece: the *Madras Athenaeum* mocked Dickens for believing that the lotus was symbol of the mutiny and chided Disraeli who "confounds lotus and lotahs"[18]).

While "Sepoy Symbols" transmits ineptitude and oblivion about India, a 26 September essay finally speaks directly to the situation on the subcontinent. Titled "A Very Black Act," the essay is by a writer who self-identifies as "the editor of a Mofussilite or provincial paper in British India." Though this sounds like Lang, the journal's office book identifies the author as John Capper.[19] The essay stridently protests the "government censorship" of the press in Calcutta, a position, as we saw in the previous chapter, much of the Anglo-Indian press protested too.[20] Three months after the passing of the Press Act, *Household Words* printed an angry reaction to it; the uprisings themselves, however, still received no attention. *Household Words*' coverage of the Uprising in the early months can best be characterized as inept, grasping, and inconsistent. "Sepoy Symbols" communicates the absence of even a passing familiarity with India and hints at editorial scrambling; "A Mutiny in India" came from a more informed pen, yet the author's account of a past mutiny, absorption in minutiae, denunciation of the incompetence and nepotism of military leaders, and support for mutinying Indian soldiers makes for a conflicting message. The major's nebulous messaging largely mirrors the periodical's inconsistency on the Uprising.

Household Words is, of course, famous for its consistency, borne of Dickens's firm hand on the editorial steering wheel. And yet, Drew has made the compelling case that even as Dickens worked hard to produce "a multi-authored journal [that might] project a powerful single identity

---

18. Qtd. in *Mofussilite*, 9 March 1858. A lotah is a small brass container for water.

19. "A Very Black Act," *Household Words*, 26 September 1857, 293. It is unclear why Capper would identify in ways that, to those familiar with the Indian press scene, make him sound like Lang (who often signed letters as "Mofussilite"). Capper had been editor of the *Ceylon Examiner*, so his claim of being the editor of "a Mofussilite" newspaper is not false, only misleading.

20. Capper dramatically declares his intention to "resign my pen and pistol for the ploughshare" (294). He did not in fact resign his pen, at least not for *Household Words*; one other essay by him appeared on 24 October 1857. Titled "Calcutta," it offers a bird's-eye view of the city and its history, the sort of background essay Merrit indicates many British periodicals published in the early days of the Uprising (3).

into the public sphere," he "often failed to make his 'corps' writers write either what or how he desired . . . They sometimes held opposing views on controversial issues" (106, 123). Indeed, Drew and his *Dickens Journals Online* team contend that central to the journal's "identity as a miscellany" was its "plasticity" or refusal to take only one stance or write in just one generic mode or voice (Drew et al. 53). Even taking into account these correctives to the orthodoxy that *Household Words* adopted an emphatically Dickensian stance and stamp on issues, the periodical's coverage of India in 1857 smacks more of ineptitude than of "plasticity" born of a diversity of perspectives.

That the editors of *Household Words* were scrambling for copy on India is evident in the roster of writers brought to weigh in on the question, a varied lot whose selection suggests less of the careful screening Dickens was famous for. E. Townsend, the author of "A Mutiny in India," "Indian Irregulars," and three other essays, was an unknown quantity in the journal's Covent Garden offices, a man who remains only vaguely identified even today. He had never published in *Household Words* prior to his August 1857 essay and after March 1858 never did again. John Robertson, the author of "Sepoy Symbols of Mutiny," was more of a known quantity: at the time of his ramblings on lotuses, he had published nineteen pieces in the journal, though his specialization was coastal living and France, where he was resident. His authority to write about India was about as robust as that of Dickens's fictional newspaper editor, Mr. Potts of the *Eatanswill Gazette*, whose essay on Chinese metaphysics was composed by reading the *Encyclopedia Britannica* "for metaphysics under the letter M, and for China under the letter C, and combin[ing] his information" (*Pickwick Papers* 646). John Capper, meanwhile, was a bona fide "expert" on the subcontinent, and prior to "A Very Black Act," Capper had published fifty-seven articles in *Household Words*. The earliest of these appeared in March 1851, within the first year of the journal's existence, and two were co-authored with W. H. Wills, Dickens's hardworking subeditor. Yet it was not on Capper but on John Lang, a relatively minor contributor with only twelve publications in *Household Words* under his belt, that Dickens bestowed a contract for copy on India.

In 1853, during Lang's first furlough in England, he had placed six pieces in *Household Words*, including "Starting a Paper in India," which I discuss in chapter 1. With one exception, all his 1853 essays are set in India and represent a mixture of fiction and travel-and-description-style prose. In a hiatus that coincides with Lang's brief return to India in 1854, his contributions to the journal cease until late 1856 or early 1857, when we see a spate of renewed publications. Of his 1857 publications prior to "Wanderings," only one took India as its subject matter. Of the rest, "Hovelling" is typical; it appeared in February 1857 and was about the "gallant conduct of the Broadstairs boatmen."[21] In his early 1857 essays, Lang adopts the style, tone, and subject matter of Dickens's own jaunty, urban sketches. Clearly, Lang had come to embrace Brand Dickens more fully in 1857 than he did in 1853. But the Uprising intervened in Lang's efforts to remake himself into a Dickens, and with "Wanderings in India" Lang was discursively returned to a place and topic that he gives every evidence of wishing to disburden himself of.[22]

"Wanderings in India" begins by quickly establishing the writer's credentials and independence:

> It is some years since I first landed in Calcutta. I was in no way connected with the government, and was consequently an 'interloper' or 'adventurer.' . . . It was not long before I made up my mind to become a wanderer in the East. I had no occupation, was my own master, and had a large tract of country to roam about in. My first step was to acquire a knowledge of Hindoostanee and of Persian . . . [In six months], with a light heart, I took my departure from the City of Palaces, and proceeded to Monghyr, on the Ganges.[23]

Credentials, including linguistic proficiency, established, the romance of the Orient—the "wanderer in the East," the "City of Palaces," the Ganges—is delivered in a breezy tone that conveys no toil or travail.[24] The "rambling" journey of an adventurer "travelling in search of the picturesque, and

---

21. "Hovelling," *Household Words*, 7 February 1857, 140.

22. After serving two months in prison in Calcutta for libel (the result of injudicious remarks at the Jyoti Prasad trial), Lang traveled to London in 1852. He returned to India briefly in 1854, but was back in London by November 1854. In short, Lang spent the better part of 1852–58 outside India and gave every indication of wishing to establish himself in London.

23. "Wanderings in India," *Household Words*, 14 November 1857, 457.

24. With the header "WANDERINGS IN INDIA" on every odd-numbered page, readers were continually reminded of the carefree note.

with a view to become acquainted with Oriental character from personal observation," this is travel writing in the picturesque mode.[25]

The incongruity of "Wanderings in India" as it appeared in *Household Words* in 1857–58 cannot be overstated. Almost everything about a piece in the picturesque mode appearing at this time and place strikes a jarring note. By mid-September 1857, as accounts of the Kanpur massacres—the Satichaura Ghat massacre of over two hundred European men and the Bibighar massacre of approximately as many European women— reached Britain, the initially subdued press responses to the insurgency turned to rage.[26] Merrit writes that prior to this news, responses in the British press "displayed a determined optimism that events were not serious and would soon be over" (2). But as events unfolded, the tenor shifted and the press began to debate "the form that British retribution should take" (Merrit 10); "humanitarian sentiments," Merrit continues, "were largely met with ridicule" (11). Gautam Chakravarty characterizes the British press's reactions as "hysterical" (40), while Graham Dawson writes that calls for the "extermination" of rebels appeared in mainstream outlets such as the *Times*, *Morning Post*, and *Lloyd's Weekly* (94).[27] Even the coolly ironic *Punch* produced a number of images of unalloyed fury and vengeance, such as its "British Lion/Bengal Tiger" or "Justice" cartoons.[28] So united was the nation that October 7–14 was declared a Week of Fast and Humiliation (Goswami 59). When "Wanderings in India" began to appear in *Household Words* on 14 November 1857, the mood in Britain was tense and bellicose. The appearance of Lang's lighthearted fare over the course of these charged months strikes an incongruous note.

In addition to the peculiarity of their appearance in London at this tense moment of crisis, the "Wanderings" essays are puzzling for their presence within Lang's oeuvre as well. For much of his career, John Lang was a provocateur. From his rustication from Cambridge to his departure

---

25. The word "rambling" in "Wanderings," *Household Words*, 14 November 1857, 461; "picturesque" in "Wanderings," *Household Words*, 30 January 1858, 148.

26. For the timing of the news' arrival, see Dawson (96–97).

27. As we saw in the previous chapter, similar calls appeared in the Anglo-Indian press.

28. 22 August and 12 September. For a discussion of the *Punch* images, see Priti Joshi ("Mutiny Echoes" 55–66).

from Sydney under a political cloud;[29] from his editing the gadfly *Mofussilite* to his audacious defense of Jyoti Prasad; from his quarrels with the East India Company's judiciary to his representation of the rani of Jhansi in 1854, Lang was not a man to shy away from controversy. Why did this man, who was involved in colonial questions and the administration of Britain's star colony, choose an apolitical form to write on a topic he had so many views on? And beyond the puzzle of Lang's choice to write a leisurely travel account lies another set of questions: Why did Dickens commission Lang to write these essays? Why did Dickens publish all twelve parts?

Formal conventions—of travel writing and of *Household Words*' house style—offer a potential explanation for the discordant appearance of these essays in 1857–58 London. In selecting the title "Wanderings in India," Lang was not only telegraphing the sense of an unhurried journey, but also working within a convention of writing about India: the picturesque. Dozens of travelers to India wrote in this mode, notably Reginald Heber, the bishop of Calcutta, who, in his 1825 *Narrative of a Journey Through the Upper Provinces of India*, spoke of himself as a "lonely wanderer" on a picturesque journey.[30] In 1850, Fanny Parkes published a feminine picturesque entitled *Wanderings of a Pilgrim in Search of the Picturesque, during Four-and-Twenty Years Residence in the East; with Revelations of Life in the Zenana*. Parkes had lived in India between 1822 and 1845, the wife of a custom's officer posted to the mofussil (in Allahabad), and her volume consists of letters to family. There is every reason to suppose that Lang had heard of or had a passing familiarity with Parkes's volume.[31] If he did not, the similarity between the title of her book and Lang's series in *Household Words* indicates that the trope of wandering in a picturesque India was established as the zeitgeist.

The picturesque mode had its origins in painting, but by the turn of the nineteenth century had developed a textual counterpart. Picturesque

---

29. For Cambridge, see Roderick and Earnshaw (110–11) and Crittenden (36–39); for Sydney, see Roderick and Earnshaw (114–19), Crittenden (48–64), and Keesing's judicious account (42–55).

30. For Heber's picturesque, see Leask (183–91).

31. Leask writes that he has been unable to locate any contemporary reviews of Parkes's book in the British press (228n73). Lang, however, was a voracious reader who took his editorial remit seriously and made it a point to read widely on and about India.

descriptions flourished particularly in travel narratives, where they served to reshape "the foreign and exotic into the familiar and tamed" (Casid 47). The hallmarks of a picturesque vision are a broad overview, a detached stance, distance from minutiae, an aesthetic composition, and a static, frozen moment. As James Buzard puts it, "What picturesque seeing yielded was not only a scene that 'looked like' a painting, but a *scene*, balanced and complete . . . [which] required some distinct slant of vision and some measure of strategic omission. Everyday features of the visited place (populations included) either fell cleanly away from the visitor's view or arranged themselves as part of the spectacle" (188). With their partial and pleasing visions, picturesque textual compositions served a purpose: Nigel Leask writes that they "commodified [the] Indian landscape for sentimental consumption in the metropolis" (175), while Sara Suleri argues that they manifested "a desire to transfix a dynamic cultural confrontation into a still life . . . that allows the colonial gaze a license to convert its ability not to see into studiously visual representations" (76). The soft-focus, zoomed-out vision of the picturesque domesticated and froze the Other, pushed conflict beyond its frame, and congratulated itself on its (in)sight.

Leask indicates that the "apogee" of the Indian picturesque was in the 1830s (167). Lang's "Wanderings," then, was a latecomer, appearing in the decline of the subgenre's life cycle and thus doubly nostalgic. Picturesque descriptions litter his text: "It was a moonlight night, and slow as was the pace at which we proceeded, I never so much enjoyed a ride in my life. The scene altogether was highly picturesque; and, as far as I was concerned, had the wonderful charm of novelty."[32] Or this textbook description that has all the hallmarks of a discursively ordered landscape view:

> It was a very pretty scene, the encampment. The tents, the arms piled in front of them; the horse under a tree, and his syce seated near him; the old buggy and harness not far off; the sepoys in groups employed in cooking their food for the mid-day meal; the numbers of brass vessels lying about in all directions; the score of squirrels hopping from branch to branch, or running up and down the trunks of the trees; the crows, the minars, and the sparrows on the look out for crumbs; the bullocks taking their rest after the fatigues of the past night;

---

32. "Wanderings in India," *Household Words*, 19 December 1857, 13.

and then, before as well as after the meal, the men crowding round the well, and washing themselves from head to foot, and washing also their under garments, which as speedily dried in that sun of that climate.[33]

The perspective is encompassing, taking in everything from arms to underwear with the same cool detachment. The resulting word picture offers a carefully composed scene with its multiple parts drawn into a harmonious whole. The tents, arms, horse, and tree all precede the syce who is as inanimate and picture-like as they and the buggy and harness he is responsible for. Even the men washing are no more agents than the squirrels hopping or the birds seeking a meal: all simply do what they are destined to. Nothing disturbs the scene. More importantly, the central figure in this composition is the absent one: the European viewer, the man of letters, the imperial I/eye, in Mary Louise Pratt's formulation. It is his composing eye—or pen—that brings harmony to the discrete and disparate elements of the landscape.

The "still life" produced in Lang's essays was anomalous in an environment of strident responses to the Uprising that were ricocheting in the press by mid-November 1857; yet it also fulfilled a function. The mutinies and civilian rebellions of 1857 were some of the earliest instances of large-scale resistance to British sovereignty. At a moment when Indians were seeking, in whatever fashion, to "represent" themselves, the aesthetic spectacle in these essays, what Buzard calls the "picture-gallery of impressions" (211) that kept the viewer at a safe distance, was deeply comforting. In the face of Indian agency, Lang's composition permitted his reader to be composed. Demands for Indian representation were met with European representations that froze India. The thrust of Lang's picturesque essays is that India, for all its current turbulence, is a static and bucolic space, a canvas on which European mastery can assert itself without violence.

Though Lang, the picturesque wanderer, presents his narrative as a factual account of a journey undertaken through the North-Western

---

33. "Wanderings in India," *Household Words*, 19 December 1857, 14. A key feature of the picturesque was contrasts of light and dark, or chiaroscuro. Such effects appear textually in Lang's essays: "It was a very picturesque scene; the white tents stand out in relief from the dark wood, lighted up by the fires, and here and there groups of coolies wrapped up in blankets, and sitting as closely as possible to the blaze" ("Wanderings in India," *Household Words*, 30 January 1858, 152).

Provinces, there is much in the essays to throw doubt upon their veracity. Lang studiously avoids situating his journey in time. Early on he indicates that shortly after landing in Calcutta and without any occupation, he began his "rambles" into the countryside, or mofussil. The itinerary sketched in the twelve installments is a familiar one, traversed by thousands of Company officials and narrated in dozens of travelogues by Anglo-Indians and Britons: from Calcutta up the Gangetic Plain to Delhi and thence into the hill stations. The earliest calendric guide Lang provides for his version of this well-worn journey is that he leaves Calcutta on an August day for Tirhoot, where he remains eight months, the guest of indigo planters; his next halts are Lucknow, where he stops five months,[34] then Bithoor, which he departs in September for Agra.[35] From this point on, we are provided with only stopping points, no dates or seasonal clues: from Delhi to Meerut to numerous stations in the interior and then into the hills to Dehradun, Mussoorie, and Almora; back in the plains, Lang visits Bijnor and Ambala before heading to Anglo-India's favorite hill station, Shimla. A tour of this nature could last anywhere from a few months to a year, depending on pace and how long a traveler stopped in each locale. Lang tells us he journeyed in a leisurely fashion and at several stops remained for weeks, such as at Bijnor, where he stopped a month to study Hindustani and Persian with a local munshi, and Meerut, where he stayed six weeks.[36] The tour as Lang narrates it here would have taken anywhere from sixteen to twenty-four months.

Any effort to map this discursive journey onto the biography of John Lang proves fruitless. Lang and his family arrived in Calcutta in June 1842; at its earliest, his tour through the plains and into the hills would not have begun before 1843. From August 1845 onward, he was the editor of a newspaper, a consuming task, particularly as he twice moved the newspaper's base, from Calcutta to Ambala in 1846, then to Meerut in 1847 (see chapter 1). The travels as Lang describes them could plausibly only have taken place between 1843 and 1845, but contextual clues in "Wanderings in India" suggest a different timeline. In the first

---

34. "Wanderings in India," *Household Words*, 14 November 1857, 458.

35. "Wanderings in India," *Household Words*, 28 November 1857, 505.

36. Bijnor: "Wanderings in India," *Household Words*, 13 February 1858, 212; Meerut: "Wanderings in India," *Household Words*, 16 January 1858, 113.

installment, our traveler meets the man known as Nana Sahib and reviled as the "Butcher of Cawnpore" for his role in the Kanpur massacres of June 1857. In the narrative, Lang discovers that Nana Sahib subscribes to the *Delhi Gazette*, the *Mofussilite*, and the *Calcutta Englishman*.[37] As the *Mofussilite* was born in 1845, the detail provides one temporal anchor point; another is that Nana Sahib complains that the Company has denied him his father's pension. Baji Rao II, Nana Sahib's adoptive father, died in January 1851, so the narrated encounter between Lang and Nana Sahib could only have occurred following 1851. A few installments later, Lang tells of his unexpected meeting with "Lallah Jooteepersâd" and mentions that "that very night, the Lallah was informed that he was, to all intents and purposes, a prisoner, and must not leave Agra."[38] As we saw in chapter 2, the charges against Jyoti Prasad were brought in November or December 1850, suggesting that the events of the fourth installment occur prior to incidents narrated in the first, which could not have occurred prior to January 1851. Later yet, in the eighth installment, the narrator shares his age which, if he were the historical person John Lang, would place the text at 1848.[39]

In short, the discursive journey does not map onto any plausible "real" journey "John Lang" could have undertaken. As the editor of a twice-weekly newspaper, Lang was busy and it is difficult to imagine that he had a year and a half or more between 1848 and 1851 during which he could take off from his editing duties and wander the countryside aimlessly. We know that during his editorship he took leaves—to defend Jyoti Prasad in 1851 or to repair to the hills for health.[40] But the notion that he established his paper in 1847 in Meerut and then abandoned it for a lengthy period is implausible. What is more likely is that Lang took many small excursions through the North-Western Provinces between 1847

---

37. "Wanderings in India," *Household Words*, 14 November 1857, 461. Lang spells the name "Nena."

38. "Wanderings in India," *Household Words*, 2 January 1858, 68.

39. "Wanderings in India," *Household Words*, 30 January 1858, 148.

40. On 5 March 1850, the *Mofussilite* announced that "declining health will compel the Editor of this paper to be absent from the plains during the hot weather, and edit the paper from Simlah" (220). And on 15 April 1850, the newspaper spoke of itself as the "Meerut Journal, edited from the Hills" (244).

and 1851, when the *Mofussilite* was based in Meerut and Lang in India. For *Household Words*, he sutured these excursions and experiences into a continuous and seamless journey. Why Lang would choose the form of a journey for his portrait of India is a question I turn to next.

In addition to the nonlinear chronology, Lang also worked hard to suppress his own role in events; he wrote not as "John Lang," but as an unnamed wanderer. When, for instance, he relates the encounter with Jyoti Prasad, Lang never mentions that it was *he* who would effectuate the acquittal he writes about. More striking yet is the episode this chapter opened with in which Lang reports on the "native newspaper" in Meerut that drew material from an Anglo-Indian newspaper. The account begins, "While at Meerut I was a guest of the editor of the journal which used to issue from that station, and as my stay extended over six weeks, during which period I frequently assisted the editor in his work, I gained some knowledge of the practical working of the press in the Upper Provinces. I am authorized to make any use I please of this knowledge."[41] That editor was, of course, the historical figure John Lang, but this fact is suppressed. The "I" of the "Wanderings" essays is separated from the writing "I"; it is not the same as the embodied John Lang, but a persona or alter ego.

The adoption of a persona for investigative reports was a feature of *Household Words*' house style. Drew describes this style as "convert[ing] raw research findings . . . into stories embroidered by Scheherezade" (115).[42] Dickens began to develop his playful yet perceptive traveling man who journeys into town and country as early as *Sketches by Boz* (1833–36) and it remained a favored form he returned to in his journalistic writing throughout his career.[43] Just weeks before the first appearance of "Wanderings," *Household Words* carried "The Lazy Tour of Two Idle Apprentices." Co-authored by Dickens and Wilkie Collins, the five-part series recounts the walking tour of Francis Goodchild and Thomas Idle, stand-ins for Dickens and Collins. Under the guise of narrating a tour of

---

41. "Wanderings in India," *Household Words*, 16 January 1858, 113.

42. See pages 113–18 and 123–25 for more on this style.

43. The urban sketches of Boz were extended to Dickens's Italian travels in the "Traveling Letters" that appeared in the *Daily News* (1846) and continued into his twilight years with the "Uncommercial Traveller" (1860–69), whose journeys appeared in *All the Year Round*.

Cumberland, the collaboration meditates on mid-century preoccupations such as the hectic pace of modern life and rapid technological developments in a seriocomic tone.[44]

Dickens exported this hallmark style to his many acolytes—or imposed it on them. *Household Words*' most prominent urbane traveler who narrates his journeys through an ironic alter ego was perhaps George Augustus Sala, whose twenty-two-part "A Journey Due North" appeared in the journal between October 1856 and March 1857 to immense acclaim. One of Dickens's most favored "young men," Sala traveled to St. Petersburg in the wake of the Crimean War at Dickens's behest.[45] Sala adopted a breezy, nonchalant tone, at one point referring to his mission as "purposeless journeying . . . a pilgrimage to the shrine of our Lady of Haphazard."[46] Drew contends that "Dickens's varied deployment in his magazines of 'Specials' as writers of sketches of travel, life and manners in Russia, Turkey, Paris, Rome, Naples, and Cologne, was a distinct innovation" (119). Though not a special correspondent sent on assignment to investigate manners and customs as Sala was, Lang was a Dickens "Special," commissioned to write about India, where he had resided for a decade and a half. The voice and persona he adopted in many of his essays—in "Wanderings" as well as in pieces such as "Hovelling," which appeared in early 1857—is detached, urbane, deliberately unserious, much like the persona adopted by so many *Household Words* writers.[47] That Lang chose a travelogue—the journey as

---

44. Drew writes that "the travel motif becomes a vehicle for social and cultural criticism, a medium for assessing that most Victorian of pre-occupations, change" (qtd. in Schlicke 588).

45. Waters writes that Sala was the most acclaimed example of Dickens using one of his "stable" of writers as a special correspondent.

46. "A Journey Due North," *Household Words*, 6 December 1856, 493. Sala even obliquely refers to Lang in the first installment, a reminder that Dickens's network of writers was tight. Speaking of his boredom and need to get away and experience hardship, Sala writes that he wishes he "could be importuned for copy by the editor of the Mofussilite, and not the Morning Meteor" ("A Journey Due North," *Household Words*, 4 October 1856, 265).

47. The eighth installment of "Wanderings," for instance, tells of the narrator's jaunt into the hills in the company of a German baron and French gentleman ("Wanderings in India," *Household Words*, 30 January 1858, 148–56). The men travel from Dehradun to Mussoorie to Almora with a retinue of 150 men who haul around cases of wine and

a frame upon which to hang an exploration of topical issues—and this voice for his series is a reflection of the genre's and style's currency in *Household Words*. Lang was adapting himself to Brand Dickens.

Indigenizing Brand Dickens

Yet while "Wanderings in India" invokes the form and conventions of a travel narrative, its substance bears little resemblance to a travelogue. Despite the liberal sprinkling of picturesque references, the adoption of an urbane and aimless wanderer, and travel to key destinations in the North-Western Provinces, the series is only tangentially about India. The narrator's occasional remarks that for months he spoke "nothing but Hindostanee or Persian" or passed long periods without encountering "a single European face" are offered to enhance his credibility, but they cannot mask the fact that his wanderings are confined almost exclusively to upper-crust, Anglo-Indian society.[48] "Wanderings," in fact, distinguishes itself from the standard Indian travelogue by containing not a single visit to a temple or mosque, no view of ruins or ancient cities (the Taj Mahal gets only a passing reference), no "nautch" or description of the Delhi durbar. Though Crittenden characterizes "Wanderings" as "stories . . . about the people of India" (73), Indians are scarce in this text. Lang mentions several elites he meets, but their names are dropped into the text in passing reference.[49] His interlocutors are largely Anglo-Indians. Dividing his

---

claret, guns and bedding, tables and leather chests. The pace is unhurried and consists of page after page that reads like this: "We were rather a temperate party; and after the second bottle of wine . . . began to play at whist" (148) or "During this march, we did not go out of our way for game; but only took such as chanced to cross our path. All we killed was ghooral [Himalayan deer] (which we did not stop to look at even) and two brace of partridges of very peculiar plumage" (152).

48. Hindostanee: "Wanderings in India," *Household Words*, 14 November 1857, 458; European: "Wanderings in India," *Household Words*, 20 February 1858, 220.

49. In the first installment, in the space of one page, Lang mentions meeting the raja of Bettiah, the raja of Durbungah, Ally Nucky Khan, and Nana Sahib ("Wanderings in India," *Household Words*, 14 November 1857, 458; I have retained his Anglicized spellings here). In the fourth installment, he meets Raja Lall Singh, commander of the Sikhs, and in the sixth installment, he meets "Maharajah Hindoo-Rao, a little fat, round Mahratta chieftain" ("Wanderings in India," *Household Words*, 16 January 1858, 112).

time between military and civilian officials of the East India Company, Lang explores not the built Indian environment nor Indian society, but Anglo-Indian society. A more accurate title for these essays would be "Wanderings in Anglo-India."

Life in the barracks and clubs our narrator moves within is frivolous and trivial—and portrayed as such. Agra society is mockingly described as "split into two sections, the civil and military," which, though "not exactly at open war," cannot agree on simple civilities.[50] Lang relates a minor incident at a ball that sets in motion a cascade of complaints to the governor general, the Court of Directors, the Board of Control, and the home government, and that produces "documents . . . [that] would, if put into type, form a volume five times as bulky as Sir William Napier's Conquest of Scinde."[51] The reference to Scinde (or Sindh), one of the final frontiers in the Company's battlefield conquests, is telling and belies the satirical posture: for the narrator, ennui ensues when the work of war and conquest is exchanged for governance; boredom feeds petty rivalries and squabbles. Other installments—the eighth, eleventh, and thirteenth—depict similarly jaded and directionless Anglo-Indian communities in the North-Western Provinces. The "character of an officer's life in India" is represented as having "an air of lassitude and satiety," the body "much too exhausted to admit of any serious mental exertion beyond that which sheer amusement can afford."[52] Though the weather is blamed for this enervation, the presentation is of a bored and aimless community, one flirting with a nabobian lifestyle.[53]

As an outsider to official Anglo-Indian society, the narrator searches for an alternative or larger purpose. That meaning is conveyed not through his behavior—the narrator too often participates in the frivolous pastimes

---

50. "Wanderings in India," *Household Words*, 2 January 1858, 67.

51. "Wanderings in India," *Household Words*, 9 January 1858, 90.

52. "Wanderings in India," *Household Words*, 20 February 1858, 222. The enervation and ennui of officers was often blamed as a cause of the disaffection among sepoys—see the letter in the *Hurkaru* referenced on page 145.

53. See David Arnold for a discussion of the environmental determinism of Western medicine in India (75–84). Arnold argues that while Ayurvedic medicine also leaned on environmental explanations for human health and disease, doctors practicing Western medicine in India in the nineteenth century believed that "the effect of environmental idiosyncrasies—such as the monsoon—were . . . aided and abetted by such peculiar rites and customs as Hindu pilgrimages and bathing festivals" (76).

he mocks—but textually by his reliance on the trope of scripted and highly contrived conversations. Lieutenant Sixtie—so-called because he has sixty first cousins serving in India and "upwards of two hundred and twenty relations and connexions" working for the government[54]—is the first of Lang's several interlocutors, and he appears over three installments (the fourth through sixth). In addition to this devil-may-care lieutenant, our narrator encounters a magistrate who "spoke Hindoostanee as well as any native"[55] and Nobinkissen, a "Bengalee Baboo" who speaks flawless English.[56] It is through exchanges with such "characters" that Lang conveys an alternative to the hollow lifestyle of the Anglo-Indians in their clubs and hill-station retreats.

The narrator's encounter with each interlocutor unfolds identically: an extended catechism-like exchange in which our wide-eyed narrator is the examiner and an informed "local" his respondent. Here, for instance, is a characteristic—and characteristically lengthy—exchange in which Nobinkissen addresses the government's financial straits:

> "Ah, sir!" he remarked, "it is a pitiful thing that the government of a great empire like this should ever be in pecuniary difficulties and put to their wits' end for a few millions annually, in order to make the receipts square with the expenditure."
> "But how can it be helped?" I asked.
> "Easily, sir," he replied. "Why not make it expedient to do away with the perpetual settlement of Lord Cornwallis, and resettle the whole of Bengal? That is by far the most fertile province in the East; but it is taxed lighter than even these poor lands of the Upper Provinces. Look at the Durbungah Rajah. Nearly the whole of Tirhoot—the garden of India—belongs to him, and he does not pay into the government treasury half a lac [five thousand pounds] per annum, while his collections amount to upwards of twenty lacs. These are the men who get hold of the money and bury it and keep it from circulating."

---

54. "Wanderings in India," *Household Words*, 2 January 1858, 64.

55. "Wanderings in India," *Household Words*, 6 February 1858, 180.

56. Lang writes that this gentleman who served time for judicial fraud "spoke English with marvellous fluency, and accuracy, and could read and write the language as well and as elegantly as any educated European" ("Wanderings in India," *Household Words*, 9 January 1858, 91).

"But all zemindarees [lands] are not so profitable in Bengal?"

"No. Many are not worth holding—especially the smaller ones, although the land is just as good and just as well cultivated."

"But how is that?"

"They are so heavily taxed. You must know, sir, that in those days—the days of Lord Cornwallis—the greatest frauds were committed in respect to the perpetual settlement. The natives who were about and under the settlement officers all made immense fortunes, and the zemindars from whom they took their bribes have profited ever since to the cost of the poorer zemindars, who could not or would not bribe, and to the cost of the British government. It is a great mistake to suppose that the whole of the landholders in Bengal would cry out against a re-settlement of that province. Only men holding vast tracts of country, at a comparatively nominal rent, would cry out."

"And tax the British government with a breach of faith?"

"Yes. But what need the government care for that cry—especially when its act is not only expedient, but would be just withal? In Bengal, all the great zemindars are rich, very rich, men. In these provinces, with very, very few exceptions, they are poor, so that the whole of Upper India would be glad to see the perpetual settlement done away with, and the land re-settled."

"Why so?"

"That is only human—and, certainly, Asiatic—nature. Few of us like to behold our neighbours better off than ourselves; so that the cry of faith-breaking would not meet with a response in this part of the world."

"Yes; but in Europe the cry would be too powerful to contend against. The Exeter Hall orators and the spouters at the Court of Proprietors would—"

"Ah, sir! India should either be governed in India or in England. It is the number of wheels in the government that clogs the movement of the machine."

"Very true."[57]

---

57. "Wanderings in India," *Household Words*, 9 January 1858, 92.

In this dialogue between a "character" and our faux-naïve narrator, Lang takes up some of the charges levied against the government of India, including land revenue and the government's reneging on treaties no longer considered convenient, issues early identified as catalysts of the Uprising. Under the guise of a conversation between himself and Nobinkissen—a man described as "the cleverest Hindoo whom I encountered during my sojourn in the East"[58]—Lang offers a polemic on the contentious topics of land revenue and fulfilling agreements.

The positions staked out—here, that the taxation system is a fraud engineered by rich Indian landowners, that old agreements between the Company and zamindars ought to be revamped, that meddlesome Britons ought to leave the business of governing India to Anglo-Indians—are not in the narrator's voice, but in the "expert's." In case after case, Lang ventriloquizes controversial positions, placing them in the mouth of a "credible" interlocutor, sometimes a native informant, sometimes an Anglo-Indian of long-standing experience in the country. The rhetorical strategy of embedded voices or invented speech was deployed regularly by Greek and Roman rhetoricians in public addresses. So valued was prosopopoeia, or speech in others' voices, that it was a standard part of the rhetorical training of young boys in the *progymnasmata* (Fahnestock 306–19).[59] Such exchanges are repeated in almost every installment of "Wanderings." With their perfectly selected "expert" and naïve prompter, they are utterly contrived; conversations supposedly from a decade prior speak directly to issues and controversies that were receiving attention in the days following the mutinies and uprisings. But it is in these contrived, temporally dissonant, and prosopopoeic moments that we get Lang's views on the governance of India.

A frequent target of his—or his handy interlocutors'—criticism is what Lieutenant Sixtie refers to as "Government logic."[60] Military orders issued by the civilian government are especially denounced. Prominent among the practices critiqued are appointing untrained officers to positions of authority, promoting "natives" according to seniority rather than merit, interfering in the relations between British officers and sepoys, and

---

58. "Wanderings in India," *Household Words*, 9 January 1858, 91.

59. That such a training was part of Lang's education is likely: he had attended Sydney College, run by William Cape, where Lang won the first medal for classics in 1835 (Roderick and Earnshaw 110).

60. "Wanderings in India," *Household Words*, 2 January 1858, 66.

"humouring . . . native soldiers."[61] (The last was a common charge directed at the Company in Anglo-Indian prints, which blamed it for "pampering" sepoys and thus sowing the seeds of the mutiny.[62]) Other charges that appear in the mouths of interlocutors include the government's shaky grasp of "principles of good government," its lack of foresight in building roads to encourage tea plantations to undercut "Mr. Chinaman," its governance by nepotism, and its indulgence of Hindus and their religious strictures.[63]

To readers of this book, many of these criticisms of the Company will sound familiar—they appeared in the *Mofussilite* throughout Lang's tenure as editor, as chapter 1 details—and not especially bold. At least since Burke's impeachment of Hastings in the late eighteenth century, criticism of the Company's policies and governance of India were unceasing, even relentless in some quarters. Denunciations even crept into travelogues such as Valentia's 1809 *Voyages and Travels in India*.[64] In both the British and the Anglo-Indian press, one did not have to look hard or dig deep to find such censure. The critic Grace Moore refers to the liberal-centrist *Household Words* as "the dominant player in exposing the East India Company's nepotism through investigative pieces like John Capper's 'The Great Indian Bean-Stalk' and 'A Pull at the Pagoda Tree'" (108). But Moore vastly exaggerates the periodical's dominance in leading charges against the Company; criticisms of the Company were widespread prior to the 1857 Uprising, and Lang's critiques in "Wanderings" would hardly have appeared either as news or as especially bold; he was treading so well-worn a path as to be rehearsing a cliché.

---

61. Untrained officers: "Wanderings in India," *Household Words*, 19 December 1857, 15, and "Wanderings in India," *Household Words*, 20 February 1858, 221; seniority: "Wanderings in India," *Household Words*, 19 December 1857, 15; officers and sepoys: "Wanderings in India," *Household Words*, 19 December 1857, 14–16; humoring: "Wanderings in India," *Household Words*, 16 January 1858, 112.

62. See *Bengal Hurkaru*, 23 April 1857, 382, and 28 April 1857, 398. The *Mofussilite*'s record of making such critiques predates the 1857 mutinies: "The fact is that the sepoy has been so petted, belauded, and indulged, that he is quite *spoilt* . . . [I]t is the pernicious fashion to pamper and applaud [the sepoy]" (8 February 1850, 92).

63. Shaky grasp: "Wanderings in India," *Household Words*, 2 January 1858, 68; lack of foresight: "Wanderings in India," *Household Words*, 30 January 1858, 152; nepotism: "Wanderings in India," *Household Words*, 2 January 1858, 68; indulgence: "Wanderings in India," *Household Words*, 9 January 1858, 93.

64. See Leask (184).

Additionally, to suggest, as Crittenden does, that such censure of the government was accompanied by sympathy for Indians is to give Lang's text more credit than it deserves.[65] Indians in "Wanderings" are secondary to Anglo-Indians, an afterthought, and presented largely as entertainment.[66] Those he favors, such as Nobinkissen, speak flawless English, are elegant and educated. Others such as his boy-servant Sham amuse him with his "quaint" English idioms and Orientalized "gay attire—a purple velvet tunic, pyjamahs of red silk trimmed with gold lace, a turban of very gorgeous aspect, and shoes embroidered all over with silver."[67] With the exception of Nana Sahib whose home decor and complaints about the Company Lang writes about at some length, most Indians are mentioned fleetingly, a name dropped into the text to enhance Lang's credibility. Mirroring this remoteness, Indians are referred to in generalities. Thus, the complaints of a *subedar* (the highest-ranking Indian in the Company's army) leads Lang to declare that a "native—especially a native commissioned officer—[will never] forget a grievance."[68] In a classic Orientalized move, a single person exemplifies an entire people or race.

Lang's most frequently repeated generalization is that Indians are complainers. In the first installment, upon meeting Nana Sahib, Lang writes, "I have been the guest of some scores of rajahs, great and small, and I never knew one who had not a grievance."[69] The remark is curious as Lang, in the previous decade, had taken up the cases of two prominent Indians with "grievances": Jyoti Prasad (in 1851) and the rani of Jhansi (in 1854). While the rani does not make an appearance in "Wanderings"—but does in *Wanderings*—Jyoti Prasad has a cameo, though Lang muzzles his own role in representing Prasad and securing his freedom. The omission is likely determined by the essays' appearance in London in the midst of the uprisings and highlights Lang's balancing act as he juggled two roles: as a

---

65. Crittenden often refers to Lang as a friend of Indians: his "sympathetic depiction of lives of [the native Indian people]" (xii) and "Lang's sympathy for the native people" (133).

66. On occasion, Lang gives "voice" to an Indian perspective as when an Indian interlocutor exposes caste as a tool used to avoid unpleasant tasks: "Wanderings in India," *Household Words*, 28 November 1857, 510, and "Wanderings in India," *Household Words*, 19 December 1857, 13.

67. "Wanderings in India," *Household Words*, 13 February 1858, 214, and "Wanderings in India," *Household Words*, 20 February 1858, 220.

68. "Wanderings in India" *Household Words*, 2 January 1858, 65.

69. "Wanderings in India" *Household Words*, 14 November 1857, 461.

guide to India and as guide to Indians. While Lang's legal representation of Indians such as Jyoti Prasad gave credence and shape to their political dissent, his textual representation personalizes dissent, reducing it to an individual's "grievances," thereby discrediting it. His depiction of Indians avoids the inflammatory and hysterical note in the more vitriolic reactions circulating in London, such as Dickens's genocidal outburst that "I wish I were Commander in Chief in India. . . . I should do my utmost to exterminate the Race upon whom the stain of the late cruelties rested . . . to blot it out of mankind and raze it off the face of the Earth" (Storey and Tillotson 8:459). But Lang's depiction is unabashedly patronizing and diminishes Indians and their aspirations. It stands in contrast to the more bellicose reactions of the day, but by leavening depictions of Indians as craven with censure of the Company and Anglo-Indian life, Lang merely offers a vision of an imperialism that is—or could be—kinder and gentler.

A final episode from "Wanderings in India" will illustrate the terrain Lang negotiated as he repackaged his colonial experiences for a metropolitan audience in 1857. The vignette this chapter opened with of the ruptured intimacy between the English-language and Urdu-language newspapers in Meerut ends on an intriguing note. To illustrate that Indian editors' "bitter irony [is wrapped] in the most complimentary phrases," Lang tells the story of an "editor of a native paper" who "never lost an opportunity of bringing British rule in India into disgrace, ridicule and contempt."[70] He did this in "flattering" language that Englishmen missed, but "Asiatics" understood; naïve Company officials, Lang continues, latched onto the editor's compliments, not his ridicule, and he was awarded a lucrative government appointment. The article that led to this man's promotion was "one descriptive of Lord Dalhousie, on the back of an elephant, proceeding to a spot appointed as the place of an interview between his Lordship and the late Maharajah Goolab Singh."[71] In 1851, when Dalhousie was governor general, Lang ran a short piece in the *Mofussilite* that we have encountered in previous chapters: under the header "From our own Correspondent with the Camp of the Governor General," the report is filed from "the darbar of Mahrag Glob Sing and the Governor General" and reports that the "G. G. was rid on eleyphant."The account is signed "Mahomed Usghur."[72]

---

70. "Wanderings in India," *Household Words*, 16 January 1858, 115.

71. "Wanderings in India," *Household Words*, 16 January 1858, 115.

72. *Mofussilite*, 7 January 1851, 12. See chapter 1 for the full report.

Though we cannot know for certain if "Mahomed Usghur" is the errant editor mentioned in "Wanderings," the reverberations between the story that appeared in the Anglo-Indian *Mofussilite* in 1851 and the episode related in *Household Words* in 1858 are compelling. If "Mahomed Usghur," the *Mofussilite*'s 1851 correspondent, is the deceptive editor Lang writes of in 1858, then the chosen correspondent whom Lang himself had promoted in 1851 had, by 1858, became a pariah. The section in "Wanderings" concludes, "I hear that he is now aide-de-camp and military secretary to Bahadoor Khan, the rebel, who is at the head of a considerable army, and, according to the latest accounts, in possession of the entire Bareilly district."[73] Given the vagaries of transliteration, "Usghur" is potentially a variant of "Asghar" or "Azhar"; if so, the *Mofussilite*'s "Mahomed Usghur" is possibly Muhammad Azhar, the Arabic teacher at Agra College who, along with his brother "Ali Asghar," joined rebel forces (Powell 94). The connections are tantalizing and suggestive: they tell a colonial story of intimacy and tutelage that had to be suppressed in the wake of the Uprising. In the "Wanderings" essays, Lang is silent about his role as guide and instructor in India, displacing responsibility for the breach between Anglo-Indian and Urdu-language newspapers upon a dummy "friend" and failing to mention that *he* had nurtured and mentored at least one Indian correspondent at the *Mofussilite*. The "native newspaper" incident, appearing almost at the very heart of the "Wanderings" series, captures with clarity the contortions Lang performed in order to camouflage and whitewash colonial experience for a metropolitan audience.

"Wanderings in India" is a curious text. In the sociopolitical climate in which it appeared, it is striking for its outmoded tone and attitude towards India. The text's discrepancy is in some measure the result of the conventions—generic and editorial—that Lang operated within, conventions that, though they did not dictate his choices, at least overdetermined them. The travelogue, penned in a detached and urbane voice, was shaped in part by Brand Dickens and in part by the picturesque mode that had dominated travel writing about India since the beginning of the nineteenth century. Working within these conventions, Lang's meandering text offers, on the one hand, a more muted response to events in India at a moment when calls for vengeance were in the air. On the other, it presents India as largely Anglo-Indian, and the few Indians who appear

---

73. "Wanderings in India," *Household Words*, 16 January 1858, 116.

in it are infantilized and in need to Anglo-Indian tutelage. If Indians are virtually absent, Anglo-Indians, with the exception of a few knowledgeable interlocutors, appear idle and incompetent, with no interest in and slim knowledge of the country they reside in. If little about "Wanderings in India" was informative or insightful about 1857, much of it was innocuous, a sedative to well-heeled and seething metropolitan readers. Lang's apolitical "Wanderings" might well have been his effort to intervene in and redirect slightly the depiction of India, while simultaneously maintaining his place in the metropolitan publishing world.

Independent *Wanderings*

The policy at *Household Words* was that essays appeared anonymously, but Dickens permitted authors the right to republish their essays after a short period without violating copyright.[74] Lang, like many others, took advantage of this clause, and in August 1859 a volume entitled *Wanderings in India and Other Sketches of Life in Hindostan* came out in London. Unlike "Wanderings" which had appeared, quite literally, under Dickens's name—on every odd-numbered page—*Wanderings* appeared with Lang's name on the title page. In addition to the lengthier title and byline, three other features mark the volume as different: the twelve parts of "Wanderings in India" are augmented with five other essays; of these, three had appeared in *Household Words* earlier and only two were previously unpublished pieces. In addition, the twelve installments of "Wanderings" now appeared under chapter titles: thus, what was before simply the 2 January 1858 installment of "Wanderings in India" is now a chapter titled "The March Continued," the 30 January installment now "The Himalayas," and so on. Finally, *Wanderings* included a frontispiece facing the title page, an image of three men in a horse-drawn carriage surrounded by attendants. The journey from serial publication in a journal to a single-authored volume marks another port—destination, for Lang—in the circulation from colony to metropole. Thus far, my discussion has highlighted the

---

74. Many complained that the journal's anonymity was uneven: Dickens's name appeared on the masthead (the full title was *Household Words. A Weekly Journal Conducted by Charles Dickens*) and on the left corner of every odd-numbered page. Douglas Jerrold quipped that items were published in *Household Words* "mononymous" (qtd. in Drew 118).

disjunctive and jarring nature of the essays as they relocated in time and place to appear in *Household Words*, a gap that allowed the pieces to slip into a reassuring role. This section discusses the serial-to-volume shift, materially and substantively.

Bibliographers have long been concerned with the book as a physical object—examining its size, paper, type, etc.—but such matters received a new direction in the 1970s in the work of D. F. McKenzie. McKenzie sought to marry the materialist emphasis of bibliographers with the textual focus of literary scholars, urging scholars to attend to the "relation between book form and textual meaning" ("Dialectics" 48). In the 1977 essay "Typography and Meaning: The Case of William Congreve," McKenzie argued that it is "quite impossible . . . to divorce the substance of the text on the one hand from the physical form of its presentation on the other. The book itself is an expressive means" (200). His insistence that the physical form of the book is central to its meanings has been distilled into the succinct formulation that "[t]he forms of texts affect their meanings" (McDonald and Suarez 9) and the "truism" in Book History: "writers don't write books, they write texts. A book is created when a text is transformed by print, when it is literally shaped into a material object whose visual and tactile features render it perceptible and accessible to others" (Gutjahr and Benton 65).

McKenzie's reorientation did not displace authors so much as de-emphasize them. As literary scholars were moving away from the Romantic-inspired Author, Book History scholars from Elizabeth Eisenstein to McKenzie, Robert Darnton to Roger Chartier were underscoring the intertwined relations between author, publisher, printer, distributor, bookseller, and reader. As Chartier notes, "If the body of the book is the result of the pressmen's labor[,] its soul is not fashioned solely by the author but shaped by all who have a hand in its punctuation, spelling, and layout, including the master printer, the compositors, the copyeditors, and the proofreaders" (77). In chapter 1, I discussed McGann's attention to features such as punctuation, spelling, and layout that he refers to as "bibliographic codes" and distinguishes from "linguistic codes," textual meanings that are author-generated. Analyzing the work of authors such as Blake and Matthew Arnold in light of such bibliographic matters, McGann demonstrates that "[m]eaning is transmitted through bibliographical as well as linguistic codes" ("Textual" 57).

Among the bibliographic codes or visual features of a book that McKenzie emphasized are the size, color, weight, and quality of the paper;

types, their size, and the ink used; the format of the book, its title page, frontispiece, and illustrations; structural divisions such as section titles, chapters, and indexes; page organizers such as columns, running titles, footnotes, pagination, and rules; and "most important of all, blank white space" ("Typography" 217). My analysis of *Wanderings* will emphasize a number of these bibliographic codes and attend to the ways in which they inform and shape the meaning of Lang's text as it continued its journey in the metropole. My aim is to augment a textual analysis with a materialist one in order to deepen our grasp of the meanings and uses of Lang's writings as they circulate across time and beyond the space they were initially conceived in.

At the macro-bibliographic level, *Wanderings in India and Other Sketches of Life in Hindostan* was published, in both 1859 and 1861, by the London firm of Routledge, Warne and Routledge. Established in 1843 by George Routledge, a bookseller and unsuccessful author, the firm became lucrative only after it started to publish cheap reprints. In 1849, it introduced the "Railway Library" series. Targeting railroad travelers, the shilling volumes by authors such as Benjamin Disraeli, Harriet Beecher Stowe, and that perennial favorite, Edward Bulwer-Lytton, were immensely popular and commercially viable (Brake and Demoor 546; Maidment). Though in the twentieth century Routledge evolved into an academic imprint, in the 1850s the firm specialized in light fare, both fiction and nonfiction. In 1859, the "Cheap Series" included titles by Longfellow, Stowe, and Defoe, as well as *The Sepoy Revolt* by someone identified only as "Mead" and the anonymous *Sebastopol, the Story of Its Fall*.[75] This is the label under which Lang's Indian picturesque, following its improbable appearance in Dickens's *Household Words* during the heat of the Uprising, appeared. Appearing in the Routledge, Warne, and Routledge catalogue, *Wanderings* was packaged and distributed as leisure reading.[76] If "Wanderings" in *Household Words* marked one departure from the political analysis and intervention that Lang's Anglo-Indian newspaper aimed for, *Wanderings*, published almost exactly a year after the dissolution of the East India Company's governance of India, underscores that the political train had left the station well and

---

75. "Routledge's Cheap Literature" [classified advertisement], *The Times* (London, England), 21 September 1859, 12.

76. Lang's novel *Too Clever by Half* was advertised under the banner "Cheap Books for the Rail" (see *The Athenaeum*, 3 December 1853, 1439).

good. The expanded title with its reference to "Sketches" underscores the leisurely and perambulatory; in volume form, Lang's text, marketed as light fare, completed its author's journey away from political commentary and analysis to easy-to-stomach fare.

In the Routledge volume, Lang's essays assume a new format and physical form. In *Household Words* they appeared in the midst of four to six other pieces that were a mix of fiction and prose essays from a broadly social-reform perspective. Packaged under Dickens's name, Lang's essays were very literally bounded by the rules—in both the admonitory and typographical senses of the word—of the *Household Words* page: contained within the double lines that surrounded each page and divided by the vertical rule that partitioned each page into two columns. Though the two-columned page of the weekly *Household Words* was more expansive than a five- or six-columned newspaper, it was more cramped than an unruled and non-columned volume page. McKenzie notes that "[t]he principle of the short prose line is one which popular newspapers still treasure as an aid to their less literate readers" ("Typography" 220). Though the readers of *Household Words* were hardly "less literate," the principle McKenzie highlights is relevant: the shorter line of the periodical format is one that both serves and induces habits of skimming or reading rapidly. Each page of *Wanderings*, on the other hand, is unbounded and surrounded by copious white space, blank real estate that encourages a slower pace of reading. Additionally, the typeface in *Wanderings* is both less condensed and lighter than that of "Wanderings," which is tighter and weightier (see figures 4.2 and 4.3). The effect of these different physical formats is that the volume, with its greater elbow room and lighter touch, encourages lingering and musing. The physical format of *Wanderings* is more congruent with the rambles or titular "wanderings" of the genre Lang chose to locate his essays in.

Released from the rules, types, and constricted page layout of *Household Words*, *Wanderings* adopted more expansive chapter titles. In keeping with house protocol, none of the parts of "Wanderings" that appeared in *Household Words* had chapter titles.[77] Chapter titles ease a reader's journey through a volume which, in contrast to serial reading, is an experience of binge reading. Titles provide readers with signposts or navigational direction. Though he utilized chapter titles in *Wanderings*, Lang neglects

---

77. For a literary analogue, each installment of Elizabeth Gaskell's *North and South* appeared in the journal under a heading such as "North and South . . . Chapter the Fifth," while in volume form each chapter was assigned a name as in "The Mutiny" or "What Is a Strike?"

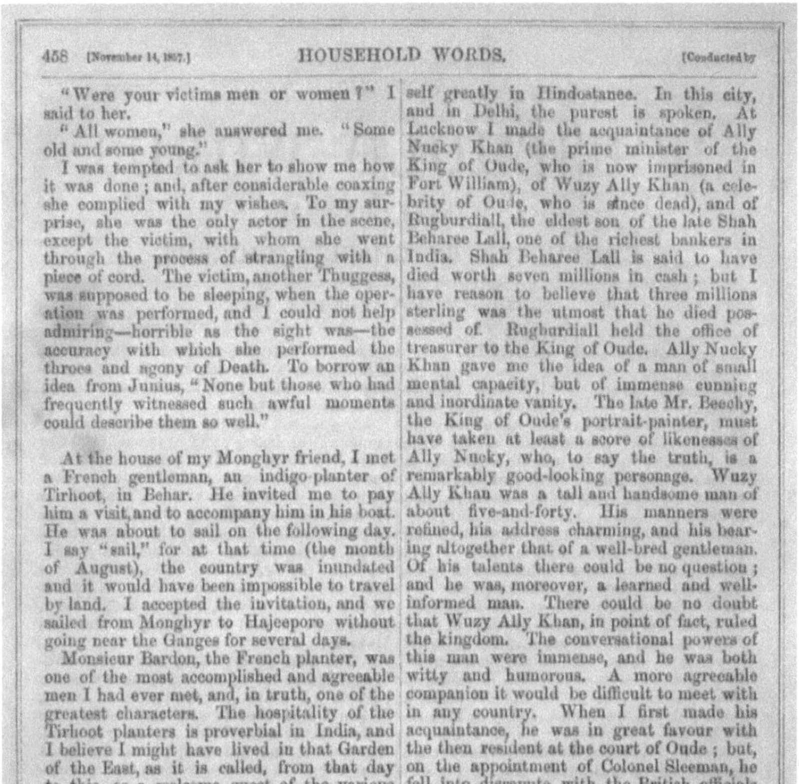

458 [November 14, 1857.] HOUSEHOLD WORDS. [Conducted by

"Were your victims men or women?" I said to her.

"All women," she answered me. "Some old and some young."

I was tempted to ask her to show me how it was done; and, after considerable coaxing she complied with my wishes. To my surprise, she was the only actor in the scene, except the victim, with whom she went through the process of strangling with a piece of cord. The victim, another Thuggess, was supposed to be sleeping, when the operation was performed, and I could not help admiring—horrible as the sight was—the accuracy with which she performed the throes and agony of Death. To borrow an idea from Junius, "None but those who had frequently witnessed such awful moments could describe them so well."

At the house of my Monghyr friend, I met a French gentleman, an indigo-planter of Tirhoot, in Behar. He invited me to pay him a visit, and to accompany him in his boat. He was about to sail on the following day. I say "sail," for at that time (the month of August), the country was inundated and it would have been impossible to travel by land. I accepted the invitation, and we sailed from Monghyr to Hajeepore without going near the Ganges for several days.

Monsieur Bardon, the French planter, was one of the most accomplished and agreeable men I had ever met, and, in truth, one of the greatest characters. The hospitality of the Tirhoot planters is proverbial in India, and I believe I might have lived in that Garden of the East, as it is called, from that day to this, as a welcome guest of the various planters, if I had chosen still to be their guest. As it was, I was eight months in the district, and then had very great difficulty in getting away. A now celebrated officer, at that time commanding the Irregular Cavalry at Segowlie, induced me to follow him; and, after leaving his abode, I went to the Bettiah Rajah, who initiated me into the mysteries of tiger-shooting. It was in the dominions of this small chief that my hands and face were so browned that I became far less fair than many natives of the country. Before leaving Tirhoot, however, I paid a visit to Rooder Singh, the Rajah of Durbungah, the richest native, perhaps, in all India. He has two hundred thousand pounds a-year net revenue; and, in a tank in his palace there is lying, in gold and silver, upwards of a million and a half sterling. Chutter Singh, the father of the Rajah of Durbungah, was a firm friend of the British Government during the Nepal war. He raised a regiment of horse and provisioned it. When asked by the authorities for his bill, he replied that the Government owed him nothing.

After leaving the Bettiah Rajah, I proceeded to Lucknow, where I improved myself greatly in Hindostanee. In this city, and in Delhi, the purest is spoken. At Lucknow I made the acquaintance of Ally Nucky Khan (the prime minister of the King of Oude, who is now imprisoned in Fort William), of Wuzy Ally Khan (a celebrity of Oude, who is since dead), and of Rugburdiall, the eldest son of the late Shah Beharee Lall, one of the richest bankers in India. Shah Beharee Lall is said to have died worth seven millions in cash; but I have reason to believe that three millions sterling was the utmost that he died possessed of. Rugburdiall held the office of treasurer to the King of Oude. Ally Nucky Khan gave me the idea of a man of small mental capacity, but of immense cunning and inordinate vanity. The late Mr. Beechy, the King of Oude's portrait-painter, must have taken at least a score of likenesses of Ally Nucky, who, to say the truth, is a remarkably good-looking personage. Wuzy Ally Khan was a tall and handsome man of about five-and-forty. His manners were refined, his address charming, and his bearing altogether that of a well-bred gentleman. Of his talents there could be no question; and he was, moreover, a learned and well-informed man. There could be no doubt that Wuzy Ally Khan, in point of fact, ruled the kingdom. The conversational powers of this man were immense, and he was both witty and humorous. A more agreeable companion it would be difficult to meet with in any country. When I first made his acquaintance, he was in great favour with the then resident at the court of Oude; but, on the appointment of Colonel Sleeman, he fell into disrepute with the British officials and continued so up to the time of his death, which occurred about two years ago. I was five months in Oude; and, during that period spoke nothing but Hindostanee, or Persian. I made a point of avoiding my own countrymen, and of associating only with the natives of India.

Previous to leaving Lucknow, a letter was despatched to Nena Sahib, informing him that a gentleman of distinction, a most intimate friend of the governor-general, and related by birth or marriage to every member of the council in Calcutta, as well as a constant guest of the Queen of England, was travelling through Hindostan in disguise, and would most probably, by his presence, illumine the abode of the Maharajah Bahadoor, and it was hoped that every respect would be paid to the dignity of the Sahib's exalted position, &c., &c. When the draft of this epistle was read aloud by the moonshee who had written it from dictation, I expostulated, on the ground that the contents were not in accordance with the truth. My scruples, however, were eventually overcome, and I took leave of my Lucknow friends, after being provided with all that I should require on my journey (of about forty-five

Figure 4.2. "Wanderings in India" in *Household Words*, November 1857 (courtesy of Dickens Journals Online).

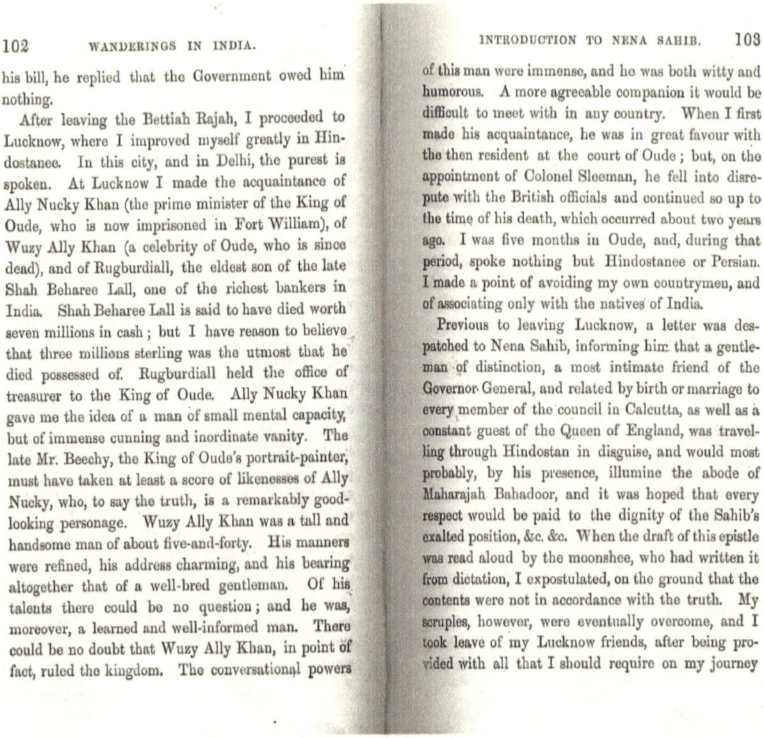
102 WANDERINGS IN INDIA.

his bill, he replied that the Government owed him nothing.

After leaving the Bettiah Rajah, I proceeded to Lucknow, where I improved myself greatly in Hindostanee. In this city, and in Delhi, the purest is spoken. At Lucknow I made the acquaintance of Ally Nucky Khan (the prime minister of the King of Oude, who is now imprisoned in Fort William), of Wuzy Ally Khan (a celebrity of Oude, who is since dead), and of Rugburdiall, the eldest son of the late Shah Beharee Lall, one of the richest bankers in India. Shah Beharee Lall is said to have died worth seven millions in cash; but I have reason to believe that three millions sterling was the utmost that he died possessed of. Rugburdiall held the office of treasurer to the King of Oude. Ally Nucky Khan gave me the idea of a man of small mental capacity, but of immense cunning and inordinate vanity. The late Mr. Beechy, the King of Oude's portrait-painter, must have taken at least a score of likenesses of Ally Nucky, who, to say the truth, is a remarkably good-looking personage. Wuzy Ally Khan was a tall and handsome man of about five-and-forty. His manners were refined, his address charming, and his bearing altogether that of a well-bred gentleman. Of his talents there could be no question; and he was, moreover, a learned and well-informed man. There could be no doubt that Wuzy Ally Khan, in point of fact, ruled the kingdom. The conversational powers

INTRODUCTION TO NENA SAHIB. 103

of this man were immense, and he was both witty and humorous. A more agreeable companion it would be difficult to meet with in any country. When I first made his acquaintance, he was in great favour with the then resident at the court of Oude; but, on the appointment of Colonel Sleeman, he fell into disrepute with the British officials and continued so up to the time of his death, which occurred about two years ago. I was five months in Oude, and, during that period, spoke nothing but Hindostanee or Persian. I made a point of avoiding my own countrymen, and of associating only with the natives of India.

Previous to leaving Lucknow, a letter was despatched to Nena Sahib, informing him that a gentleman of distinction, a most intimate friend of the Governor-General, and related by birth or marriage to every member of the council in Calcutta, as well as a constant guest of the Queen of England, was travelling through Hindostan in disguise, and would most probably, by his presence, illumine the abode of Maharajah Bahadoor, and it was hoped that every respect would be paid to the dignity of the Sahib's exalted position, &c. &c. When the draft of this epistle was read aloud by the moonshee, who had written it from dictation, I expostulated, on the ground that the contents were not in accordance with the truth. My scruples, however, were eventually overcome, and I took leave of my Lucknow friends, after being provided with all that I should require on my journey

Figure 4.3. *Wanderings in India and Other Sketches of Life in Hindostan*, 1859 (from Boston Public Library).

to optimize them. With a few exceptions, most of *Wanderings*' chapter titles are unimaginative, as for example "Miscellaneous" or "Forward." Only three of seventeen titles are cued to readers' or marketers' needs. "Tirhoot, Lucknow, Bhitoor, Etc." is one: to a reader in 1859, the title would resonate as it was common knowledge at this point that Nana Sahib, the "arch villain of Cawnpore," was from Bithoor. Other chapter titles—"Marching," "Returning"—seem deliberately designed to avert attention from the events of 1857–58. It is as if Lang were working hard to publish a *non*-Mutiny book. In light of the rush to publish accounts of 1857—the earliest began to appear in 1858[78]—Lang's decision to continue

78. Colin Campbell, commander in chief of the army that led the relief of Lucknow, came out with the 450-page *Narrative of the Indian Revolt: From Its Outbreak to the Capture of Lucknow* in 1858, and Martin Gubbins, besieged in Lucknow, published

to underplay the political and topical aspects of his writings underscores what was hinted at in "Wanderings": that Lang was working to offer a non-crisis, sentimental, and Orientalized vision of India. That he chose not to highlight the Mutiny or the sensationalist aspects of the events, either in *Household Words* or *Wanderings*, indicates that he was making a deliberate choice to convey a picturesque image of India. This version, as I have argued, did not instruct or even speak directly about the events. But neither did it inflame. The picturesque travelogue that froze India was Lang's intervention; he was being "political" by ostentatiously avoiding political matters.

Wanderings consists of seventeen chapters; twelve are textually almost identical to the installments of "Wanderings in India."[79] The substantive difference is that in the volume they are preceded by three chapters, pieces that had appeared in *Household Words* prior to the events of 1857: "The Himalayan Club" had appeared on 21 March 1857; "The Mahommedan Mother" on 11 June 1853; and "Black and Blue" on 3 October 1856. Unlike the twelve parts of "Wanderings," which adopt the feint of a first-person travelogue, these pieces are fiction. The narrator of "The Himalayan Club" is a Captain Wall, while "The Mahommedan" mother is narrated by a man named Longford. To an even greater extent than the "Wanderings in India" essays, the stories that open *Wanderings* are concentrated on Anglo-Indian life and concerns. "The Himalayan Club" is an account of the "idle" life of well-heeled Anglo-Indians in Mussoorie, their meals and pastimes, affairs and flirtations, rides on the mall and seasonal balls. In a discussion of William Hodges's 1793 *Travels in India*, Beth Fowkes Tobin argues that Hodges focuses on Indian ruins in order "to construct the Mughal imperium as decadent and decayed, as an entropic force of ruination and devastation that invited British intervention and eventual usurpation" (118). In Lang's story, half a century later, it is not the Mughals who are decadent, but the *British*. Capt. Wall partakes in all the Club's activities with relish and yet the story closes on this polemical note: "Twenty years ago [during the time of the Company's nabobs] India was famous for its infamy. Ten years ago it was very bad. It is now tolerable" (*Wanderings* 28). Progress, but not enough. To repair the "tone of Indian society," the

---

An Account of the Mutinies in Oudh the same year. Mowbray Thomson, one of the few survivors of the Satichaura Ghat massacre in Kanpur, published *The Story of Cawnpore* in 1859.

79. Punctuation is occasionally altered and the final installment of "Wanderings" is, in the book, augmented with a section on Anglo-Indians relaxing in Shimla.

narrator suggests that the "East India Company should . . . encourage young officers to spend a certain time every seven years in Europe" in order to reverse the "bad habits" officers "contract" in India (28–29).[80] As the opening chapter, the story sets the tone and focus for the volume: an emphasis on Anglo-Indians, their languid lifestyle, and India as a place of contamination for Britons.

The next two chapters expand on the theme of contagion. "The Mahommedan Mother" and "Black and Blue" are stories of mixed-race children. The first tells of a mourning Indian mother whose son is whisked away to be reinstated into Anglo-Indian society where he "belongs." The sentimental Longford allows the mother one meeting with her son before he sternly whisks the boy away. The story both hearkens back to the Oriental tale and anticipates *Kim*. The next story, "Black and Blue," is less sanguine about the integration of the miscegenated child. The story is about the younger son of an English aristocrat who "goes native," marries a local woman, and produces a dark-skinned child with blue eyes. This mixed-race boy is "rescued" by a caring English doctor who attempts to bring him into the fold. The boy, however, is "hideous" in his "black trousers, black waistcoat, black surtout coat, white neckcloth, black beaver hat, and Wellington boots . . . [and] slouching Indian gait" (82) and cannot be integrated into Anglo-Indian, much less British, society. His efforts to claim his title and inheritance come to naught, and at the close of the tale nobody knows "what on earth became of that black earl" (83).[81]

Both are colonial stories of intimate relations across the color line. Such relations were more prevalent in the earlier days of the Company, the heyday of "white Mughals," as William Dalrymple romantically refers to them. By mid-century, as Lang's stories manifest, Anglo-Indian and Indian society were asunder. Ann Stoler writes about the imperial panic

---

80. This advice runs contrary to the many commentaries in the *Mofussilite* that British officers should learn Indian languages and know the people better in order to bridge the gap between them.

81. Both stories anticipate many of Kipling's Anglo-Indian stories and *Kim*, and "Black and Blue" is a grotesque, reverse parody of the "Man Who Would Be King." It has been proposed that the model for the latter story is Frederick "Pahari" Wilson, a colorful former private in the British-India army who settled in Mussoorie as did Lang (Hutchinson). Although Lang never mentions Wilson in his published works, Hutchinson imagines them drinking together. For a more sober account of Wilson's life, particularly his role in the deforestation and "ecocide" of the western Himalayas, see Kala's *Frederick Wilson ("Hulson Sahib") of Garhwal, 1816–83* (176).

that mestizos aroused in the Dutch East Indies in the nineteenth century, giving rise to an increasingly detailed regulatory system to manage the "contamination" of bloodlines (43–49). In contrast to the Dutch colonies, the British in nineteenth-century India attempted to maintain the color line socially, not legally. Taken as a pair, Lang's stories mark the shift from an uneasy acceptance of the intimacies of colonial desire to a growing conviction that the outcome of such intimacies were irredeemable.[82] "The Mahommedan Mother" subscribes to the belief than an ounce of British blood makes a Briton, and the doctor in "Black and Blue" subscribes to that notion as well. But the narrative of the latter story rejects that view; social conditioning—the "slouching Indian gait" the boy has acquired—trumps blood. The story captures the bifurcation between Indians and Anglo-Indians, a division that was entrenched by 1857.

As the portal into the "Wanderings in India" essays, these three fictional accounts highlight the costs of empire. The arc of the stories suggests that the price to pay for the "idleness" of life in Anglo-Indian hill stations is the messy intricacy of miscegenation, misrecognition, mésalliances, and mourning. To a greater extent than Lang's essays written during the Uprising itself, these stories grapple with the social relations borne of empire. Although the tales are sentimental and not altogether accomplished literary works, fiction allowed Lang a more complicated exploration of the costs of empire. Together with the previously unpublished "political" piece that closes the volume, this opening allowed Lang—or his publishers—to frame his travelogue as a commentary on race relations, a matter much on the minds of Britons as, in 1859, they returned to the business of ruling a people whom they felt a murderous rage towards, having discovered that many did not wish to be ruled by them.

Following these fictional accounts, Lang returns to travel memoir and himself in a chapter entitled "The Ranee of Jhansi." This is the first of two unpublished and explicitly topical chapters in this volume, the first to directly reference the events of 1857-58. Laxmibai, the rani of Jhansi entered into Britons' consciousness during the Uprising and was an ambivalent figure. A displaced queen who led the *sipahis* and people of Jhansi in revolt, she was a warrior who fought and was killed on the battlefield.

---

82. Things were a bit different in the biographical sphere: in Mussoorie, Lang (possibly bigamously), married a woman named Margaret Wetter, who Crittenden speculates may have been mixed race (198–99; Roderick and Earnshaw 129–30). Lang's will named her sole beneficiary, but here the trail goes cold; she is not buried beside him in Camel Back Cemetery.

Laxmibai was a Joan of Arc figure who complicated narratives of gender rescue that, at least since the abolition of sati in 1829, were foundational to the British civilizing mission. Lang's chapter in *Wanderings* relates his meeting with the rani in 1854 when she summoned him to her palace. At the time, Laxmibai was the young widow of the recently deceased raja of Jhansi, a small principality that was an ally of the British. Shortly before his death in 1853, the issueless raja adopted, as was customary at the time, a young boy as his heir. Since 1848, Dalhousie, the governor general, had implemented the "doctrine of lapse," a policy that stated that any princely territory under British influence could be annexed if the ruler was deemed incompetent or died without a male heir (Wolpert 226–28). An alternative to battlefield conquests, annexation by lapse was far less costly and, once deemed "legal," much used throughout the 1850s.[83] Under the doctrine of lapse, Jhansi was annexed upon the death of the raja, and the rani, as regent, displaced. Almost immediately, Laxmibai appealed the annexation and sought Lang's aid to make her case.

Lang, as a result of his successful defense of Jyoti Prasad in 1851, had a reputation both as a highly capable attorney and as an advocate of Indians defrauded by the government. In his account in *Wanderings*, Lang tells us that "a month after the order had gone forth for the annexation of the little province of Jhansi (in 1854), and previous to a wing of the 13th Native Infantry occupying the country," the young rani summoned him for advice on appealing the annexation (*Wanderings* 84). Early in the chapter, Lang informs us that "many . . . officials of rank in India, regarded the annexation of Jhansi—'a trumpery state after all'—not only as impolitic, but unjust and without excuse" (85). The remainder of the chapter (ten pages) veers from the case at hand into Orientalist fantasy. Lang describes the horse and elephants used to escort him to Jhansi, the carpeted rooms with chandeliers, mirrors, and flowers, the young heir dressed in fine clothes and jewels, and the woman speaking from behind purdah. Of the conversation we are told nothing but that "she began to pour forth her grievances" (93). Instead of details of those "grievances," we segue into *Arabian Nights* territory:

---

83. The policy's most audacious implementation occurred in 1856, when Awadh was annexed based on its ruler's incompetence. Dalhousie extended the doctrine of lapse to pensions as well: in 1853, upon the death of Baji Rao II, the deposed peshwa of Poona, the Company determined that his adopted son, Dhondu Pant, would not receive his father's pension (Wolpert 228). This disaffected son was later known as Nana Sahib.

> I was very curious indeed to get a glimpse of her; and whether it was by accident, or by design on the Ranee's part, I know not, my curiosity was gratified. The curtain was drawn aside by the little boy, and I had a good view of the lady. It was only for a moment, it is true; still I saw her sufficiently to be able to describe her. She was a woman of about the middle size . . . (93)

The voyeuristic, Oriental fantasy is temporarily curbed by the rani's voice, "something between a whine and a croak" (94). Though Lang is credited with helping Laxmibai craft an appeal to the governor general, and though he tells us that they spoke for some eight hours, here he relates none of the substance of the conversation.[84] Instead the account closes with his parting and patronizing words to her: "[I]f the Governor-General could only be as fortunate as I have been, and for even so brief a while, I feel quite sure that he would at once give Jhansi back again to be ruled over by its beautiful Queen" (94).

That Lang in 1859 would wish to suppress the extent of his involvement with and advice to the rani of Jhansi is unsurprising; though dead, she was allied with Nana Sahib and Tatya Tope, the other "archvillain" of 1857. The insertion of this autobiographical narrative of his encounter with her is patently an effort at marketing the book by featuring the least objectionable of the Indians who opposed the British. But once again, Lang's text works at cross-purposes with his publisher's or editor's needs and aims. Just as "Wanderings in India" obdurately offered little insight into Indian affairs and took no position on events, so here the rani of Jhansi chapter fails to meet the expectations raised by its inclusion in the volume. Rather than offering analysis or commentary, we get an all-too-familiar image of a shrouded woman; Lang's own part and politics are similarly shrouded. This is railway fare indeed, with an Orientalized cast.

The final chapter of *Wanderings*, "Tantia Topee," is devoted to the man who served as Nana Sahib's general. This chapter, also previously unpublished, is just over five pages, the only pages in the volume that directly and explicitly refer to the Uprising. Tatya Tope, whom Lang tells us he met when he visited Nana Sahib, is described as a "miscreant" with a low forehead, broad nose, irregular teeth, and "eyes . . . full of cunning, like those of most Asiatics" (410–11). Lang's purpose in this brief chapter is to offer two arguments. "[I]n the absence of some proof [to the con-

---

84. Of the letters Dalhousie's office received from the rani, only one, dated 22 April 1854, was in English (rather than Persian); this is potentially the appeal Lang helped her craft.

trary]," he argues, it was Tatya Tope, not Nana Sahib, who ordered "the fiendish treachery and horrible massacre which took place at Cawnpore in July, 1857" (412). Lang's reasoning is curious:

> Nena Sahib had seen so much of English gentlemen and ladies[,] was personally (if not intimately) acquainted with so many of the sufferers, that it is only fair to suppose, when he ordered boats to be got ready, he was sincere in his desire that the Christians should find their way to Calcutta, and that what ensued was in violation of his orders, and the act of those who wished to place for ever between Nena Sahib and the British Government an impassable barrier, so far as peace and reconciliation were concerned. No one knew better than Nena Sahib that, in the event of the British becoming again the conquerors of India, the very fact of his having spared the lives of those who surrendered, would have led to the sparing of his own life, and hence the promise he made to Sir Hugh Wheeler. (412–13)

This is not only a defense of Nana Sahib, but also the strongest political commentary Lang has made—in "Wanderings" or *Wanderings*. It is followed by his only other piece of commentary, that "[i]t is to be regretted that previous to hanging 'Tantia Topee,' some statement was not extracted from him touching what took place in Cawnpore" (412–3).

As a coda to 409 lighthearted and insistently non-topical pages, this chapter is an anomaly. Little has prepared us for such purposeful commentary on the current events. The twelve parts of "Wanderings in India" appeared in a different sociopolitical moment than the world they described and occurred in; similarly, the opening chapters of *Wanderings* reach into Lang's published oeuvre and deal either with the leisurely life of nabob-like "idlers" or with mixed-race progeny, themselves a phenomenon of the past. Only at the very end of the volume does Lang refer directly to the Uprising itself and to the recent hanging of Tatya Tope (though, significantly, he does not connect what he says to the broader topic of justice for rebels). It is as if only in this small space of five pages, written as he is boarding the steamer to return to India, that Lang resumes his editorial habit.[85]

One final addition to *Wanderings* is a frontispiece (see figures 4.4 and 4.5). Facing the title page is an image of several men in an open,

---

85. Lang departed England on 6 February 1858 (see ships' arrival data in the *Calcutta Directory of 1858* in FIBIS).

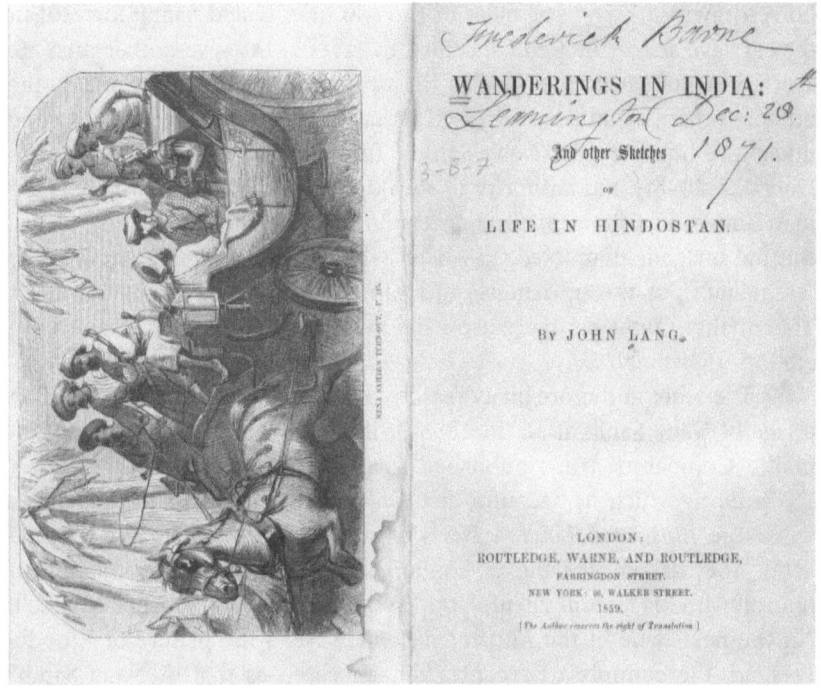

Figure 4.4. *Wanderings in India* title page and frontispiece (from Boston Public Library).

Figure 4.5. *Wanderings in India* frontispiece (from Boston Public Library).

horse-drawn carriage. The faces of the two men seated facing forward in the carriage are distinct and specific; the faces of the seven other men are averted or indeterminate. One of the two seated men is a European, the other a turbaned and neatly dressed Indian leaning on his sword. The copy under the image reads "Nena Sahib's Turn-out." The etching establishes Lang's credibility and authority to speak about India: here, after all, is the man known to Britons as the mastermind behind the Kanpur massacres. But the image is double-edged—here is Lang in easy familiarity with the "archvillain" of the uprisings—and hints at a too-dangerous intimacy. This duality might be one reason the image did not appear in the 1861 edition of *Wanderings*.

The other and more likely reason for its removal is that it was not an image of Nana Sahib at all. In 1893, William Forbes-Mitchell, a sergeant in the Company's army, published *Reminiscences of the Great Mutiny, 1857–59*, in which he recounts that, during the height of the rebellion, when the *Illustrated London News* was looking for an image of Nana Sahib, they called on Lang in London. Lang showed them a portrait of himself with his famous client, Jyoti Prasad. According to Forbes-Mitchell, "in the next issue of the *Illustrated London News* the picture of Ajoodia Pershâd, the commissariat contractor, appeared as that of Nana Sâhib" (159). "To the day of his death," Forbes-Mitchell continues, "John Lang was in mortal fear least Ajoodia Pershâd should ever come to hear how his picture had been allowed to figure as that of the arch-assassin of the Indian Mutiny" (159). The tale makes for a good yarn, and Forbes-Mitchell, who was in India at the time the episode occurred in London, does not offer a source.[86] How much fear Lang was in is unclear: after the image appeared in the *Illustrated London News* on 26 September 1857 (see figure 4.6), it appeared in *Wanderings* almost two years later, again identified as depicting Nana Sahib.

It is possible that Lang never sanctioned the inclusion of the image in *Wanderings*—nor had much to do with the volume's final shape. The Routledge, Warne, and Routledge archive contains a signed and stamped contract, dated June 28, 1858, in Lang's hand, that reads, "I agree to sign over to them [Meſr. Routledge Warne and Routledge] my copyright of

---

86. Malik repeats this story in *1857* (8).

Figure 4.6. "Nana Sahib" from *Illustrated London News*, September 1857 (from *ILN* microfilm).

'Wanderings in India' [sic] which appears in 'Household Words.'"[87] Quite possibly, an editor at the press made a last-minute decision to include the image for marketing purposes without consulting Lang, who was, in any case, back in India. The inclusion in the 1859 edition of *Wanderings* of the image that Forbes-Mitchell says was of Jyoti Prasad, however instrumental and unsanctioned by Lang it might have been, underscores my argument that *Wanderings*—and "Wanderings"—attempted to capitalize on the political moment even as it shied away from political commentary. In the metropole and in the aftermath of the crisis of 1857, the gadfly colonial editor morphs into a bland, derivative writer. The image also illuminates the balancing act Lang was involved in: his familiarity with "Nana Sahib" burnished his "cred," but it also threatened to taint him. This might be one reason the image does not appear in the 1861 edition of *Wanderings*.

The image of Jyoti Prasad—in 1857 in the *Illustrated London News* and in 1859 in *Wanderings in India*—instantiates the circulation that lies at the heart of this book. As with other unauthorized circulation—"piracy"— this episode highlights questions of property rights and ownership. But it differs from intellectual property and copyright, as the material circulated in this case is not a text or excerpts, but a reprint of an image and person it purports to represent. The mislabeling of the man in the image speaks to the interchangeability of Indians in the mind of Britons, as well as underscores their lack of representation. In this narrative, the English-trained barrister can only legally represent the Indian, but not represent him in anything like fidelity outside the courtroom. The story of Indians' self-representation and voice requires another archive and volume.

CODA: WANDERING ON

A coda to this chapter that traces the travels of Lang's Indian experiences from colony to metropole, periodical to volume, and journalist and editor to commissioned author: in 2015, an elegant volume appeared in New Delhi. Entitled *In the Court of the Ranee of Jhansi and Other Travels in India* and published by the well-credentialed press Speaking Tiger, the volume is a selection from Lang's *Wanderings in India*. Lang's encounter with the rani is the volume's selling point, and it begins with the rani of Jhansi chapter—retitled "In the Court of the Ranee of Jhansi"—followed

---

87. *Archives of George Routledge and Co.* The book *Wanderings* appeared in print on 5 August 1859.

by "Black and Blue" and "The Mahommedan Mother," the two stories about mixed-race children, followed by six installments/chapters from "Wanderings"/ *Wanderings*. The volume includes no editorial apparatus and its back cover reads, "Novelist, intrepid traveller, barrister-at-law, newspaper editor and uninhibited gossip, John Lang lived for a number of years in pre- and post-Mutiny British India, and his writings constitute some of the most vivid records of the time. . . . Written with a historian's sense of detail, a raconteur's delight in the unexpected, and a keen sense of the absurd, John Lang's travel diary is a riveting read."

The latest in the global travels of Lang and his prose, the appearance of this book at this time and place speaks volumes about the uncertainties of who John Lang was and what he stood for. Hailed in contemporary India as a "friend of Indians," he is credited with a critique of empire that never emanated from his pen or appeared in his newspaper. In such accounts, Lang's high imperialism is effaced and his defense of Jyoti Prasad and counsel to the rani of Jhansi emphasized. While the reasons for his elevation are multiple, this chapter offers one textual answer: the essays in "Wanderings"/*Wanderings* are cautions and refrain from wading into controversial territory. By settling on a dying generic representation, Lang managed to capture an India that was in the past, but was also innocuous. If in 1857–58 he did not offer any insights, he did not unsettle any beliefs either. The ironies of globalization are such that in 2015 his text reverses its journey and is now, from India, seen to offer a "vivid record" of a colonial moment that postcolonials can now afford to regard as picturesque.

Conclusion

Mofussil News

I began this book with Walter Moody, Eleanor Catton's dandified, metropolitan naïf, who condescendingly chuckles at the "parish gazette" on his tea tray. Where Moody sees naught but rubbish advertisements, dreary campaign speeches, and dry shipping notices, Catton offers a vibrant account of life in a New Zealand frontier town. With that gazette and its editor as one of the forces shaping the relationship of the town's indigenous and transplanted inhabitants, *The Luminaries* amplifies what periodical studies scholars have been insisting for two decades: that "parish gazettes" were anything but "a delayed and passive replica of attitudes in the capital" (H. Barker 114). Such scholarship—of which Andrew Hobbs's *A Fleet Street in Every Town: The Provincial Press in England, 1855–1900* (2018) is only the latest—rewrites the metropolitan narrative of itself as cynosure. This book augments and thickens that conversation by turning to a press that is doubly provincial: the mofussil press. The newspapers I have focused on were mofussil in two senses: they lay on the colonial periphery (in India) and one appeared from deeper in the hinterland, far from the colonial capital. With the mofussil—a geographical location but also an ethos—at its center, this book examines the circulation and exchange that brought global and local events and relations in India into the same, sometimes contentious, frame.

My account's Walter Moody may be Charles Dickens, whose only known comment on John Lang's work neatly telescopes the double burden the mofussil newspaper and editor faces in the metropole. Lang's essay "Starting a Paper in India" appeared in *Household Words* on 26 March 1853. Two weeks before its appearance, Dickens complained about the submission in a letter to his subeditor, W. H. Wills:

> Starting a paper in India is very droll—to us. But it is full of references that the public don't understand, and don't in the least care for. Bourgeois, brevier, minion, and nonpareil, long primer, turn-ups, dummy advertisements and reprints, back form, imposing stone, and locking up, are all quite out of their way and a sort of slang that they have no interest in. (Storey and Tillotson 7:48)[1]

"Don't in the least care for"; "have no interest in": Dickens's comments confirm Anglo-Indians' persistent complaint that Britons knew little about India and cared even less to learn. That Dickens's directive to Wills to "revise" and "strengthen" the submission was heeded is apparent in the final product: of the eleven terms Dickens objected to, six were excised. The remnant—long primer, dummy advertisements, reprints, imposing stone, and locking up [chases]—are all terms of art for the work of printers and press operators. For long, the technical details of putting together printed materials were treated as a vocational enterprise, distinct from the products of the presses, the newspapers, magazines, and books. In the late twentieth century, Book History brought into the same intellectual circuit what had been disparate affordances—the creation of a text and the production of a book—as scholars such as Eisenstein, McKenzie, McGann, and others argued that the meanings of a text lie not just in its words, but also in the arrangement of those words, in its format.

The resulting incorporation of material factors in the analysis of text has, until recently, not been adopted by postcolonial studies, a field that during much of its high noon was concerned largely with matters of discourse analysis. As the study of colonialism and colonial relations has come to incorporate a textual-materialist approach, a previously neglected archive—of newspapers and periodicals—has become comprehensible and available for analysis. This book has drawn upon these intellectual dispensations to guide my journey through the archives of nineteenth-century English-language newspapers of the mofussil. Yet, because that archive is fragmented, I have had to be methodologically nimble; in doing so I have drawn inspiration from historians and anthropologists, political scientists

---

1. Dickens was harsher yet on one of his favored "young men": the same 10 March 1853 letter in which he comments on Lang's essay begins simply, "Sala, very poor" (7:46). Though Dickens is listed as sole editor of *Household Words* and Wills as "sub-editor," the latter made many of the day-to-day decisions (Schlicke 598–600).

and literary scholars who work in cratered archives. In his powerful account of the making and accounting of history, *Silencing the Past: Power and the Production of History* (1995), Michel-Rolph Trouillot writes,

> Silences enter the process of historical production at four crucial moments: the moment of fact creation (the making of *sources*); the moment of fact assembly (the making of *archives*); the moment of fact retrieval (the making of *narratives*); and the moment of retrospective significance (the making of *history* in the final instance). (26)

The newspapers this book studies are sources—they created facts—that at the moment of their production also created an archive and narratives as they gathered, reprinted, and produced accounts of British colonialism in India. As source, archive, and narrative, these newspapers are, to use the oft-repeated phrase, the "first rough draft of history." That they are "officially" archived in libraries is the outcome of the consolidation and cataloguing power of the colonial state with its deposit requirements. That these archives are fragmented and their provenance difficult to trace is a mark of their mofussil condition.

While Trouillot addresses literal and metaphoric "silences" in the historical record—his reading of Columbus is drawn not from "an absence of facts or interpretations as through conflicting interpretations of Columbus's persona" (28)—Saidiya Hartman encounters in present-day Ghana thinly veiled antipathy as she searches for slave origins. Continually coming up empty-handed as she attempts to grasp the workings of the slave trade, she poignantly concludes near the end of *Lose Your Mother: A Journey along the Atlantic Slave Route* (2007): "It is said that when you spot a cluster of baobab trees it's the sign a village existed in that spot . . . These islands of baobab, shea butter, locust bean, and fig trees preserved the history of the stateless; they are the archive of the defeated" (219). "The archive of the defeated": in reading in a cluster of baobab trees the story of a village that was wiped out by the slave trade, Hartman not only expands the archive, but does so by drawing on an astonishing array of tools. Oral accounts—"It is said"—are brought into conversation with ecological traces, records in the national archives, prison log books, abolitionists' memoirs, and coastal and inland Ghanaians' memories of and evasions about the region's slave history. The result is a genre-defying account of the differing meanings of the slave trade, each inflected by local pasts and present accounts of the past. Hartman has called her method of filling in blanks of a partial archive "critical fabulation" ("Venus" 11).

Closer to my research area, the work of Subaltern Studies scholars to write histories for which there are no sources and nonexistent records offers another model for working around and in a fragmented archive. As peasants—subalterns par excellence—left no written records, how were their voices to be excavated, their histories written? Through "innovation in historians' practices," Dipesh Chakrabarty writes (100). As Ranjit Guha, the guiding force of the collective, famously demonstrated, historians could tease out stories of peasant consciousness by reading against the grain of the existing archive. The records of the colonial state are full of accounts of peasant insurgency; these, Guha illustrated, simply had to be understood as an archive of *counter*-insurgency, thus opening up space to see and read the resistance and consciousness of peasants. Reading the colonial archive aslant, as well as drawing on narrative, folklore, ethnography, and oral history, the Subaltern Studies Collective came up with "ingenious methods for uncovering fragments of subaltern [subjectivity]" (Ludden 19).

Anglo-Indian newspapers, their editors, and their readers are not subaltern by any stretch of the imagination. This study relies on a less literal understanding of "subaltern." Dipesh Chakrabarty has argued that "subaltern pasts" are something that "[e]lite and dominant groups can also have . . . to the extent that they participate in life-worlds subordinated in the 'major' narratives of the dominant institutions" (101). Anglo-Indian newspapers, long read as "delayed replicas" of metropolitan news and ideas, were subordinate to dominant metropolitan journals and suffered the condescension of the metropole and of scholars. Their mofussil status on the margins earned them their share of neglect, resulting in an archive that is filled with gaps. By centering mofussil newspapers and attending to the premise that the "colonial domain was distinct from the metropolitan one" (Stoler and Cooper 3), that colonizers *in the colonies* were continually refashioning metropolitan ideas, this book crafts a richer story of how empire functioned. It illustrates that while in some cases mofussil newspapers were metropolitan mimickers—the adoption of the white-lined, Old English typeface of the *Times* for the masthead of almost every newspaper in my sample—in more substantive matters they charted their own path. The year 1851 is a case in point: as British newspapers were preoccupied with the Great Exhibition, Anglo-Indian newspapers were absorbed in assembling an archive and producing a narrative that came far closer to interrogating the sources of industrial ascendency than the exhibition itself did. Drawing a direct link between the Kohinoor and the quotidian—bullocks!—that made the gem's journey to London possible, Anglo-Indian newspapers told a story of 1851 that placed the East India Company on trial in their pages. The Company lost in the courtroom and in the pages of Anglo-Indian newspapers, and Anglo-Indian newspapers felt vindicated. But the crimes of colonialism some commentators came close to articulating went unheeded, lost in legalese and self-congratulation.

These newspapers all subscribed to an imperial vision—India required tutelage—but were not tethered to the Company; indeed, well before 1857, much of the Anglo-India media had written the Company's obituary several times over.[2] The relation between the global (in this case, an imperial vision) and its local application was uneven. Newspapers, which contain on-the-spot accounts filled with inconsistencies, reversals, and flux, chart the instability of what otherwise appears as a monolithic and all-powerful imperial agenda. The tensions and cracks matter because in the interstitial—and sometimes infinitesimal—spaces between them we see instances of relations between Indian and Anglo-Indians, relations that took tutelage to mean something other than intended. The universe of print culture—which includes not simply editors, writers, and translators, but also the vast operation of printers, compositors, typefounders, and more—offers a rich arena in which we see the "taking, snatching, pilfering, plundering . . . giving, exchanging, and unevenly borrowing" that Priya Joshi speaks of in her striking analogy of Britain and India as "two sides facing each other with their arms outstretched" (*In Another Country* 7). Much work remains to excavate these exchanges; the story of "Mahomed Usghur," a skein running through his book, offers a tantalizing—and incomplete—glimpse of the knotty relations of confederacy and contestation across colonial lines that are a feature of colonialism. If my conjectures are correct—that "Mahomed Usghur," a once favored correspondent, started his own vernacular-language newspaper, and eventually joined rebels in 1857—he would hardly be the first to mix or shift allegiances.[3]

---

2. Criticisms of the Company were almost as old as the Company itself and a minor sport in late eighteenth-century Britain. The Anglo-India press of the nineteenth century has long been regarded as the handmaiden of the Company as it became more of a governing entity. This book has argued that in the years before its demise, the Company had few friends in the Anglo-Indian media.

3. Farooqui writes that Mohammed Baqar, the editor of the Urdu-language *Delhi Urdu Akhbar*, who espoused the cause of rebels, was also in correspondence with British intelligence in 1857 and possibly a spy for them (403).

Harish Chandra Mukherjee of the *Hindoo Patriot* is a more visible nodal point in the history of the exchanges between Indian and Anglo-Indian newspapers. Our encounter with him begins with the rupture of those relations—but it also reveals that ruptures in the colonial domain did not necessarily extend into the imperial one. Mukherjee's rejection of his Anglo-Indian contemporaries and turn to imperial elites in London might signal naïveté or poor judgment—or the lived contradictions of an intermediary, what Dharwadker calls "incompletely translated and substantially hybridized Enlightenment activism" (120). Stoler and Cooper refer to colonies as "laboratories of modernity" (5), and the Indians in this account who engaged with Anglo-Indians in the public sphere straddled this modernity. In this account they are not central actors—the silence in the English-language archive about a Jyoti Prasad ensures this—but they point to further research directions.

If relations between Indians and Anglo-Indians became increasingly distant over the course of this period, what of relations between Anglo-Indians and Britons? Throughout this book I have argued that, contrary to previous accounts, Anglo-Indian newspapers of this period were far from simply mouthpieces of British prints or opinions. The Anglo-Indian newspapers in my sample certainly reprinted literature from the English prints, and if one focused only on fiction, it might appear that they were beholden to the "mother country." James Mulholland, who focuses on literature, challenges even that notion when he refers to Anglo-India as "defined by its partial autonomy from British norms" ("Translocal" 274). Beyond the literature pages of newspapers, we see even more autonomy. While Anglo-Indian newspapers reprinted political items from British prints, they did so far less than one might expect and far more pugnaciously. Granular attention to bibliographic codes in conjunction with textual analysis indicates that Anglo-Indian newspapers reprinted, referenced, engaged, and debated with one another far more than they did with British newspapers and periodicals and that they challenged—even at times mocked—British prints' account of India. Part of the reason for Anglo-Indian newspapers' distance from the British media was quite literally distance: well into the 1850s, the steamer between London and Calcutta took thirty-five to forty-five days.[4] But partly, too, the distance

---

4. The first direct telegraph line between Britain and India did not exist until 1870; a telegraphic link was established in 1860, but it consisted of a series of patchworks (see Boyce 142 and Mann).

is the result of Anglo-Indian newspapers' conviction that official and public opinion in Britain was largely ignorant about India. On political matters, they viewed themselves as watchdogs and gatekeepers in the flow of information about the British Indian empire on the day-to-day.

In this period in India, very little flowed or circulated in a smooth or direct line. Whether relations between Anglo-Indians and Indians, exchanges between newspapers, or traffic in technologies and ideas, the circulations that have been a central preoccupation and heuristic of this book were as often unsuccessful as tidily completed. Like the many private letters that arrived on editors' desks through circuitous routes in 1857 when roads in north-central India were blocked, the circuits of exchange and networks this book has uncovered were fractured and fleeting, often incomplete or dead on arrival. Newspapers (and newspaper personnel) circulated, but the transformations that occurred in the process of their texts circulating always exceeded where they started. The journey of the story of the British magistrate who indiscriminately torched an Indian village from English to Urdu back to English, from the hands of Anglo-Indians to Indians to Britons, from Indian readers to metropolitan ones is but one of the knotty circuits this book uncovers. The journey elucidates the reasons we must study circulation as much as about movement as about blockage, as connection and also rupture, as harmony and fracture.

Nowhere is fracture more evident than in moments of crisis, the stock-in-trade of newspapers. Yet, as *Empire News* has argued, attention to Anglo-Indian newspapers allows us to grasp that local crises—even news—varied greatly from global ones. Of course, every Anglo-Indian newspaper in my sample covered the Crimean War (though none appear to have had their own correspondents in the region). But their accounts of what counted as newsworthy seldom aligned with British newspapers': thus, the trial of Jyoti Prasad, a mere blip in British prints, dominated Anglo-Indian newspaper real estate for much of 1851. In 1857, the "local" story was the global one, of course; but here, too, the Anglo-Indian account did not align with the British. Historians tell us that British newspaper and public reactions to the events of 1857 on the subcontinent were shrill, hysterical, vitriolic; Anglo-Indian accounts are these, but they were confused and contradictory as well, telegraphing inconsistency. In "the moment of fact creation" as Trouillot refers to it (26), Anglo-Indian newspapers conveyed anything but imperial certitude.

Imperial certitude had been a feature of Anglo-Indian newspapers up to this point (and in 1857, its fracturing was only temporary as editors, short of copy, allowed a plethora of voices to appear). But that certainty was coupled with noisy debate in the public prints. With the exception of the most pro-government paper, the *Englishman*, every other newspaper under examination debated and challenged the administration of India in a public space that expanded with the lifting of direct censorship of newspapers in 1835. Those critiques came from firmly within an imperial mindset: that Britain—though not the Company—belonged in India and that Indians required British guidance and tutelage. Anglo-Indian newspapers challenged *this* colonial administration, particularly in regards to reforms of the judiciary, as we saw in the coverage of the 1851 trial of Jyoti Prasad and mockery of the Company's courts or *sadr adalats*. The mofussil mentality this book set out to explore consists of imperial certitude combined with colonial critique.

As so many commentators and scholars have noted, the events of 1857 changed much in the landscape of and relationships in India. (McBryde, the police superintendent in *A Passage to India*, famously tells Fielding, "Read any of the Mutiny records; which, rather than the Bhagavad Gita, should be your Bible in this country" [Forster 187].)[5] Relations that had been cooling cemented into hard barriers, a process charted in Harish Chandra Mukherjee's *Hindoo Patriot*. The paper clung to its belief that British imperialism could reform India for the better, even as it balked at the arrogance of Anglo-Indians. That a hard line had formed is perhaps nowhere clearer than in this pair of passages, some fifteen years apart, describing life in Anglo-India. Writing of his arrival in India in 1842, Lang declared, "I was in no way connected with the government, and was consequently an 'interloper' or 'adventurer.'"[6] Proudly donning this outsider status—what I have called a mofussil mentality—Lang ventured into the mofussil of India to comment on the British empire. With his newspaper as our centerpiece, I have charted the limits, as well as shape, of colonial certitude in the years before 1857. After the Uprising, the landscape had altered: in 1858, a new print, the *Indian Empire*, appeared in Calcutta. In its manifesto, the daily notes that Anglo-Indian newspapers have always

---

5. In a similar vein, but closer to events, John W. Kaye, Britain's first historian of the Uprising, wrote that 1857 "roused English manhood in India to a pitch of national hatred that took years to allay" (qtd. in Chakravarty 40).

6. "Wanderings in India," *Household Words*, 14 November 1857, 457.

looked for "patronage" among two populations: "[t]he army and civil service and the adventurers and interlopers." Until recently, the manifesto continues, the adventurers and interlopers were too few in number, "[b]ut now there is already dawning in the East a new day, and countless numbers of hitherto so called adventurers daily attracted to our shores will prove the formation of a strong body of free and independent men which will show that an Indian Public is no longer a matter of despair."[7] With the demise of the Company, so-called adventurers indeed poured in. Given what we know of the high noon of the Raj, few would call them free or independent; on the contrary, the "adventurers and interlopers" of the post-Uprising period were firm imperialists who supported the Crown and made not even the feint at a mofussil mentality that Lang had attempted in 1845. A new day had indeed dawned—an imperialist one. But in that dawn sky was also a star: the many new prints of an "Indian Public"—though not the one the *Indian Empire* had in mind—that rose steadily in the firmament during the second half of the nineteenth century.

---

7. Qtd. in *Mofussilite*, 6 April 1858, 215; see Chanda (*History* [2008] 32).

Appendix

Press Regulations and Significant Events in Indian Press History, 1780–1857

Date	Relevant Act or Event	Description/Comments	Source(s)
1794	William Duane, editor of the *World*, deported	(Duane subsequently edited the Philadelphia *Aurora*)	Chanda (*History* [1987] 23–24, 363)
May 1799	Regulation of the public press	—All papers must be "inspected" by the secretary to the government; require name of printer on the paper; editor and proprietor to deliver name to the secretary	Chanda (*History* [1987] 363, 415–16); Khan (10–11)
October 1813	Document clarifying censorship rules issued	—Proof-sheets and notices must be sent to the secretary for revision	Chanda (*History* [1987] 417–18); Ahmed (54–56)
August 1818	Press regulations of 1818	—Lifted direct censorship of 1799; paper does not have to be submitted to secretary prior to publication, but ban on certain topics remains —Shift in responsibility for content from printer to editor —Required deposit of one copy of every paper with secretary	Chanda (*History* [1987] 364, 418–20); Ahmed (56); Khan (14)
February 1823	James Silk Buckingham, editor and proprietor of the *Calcutta Journal*, deported	(Buckingham subsequently established and edited the *Oriental Herald* in London)	Chanda (*History* [1987] 53–58, 421–24); Khan (15–18)
March 1823	New regulation for the press, Regulation III of 1823	—Strong restrictions imposed —Required license by proprietor (not editor), issued upon sworn affidavit before magistrate —License required press, printer, publisher, proprietor, and contents named —No distinction made between English & Indian press —In protest, Rammohan Roy stopped publication of *Mirat-ul-Akhbar*	Chanda (*History* [1987] 425–29); Boyce (34); Khan (18); Ahmed (63) —(Protest): Boyce (35); Bhatnagar (12)

1826		—Court of directors (London) prohibits East India Company servants from "association" with the press	Chanda (*History* [1987] 395); Chakraborti (70); Khan (22)
September 1835	Press Act XI	—Repealed press regulations of 1823 —Required printer and publisher to sign a declaration before a magistrate (abolished oath of 1823) and list their name and address on publication	Cassels (376–78); Boyce (39)
1841		—Withdrawal of 1826 prohibition of Company servants' connection with press	Chanda (*History* [1987] 444)
1848	Annual reports	—Compilation of annual reports summarizing the sentiments of the vernacular-language press	Boyce (45–46)
June 13, 1857	Act XV ("Gagging Act")	—Required all printing presses to obtain a license which could be revoked if paper published material that "excite[d] disaffection or unlawful resistance to [Government] orders," created "alarm or suspicion among the Native population," or "weaken[ed] the friendship . . . of Native Princes, Chiefs or States" towards the Government —Imposed on both English- and vernacular-language press	United Kingdom, House of Commons ("Papers" 37–38)
1863	Weekly report on native papers	—Weekly monitoring of vernacular-language press	
1878	Vernacular Press Act	—Restricted freedom of Indian-language (i.e., non-English) press	

Bibliography

Nineteenth-Century Indian Newspapers
(Archival location and medium)

Allen's Indian Mail (bound volumes, printed by W. H. Allen, London; British Library, microfilm)
**The Bengal Hurkaru* (British Library, microfilm)
The Bombay Gazette (British Library, microfilm)
The Bombay Times (British Library, microfilm)
The Delhi Gazette (British Library, microfilm)
*The Englishman (British Library, microfilm)
**The Friend of India* (British Library, microfilm; bound volumes; limited run digitized in Gale's *19th Century British Library Newspapers*)
**The Hindoo Patriot* (selections in Benoy Ghose, *Selections from English Periodicals of 19th Century Bengal, Volume IV (1857)*, Calcutta, Papyrus, 1979; and Nares Chandra Sen-Gupta, *Selections from the Writings of Hurrish Chunder Mookerji: Compiled from the Hindoo Patriot*, Calcutta, Cherry Press, 1910).
The Lahore Chronicle (British Library, microfilm)
*The Mofussilite (British Library, microfilm)
The Times of India (British Library, microfilm; limited run digitized in Gale's *19th Century British Library Newspapers*)

British Newspapers and Periodicals

Household Words (digitized at Dickens Journals Online, http://www.djo.org.uk/)

> Though every item appeared anonymously in the journal, scholars have identified authors by cross-checking the journal's office books and Dickens's letters.

---

*indicates prints discussed in depth

[Capper, John], "A Very Black Act," *Household Words*, 26 September 1857, 293–94.

[Lang, John], "Hovelling," *Household Words*, 7 February 1857, 139–42.

———, "Starting a Paper in India," *Household Words*, 26 March 1853, 94–96.

———, "Wanderings in India [i]," *Household Words*, 14 November 1857, 457–63.

———, "Wanderings in India [ii]," *Household Words*, 28 November 1857, 505–11.

———, "Wanderings in India [iii]," *Household Words*, 19 December 1857, 12–20.

———, "Wanderings in India [iv]," *Household Words*, 2 January 1858, 64–70.

———, "Wanderings in India [v]," *Household Words*, 9 January 1858, 87–94.

———, "Wanderings in India [vi]," *Household Words*, 16 January 1858, 112–18.

———, "Wanderings in India [vii]," *Household Words*, 23 January 1858, 135–44.

———, "Wanderings in India [viii]," *Household Words*, 30 January 1858, 148–56.

———, "Wanderings in India [ix]," *Household Words*, 6 February 1858, 179–86.

———, "Wanderings in India [x]," *Household Words*, 13 February 1858, 212–16.

———, "Wanderings in India [xi]," *Household Words*, 20 February 1858, 220–24.

———, "Wanderings in India [xii]," *Household Words*, 27 February 1858, 254–60.

[Robertson, John], "Sepoy Symbols of Mutiny," *Household Words*, 5 September 1857, 228–32.

[Sala, George Augustus], "A Journey Due North [i]," *Household Words*, 4 October 1856, 265–76.

———, "A Journey Due North [x]," *Household Words*, 6 December 1856, 493–98.

[Townsend, E.], "Indian Irregulars," *Household Words*, 12 September 1857, 244–46.

———, "A Mutiny in India," *Household Words*, 15 August 1857, 154–56.

The Illustrated London News (digitized)
The Times (London) (digitized)

Other Nineteenth-Century Archival Sources

The Bengal and Agra Directory and Annual Register for the Year 1844. Calcutta, Bengal Hurkaru Press / Samuel Smith, 1844.

The Bengal Directory and General Register for the Year 1825. Calcutta, Bengal Hurkaru Press / Samuel Smith, 1825.
Maidment, Brian, editor. *The Archives of George Routledge and Co., 1853–1902.* Chadwyck-Healy, 1973. Microfilm.
Official Descriptive and Illustrated Catalogue of the Great Exhibition of the Works of Industry of All Nations, 1851. London, Spicer Brothers, 1851.
Prize and Batta Rolls, 1793–c1886 for "Indus, Sutlej, and Punjab, 1846–1849." L/LMIL/5/276. British Library.
The Trial of Lalla Jotee Pershad and Others. Reported for the Delhi Gazette. Delhi, Delhi Gazette Press / Kunniah Lall, 1851.
United Kingdom, House of Commons. *East India Acts for the Year 1850, with Index.* 1852.
———, ———. "Papers Relating to the Public Press in India." *Accounts and Papers of the House of Commons,* vol. XLIII, 1857–58, East India; China. London, HMSO, 1858, pp. 1–69.
———, ———. "Petition of the Inhabitants of Calcutta for the Recall of the Governor General." *Accounts and Papers of the House of Commons,* vol. XLIII, 1857–58, East India; China. London, HMSO, 1858, pp. 1–18.
———, ———. "Returns Relating to the Restriction of the Liberty of the Press in India." *Accounts and Papers of the House of Commons,* vol. XXIX, 1857, Sess. 2, East India. London, HMSO, 1858.

Other Published Sources

Agathocleous, Tanya. "Criticism on Trial: Colonizing Affect in the Late-Victorian Empire." *Victorian Studies,* vol. 60, no. 3, 2018, pp. 434–60.
Ahmed, Salahuddin A. F. *Social Ideas and Social Change in Bengal 1818–1835.* E. J. Brill, 1965.
Allen, Joan, and Owen R. Ashton. *Papers for the People: A Study of the Chartist Press.* Merlin Press, 2005.
Altick, Richard D. *Punch: The Lively Youth of a British Institution, 1841–1851.* Ohio State UP, 1997.
Anderson, Benedict R. *Imagined Communities: Reflections on the Origin and Spread of Nationalism.* Rev. ed., Verso, 1991.
Appiah, Kwame Anthony. "Is the Post- in Postmodernism the Post- in Postcolonial?" *Critical Inquiry,* vol. 17, no. 2, 1991, pp. 336–57.
Arnold, David. *Science, Technology and Medicine in Colonial India.* Cambridge UP, 2000.
Auerbach, Jeffrey A. *The Great Exhibition of 1851: A Nation on Display.* Yale UP, 1999.
Bandyopadhyay, Sekhar. "Eighteen-Fifty-Seven and Its Many Histories." *1857: Essays from* Economic and Political Weekly, Hyderabad, Orient Longman, 2008, pp. 1–22.

Barker, G. F. R. "Buckingham, James Silk (1786-1855)." Revised by Felix Driver, *Oxford Dictionary of National Biography*, Oxford UP, January 2008, http://www.oxforddnb.com/view/article/3855. Accessed 25 September 2014.

Barker, Hannah. *Newspapers, Politics and English Society, 1695-1855*. Longman, 2000.

Bayly, C. A. *Empire and Information: Intelligence Gathering and Social Communication in India, 1780-1870*. Cambridge UP, 2007.

Beetham, Margaret. "In Search of the Historical Reader; The Woman Reader, the Magazine and the Correspondence Column." *SPIEL: Siegener Periodicum zur Internationalen Empirischen Literaturwissenschaft*, vol. 19, no. 1, 2000, pp. 89-104.

Beredo, Cheryl. *Import of the Archive: U.S. Colonial Rule of the Philippines and the Making of American Archival History*. Litwin Books, 2013.

Bhabha, Homi K. "DissemiNation: Time, Narrative and the Margins of the Modern Nation." *The Location of Culture*, Routledge, 1994, pp. 139-70.

Bhatnagar, Ram Ratan. *The Rise and Growth of Hindi Journalism (1826-1945): Being an Attempt at a History of Hindi Journalism in Historical, Chronological and Evolutionary Perspective*. Allahabad, Kitab Mahal, 1947.

Black, Jeremy. *The English Press in the Eighteenth Century*. U of Pennsylvania P, 1987.

Blanchard, Sidney Laman. *Yesterday and To-Day in India*. W. H. Allen, 1867.

Boyce, Merrill Tilghman. *British Policy and the Evolution of the Vernacular Press in India, 1835-1878*. Delhi, Chanakya Publications, 1988.

Brake, Laurel. "The Longevity of 'Ephemera': Library Editions of Nineteenth-Century Periodicals and Newspapers." *Media History*, vol. 18, no. 1, 2012, pp. 7-20.

———. "Lost and Found: Serial Supplements in the Nineteenth Century." *Victorian Periodicals Review*, vol. 43, no. 2, Summer 2010, pp. 111-18.

———. *Print in Transition, 1850-1910: Studies in Media and Book History*. Palgrave, 2001.

———. *Subjugated Knowledges: Journalism, Gender, and Literature in the Nineteenth Century*. New York UP, 1994.

———. "'Time's Turbulence': Mapping Journalism Networks." *Victorian Periodicals Review*, vol. 44, no. 2, Summer 2011, pp. 115-27.

Brake, Laurel, and Marysa Demoor, editors. *Dictionary of Nineteenth-Century Journalism in Great Britain and Ireland*. Academia Press / British Library, 2009.

Brake, Laurel, and James Mussell. "Digital Nineteenth-Century Serials for the Twenty-First Century: A Conversation." *19: Interdisciplinary Studies in the Long Nineteenth Century*, no. 21, 2015, https://19.bbk.ac.uk/article/id/1694/print/.

Breckenridge, Carol. "The Aesthetics and Politics of Colonial Collecting: India at World Fairs." *Comparative Studies in Society and History*, vol. 31, no. 2, 1989, pp. 195-216.

Brodkin, E. I. "The Struggle for Succession: Rebels and Loyalists in the Indian Mutiny of 1857." *Modern Asian Studies*, vol. 6, no. 3, 1972, pp. 277–90.

Brooker, Peter, and Andrew Thacker, editors. *The Oxford Critical and Cultural History of Modernist Magazines: Volume I: Britain and Ireland 1880–1955*. Oxford UP, 2009.

Brown, Lucy. *Victorian News and Newspapers*. Clarendon Press / Oxford UP, 1985.

Burke, Edmund. *Edmund Burke on Government, Politics, and Society*. Selected and edited by B. W. Hill, International Publications Service, 1976.

Burton, Antoinette. "Archive Stories: Gender in the Making of Imperial and Colonial Histories." *Empire in Question: Reading, Writing, and Teaching British Imperialism*, Duke UP, 2011, pp. 94–105.

Buzard, James. *The Beaten Track: European Tourism, Literature, and the Ways to Culture, 1800–1918*. Oxford UP, 1993.

Carey, W. H. *The Good Old Days of the Honorable John Company; Being Curious Reminiscences during the Rule of the East India Company from 1600 to 1858*. 1882. Calcutta, Quins Book Company, 1964.

Carter, Mia, and Barbara Harlow. *Archives of Empire: Volume I. From the East India Company to the Suez Canal*. Duke UP, 2003.

Casid, Jill H. *Sowing Empire: Landscape and Colonization*. U of Minnesota P, 2005.

Cassels, Nancy Gardner. *Social Legislation of the East India Company: Public Justice versus Public Instruction*. Sage Publications, 2010.

Catton, Eleanor. *The Luminaries*. Granta Books, 2013.

Chakrabarty, Dipesh. *Provincializing Europe: Postcolonial Thought and Historical Difference*. Princeton UP, 2000.

Chakraborti, Smarajit. *The Bengali Press, 1818–1868: A Study in the Growth of Public Opinion*. Calcutta, Firma KLM, 1976.

Chakravarty, Gautam. *The Indian Mutiny and the British Imagination*. Cambridge UP, 2005.

Chakravorty, Swapan. "Educational Texts in Bengal, 1830–1900: Some Problems Relating to British Imports." *Founts of Knowledge: Book History in India*, edited by Swapan Chakravorty and Abhijit Gupta, New Delhi, Orient Blackswan, 2016, pp. 317–33.

Chanda, Mrinal Kanti. *History of the English Press in Bengal, 1780 to 1857*. Calcutta, K. P. Bagchi, 1987.

———. *History of [the] English Press in Bengal, 1858–1880: With List of Papers Published in India (Including Burma and Ceylon)*. Kolkata, K. P. Bagchi, 2008.

Chartier, Roger. "The Press and Fonts: Don Quixote in the Print Shop." *The Broadview Reader in Book History*, edited by Michelle Levy and Tom Mole, Broadview, 2015, pp. 73–92.

Chatterjee, Partha. "After Subaltern Studies." *Economic and Political Weekly*, vol. 47, no. 35, 2012, pp. 44–49.

———. *The Black Hole of Empire: History of a Global Practice of Power*. Princeton UP, 2012.

Chaudhary, Zahid. *Afterimage of Empire: Photography in Nineteenth-Century India*. U of Minnesota P, 2012.

Chaudhuri, Bhrahma. "India." *Periodicals of Queen Victoria's Empire: An Exploration*, edited by J. Don Vann and Rosemary VanArsdel, U of Toronto P, 1996, pp. 175–200.

Chaudhuri, Rosinka. *The Literary Thing: History, Poetry, and the Making of a Modern Cultural Sphere*. Delhi, Oxford UP, 2014.

Choudhury, Deep Kanta Lahiri. " 'Clemency' Canning, the Telegraph, Information and Censorship During 1857." *Mutiny at the Margins: New Perspectives on the Indian Uprising of 1857*, edited by Marina Carter and Crispin Bates, vol. 3, New Delhi, Sage Publications, 2013, pp. 67–86.

Codell, Julie. "Introduction: The Nineteenth-Century News from India." *The Nineteenth-Century Press in India*, special issue of *Victorian Periodicals Review*, vol. 37, no. 2, 2004, pp. 106–23.

Conboy, Martin. *The Press and Popular Culture*. Sage Publications, 2002.

Connors, Linda E., and Mary Lu MacDonald. *National Identity in Great Britain and British North America, 1815–1851: The Role of Nineteenth-Century Periodicals*. Ashgate, 2011.

Cooper, Fredrick. "Postcolonial Studies and the Study of History." *Postcolonial Studies and Beyond*, edited by Ania Loomba, et al., Duke UP, 2005, pp. 401–22.

Coopland, R[uth] M. *A Lady's Escape from Gwalior and Life in the Fort of Agra during the Mutinies of 1847*. Smith, Elder, 1859.

Cordell, Ryan. "Reprinting, Circulation, and the Network Author in Antebellum Newspapers." *American Literary History*, vol. 27, no. 3, Fall 2015, pp. 417–45.

———. "Viral Textuality in Nineteenth-Century US Newspaper Exchanges." *Virtual Victorians: Networks, Connections, Technologies*, edited by Veronica Alfano and Andrew Stauffer, Palgrave Macmillan, 2015, pp. 29–56.

Crittenden, Victor. *John Lang: Australia's Larrikin Writer: Barrister, Novelist, Journalist, and Gentleman*. Canberra: Mulini Press, 2005.

———. "The Missing 1846 Copies of The Mofussilite. Was It Censored?" *MARGIN: Monash Australiana Research Group Informal Notes*, vol. 62, 1 April 2004, pp. 10–12.

Dalrymple, William. *The Last Mughal: The Fall of a Dynasty: Delhi, 1857*. Alfred A. Knopf, 2007.

Darnton, Robert. "What Is the History of Books?" *Daedalus*, vol. 111, no. 3, 1982, pp. 65–83.

Das, Sisir Kumar. *A History of Indian Literature: 1800–1910, Western Impact: Indian Response*. New Delhi, Sahitya Akademi, 1991.

Dawson, Graham. *Soldier Heroes: British Adventure, Empire, and the Imagining of Masculinities*. Routledge, 1994.
De Nie, Michael Willem. *The Eternal Paddy Irish Identity and the British Press, 1798–1882*. U of Wisconsin P, 2004.
Derrida, Jacques. "Archive Fever: A Freudian Impression," translated by Eric Prenowitz. *Diacritics*, vol. 25, no. 2, Summer 1995, pp. 9–63.
Dharwadker, Vinay. "Print Culture and Literary Markets in Colonial India." *Language Machines: Technologies of Literary and Cultural Production*, edited by Jeffrey Masten et al., Routledge, 1997, pp. 108–33.
Dickens, Charles. *Pickwick Papers*. 1836. Edited and introduction by James Kinsley, Oxford World's Classics, 2008.
Dirlik, Arif. "Rethinking Colonialism: Globalization, Postcolonialism, and the Nation." *Interventions*, vol. 4, no. 3, 2002, pp. 428–48.
Drew, John. *Dickens the Journalist*. Palgrave MacMillan, 2003.
Drew, John, et al. "Introduction to *Household Words*, Volume I, March 30–Sept 21, 1850." *Dickens Quarterly*, vol. 29, no. 1, March 2012, pp. 50–67.
Fahnestock, Jeanne. *Rhetorical Style: The Uses of Language in Persuasion*. Oxford UP, 2011.
Families in British India Society [FIBIS] Database. https://search.fibis.org/frontis/bin/.
Farooqui, Mahmood. *Besieged: Voices from Delhi 1857*. New Delhi, Penguin Books India, 2010.
Farrington, Anthony. *Guide to the Records of the India Office Military Department, 10R L/MIL & L/WS*. India Office Library and Records, 1982.
Finkelstein, David, and Douglas M. Peers. "'A Great System of Circulation': Introducing India into the Nineteenth-Century Media." *Negotiating India in the Nineteenth-Century Media*, edited by David Finkelstein and Douglas M. Peers, Macmillan Press, 2000, pp. 1–22.
Forbes-Mitchell, William. *Reminiscences of the Great Mutiny, 1857–59: Including the Relief, Siege, and Capture of Lucknow, and the Campaigns in Rohilcund and Oude*. Macmillan, 1893.
Forster, E. M. *A Passage to India*. Harcourt, 1924.
Fraser, Robert. *Book History through Postcolonial Eyes: Rewriting the Script*. Routledge, 2008.
Fyfe, Paul. "Access, Computational Analysis, and Fair Use in the Digitized Nineteenth-Century Press." *Victorian Periodicals Review*, vol. 51, no. 4, Winter 2018, pp. 716–37.
Ghose, Benoy. *Selections from English Periodicals of 19th Century Bengal, Volume I (1815–33)*. Calcutta, Papyrus, 1978.
———. *Selections from English Periodicals of 19th Century Bengal, Volume IV (1857)*. Calcutta, Papyrus, 1979.

Ghosh, Anindita. "An Uncertain 'Coming of the Book': Early Print Cultures in Colonial India." *Book History*, vol. 6, 2003, pp. 23–55.

Gilmartin, Kevin. *Print Politics: The Press and Radical Opposition in Early Nineteenth-Century England*. Cambridge UP, 1996.

Goldberg, David Theo. "Liberalism's Limits: Carlyle and Mill on 'the Negro Question.'" *Nineteenth-Century Contexts*, vol. 20, no. 2, 2008, pp. 203–16.

Goswami, Manu. "'Englishness' on the Imperial Circuit: Mutiny Tours in Colonial South Asia." *Journal of Historical Sociology*, vol. 9, no. 1, March 1996, pp. 54–84.

Granth: South Asia Print Resources. School of Cultural Texts and Records, Jadavpur University, https://granthsouthasia.wordpress.com/.

Guha, Ranjit. "A Colonial City and its Time(s)." *The Indian Postcolonial: A Critical Reader*, edited by Elleke Boehmer and Rosikna Chaudhuri, Routledge, 2010, pp. 334–54.

Gutjahr, Paul, and Megan Benton. "Reading the Invisible." *The Broadview Reader in Book History*, edited by Michelle Levy and Tom Mole, Broadview, 2015, pp. 63–72.

Habib, Irfan. "The Coming of 1857." *Social Scientist*, vol. 26, no. 1, 1998, pp. 6–15.

Hainsworth, D. R. "Underwood, Joseph (1779–1833)." *Australian Dictionary of Biography*, vol. 2, 1967, http://adb.anu.edu.au/biography/underwood-joseph-2752. Accessed May 2015.

Hartman, Saidiya. *Lose Your Mother: A Journey along the Atlantic Slave Route*. Farrar, Straus and Giroux, 2007.

———. "Venus in Two Acts." *Small Axe*, vol. 26, 2008, pp. 1–14.

Helgesson, Stefan. "Post-anticolonialism." *PMLA*, vol. 132, no. 1, 2017, pp. 164–70.

Hensley, Nathan. "Empire." *The Encyclopedia of Victorian Literature*, edited by Dino Franco Felluga et al., John Wiley & Sons, 2015, pp. 521–31.

Hewitt, Martin. *The Dawn of the Cheap Press in Victorian Britain: The End of the 'Taxes on Knowledge,' 1849–1869*. Bloomsbury, 2013.

Hirschmann, Edwin. *Robert Knight: Reforming Editor in Victorian India*. Oxford UP, 2008.

Hobbs, Andrew. *A Fleet Street in Every Town: The Provincial Press in England, 1855–1900*. Open Book Publishers, 2018.

Hofmeyr, Isabel. *Gandhi's Printing Press: Experiments in Slow Reading*. Harvard UP, 2013.

Hosking, Rick. "A Traveller's Eye: John Lang's *Wanderings in India*." *Wanderings in India: Australian Perceptions*, edited by Rick Hosking and Amit Sarwal, Monash U Publishing, 2012, pp. 89–104.

Hughes, Linda. "*SIDEWAYS!*: Navigating the Material(ity) of Print Culture." *Victorian Periodicals Review*, vol. 47, no. 1, Spring 2014, pp.1–30.

Humpherys, Anne, and Louis James. *G. W. M. Reynolds: Nineteenth-Century Fiction, Politics, and the Press*. Ashgate, 2008.

Hussain, Nasser. *The Jurisprudence of Emergency: Colonialism and the Rule of Law*. U of Michigan P, 2003.
Hutchinson, Robert. *The Raja of Harsil: The Legend of Frederick "Pahari" Wilson*. Roli Books, 2010.
Hutt, Allen. *The Changing Newspaper: Typographical Trends in Britain and America 1622–1972*. Gordon Fraser, 1973.
Jones, Aled. *Powers of the Press: Newspapers, Power and the Public in Nineteenth-Century England*. Ashgate, 1996.
Joshi, Priti. "Audience Participation: Advertisements, Readers, and Anglo-Indian Newspaper." *Victorian Periodicals Review*, vol. 49, no. 2, 2016, pp. 249–77.
———. "1857; or, Can the Indian 'Mutiny' Be Fixed?" *BRANCH: Britain, Representation and Nineteenth-Century History*, edited by Dino Franco Felluga, 2013, https://www.branchcollective.org/?ps_articles=priti-joshi-1857-or-can-the-indian-mutiny-be-fixed. Accessed 10 July 2017.
———. "Heads Up: Anglo-Indian Newspaper Mastheads." *Victorian Review*, vol. 43, no. 2, Fall 2017, pp. 173–78.
———. "Miles Apart: The India Display at the Great Exhibition." *Museum History Journal*, vol. 9, no. 2, 2016, pp. 136–52.
———. "Mutiny Echoes: India, Britons, and Charles Dickens's *A Tale of Two Cities*." *Nineteenth-Century Literature*, vol. 62, no. 1, 2007, pp. 48–87.
———. "Scissors-and-Paste: Ephemerality and Memorialization in the Archive of Indian Newspapers." *Amodern*, vol. 7, 2017, http://amodern.net/article/scissors-and-paste/.
Joshi, Priya. "Globalizing Victorian Studies." *The Yearbook of English Studies*, vol. 41, no. 2, 2011, pp. 20–40.
———. *In Another Country: Colonialism, Culture, and the English Novel in India*. Columbia UP, 2002.
Kala, D. C. *Frederick Wilson ("Hulson Sahib") of Garhwal, 1816–83*. Delhi, Ravi Dayal Publisher, 2006.
Kanjilal, Pratik, "Book Review: In the Court of the Ranee of Jhansi and Other Travels in India." *Indian Express*, 4 October 2015, https://indianexpress.com/article/lifestyle/books/book-review-in-the-court-of-the-ranee-of-jhansi-and-other-travels-in-india/.
Kaul, Anjuli, "The Raj Retold." *OPEN*, 27 August 2015, https://openthemagazine.com/lounge/books/the-raj-retold/.
Kaul, Chandrika. *Reporting the Raj: The British Press and India, c. 1880–1922*. Manchester UP, 2003.
———. "'You Cannot Govern by Force Alone': W. H. Russell, *The Times* and the Great Rebellion." *Mutiny at the Margins: New Perspectives on the Indian Uprising of 1857*, edited by Marina Carter and Crispin Bates, vol. 3, Sage Publications, 2013, pp. 18–35.
Keene, Henry George. *A Servant of "John Company"; Being the Recollections of an Indian Official*. London, W. Thacker, 1897.

Keesing, Nancy. *John Lang and "The Forger's Wife": A True Tale of Early Australia*. Sydney, John Ferguson, 1979.

Khan, Iqtidar Alam. "The Gwalior Contingent in 1857–58: A Study of the Organisation and Ideology of the Sepoy Rebels." *Social Scientist*, vol. 26, no. 1, 1998, pp. 53–75.

Khan, Nadir Ali. *A History of Urdu Journalism (1822–1857)*. Delhi, Idarah-i Adabiyat-i Delli, 2009.

King, Andrew. *The London Journal 1845–83: Periodicals, Production, and Gender*. Ashgate, 2004.

Kipling, Rudyard. *The Man Who Would Be King and Other Stories*. Edited and introduction by Louis L. Cornell, Oxford World's Classics, 2008.

Koselleck, Reinhart. "Crisis." *Journal of the History of Ideas*, vol. 67, no. 2, April 2006, pp. 357–400.

Kriegel, Lara. "Narrating the Subcontinent in 1851: India at the Crystal Palace." *The Great Exhibition of 1851: New Interdisciplinary Essays*, edited by Louise Purbrick, Manchester UP, 2001, pp. 146–78.

Lang, John. *In the Court of the Ranee of Jhansi and Other Travels in India*. New Delhi, Speaking Tiger, 2015.

———. *Wanderings in India and Other Sketches of Life in Hindostan*. London, Routledge, Warne, and Routledge, 1859.

Latham, Sean, and Robert Scholes. "The Rise of Periodical Studies." *PMLA*, vol. 121, no. 2, 2006, pp. 517–31.

Law, Graham, and Robert L. Patten. "The Serial Revolution." *The Cambridge History of the Book in Britain: Volume VI, 1830–1940*, edited by David McKitterick, Cambridge UP, 2009, pp. 144–71.

Leary, Patrick. *The Punch Brotherhood: Table Talk and Print Culture in Mid-Victorian London*. British Library, 2010.

Leary, Patrick, and Andrew Nash. "Authorship." *The Cambridge History of the Book in Britain: Volume VI, 1830–1940*, edited by David McKitterick, Cambridge UP, 2009, pp. 172–213.

Leask, Nigel. *Curiosity and the Aesthetics of Travel-Writing, 1770–1840: "From an Antique Land."* Oxford UP, 2004.

Legg, Marie-Louise. *Newspapers and Nationalism: The Irish Provincial Press, 1850–1892*. Four Courts Press, 1999.

Lewis, Franklin. "Golestān-e Saʿdi," *Encyclopaedia Iranica*, XI/1, pp. 79–86, http://www.iranicaonline.org/articles/golestan-e-sadi. Accessed December 2014.

Liddle, Dallas, "Who Invented the 'Leading Article'? Reconstructing the History and Prehistory of a Victorian Newspaper Genre." *Media History*, vol. 5, no. 1, 1999, pp. 5–18.

Logan, Deborah. *The Indian Ladies Magazine, 1901–1938*. Rowman and Littlefield, 2017.

Long, James. "Report on the Native Press in Bengal." *Selections from the Records of the Bengal Government*, No. 33. Calcutta, John Grey, 1859.
Loomba, Ania, et al., editors. *Postcolonial Studies and Beyond*. Duke UP, 2005.
Lowe, Lisa. *The Intimacies of Four Continents*. Duke UP, 2015.
Ludden, David. "A Brief History of Subalternity." *Reading Subaltern Studies: Critical History, Contested Meaning and the Globalization of South Asia*, edited by David Ludden, Anthem Press, 2002, pp. 1–39.
Malik, Salahuddin. *1857: War of Independence or Clash of Civilizations? British Public Reactions*. Oxford UP, 2008.
———. "Popular British Interpretations of 'The Mutiny': Politics and Polemics." *Mutiny at the Margins: New Perspectives on the Indian Uprising of 1857*, edited by Andrea Major and Crispin Bates, vol. 2, Sage Publications, 2013, pp. 25–49.
Mann, Michael. *Wiring the Nation: Telecommunication, Newspaper-Reportage, and Nation Building in British India, 1850–1930*. Oxford UP, 2017.
Masih, Archana. "The Aussie Who Took on the British for Rani Laxmibai," *Rediff News*, https://www.rediff.com/news/special/the-aussie-who-took-on-the-british-for-rani-laxmibai/20161226.htm. Accessed 26 December 2016.
Masselos, Jim. "The Dis/Appearance of Subalterns: A Reading of a Decade of Subaltern Studies." *South Asia*, vol. 15, no. 1, 1992, pp. 105–25.
McDonald, Peter, and Michael Suarez. "Editorial Introduction." *Making Meaning: "Printers of the Mind" and Other Essays*, edited by Peter McDonald and Michael Suarez, U of Massachusetts P, 2002, pp. 3–10.
McGann, Jerome J. *A New Republic of Letters: Memory and Scholarship in the Age of Digital Reproduction*. Harvard UP, 2014.
———. *The Textual Condition*. Princeton UP, 1991.
McGill, Meredith. *American Literature and the Culture of Reprinting, 1834–1853*. U of Pennsylvania P, 2003.
McKenzie, D. F. *Bibliography and the Sociology of Texts*. 1986. Cambridge UP, 1999.
———. "The Dialectics of Bibliography Now." *The Broadview Reader in Book History*, edited by Michelle Levy and Tom Mole, Broadview, 2015, pp. 45–61.
———. "Typography and Meaning: The Case of William Congreve." 1977. *Making Meaning: "Printers of the Mind" and Other Essays*, edited by Peter McDonald and Michael Suarez, U of Massachusetts P, 2002, pp. 198–236.
McKitterick, David. "Introduction." *The Cambridge History of the Book in Britain: Volume VI, 1830–1940*, edited by David McKitterick, Cambridge UP, 2009, pp. 1–74.
Medcalf, Rory. "John Lang, Our Forgotten Indian Envoy." *The Spectator*, 31 March 2010, http://www.spectator.co.uk/australia/5880088/john-lang-our-forgotten-indian-envoy/.

Mehta, Uday Singh. *Liberalism and Empire: A Study in Nineteenth-Century British Liberal Thought*. U of Chicago P, 1999.

Merrit, Rebecca. "Public Perceptions of 1857: An Overview of British Press Responses to the Indian Uprising." *Mutiny at the Margins: New Perspectives on the Indian Uprising of 1857*, edited by Andrea Major and Crispin Bates, vol. 2, Sage Publications, 2013, pp. 1–24.

Metcalf, Barbara, and Thomas Metcalf. *A Concise History of India*. Cambridge UP, 2002.

Mill, John Stuart. *Utilitarianism and On Liberty: Including "Essay on Bentham" and Selections from the Writings of Jeremy Bentham and John Austin*, edited by Mary Warnock, New American Library, 1974.

Misra, Anand Swarup. *Nana Saheb Peshwa and the Fight for Freedom*. Uttar Pradesh Government, 1961.

Moore, Grace. *Dickens and Empire: Discourses on Class, Race and Colonialism in the Works of Charles Dickens*. Ashgate, 2004.

Mufti, Aamir R. "Orientalism and the Institution of World Literatures." *Critical Inquiry*, vol. 36, no. 3, 2010, pp. 458–93.

Muir, William. *Records of the Intelligence Department of the Government of the North-West Provinces of India during the Mutiny of 1857*. Edinburgh, T. & T. Clark, 1902.

Mukherjee, Mithi. "Justice, War, and the Imperium: India and Britain in Edmund Burke's Prosecutorial Speeches in the Impeachment Trial of Warren Hastings." *Law and History Review*, vol. 23, no. 3, 2005, pp. 589–630.

Mukherjee, Rudrangshu. "Awadh in Revolt." *The 1857 Rebellion*, edited by Biswamoy Pati, Oxford UP, 2007, pp. 221–34.

———. *Awadh in Revolt 1857–1858: A Study of Popular Resistance*. Anthem Press, 2002.

———. "The Sepoy Mutinies Revisited." *India's Colonial Encounter: Essays in Memory of Eric Stokes*, edited by Mushirul Hasan and Narayani Gupta, New Delhi, Manohar, 1993, pp. 121–32.

Mukhopadhyay, Tarun Kumar. *Hicky's Bengal Gazette: Contemporary Life and Events*. Calcutta, Subarnarekha, 1988.

Mulholland, James. "An Indian It-Narrative and the Problem of Circulation: Reconsidering a Useful Concept for Literary Study." *Modern Language Quarterly*, vol. 79, no. 4, December 2018, pp. 373–96.

———. "Translocal Anglo-India and the Multilingual Reading Public." *PMLA*, vol. 135, no. 2, 2020, pp. 272–98.

Mussen, Deidre. "Catton's Novel Brings Old Family Links to Life." *The Press*, 26 March 2014, http://www.stuff.co.nz/entertainment/arts/9867720/Cattons-novel-brings-old-family-links-to-life. Accessed 10 July 2017.

Nair, P. Thankappan. "The Growth and Development of Old Calcutta." *Calcutta: The Living City, Volume I: The Past*, edited by Sukanta Chadhuri, Oxford UP, 1990, pp. 10–23.

———. *Hicky and his Gazette*. Kolkata, S&T Book Stall, 2001.
———. *A History of the Calcutta Press: The Beginnings*. Calcutta, Firma KLM, 1987.
Nakazato, Nariaki. "Harish Chandra Mukherjee: Profile of a 'Patriotic' Journalist in an Age of Social Transition." *South Asia: Journal of South Asian Studies*, vol. 31, no. 2, 2008, pp. 241–70.
Narain, Prem. *Press and Politics in India, 1885–1905*. Delhi, Munshiram Manoharlal, 1970.
Natarajan, Swaminath. *A History of the Press in India*. Asia Publishing House, 1962.
O'Hanlon, Rosalind, and David Washbrook. "Histories in Transition: Approaches to the Study of Colonialism and Culture in India." *History Workshop*, vol. 32, no. 1, Autumn 1991, pp. 110–27.
Onslow, Barbara. *Women of the Press in Nineteenth-Century Britain*. St. Martin's Press, 2000.
Orsini, Francesca. "Pandits, Printers and Others: Publishing in Nineteenth-Century Benares." *Print Areas: Book History in India*, edited by Swapan Chakravorty and Abhijit Gupta, Delhi, Permanent Black, 2004, pp. 103–38.
———. *Print and Pleasure: Popular Literature and Entertaining Fictions in Colonial North India*. Ranikhet, Permanent Black / Orient Blackswan, 2009.
Otis, Andrew. *Hicky's Bengal Gazette: The Untold Story of India's First Newspaper*. Chennai, Tranquebar, 2018.
Ozmet, Kate. "Rationale for Feminist Bibliography." *Textual Cultures*, vol. 13, no. 1, 2020, pp. 149–78.
Paul, Debapriya. "*Hindoo Patriot* and Hurish Chunder Mookherjea: A Study in Colonial Resistance." *Victorian Periodicals Review*, vol. 37, no. 2, 2004, pp. 161–75.
Peers, Douglas. "'There is Nothing More Poetical than War': Romanticism, Orientalism, and Militarism in J. W. Kaye's Narratives of the Conquest of India." *Imperial Co-Histories: National Identities and the British and Colonial Press*, edited by Julie Codell, Fairleigh Dickinson UP, 2003, pp. 273–99.
Pitts, Jennifer. *A Turn to Empire: The Rise of Imperial Liberalism in Britain and France*. Princeton UP, 2005.
"PM Gifts Rani of Jhansi's Petition to Abbott." *The Hindu*, 18 November 2014, https://www.thehindu.com/news/national/prime-minister-narendra-modi-gifts-rani-of-jhansis-petition-to-abbott/article6612039.ece.
Potter, Simon James. *Newspapers and Empire in Ireland and Britain: Reporting the British Empire, c. 1857–1921*. Dublin: Four Courts, 2004.
Powell, Avril. "Questionable Loyalties: Muslim Government Servants and Rebellion." *Mutiny at the Margins: New Perspectives on the Indian Uprising of 1857*, edited by Crispin Bates, vol. 5, Sage Publications, 2014, pp. 82–102.
Pratt, Mary Louise. *Imperial Eyes: Travel Writing and Transculturation*. Routledge, 1992.
Price, Leah. *The Anthology and the Rise of the Novel: From Richardson to George Eliot*. Cambridge UP, 2000.

———. *How to Do Things with Books in Victorian Britain*. Princeton UP, 2012.
Raj, Kapil. "Beyond Postcolonialism . . . and Postpositivism: Circulation and the Global History of Science." *Isis*, vol. 104, no. 2, June 2013, pp. 337–47.
Ramakrishnan, R. *Press and Politics in an Indian State: Mysore, 1859-1947*. New Delhi, Delta Publishing House, 1994.
Ranjan, Amit. "John Lang: The Lawyer Who Defeated the East India Company." *Daily O*, 24 November 2014, https://www.rediff.com/news/special/the-aussie-who-took-on-the-british-for-rani-laxmibai/20161226.htm.
Ray, Deeptanil, and Abhijit Gupta. "The Newspaper and the Periodical Press in Colonial India." *Journalism and the Periodical Press in Nineteenth-Century Britain*, edited by Joanne Shattock, Cambridge UP, 2017, pp. 245–62.
Rodensky, Lisa. *The Crime in Mind: Criminal Responsibility and the Victorian Novel*. Oxford UP, 2003.
Roderick, Colin, and John Earnshaw. "John Lang (1816–1864): First Australian-Born Novelist." *Royal Australian Historical Society Journal*, vol. 49, no. 2, 1963, pp. 100–35.
Roitman, Janet. *Anti-Crisis*. Duke UP, 2013.
Rooney, Paul. "Readers and the Steamship Press: *Home News for India, China, and the Colonies* and the Serialization of Arthur Griffiths's *Fast and Loose*, 1883–84." *Victorian Periodicals Review*, vol. 47, no. 1, 2014, pp. 31–49.
Roorbach, Bill. "When the Gold Dust Settles." *New York Times*, 16 October 2013, https://www.nytimes.com/2013/10/17/books/review/eleanor-cattons-book-er-prize-winning-luminaries.html. Accessed 10 July 2017.
Roy, Tapti. "Disciplining the Printed Text: Colonial and Nationalist Surveillance of Bengali Literature." *Texts of Power: Emerging Disciplines in Colonial Bengal*, edited by Partha Chatterjee, U of Minnesota P, 1995, pp. 30–62.
———. "Vision of the Rebels: A Study of 1857 in Bundelkhand." *Modern Asian Studies*, vol. 27, no. 1, 1993, pp. 205–28.
Ruymbeke, Christine van. "Kashefi's Forgotten Masterpiece: Why Rediscover the Anvar-i Suhayli?" *Iranian Studies*, vol. 36, no. 4, 2003, pp. 571–88.
Said, Edward. *Culture and Imperialism*. Alfred A. Knopf, 1993.
Sanial, S. C. "History of Journalism in India, III." *Calcutta Review*, vol. 125, no. 251, January 1908, pp. 92–144.
———. "History of Journalism in India, IV." *Calcutta Review*, vol. 125, no. 252, April 1908, pp. 195–247.
Sanyal, Ram Gopal. *Reminiscences and Anecdotes of Great Men of India*. Calcutta, Herald Printing Works, 1894.
Sarkar, Nikhil, "Printing and the Spirit of Calcutta." *Calcutta: The Living City, Volume I: The Past*, edited by Sukanta Chadhuri, Oxford UP, 1990, pp. 128–36.
Sarkar, Sumit. "Calcutta and the 'Bengal Renaissance.'" *Calcutta: The Living City, Volume I: The Past*, edited by Sukanta Chadhuri, Oxford UP, 1990, pp. 95–105.
———. "The Decline of the Subaltern in *Subaltern Studies*." *Writing Social History*, Oxford UP, 1997, pp. 82–108.

Schlicke, Paul, editor. *The Oxford Companion to Charles Dickens*. Anniversary ed., Oxford UP, 2011.
Scott, David. "The Social Construction of Postcolonial Studies." *Postcolonial Studies and Beyond*, edited by Ania Loomba et al., Duke UP, 2005, pp. 385–400.
Sen-Gupta, Nares Chandra. *Selections from the Writings of Hurrish Chunder Mookerji: Compiled from the Hindoo Patriot*. Calcutta, Cherry Press, 1910.
Seville, Catherine. *The Internationalisation of Copyright Law: Books, Buccaneers and the Black Flag in the Nineteenth Century*. Cambridge UP, 2006.
———. *Literary Copyright Reform in Early Victorian England*. Cambridge UP, 1999.
Slauter, Will. *Who Owns the News? A History of Copyright*. Stanford UP, 2019.
Stanley, Peter. *White Mutiny: British Military Culture in India, 1825–1875*. London, Hurst, 1998.
Stark, Ulrike. *An Empire of Books: The Naval Kishore Press and the Diffusion of the Printed Word in Colonial India*. Ranikhet, Permanent Black / Orient Longman, 2007.
Stokes, Eric. *The Peasant Armed: The Indian Revolt of 1857*. Edited by C. A. Bayly, Oxford UP, 1986.
Stoler, Ann Laura. *Race and the Education of Desire: Foucault's History of Sexuality and the Colonial Order of Things*. Duke UP, 1995.
Stoler, Ann Laura, and Frederick Cooper. "Between Metropole and Colony: Rethinking a Research Agenda." *Tensions of Empire: Colonial Cultures in a Bourgeois World*, edited by Frederick Cooper and Ann Laura Stoler, U of California P, 1997, pp. 1–55.
Storey, Graham, and Kathleen Tillotson, editors. *The Letters of Charles Dickens*. Clarendon Press, 1993–95. 8 vols.
Streets, Heather. *Martial Races: The Military, Race and Masculinity in British Imperial Culture, 1857–1914*. Manchester UP, 2004.
Suleri, Sara. *The Rhetoric of English India*. U of Chicago P, 1992.
Taylor, P. J. O. *A Companion to the "Indian Mutiny" of 1857*. Oxford UP, 1996.
Tobin, Beth Fowkes. *Colonizing Nature: The Tropics in British Arts and Letters, 1760–1820*. U of Pennsylvania P, 2005.
Topham, Jonathan R. "John Limbird, Thomas Byerley, and the Production of Cheap Periodicals in the 1820s." *Book History*, vol. 8, no. 1, 2005, pp. 75–106.
Trotter, Lionel James. *Life of the Marquis of Dalhousie*. W. H. Allen, 1889.
Trouillot, Michel-Rolph. *Silencing the Past: Power and the Production of History*. Beacon Press, 2015.
Vann, J. Don, and Rosemary T. VanArsdel, editors. *Periodicals of Queen Victoria's Empire: An Exploration*. U of Toronto P, 1996.
Venkatachalapathy, A. R. "Wandering in Hindostan." *The Hindu*, 8 August 2015, https://www.thehindu.com/books/literary-review/a-r-venkatachalapathy-reviews-in-the-court-of-the-ranee-of-jhansi-and-other-travels/article7512440.ece.
Viswanathan, Gauri. *Masks of Conquest: Literary Study and British Rule in India*. Columbia UP, 1989.

The Waterloo Directory of English Newspapers and Periodicals, 1800–1900. Series 3, http://www.victorianperiodicals.com/series3/index.asp. Accessed 8 June 2017.

Waters, Catherine. "'Much of Sala, and but Little of Russia': 'A Journey Due North,' *Household Words*, and the Birth of a Special Correspondent." *Victorian Periodicals Review*, vol. 42, no. 4, 2009, pp. 305–23.

Wiener, Joel H. *The War of the Unstamped: The Movement to Repeal the British Newspaper Tax, 1830–1836.* Cornell UP, 1969.

Wiener, Martin J. *An Empire on Trial: Race, Murder, and Justice under British Rule, 1870–1935.* Cambridge UP, 2009.

Wolpert, Stanley. *A New History of India.* 5th ed., Oxford UP, 1997.

Young, Paul. "'Carbon, Mere Carbon': The Kohinoor, the Crystal Palace, and the Mission to Make Sense of British India." *Nineteenth-Century Contexts*, vol. 29, no. 4, 2007, pp. 343–58.

Yule, Henry, and Arthur C. Burnell. *Hobson-Jobson: The Anglo-Indian Dictionary.* 1886. Ware, Wordsworth Editions, 1996.

Index

Locators in *italic* refer to figures or tables.
Thus *41*f1.3 refers to figure 1.3 on page 41;
230 refers to page 230 of the table in the appendix.

1851 trial. *See* Prasad, Jyoti—TRIAL OF (1851)
1857 Uprising (aka Sepoy Mutiny or Indian Mutiny):
  British newspapers and public reactions to the events of, 139, 146, 161, 174–175, 179–181, 184, 225–226
  and contradictory views of in Anglo-Indian newspapers, 139–147, 154–162
  coverage by the *Bengal Hurkaru*, 144–146, 154–156, 160
  coverage by the *Bombay Times*, 155
  coverage by the *Hindoo Patriot*, 137, 166–171
  coverage by the *Mofussilite*, 146–147, 156–162
  and expansion of sources, 27, 139–144
  and *Friend of India*'s provocative leader, 151–153
  and gaps in the archival record, 27, 130–135, 140–144
  in *Household Words*, 179–181
  and ordinary Delhiites, 169
  and Prasad (Jyoti), 120–122, 133, 214–216
  presses attacked by insurgents during, 141–142
  See also Act XV

Act XV ("Gagging Act" of 1857):
  Anglo-Indian press reaction to, 149–154
  passage, purpose, and effect of, 148–150, *231*
Act XXXVIII of 1850 (right of counsel in *sadr adalat* or Company court), 111–112
advertisements and advertisement sections:
  and archival holes, 5
  and prize-property auctions in Anglo-Indian newspapers, 95
  proportion of newspapers devoted to and revenue from, 45–46
Agra:
  and the 1857 Uprising, 133–134, 135, 140–142, 156

Agra *(continued)*
  English papers appearing from, 31
    and *Jam-e-Jamshed,* 176n7
  Mofussilite based in, 120–121, 129,
    131–135, 146
  Multa-ool-Akbar based in, 52
  postal communications with
    Calcutta, 140
  Prasad trial at *sadr* court in, 88,
    100–103, 105–106, 109–114,
    118n71
  relocation of provincial capital to
    Allahabad, 54, 57
  in "Wanderings in India," 188–189,
    193
  See also Usghur, Mohamed
Agra Messenger, coverage of Prasad
  trial, 51, 53, 105–106, 112, 114,
  117, 133
akhbarat (scribal newsletters), 9, 143
Allen's Indian Mail, 13, 30n3, 35n17,
  36n22, 120n74, 121n77
Anderson, Benedict R., 4, 48–49
Andrews, Thomas, as printer and
  publisher of the *Mofussilite,*
  31–34
"Anglo Indian," use of, ix, 2n2
Anglo-Indian newspapers:
  coverage and commentary of
    Prasad trial, 98–117, 123–126
  critiques of East India Company/
    Government of India, 25, 60,
    61n83, 74–81, 100, 108–117,
    123–124, 149, 153, 157, 167n121
  editors of, 32, 55–58, 60–61, 72–74,
    106, 130–134, 136–137, 141–144
  and relation with Britons, 123,
    180–181, 224–225
  and relation to vernacular-language
    presses, 11–13
  and vernacular-language
    correspondents and material, 52,
    64–65, 67–68

  *See also Agra Messenger; Bengal
    Hurkaru; Bombay Times;
    Englishman; Friend of India;
    Mofussilite*
Anglo-Sikh wars:
  and the Kohinoor diamond, 93–
    96
  and Prasad (Jyoti), 100
  and prize property, 94–95
Appiah, Kwame Anthony, 18–19
archive:
  and Burton (Antoinette), 12n6
  and Catton's (Eleanor) use of, 2n1
  and excess in Prasad trial, 99
  gaps in, 4–6, 8, 23–5, 35–36, 103,
    130–135, 140–144
  and silence on Prasad, 120, 122,
    126, 216, 224
  of *Hindoo Patriot,* 163–164
  and historical method, 25–26, 38,
    220–222
Atlas for India, 51, 158
Awadh (or Oude, Oudh), annexation
  of, 54, 62, 80–81, 145, 159–160,
  210n83

Bayly, Christopher A.:
  on *akhbarats,* 8–9, 143
  on information blackout in Agra in
    1857, 140n31
  on print media in the 1830s and
    1840s, 11
Bengal Hurkaru:
  attack on *Hindoo Patriot,* 167n121
  censored in 1857, 153–154
  circulation and subscribers, 13–
    14
  correspondents, 63–64
  coverage of 1857 Uprising, 143–
    146, 154–156, 160
  criticism of Company/government,
    197n62
  editors of, 136

and the Great Exhibition (1851),
91–92, 98
and the Kohinoor diamond, 96
letters to the editor in, 58–62,
142–147, 160
literature in, 69
masthead, 42, 42fl.5
Prasad trial, coverage of, 98,
105–106
Prasad trial, reaction to, 89, 107–
119, 123
printer and publisher of, 43
reprints in, 49–55
reprints from vernacular-language
papers, 52, 54
response to Act XV ("Gagging Act"
of 1857), 149–150
as source of reprints, 51
Tagore's (Dwarkanath) ownership
of, 12–13, 145, 165
bibliographic codes:
and Brooker (Peter) and Thacker
(Andrew) on periodical codes,
40, 71
and McGann (Jerome), 39–40, 202,
220
and the text of "Wanderings in
India," 203–204, 206–207
See also advertisements and
advertisement sections; headlines;
leaders and leader sections;
mastheads
Blanchard, Sidney Laman:
as editor of the *Bengal Hurkaru*,
136, 146, 153
as editor of the *Mofussilite*, 72,
73fl.7, 131–134
"The Road in India" (in *Household Words*), 69
Bombay Gazette, 48n40, 51, 147,
148–149
Bombay Times:
and the 1857 Uprising, 155

masthead, 42, 42fl.4
and the Prasad trial, 100, 108–110,
118, 123
as source of reprints, 51
Brake, Laurel, 4, 5, 128
Brooker, Peter, on periodical codes,
40, 71
Broughton, Baron (president of
Company's Board of Control):
and the Prasad trial, 107n38, 115,
118
and the Punjab prize property
debates, 96
Buckingham, James Silk:
criticisms of the Company, 61n83, 76
deportation of, 11, 32, 32n8, 33n11,
76, *230*
career in Britain, 132n11
Burke, Edmund, 82–83
on colonial relations, 116
evoked in Prasad trial, 109, 113–
115
impeachment of Hastings (Warren),
89, 96–97, 113, 116, 197
Buzard, James, on picturesque, 186,
187

Canning, Viscount (governor general
in 1857), 139n27
and Act XV of 1857, 150–151
and fears of proselytization, 152
the *Friend*'s license revoked by,
153nn75–76
and the *Hindoo Patriot*, 137, 166–
167, 171
on vernacular-language newspapers'
language, 150–151, 175n5
Caper, John, articles for *Household Words*, 181, 182, 197
Carlyle, Thomas, "Occasional Discourse
on the Negro Question," 81
Catton, Eleanor, *The Luminaries*, 1–2,
219

censorship:
  of *Bengal Hurkaru*, 153–154
  of *Friend of India*, 151–153
  of vernacular press advocated by the *Mofussilite*, 147–148
  See also Act XV ("Gagging Act" of 1857); Press Act XI (1835); press regulations; Press Regulations of 1818; Press Regulations of 1823; Vernacular Press Act of 1878
Chanda, Mrinal Kanti:
  on the *Bengal Hurkaru*'s censorship in 1857, 153
  on the mortality of English-language newspapers, 128n2
  on preservation of Indian newspapers, 8
  on press regulations and editors, 32–33
  on printers, 33
  on print runs and circulation, 13–14, 37, 137n23
  on reporters, 63n91
Chartier, Roger, 202
Chatterjee, Partha:
  on empire as practice, 84
  on *Hicky's Bengal Gazette* and the public sphere, 9
  on J. S. Mill and despotism, 82
  on modernity and nationalists, 22
  on populism, 21
  on Roy's (Rammohan) involvement with Anglo-Indian presses, 12
Chaudhuri, Rosinka, 44n32, 171n140
circulation:
  between colony and metropole, 173–177
  and cultural dispersal or exchange, 18, 22–23, 66–68
  of editors and pressmen, 65, 127–128, 132–134
  numbers of Indian newspapers, 13–14, 136, 137n23
  obstruction of, 24, 27–28, 129n3, 139–144, 162, 225
  and reprints, 36, 50–58, 68–71, 134–135, 201–216
civilizing mission of the British in India, 79–85, 151–152, 209–211
Company, the. *See* East India Company (EIC, or "the Company")
Cooper, Fredrick:
  reorientation of postcolonial studies advocated by, 19–21
  on "tensions of empire," 19, 85, 124
copyright law:
  Colonial Copyright Act of 1847, 69
  Copyright Act of 1842, 69
  and reprints, 49–51, 69–71, 106
Cordell, Ryan, 23, 49n45, 57n66
courts in India—COMPANY COURTS. *See sadr adalat* or Company court (also "sudder")
courts in India—CROWN COURTS:
  jurisdiction of, 110
  and the Prasad case, 113
crisis:
  of 1857 Uprising deflected in "Wanderings"/*Wanderings*, 184–188, 207, 216
  and failed circulation during, 140–142
  Koselleck (Reinhart) on, 24
  and narratives of empire, 3, 21, 84, 89, 122–126
  and the newspaper trade, 4, 24–25, 225–226
  as productive of print, 98–99, 105–106, 113–115, 123, 142–144, 162

See also 1857 Uprising (aka Sepoy Mutiny or Indian Mutiny); Prasad, Jyoti—TRIAL OF (1851)

Crittenden, Victor:
  error about Lang's whereabouts in 1851, 88, 101
  on gaps in the archive of the *Mofussilite*, 35–36, 130
  on Lang's depiction of Indians, 17, 130, 192, 198
  unsigned texts in the *Mofussilite* identified as Lang's, 65n96, 68
Crystal Palace. *See* Great Exhibition (1851)

Dalhousie, Earl of (governor general in 1851):
  and annexation of Awadh, 210
  compared to Hastings (Warren), 114
  and "doctrine of lapse," 80, 94n13, 210
Darnton, Robert, communications circuit, 38–39, 58, 128, 202
Das, Sisir Kumar, 64–65n95, 104
Delhi Gazette, 37n25, 103n30, 127, 131, 136
  and the 1857 Uprising, 142, 154n80
  accused of plagiarism, 70n113
  Nana Sahib subscribed to, 189
  and the Prasad Trial, 89n4, 104, 105n34, 105n36, 107n40, 123
  as source of reprints, 51, 53
Dharwadker, Vinay:
  on introduction of print to India, 8, 10
  on subject positions created by colonial print culture, 126, 165, 171, 224
Dickens, Charles:
  and Blanchard (Sidney Laman), 131–132
  as editor, 181–183, 191–192
  and Lang (John), 71, 177–178
  persona in nonfiction essays, 190–191
  reaction to 1857 Uprising, 199
  works reprinted in Indian newspapers, 69–70
  See also Household Words
directories of Bengal and the mofussil, 31, 33, 35n17, 38, 88n2, 212n85
  See also Families in British India Society [FIBIS]
"doctrine of lapse," 80, 94n13, 210
  See also Awadh; Dalhousie
Drew, John, 179, 181–182, 190–191
D'Rozario, Peter Stone:
  and heritage-Portuguese publishers, 33
  as printer and publisher of the *Mofussilite*, 31–34, 43

East India Company (EIC, or "the Company"):
  and annexations on the subcontinent, 36–37, 67–68, 80, 93–94, 100, 210
  criticisms of in Anglo-Indian newspapers, 25, 60, 61n83, 74–81, 100, 108–117, 123–124, 149, 153, 157, 167n121, 194–197
  and "doctrine of lapse," 80, 94n13, 210
  and Mill (J. S.), 82n135
  See also Broughton; Canning; Dalhousie; Ellenborough; Nandakumar; *sadr adalat* or Company court
East India Company v. Jootee Persaud. *See* Prasad, Jyoti—TRIAL OF (1851)

Edinburgh Review:
   Macaulay's essay on Hastings (Warren) in (1841), 114n61
   and public opinion-style leaders, 46–47
editors:
   and the 1857 Uprising, 139–147, 159–162
   circulation of, 65, 127–128, 132–134
   and the compilation of news items from other newspapers, 49–50, 52–57
   and the energy Lang brought to the task, 73–74
   and leaders or opinion pieces, 46–48, 57–58, 74–82, 105–106
   politics of Anglo-Indian newspapers determined by, 72
   and press regulations in India, 32–33, 76–77
   and the publishing of letters, 60–63, 153–158
   Stocqueler (J. H.) on a typical day, 56
   See also Blanchard, Sidney Laman; Buckingham, James Silk; Dickens, Charles; Lang, John; Mukherjee, Harish Chandra; Townsend, Meredith; Wilby, G. H.
Ellenborough, Earl of (governor general and on Board of Control):
   on the impounding of *Mofussilite*'s presses, 102–103
   on Prasad (Jyoti), 115
   and the Punjab prize property debates, 94–98
Englishman:
   circulation and subscribers, 13–14
   correspondents, 63–64
   editors of, 56, 136
   on the *Mofussilite*, 30n3
   Mukherjee's (Harish Chandra) apprenticeship at, 137, 163
   Nana Sahib subscribed to, 189
   on the Prasad trial, 111, 118, 121n77
   printer and publisher of, 43
   rivalry with *Bengal Hurkaru*, 150
   as source of reprints, 51
   Tagore's (Dwarkanath) purchase of, 11–12

Families in British India Society [FIBIS], shipping lists, 88n2
Farooqui, Mahmood, 2n2, 169n133, 223n3
Finkelstein, David, 7, 123
Forbes-Mitchell, William:
   image of Nana Sahib labeled as Prasad by, 214–216
   on Lang's closing remarks at Prasad trial, 119–120
Forster, E. M., 21, 226
Friend of India:
   on the 1857 Uprising, 145
   censored for "Centenary of Plassey" in 1857, 151–153
   circulation and subscribers, 13–14, 136
   defense of the government of India, 123
   editors of, 132n11, 136–137
   on the Great Exhibition (1851), 90–91, 98–99
   headlines, use of, 48
   masthead, 41, 41fl.3
   on the *Mofussilite*, 36
   on the Prasad case, 100–102, 115–117, 120–122
   on press regulations, 147–148

printed and published at the
Serampore Press, 44, 136
on fewer advertisements, 45–46
as source of reprints, 51, 53–54

Gagging Act. *See* Act XV
Ghosh, Anindita, 8n8, 12
Gibbons, John A., printer of the
Mofussilite, 34–35, 43n30, 87,
133–134, 142n35, 154
Great Exhibition (1851):
coverage in contrast to Prasad trial,
26, 88–90, 98–99, 105, 122–126,
222
and the India exhibit of, 90–93
and the Kohinoor diamond, 26,
93–97, 100, 125, 223
Official Catalogue of, 93–94
Gubbins, Martin, 60, 206–207n78
and the Prasad trial, 102–103, 109,
117
in Usghur letter, 85, 103
Guha, Ranjit, 27, 222
Gupta, Abhijit, 2n2
Gupta, Iswarchandra, 171n140

Hartman, Saidiya, 221–222
Hastings, Warren:
Burke's (Edmund) impeachment of,
26, 89, 96–97, 109, 113–114,
116
and *Hicky's Bengal Gazette*, 9,
76
Macaulay's essay in the *Edinburgh
Review* on (1841), 114n61
and the Nandakumar episode,
113–114
headlines, use of, 48
Hicky's Bengal Gazette, established
by Hicky (James Augustus), 9,
14–15, 76–77

Hindoo Patriot:
circulation and subscribers, 13–14,
137n23
coverage of 1857 Uprising, 137,
167–171
dominance of print sphere by
Anglo-Indians challenged, 165–
166, 171
editor of, 13, 137–138
headlines eschewed by, 48
masthead and endcap, 42–44, 44fl.6
printed and published in
Bhowanipore, 44, 44fl.6
relation to Anglo-Indian presses,
37, 162–163
in relation to Press Regulations of
1823, 166–167
support of Canning during 1857
Uprising, 137, 166–167, 171
See also Mukherjee, Harish
Chandra
Hindustani (Hindostanee or
Hindoostanee):
Lang's (John) understanding of, 65,
68, 104–105, 175–176, 183, 188,
192
as a language, 64–65, 104n32,
176n6
and *nasta'liq* (or Perso-Arabic)
script, 64–65, 104n32
and the Sanskritization of tradition,
67
and text published in *Mofussilite*,
64–67
and "Wanderings in India," 175–
176, 183, 192, 194
See also Persian; Urdu
history and method:
archival gaps and silences, 4–6,
8, 12n16, 24, 25–26, 30, 35–38,
120–122, 130, 163–164, 221–222

history and method *(continued)*
and creativity with archives, 23, 38, 221–222
human actors as makers and narrators of history, 100
newspapers as "the first rough draft of history," 21, 85, 221
See also Hartman, Saidiya; Postcolonial studies; Subaltern Studies; Trouillot, Michel-Rolph

Household Words:
and the 1857 Uprising, 179–184
anonymity of contributors, 29, 177, 201
reprints in *Mofussilite*, 51, 69–71
See also Dickens, Charles; "Wanderings in India"

Household Words—ESSAYS:
"Hovelling" (by John Lang), 183, 191
"An Indian Court Martial," 69
"Indian Irregulars" (by E. Townsend), 180, 182
"A Journey Due North" (by G. A. Sala), 191
"A Mutiny in India" (by E. Townsend), 179, 181–182
"The Road in India" (by Sidney Laman Blanchard), 69
"Sepoy Symbols of Mutiny" (by J. Robertson), 180–182
"Starting a Paper in India" (by John Lang), 5–6, 29, 34–35, 65n98, 182, 219–220
See also "Wanderings in India"

Hughes, Linda, 4
Hurkaru. *See Bengal Hurkaru*

Impey, Elijah:
and *Hicky's Bengal Gazette*, 9
and Nandakumar case, 113
See also courts in India–CROWN COURTS

Indian Mutiny. *See* 1857 Uprising

Jam-e-Jamshed, 65, 173–177
Jhansi, rani of (Laxmibai), 16, 84, 131, 171n140, 185, 198, 209–211, 216–217
Jooteepersâd, Lallah. *See* Prasad, Jyoti
Joshi, Priya, 8n9
Britain and India in transactional relation, 22, 223
circulation records of Indian libraries studied by, 22n31, 23
Joteepershad, Lalla. *See* Prasad, Jyoti
Jyoti Prasad trial. *See* Prasad, Jyoti—TRIAL OF (1851)

Kaul, Chandrika, 7, 139n27, 150
Kaye, John W., 84–85, 226n5
Keene, Henry George, on Lang, 38
Khan, Nadir Ali, on Urdu newspapers, 53, 65, 76
Kipling, Rudyard:
Lang compared with, 17–18
Lang's stories compared to, 208n81
Kohinoor diamond, 26, 93–97, 100, 125, 223
Koselleck, Reinhart, on crisis, 24

Lahore Chronicle, 51, 100–101, 127
accusation of "literary piracy" by the *Mofussilite*, 69–70
Lang, John:
as attorney for Prasad (Jyoti), 26, 88, 101–104, 109, 112, 117–120, 177, 198–199
biography and family, 15–16, 184–185, 196n59, 209n82
depiction of Indians, 17, 130, 192, 198
as editor of the *Mofussilite*, 72–73, 73f1.7, 85–86, 131–132

"Hovelling" (*Household Words*), 183, 191
  interest in Indian languages of, 65, 68, 104–105, 175–176, 188, 192
  Kipling compared with, 17–18
  as legal counsel to the rani of Jhansi, 84, 210–211
  pseudonym "Le Juif Errant" used by, 65n96, 104
  and revival of interest in in India, 16–17, 216–217
  "Starting a Paper in India" (*Household Words*), 5–6, 29, 34–35, 65n98, 182, 219–220
  See also "Wanderings in India"; *Wanderings in India*; *Wanderings in India*—INDIVIDUAL CHAPTERS
Latham, Sean (and Robert Scholes):
  on holes in the archive of nineteenth-century newspapers and periodicals, 4–5
  on newspapers as "the first rough draft of history," 21, 85, 221
leaders:
  on 1857 Uprising, 144–147, 151–161, 167–170, 179n12
  "The Centenary of Plassey" in *Friend of India*, 151–153
  characteristics of, 46–49, 54–55
  on the Prasad case, 99, 105–106, 108–109, 114, 116–118, 125–126
  public-opinion style, 46–47, 57, 99, 106, 144
  samples from the *Mofussilite*, 75–81, 125–126, 146–147, 154–159
  shift from letters to leaders in the *Mofussilite*, 62–63
Leask, Nigel:
  on Fanny Parkes, 185n31
  on the Indian picturesque, 186

Liddle, Dallas:
  on letters from pseudonymous correspondents, 61n82
  on public opinion-style leaders, 46–47, 57, 99, 106, 144
Long, James, 14n18, 22, 33, 59, 147–148
Loomba, Ania, 81n132

McGann, Jerome J., on bibliographic codes, 39–40, 202, 220
McGill, Meredith, 49n45, 55n61, 55n63
McKenzie, D. F., on bibliographic codes, 26, 39–40, 202–204, 220
McKitterick, David, 5–6
Malik, Salahuddin, on causes of the 1857 uprising, 146, 161
Marshman, John (of the *Friend of India*), 136, 146n45, 153n76, 164
mastheads, 40–43, 47
  of the *Bengal Hurkaru and Chronicle*, 42, 42fI.5
  of the *Bombay Times*, 42, 42fI.4
  Dickens's name on *Household Words*, 201n74
  of the *Friend of India*, 41, 41fI.3
  of the *Hindoo Patriot*, 42n28, 44n32
  of the *Mofussilite*, 30, 40–41, 41ffI.1–1.2, 134
  and the *Times*' Old English typeface, 40–43, 222
Mehta, Uday Singh, on tensions between liberalism and empire, 82–83
Merrit, Rebecca, 161, 178, 181n20, 184
Mill, John Stuart:
  and contradictions of liberalism, 81–83, 116
  as examiner of the Company's correspondence, 82n135
  "The Negro Question," 81–82

Mofussilite:
- archival fissures of, 30–38, 130–135
- based in Agra, 129, 131, 133, 146
- based in Meerut, 34n15, 37, 37n24, 65, 129–130, 189–190
- on censorship of vernacular press in 1857, 147–148
- circulation and subscribers, 13–14
- civilizing mission, 79–84
- and copyright, 68–71
- correspondents, 62–64
- correspondents, Indian, 64, 85–86, 103–105, 199–200
- *See also* Usghur, Mohamed
- coverage of 1857 Uprising, 146–147, 156–162
- criticism of the Company/government, 71–81, 111–112, 125–126, 197n62
- editors of, 15–16, 72–74, 73fI.7, 100, 130–134
- and the Great Exhibition (1851), 91–92, 94, 98, 125–126
- and the Kohinoor diamond, 94
- and letters to the editor in, 58–62, 143–144
- literature in, 66–69
- masthead of, 30, 40–41, 41ffI.1–1.2
- missing numbers for 1846, 35–36
- missing numbers in 1857, 130–135
- name, meaning of, 14–15, 29–30
- Nana Sahib subscribed to, 189
- Prasad trial, coverage of, 106n37
- Prasad trial, reaction to, 123, 125–126
- press impounded or shut down, 102–103
- printer and publisher of, 31–35, 43n30
- relocation to Agra, 129, 131
- relocation to Ambala, 30, 36–37
- relocation to Meerut, 37
- reprints in, 49–55, 57, 68–71
- as source of reprints, 51
- vernacular-language material in, 64–68

Moore, Edward P., as editor of the *Hurkaru*, 136, 154
Moore, Grace, 197
Mukherjee, Harish Chandra (also Hurrish Chunder Mookerji), 12
- on 1857 Uprising, 167–171
- as editor and proprietor of the *Hindoo Patriot*, 13, 137–138
- on the English press in India, 37
- relations with Anglo-Indian presses, 162–163, 165–166
- support of Canning, 166–168

Mukherjee, Rudrangshu, on 1857 Uprising, 139, 159, 161
Mulholland, James, 23, 65n97, 66n102, 224
Mussell, James, on gaps in the newspaper archive, 5
Mutiny. *See* 1857 Uprising

Nakazato, Nariaki:
- on the *Hindoo Patriot*'s circulation, 137n23
- on the *Hindoo Patriot*'s move to Bhowanipore (1855), 44n31
- on Mukherjee as editor of the *Hindoo Patriot*, 138, 163n110, 169, 170

Nandakumar (or Nuncomar) episode (1775), 113–114

Orsini, Francesca, 65n97
Oude. *See* Awadh

Parkes, Fanny, on the feminine picturesque, 185
Paul, Debapriya, 137n23
Peers, Douglas, 7, 84–85, 123, 131

Persand, Jotee. *See* Prasad, Jyoti
Persian:
   and the Indian Civil Service exam, 66–67
   translated tales published in the *Mofussilite,* 66
   and the word *mufaṣṣal,* 14
   See also Hindustani (Hindostanee or Hindoostanee); Urdu
Persuad, Lallah Jootee. *See* Prasad, Jyoti
picturesque mode, 185–187
   and Lang's essays for *Household Words,* 183–188, 207
Pitts, Jennifer, on tensions between liberalism and empire, 82–83, 97n19, 113
Postcolonial studies, 2n3, 18–22
   See also Subaltern Studies
Prasad, Jyoti:
   absence from the print archive, 120, 126, 224
   and Anglo-Indian conception of a "good Indian," 120–122
   and image of Nana Sahib, 214–216, 215f4.6
   irregularities in spelling of name, 88–89n3
   obituary of, 118–119
Prasad, Jyoti—TRIAL OF (1851), 105–106
   acquittal of, 107–108, 114–115
   Anglo-Indian newspaper coverage and commentary of, 105–115, 118–120, 123–126
   charge against Prasad, 106–107
   coverage of Great Exhibition in Indian press subsumed by, 88–90, 98–99, 105, 122–126, 222
   and Hindustani as language of the Court, 104
   Lang's closing remarks, 119–120
   and Nandakumar (or Nuncomar) episode, 113–114
   transcription of the testimony of, 105–106
Press Act XI (1835):
   censorship laws repealed by, 10, 11, 36, 77, 226
   stipulations of, 32–33, *231*
   surveillance of printers and publishers in the aftermath of, 43
press regulations, *230–231*
   See also Act XV ("Gagging Act"); censorship; Press Act XI (1835); Press Regulations of 1818; Press Regulations of 1823; Vernacular Press Act of 1878
Press Regulations of 1818, 10, 37, *230*
Press Regulations of 1823:
   deportation of James Silk Buckingham due to, 32, 33n11, 76
   Roy's (Rammohan) protest of, 164, 166
Price, Leah, 56–57, 135n19
price or subscription rate of newspapers, 45–46
prize property (or prize money or batta), 95–96, 98, 115, 125

reprinting or scissors-and-paste journalism, 49–57, 68–71, 106
   and the endurance of news stories, 55
   and the *Mofussilite*'s archival gaps, 35–36, 134–135
   and the stamp tax, 50, 179n11
   See also copyright law
Robertson, John, "Sepoy Symbols of Mutiny" (*Household Words*), 180–182
Roy, Rammohan:
   1823 press restrictions protested by, 164, 166

Roy, Rammohan *(continued)*
  and the "Bengal Renaissance," 44n31
  Sambad Kaumudi founded by (1821), 164
  and transactional exchanges with Anglo-Indians, 11–13, 22, 71–72, 164
Roy, Tapti, 22
Russell, William Howard, coverage of 1857 Uprising, 63–64, 139

sadr adalat or Company court (also "sudder"):
  and the Company's judicial system, 109–112
  Prasad trial in, 88, 100–106, 109–113
  reforms proposed in 1851 leader in *Mofussilite*, 78
Sala, George Augustus:
  "A Journey Due North" (*Household Words*), 191
  special correspondent for Dickens, 191
Sambād Prabhākar, 44n32, 171n140
Sanyal, Ram Gopal, 131n8, 137–138
Sarkar, Sumit, 19n28, 21
Saunders, Patterson, as editor of the *Hurkaru*, 136, 154
Scholes, Robert (and Sean Latham):
  on holes in the archive of nineteenth-century newspapers and periodicals, 4–5
  on newspapers as "the first rough draft of history," 21, 85, 221
scissors-and-paste journalism. *See* copyright law; reprinting
Scott, David, 18–19
Sepoy Mutiny. *See* 1857 Uprising
Serampore/Baptist Mission Press, 67
  Friend of India printed and published by, 44, 136

  and Gangakishore Bhattacharya, 12n16, 164
shipping intelligence (arrivals and departures):
  as archive, 38
  Lang's name on, 88, 212
  as newspaper section, 49
Slauter, Will, 49n45, 55n62
Stark, Ulrike, 8, 13n17
Stocqueler, J. H., 11, 12, 56
Stoler, Ann Laura:
  on colonial modernity, 22, 224
  reorientation of postcolonial studies advocated by, 19–20
  on "tensions of empire," 19, 85, 124
Subaltern Studies:
  criticism of, 19
  and innovations in historians' practices, 222
sudder court. *See sadr adalat*
Suleri, Sara, 116, 186

Tagore, Dwarkanath:
  and the *Bengal Hurkaru*, 13, 145, 164
  and the colonial early modern, 22
  and the *Englishman*, 11, 12, 13
Thacker, Andrew, on periodical codes, 40, 71
Thomas, George Powell, and the *Mofussilite*, 133
Times (London):
  coverage of Prasad trial, 88–89, 99n21, 101–104, 107nn38–39, 108–110, 114–115, 118, 118n71
  coverage of India exhibit at the Great Exhibition, 92
  on the mutiny at Meerut, 179n12
  Old English typeface of masthead, 40–43, 42n29, 222

on proprietorship of the Kohinoor diamond, 94, 97, 125
"The Punjab Booty," 95
and reprinting of news by Anglo-Indian newspapers, 51, 56
Robinson (Henry Crabb) on writing leaders of, 46n38
Russell's (William Howard) coverage of the Uprising, 63–64, 139
Townsend, Meredith, as editor of the *Friend of India*, 132n11, 136, 153
Trouillot, Michel-Rolph, on archives, 38, 100, 221, 226

Urdu, 2n2, 14, 64–65, 67, 104, 176n6
See also Hindustani (Hindostanee or Hindoostanee)
Urdu-language newspapers, 7, 10, 52–53, 65, 151n70, 173–177, 199–200, 223n3
See also *Jam-e-Jamshed*
Usghur, Mohamed (also Asghar or Azhar):
correspondent for the *Mofussilite*, 85–86, 103–105
as possibly Arabic teacher at Agra College, 200
as possibly referenced in "Wanderings in India," 199–200
and relations across colonial lines, 223

vernacular languages:
the *Mofussilite*'s promotion of, 65–67
and the Sanskritization of tradition, 67
See also Hindustani (Hindostanee or Hindoostanee); Urdu

Vernacular Press Act of 1878, and censorship of Indian-owned and -edited newspapers, 10–11
vernacular presses:
and Bhowanipore, 44n31
cited in the *Hurkaru*, 52
and collaboration with Anglo-Indians, 11–12
emergence between 1800 and 1835 of, 10
independence from Anglo-Indian presses, 12–13
Indian proprietors of, 12
See also *Jam-e-Jamshed*

"Wanderings in India," 27
and the picturesque mode, 183–188
recourse to Orientalized India in, 184–188, 207, 216
Wanderings in India:
bibliographic codes (format and layout), 202–207
published in Routledge's "Cheap Series," 203–204
title page frontispiece, 212–213, 213ff4.4–4.5
Wanderings in India—INDIVIDUAL CHAPTERS:
"Black and Blue," 208–209, 217
"The Ranee of Jhansi," 209–211, 216–217
"The Himalayan Club," 207
"The Mahommedan Mother," 208–209, 217
Wilby, G. H.:
as editor of the *Mofusilite*, 72, 73f1.7, 127, 131
and the network of Anglo-Indian pressmen, 127–128, 131–132, 134
Wilson, Frederick "Pahari," 208n81

www.ingramcontent.com/pod-product-compliance
Lightning Source LLC
Chambersburg PA
CBHW030532230426
43665CB00010B/853